RHETORICAL DARWINISM

Studies in Rhetoric and Religion 11

RHETORICAL DARWINISM

Religion, Evolution, and the Scientific Identity

THOMAS M. LESSL

BAYLOR UNIVERSITY PRESS

Cover Design by theBookDesigners
Cover Image: Cover images © Shutterstock/fivespots, MarcelClemens, Bill McKelvie

Library of Congress Cataloging-in-Publication Data

Lessl, Thomas M., 1954–
  Rhetorical darwinism : religion, evolution, and the scientific identity / Thomas M. Lessl.
     p. cm.
  Includes bibliographical references and index.
  ISBN 978-1-60258-403-7 (hardback : alk. paper)
  1. Science--Public opinion. 2. Religion and science. 3. Science--Philosophy. I. Title.
  Q172.5.P82L47 2011
  261.5'5--dc23

                          2011021757

BAYLOR
UNIVERSITY

Printed in the United States of America on 30% pcw recycled acid-free paper.

For Ruth

CONTENTS

List of Figures

PREFACE

It would be hard to miss the fact that the concept of evolution lives a double life, that it references a body of technical knowledge developed through careful scientific study but also evokes a cluster of more intangible meanings at once emotive, ideological, perhaps even religious, that move in orbit around the notion of progress. But what is the relationship between these two senses of evolution—between what we might call "evolution" and "evolutionism"? In answering this question I mean to argue that, while evolutionary science certainly stands by itself as a biological research program, it is also vitally connected to evolutionism. Like the Colossus of Rhodes, the idea of evolution has a foot on two shores, one scientific and another mythic. The main argument of this book is that this connection exists because the persuasive work that is performed by evolutionism sustains science's place in the world, and this work can only succeed when evolutionism is taken to mean the same thing as evolutionary science.

The term "Rhetorical Darwinism" in my title might be regarded as a synonym for evolutionism, and I use it here to accentuate the fact that my concern is with evolutionism's public rather than personal aspects. Rhetoric is the heading under which scholars typically categorize efforts of communication that work to establish or uphold institutional interests, and I believe that it is for such ends that evolutionism exists. Although it certainly also has personal appeal for scientists as a kind of spiritualization of scientific knowledge, I aim to explore only its rhetorical blandishments. I believe that it represents a configuration of symbols with unique potential for establishing science's place and importance in the world. This is because the primary effect of evolutionism is scientism. To believe that evolutionary science is capable of explaining not just the development of biological organisms but also the origins of moral values, historical meaning, and societal purpose, is to believe that science is destined for absolute authority.

Readers will likely associate evolutionism with the concept of social Darwinism, and certainly my subject encompasses this movement from a century ago as well as much of what now comes under such headings as "sociobiology" and "evolutionary psychology." But evolutionism is a broader phenomenon. Many have advanced it as an explicit extension of the doctrine of natural selection, but it manifests in many less formal ways as well. A more encompassing way to describe evolutionism would be to say that it is detected whenever the language of evolution comes loose from its scientific moorings through various metaphorical expressions. When it does so, the term "evolution" transcends its merely descriptive and explanatory meaning as a biological concept, most typically by becoming a synonym for "progress."

Most readers will agree (and I do too) that evolutionism is not evolutionary science, and for this reason, they may also assume that it is found only at the margins of science. This supposition is reinforced, so far as social Darwinism is concerned, by a website called "Understanding Evolution for Teachers," sponsored by the University of California, Berkeley. These Berkeley educators tell us that, while social Darwinists once supposed that "evolution by natural selection provided support for these ideas," it was merely science distorted by the "pre-existing prejudices" of unnamed individuals who wanted to "promote social and political agendas." The site dramatizes this point through an illustration that shows Charles Darwin standing, with cane in hand, before the arched doorway of a building called "Darwin" from which he is driving away a fat, cigar-smoking man labeled "laissez faire" (who looks like the character from the Monopoly game) and a bald spectacled one called "eugenics" (figure 1).[1]

This represents what we might call the official view of scientific history, the idea that scientists jealously guard the epistemic borders of science against such ideological impostors. This view is formally expressed elsewhere on the Berkeley site, where we learn that scientific inquiry is always bounded by three questions: "What is there?" "How does it work?" and "How did it come to be this way?"[2] Science does not let in speculations about value or purpose, and so those who promulgated social Darwinism must have been outsiders.

While what the Berkeley educators teach us may be true to a *formal* understanding of what distinguishes science from other enterprises of

Figure 1

inquiry, it is certainly not true to scientific history. Social Darwinism, like all the variant forms that might be grouped under the heading of evolutionism, has been just as likely to be promulgated by scientists as by pseudoscientific thinkers. This is because the outer boundaries of the scientific enterprise are not defined by what scientists do in laboratories or by what they publish in academic journals. Science is more than inquiry; it is an institutional culture that expresses its identity—as all cultures do—in the totality of its products.[3] Some of these products, mainly its technical and scholarly discourses, are formal, rigorous, and closed to all but the specialists in each given field, but other products of scientific communication are not. In addition to *technical communication*, the scientific community also produces vast amounts of *public communication* in textbooks, magazines, public lectures, books, museum exhibits, and other diverse outlets. What the official view tends not to recognize is that, while scientists may abjure questions of value and purpose in the pursuit of technical knowledge, they cannot afford to do so when communicating in the public sphere.

The Berkeley site itself illustrates this point: although it speaks on science's behalf, the heroic image of science that it communicates is itself not a scientific message. Its creators have stepped outside of their own definition of science in their effort to absolve it of responsibility for the social and political schemes of social Darwinism. In this regard, they provide a compact illustration of the central problem that draws my attention. Much of the public esteem that science has enjoyed in recent centuries is tied up with what it claims on the technical side, namely that scientists operate in an arena of inquiry unspoiled by the dubious human motives that govern other affairs. We have special regard for science because we believe that it approaches nature on nature's own terms. But while public support for such work depends on upholding this image, it also demands that science should mean more than this. Scientists respond to this dilemma by creating public messages that continue to have scientific content, thus retaining some sense of their profession's epistemic purity, but these messages also seem to advance social and political arguments that could never in reality have such a grounding.

One body of technical knowledge that especially lends itself to such efforts is evolutionary science. Because evolutionary symbols pertain to life and history as it is understood in the scientific realm, they also sustain analogous but qualitatively different meanings in the public realm—while still retaining a sense of the scientific.

When this occurs, the "story" of biological evolution becomes the story of science's ascent. Evolutionism in this way presents one particular body of scientific knowledge as a historical justification for the scientific enterprise itself. It writes the history of science back into natural history.

This is supported by the fact that rhetorical Darwinism is, just as often as not, the work of scientists rather than nonscientists. The philosopher Michael Ruse demonstrated this when he showed that biological evolution and human progress have been drawn together in the thinking of nearly every leading figure in evolutionary science since (and including) Darwin.[4] What is different about my take on this is that, while Ruse supposes that this occurs merely for personal reasons, I believe that it has rhetorical purposes that make it a matter of public concern. This argument rests upon the premise that one of evolutionism's chief attractions is its power to address the perennial problem of scientific patronage. By patronage I mean something that is primarily symbolic and social rather than material. Patronage may end by pouring cash into labs and salaries, but it begins symbolically in the formation of a scientific identity that is also part and parcel of some larger social identity.

For this reason, modern science could not have arisen simply because new techniques of inquiry were discovered or fundamental physical truths overturned; it depended more fundamentally upon a symbolic revolution that enlarged science's position in the world. England's early lead in science, as I argue in chapters 2 and 3, was encouraged by a cultural linkage that tied the scientific ethos or identity to an altered theological understanding of history that was arising within the Protestant Reformation. The leaders of this movement surmised that the reforms they were promulgating were also putting the Christian faith back on the course of providential history, and science, thanks in no small part to the creative artistry of Francis Bacon (1561–1626), also came to symbolize this restoration. Science gained unprecedented social significance in seventeenth-century England because it also had achieved unprecedented spiritual meaning as a sign of the restoration of the creation that the Creator was bringing about in coincidence with the church's final millenarian purification.

I begin by exploring the religious rhetoric that fostered this change because my main argument is itself an evolutionary one—an evolutionary explanation of evolutionism. If evolutionism is pervasive now because it is the central part of a symbol system that sustains scientific patronage, it might be illuminating to consider the symbolic structures that sustained social support for science in other times and places. But this is not my primary reason for beginning in Bacon's century. The more vital reason is my belief that evolutionism descends from this religious rationale. The symbolic means by which patronage was first sustained were not abandoned as science developed; they instead developed in step with it. Societies change through human invention, and because a major part of invention is creative imitation, *mimesis* as the ancients called it, important elements of past cultures always endure within present ones. For this reason, I believe that to understand why evolutionism remains vital to the scientific identity we first need to understand its rhetorical ancestry, the older theological vision of science's place in the world from which that identity descends.

Some readers will find this implausible. But if everything evolves from something else, though often through indiscernible increments, what are we to say of science? If there is nothing surprising in supposing that we have descended from primates as seemingly different from us as we now are from the great apes, why should we be surprised to discover that the contemporary scientific ethos has descended from a religious one? If blind evolutionary dynamics can turn apes into humans in just a few million years, what reason do we have for doubting that intentional ones might turn religious ideas into secular ones in the course of a few hundred years?

An important support for my thesis is the fact that evolutionism shares symbolic features with the religious worldview that first established science's place in English society four centuries ago. We might say that evolutionism is *homologous* with an older Baconian worldview. Like the anatomical and genetic similarities that living organisms share with their extinct ancestors, the abiding ethical and historical consciousness that we now detect in rhetorical Darwinism demonstrates its descent from an explicitly religious rationale for science that came into dominance in the seventeenth century. The worldview reflected in evolutionism may seem quite different from the explicitly religious rationale for science that Bacon so successfully promulgated, but the symbolic features that these worldviews share also perform similar functions. Moreover, we can trace the development of the contemporary worldview of evolutionism from its Baconian antecedent step by step. In this last respect, my argument from cultural homology stands on strong empirical ground. Biologists can demonstrate genetic and anatomical similarities of form and function, and they can show evolutionary descent to the extent that it is reflected in fossil records. But they cannot witness firsthand the operations of biological change that produced these homologies. Since I am trying to account for gradual changes brought about through various recorded acts of public communication, the cultural evolutionary process treated in this book remains quite visible.

The materials reworked through this process are various symbolic expressions of the priestly authority that first enabled the Christian church to establish its secular patronage. Although the period examined in this book goes back only to Bacon's time, the religious formula that he applied to science descended from a Catholic one that is in its own way homologous with evolutionism. The Catholic Church established its patronage in feudal Europe by successfully engendering the belief that even secular power was sustained by the knowledge mediated through its priestly labors. So long as the church was recognized as the authorized interpreter of a universal historical blueprint, all dominions and powers came under its control. Once in place, Catholic authority was as necessary and attractive to princes as it was to popes. The secular rulers that had forged this bargain with Rome became as deeply invested in its spiritual authority as the clergy themselves, and this meant that kings and princes were just as committed to upholding the church's teaching authority, its magisterium.

My study picks up in the seventeenth century as the unfolding Protestant reform movement was reworking this magisterium. This reshuffling of Christian notions of authority provided the arguments for scientific patronage that Bacon was turning to science's advantage. Because spiritual authority was now measured by one's obedience to Scripture rather than to Rome, the manner in which that authority extended into the secular realm was being similarly altered. Secular interests that could be aligned with this hermeneutical ideal could enlarge their social privileges proportionately, and this put science in a particularly advantageous position. Since nature, the book of God's creation, had traditionally been regarded as an analogue to the Bible, to show that science represented a particularly faithful reading of this revelation was to give it a place analogous to that of Protestant clergy in societies now under the sway of the Reformation.

To realize this potential required a certain kind of creative genius, and it is for this reason that Francis Bacon figures so prominently in this book. In his writing campaign on science's behalf, the Lord Chancellor counterposed the new experimental philosophy against Catholic Aristotelianism, and in doing so he aligned it with the rigorous spiritual discipline that Protestants were championing. The newly reformed church was a purer prophetic and priestly institution, the ordained mediator of God's Word, and Bacon was simply pointing out that the new experimental philosophers occupied an adjacent office as faithful readers of the book of "God's Works." This was not a new idea. But it was an especially timely one, and it was now being voiced by one of England's most influential public figures. The implications of this association for scientific patronage were clear: the new natural philosophers were advancing their own work of reform and were therefore entitled to commensurate support. Science was the philosophical arm of a new hermeneutical magisterium and was thus imbued with a spiritual authority nearly equal to that of Protestant divines.

I am not denying that Bacon also was, as is now customarily thought, an important advocate for the new experimentalism that continues to be featured even today in public portrayals of the scientific identity. What we are likely to miss is the fact that some of the original religious meaning with which Bacon surrounded these ideas persists as well. It was not just on technical epistemological grounds that Bacon advocated the notion that philosophers ought to humble themselves before natural fact; this was also an explicit effort to put science at the ethical center of an emerging Protestant worldview. Bacon also had assigned science a spiritual *role* in English life. It was assured of such a place because it was grounded in the faithful reading of God's revelation, and this also meant that it was imbued with special historical significance as an instrument of divine providence.

Bacon's efforts to transform the experimental philosopher into a priest of nature and prophet of history were followed by a notable rise in the fortunes of science in the latter part of the seventeenth century. When Bacon played his chips in its early decades, he laid them on the Calvinist world-view that his mother and some of his Cambridge professors had impressed upon him. This wager paid such enormous dividends that by the time Isaac Newton died a century later, science had become a crucial symbol of both church and state. The marble memorial erected over Newton's remains in Westminster Abbey is one of the most conspicuous of that great church's monuments, and I am convinced that this tells us as much about the rhetorical revolution that had occurred in the previous century as it does about the intellectual achievements of this scientific thinker. Only such a grand funereal monument as this could do justice to what science meant for those who had came to power in the decades after the English Revolution, and what it meant was expressed in the theological daring of Alexander Pope's familiar epitaph:

> Nature and Nature's laws lay hid in night:
> God said, "Let Newton be!" and all was light.

These lines took hold of the English imagination because they summed up a perspective on science that had come into ascendancy. With the universal explanatory range of the *Philosophiæ Naturalis Principia Mathematica* now wedded in the British imagination to Christian universalism, it was not surprising that Newton would be regarded as a messianic figure.

Such theological understandings empowered science, and that which empowers is not likely to be cast aside. If I may take the liberty of altering Lord Acton's famous saying: Power tends to perpetuate itself, and absolute power perpetuates itself absolutely. No alternative basis for scientific patronage could do for science what Bacon's religious one had done—except of course one that sustained similar theological meanings. Thus as the Baconian scientific ideology gradually began to lose its efficacy, evolutionism was already beginning to take its place—evolving, this is to say, from Baconianism.

The middle section of this book traces the cultural evolutionary progression through which these priestly and millenarian meanings were reworked to sustain a similar scientific ethos. The developmental process leading from Baconianism to evolutionism was mediated by Enlightenment thinkers and their early nineteenth-century progeny who wished to repudiate the older religious worldview. In doing so, they proposed (and probably often believed) that what they were advancing was merely reason or science. My task in these middle chapters is to show how religious concepts that continued to abide in their messages also continued to sustain an emerging scientific ethos. This requires careful dissection. To separate out the religious meanings that were becoming intertwined with scientific ones in this transitional period, I apply an insight into the nature of religious meaning, the efficacy of which has already been demonstrated by numerous scholars. In short, this turns upon the recognition that religious *meaning* abides in particular language *forms*. Thus when I say that evolutionism sustains patterns of religious meaning that descend from a seventeenth-century archetype, I mean that, as John Angus Campbell first put this, the scientific culture continues to employ a "Baconian grammar."[5] The message patterns that gave rise to evolutionism certainly did reference scientific meanings, but because these meanings continued to be worked into the language forms of religion, they expressed something more.

This is analogous to what occurs when we encounter such playful nonsense as this from Lewis Carroll's "Jabberwocky."

> 'Twas brillig, and the slithy toves
> Did gyre and gimble in the wabe;
> All mimsy were the borogoves,
> And the mome raths outgrabe.

Upon close examination, we will notice that Carroll's invented language is not entirely new, that it borrows from traditional semantic and syntactic forms. Although words like "brillig" and "slithy" might at first seem to have been pulled out of the blue, their phonemic forms echo familiar words like "brilliant" and "slippery," thus hinting at some similar meaning. Something like this is achieved by Carroll's borrowing of conventional syntax as well. We may not know what "toves" are, but we do know that when they "gyre and gimble," they are *doing* something and that they are doing it "in the wabe."

The counterpart forms of diction and syntax that transform evolutionary symbols into religious ones in the scientific arena are traditional patterns of metaphor and myth—the latter of which we might regard as metaphor working on a narrative scale. Religious language is always metaphorical in the sense that religion, by its very nature, is about things not of this world, and things not of this world are only capable of being represented (at least for mortals such as ourselves) in terms of things that are. It is impossible to speak of God's "thoughts" or "purposes" without using anthropomorphic terms—human experiences of cognition metaphorically stretching into abstract regions of theology. Metaphors do not always invoke religious meanings, but they will tend to do so when their context of expression will not allow us to suppose that they have a merely natural referent. Since the scientists who labored in Bacon's shadow assumed that natural objects were God's creations, we have little reason to doubt that they intended to convey theological as well as scientific meaning when they applied, as William Paley famously did, the metaphor of "contrivance" to biological organisms. But did this theological meaning disappear when Darwin used this term? Certainly he did not intend to posit a "contriver" behind the mechanisms of biology, but human intentions do not necessarily obstruct the tendencies of metaphor. Whether or not such metaphors continue to have religious significance will depend upon how we judge the interpretive process that audiences bring to them. Context is the crucial determinant. When the metaphor of "natural selection" is typically used, its obvious utility as a figurative device enabling us to instantly grasp the essence of Darwin's theory weighs against any assumption that it could mean more than this. Its clear scientific purposes show that the "design" it implies is only a useful fiction. But in those contexts where evolutionism and its various ancestral forms manifest we cannot assume this.

The middle chapters of this book follow the progress of such adaptations of Baconian natural theology through the eighteenth-century Enlightenment and the positivist movement that succeeded it in France. The historical visions examined in this part of the project represent some of the transitional forms that bridged Baconianism with evolutionism. Like Bacon, Enlightenment philosophers and positivists continued to promote the idea that science was called upon to play a key role in achieving history's predestined ends, and like the rhetorical Darwinists, they surmised that the plan of history they were interpreting had arisen from nature rather than from providence.

What these evolutionary views still lacked was an explicit connection between biology and history, and in part we might attribute this to the fact that the architects of the Enlightenment and positivism had little direct interest in the natural sciences. Nevertheless, the attraction of such narratives for scientists should be obvious. Where scientific advancement was a signal of historical progress, science was sure to enjoy certain entitlements. But in the short run, these emerging narratives could do little to advance science's professional establishment. One might even argue that they became an obstacle to its growth. The Enlightenment philosophers and positivists who constructed them, regarded themselves as the pioneers of this emerging scientific order, as the social scientific counterparts to Newton and Galileo who were bringing human society under nature's command. Even though they heralded science as universal and henceforth destined for unlimited prestige, they also constructed a scientific division of labor that put sociology, rather than physics or geology, at the top of this evolutionary hierarchy.

The sociological bent of positivism made it impractical as a rhetorical basis for scientific patronage. Thus it should not surprise us to find that the leading architect of science's professionalization in nineteenth-century England, Thomas Henry Huxley, became its most vocal opponent. No less surprising is the fact that Huxley was simultaneously reinventing positivism as rhetorical Darwinism. While the English positivists eagerly sought his blessing, since they regarded him as the most eloquent and respected proponent of their own worldview, he rebuffed every such overture. Positivism may have matched up generally well with the scientism expressed in Huxley's own agnostic stance, but as a historical narrative it did not uphold the supremacy of the natural sciences. He was thus determined to neutralize its influence, and he found that he could do this most effectively by embarrassing the positivists, by drawing attention to the very thing we will discover in his public treatments of evolution—that positivism (like the evolutionism that succeeded it) derived much of its meaning from its imitations of religious speech forms. The religious aspirations of positivism, in fact, were no secret. An explicit argument of the movement's French founders was that the sociological science they were developing was theology's direct descendant. Formally this only meant that supernatural religion had been a prescientific step en route to the natural theory of social existence that was the destined end of social evolution, but the fact that theology and science occupied the same evolutionary continuum also created some ambiguity. If sociology had evolved from theology, it also carried theology forward in some sense and could be said to share its religious essence. It was this implication that Huxley took aim at in 1868 when he fired off his most famous and devastating shot at positivism, calling it "Catholicism minus Christianity."

But if Huxley found positivism repulsive, it was only because he had scientistic aspirations of a similar kind. Even as he rebuffed the entreaties of its English proponents, sometimes with scintillating onslaughts of eloquence and sometimes with droll cajolery, he was also laboring to engineer a similar narrative—one more capable of propelling science's rise within the indigenous social order. Such a philosophy of history would need to come from science, and some ideal material happened to be available now that a legitimate biological theory of evolution had emerged. Darwin's great achievement had given natural history a scientific basis, and Huxley was one of the first to recognize the rhetorical payoffs that might be realized if this natural history were to shade into evolutionism. Even as he discussed the evidence supporting the evolutionary hypothesis in his public life, Huxley was also stretching the scope of its meaning so as to naturalize traditional notions of human history. We will see upon close inspection that the word "place" in the title of Huxley's book on human evolution, *Man's Place in Nature*, operates on two levels. With regard to the book's scientific subject matter, it denotes the relationship of humans to ancestral primates as revealed by comparative anatomy. But it simultaneously gives science a "place" atop a new understanding of social hierarchy, a biologically inspired Great Chain of Being structured in accordance with evolutionary progress. *Man's Place in Nature* is as much about science's place in history as it is about biological evolution. This is because in evolutionism, the two subjects always converge.

Myths that are recognized as myth lose their efficacy, and evolutionism avoids this by constantly folding itself back into evolutionary biology. This explains an odd anomaly in Huxley's professional life. Although certainly an evolutionist, he remained ambivalent about Darwin's theory and hardly ever treated the question of evolution in the classroom, but he actively addressed it in his influential public lectures and writings. This inconsistency makes sense once we understand what evolutionism does for the scientific ethos. Huxley needed to advance evolution as a public figure because it was tied up with the mythical vision through which he hoped to advance science's public fortunes.

Those who now carry on this rhetorical legacy must also uphold evolutionism's scientific appearances, and this may explain why Huxley is now fashioned as "Darwin's bulldog" in popular memory. Examine *any* of the public discourses which are supposed to have earned him this title, and you will find that Darwin's work is scarcely mentioned and only tepidly assented to. When we do find Huxley treating Darwin's mechanism of natural selection, we are likely to find him outlining his scientific reservations about that theory. Huxley did advance evolutionary science as a public figure— just not on Darwinian grounds. But if evolutionism is going to work for our scientific culture, the attributes of this myth's characters have to be integrated into its main story lines. In reality it would be more accurate to say that Huxley was *evolutionism's bulldog*, but since evolutionism gains its authority from the truth of evolutionary science (which is now even more closely identified with Darwin's achievements), the Huxley of history has been absorbed into myth as Darwin's greatest supporter. For true believers, evolution and evolutionism are the same thing, and the symbolic force that holds them together would lose its power if the fidelity of one of this narrative's greatest heroes was called into question.

Huxley's own efforts to develop a narrative of evolutionism differed from those of his positivist rivals in two vital and enduring ways. First, by playing upon a stock of associations that already linked science's empirical rigors with a Protestant ethos deeply rooted in the English psyche, Huxley could more easily back the public into a naturalistic corner. Since the audiences he appealed to were accustomed to equating science's disciplined factuality with the Protestant devotion to God's revelations, Huxley's constant accentuation of science's moral courage in facing the facts of evolutionary naturalism made religious opposition largely untenable for his English audiences: to oppose such evidences was to deny their own cultural being. Second, by carefully managing the symbolic expansion of evolutionary science into evolutionism, he was less likely to draw attention to the unscientific bases of the latter position. The positivists had boldly and openly asserted that positive science was religion's successor—the revelation of its true essence. Privately, as the English positivists well knew, Huxley was of the same opinion, but rhetorically he was more astute than these rivals. He was better able to maintain the appearance of a clear separation between science and religion, most famously by inventing the concept of "agnosticism," even as he drew these realms together by casting evolutionary ideas in the Baconian idiom of his culture.

Although this study ends with Huxley, I believe that to understand the rhetorical campaigns of this Victorian scientist is to understand a defining pattern of public communication that endures in our own scientific culture. Once we recognize that the such pseudoscientific ideas have a serious professional purpose for scientists, we can begin to understand why the maturation of evolutionary science has done so little to diminish scientists' attraction to evolutionism. In my concluding chapter, I explore some subsequent manifestations of evolutionism, and I consider its implications, not only as a kind of meta-paradigm for science, but also as a symbolic resource likely to impact public audiences that now lean more heavily than ever before upon science for their understanding of the world.

Any book that is critical of what evolutionary scientists say is likely to be taken as a book against evolutionary science—and thus as an effort to advocate something like creationism or intelligent design. This suspicion is likely to be heightened once it is known that the author of that book is a religionist of some kind—in this case a religionist of the Roman Catholic kind. But while I do question the public behavior of evolutionary scientists, this book is only indirectly concerned with the substance of their work. Although I do believe that evolutionism only attains its desired rhetorical effects when it is thought to be identical with evolutionary science, I certainly do not believe that evolution and evolutionism are the same thing. To discover that evolutionary science sometimes becomes myth is not to say that it always does. Myths always tend to absorb regnant natural truths. Sometimes the natural understandings from which they spring are as imaginary as the myths, but not always. For this reason, my claim that evolutionary science sustains a prevalent myth should not be regarded as a challenge to this scientific field. To challenge evolutionism (as I certainly do) is not to contend that evolution is pseudoscience (which is certainly not my position).

I am operating upon the assumption that the descriptions and understandings of biological evolution put forth by my contemporaries are basically correct. This is not because I know that they are or because I think that evolutionary science should not be subject to honest criticism. It simply means that I do not have the expertise to say otherwise and that it would be presumptuous for me to suppose that those who know best have got it wrong. Criticism of the technical substance of scientific knowledge ought to be carried out by technical experts. Since I am not a scientist, I have simply surrendered all questions about biological evolution to those best qualified to address them. My criticism is directed at science as a public matter, and that is where my expertise lies.

Support for this undertaking has come from many quarters. I am especially grateful to my wife, Ruth Lessl, whose constant cheerful encouragement and friendship does so much to sustain my happiness and peace of mind. Ruth began an undergraduate course of study around the time I began this project, and she won (with several years to spare) the wager we made regarding who would finish first. My parents, Mildred and Robert Lessl, encouraged me to love both science and their Catholic faith. Their example of generosity, goodwill, and abiding practical sense is the most precious inheritance any human being could hope for. It has been my great good fortune to be able to work within range of the warming fire of a family that has now enlarged to include not only my two children, Jay and Amy, but also their wonderful spouses, Sandi and Skip, three granddaughters—Evelyn, Adeline, Emily, and one grandchild soon to come.

The Department of Communication Studies at the University of Georgia, which took me in some years ago, has proved to be a stimulating work environment for my research—a place that encourages competitive daring but also stretches out a safety net of collegiality. Each of those who have been around long enough to become pillars of this department, such as Ed Panetta, Celeste Condit, and Jennifer Monahan, have inspired me in their own unique ways. But the young Turks, Roger Stahl and Kelly Happe, inspire me too. I am especially grateful to Don Rubin, our former department head, for his humanity, optimism, and patient prodding, and to his successors, Jerry Hale and Barbara Biesecker, for carrying on that tradition.

The opportunity to participate in a summer seminar sponsored by the National Endowment for the Humanities and conducted at Cambridge University in 2002, enabled me to examine many primary materials pertaining to the career of Thomas Huxley. The directors of the NEH seminar, Professors Jan Swearingen and Carol Poster, offered much helpful feedback as my thinking about Huxley was in its early stages. While in residence in England, I also received much generous assistance from Anne Barrett, the Huxley archivist at Imperial College. Thanks are extended also to Courtney Caudle for her cheerful assistance on this end with various aspects of the manuscript's preparation. A travel grant provided by the University of Georgia's Center for the Humanities as well as funds generously endowed by a trust of the Karl Wallace family have enabled me to examine museum exhibits on evolution around the country. I was given the opportunity to present some of the themes of this book at a conference entitled "God, Science and Design," hosted by St. Anne's College, Oxford, in 2008, and at the meeting of the International Society for the History of Rhetoric, in Strasbourg (France) in 2007.

John Angus Campbell's work has provided vital inspiration for this book, and his comments on an early draft of the first chapter helped considerably in putting this project on course. But I am mostly grateful to him just for being John Campbell. He is the living spirit of our discipline. I owe similar thanks to Kenneth Zagacki, not only for his generosity in reading and commenting on the entire manuscript but also for many hours of stimulating conversation that have helped to sustain my faith in this project. Roderick Hart, my major professor at the University of Texas, has been an abiding source of encouragement as well. More locally, such support has come from my colleague Edward Larson and (undoubtedly without their knowing it) Howard and Linda Abney.

None of this would have been possible without Marty Medhurst's deft management of the review process and his patience in seeing this project through to the end. Finally, I wish to thank Carey Newman, the director of the Baylor University Press, and his outstanding staff for all their hard work in bringing this book to life.

1

The Social Meaning of Evolutionary Science

The theory of evolution is not just an inert piece of theoretical science. It is, and cannot help being, also a powerful folktale about human origins. . . . Facts will never appear to us as brute and meaningless; they will always organize themselves into some sort of story, some drama. These dramas can indeed be dangerous. They can distort our theories, and they have distorted the theory of evolution perhaps more than any other. The only way in which we can control this kind of distortion is to bring the dramas themselves out into the open, to give them our full attention, understand them better and see what part, if any, each of them ought to play both in theory and in life.

–Mary Midgley

Museum exhibits on human evolution are a familiar sight. They typically include some version of what Stephen Jay Gould once called the "march of progress," hominids in procession leading from the most ancient up to some representation (usually male and weapon-bearing) of the modern human form.[1] In the summer of 2006, I ran upon a particularly interesting version of this in the Musée de l'Homme, the Parisian museum of anthropology housed within the Palais de Chaillot. The skulls displayed here represent only the most recent phase of human evolution. They progress from a Cro-Magnon specimen dating from 100,000 years ago on the far right to a modern human cranium on the left. This evolutionary snapshot may not illustrate the sort of striking physical alterations one would see in similar displays that begin with our most remote bipedal ancestors, but its symbolic markers are familiar enough to assure visitors that each specimen represents a distinct stage of biological and cultural history. Laid out on ledges just below each skull are various artifacts associated with each of these stages of development. Their evolution progresses in step with these human remains, leading from the crude stone tools of our Cro-Magnon ancestors and culminating with a single modern artifact—a book, but not just any book. In fact it is a great scientific work, the *Discours de la méthode* (1637), and the skull on display above it once belonged to its author, the mathematician and scientist René Descartes (figure 2).

Figure 2

This might be interpreted in a number of different ways. In choosing a native son to symbolize the end of evolution, the exhibit's curators recognizably display a kind of national pride that one often sees in public museums. Indeed, a nationalistic motive is suggested by the plaque that indicates whose skull this is. The great mathematician is identified as a "Philosophe et savant français." Other exhibits in the museum, such as one depicting France as the world's leader in population control, send a similar message. But what draws my attention is the manner in which this particular exhibit brings together the notions of biological evolution and cultural progress. Jeanne Fahnestock regards science exhibits of this kind as visual instances of *incrementum*, that rhetorical figure that orders elements into some climactic structure on the principle of "the more and the less." She notes that the sense of natural continuity created by such figures enables them to integrate items into some single progression in which they might not otherwise belong.[2] In the Musée de l'Homme exhibit, this occurs because its curators have brought into parallel arrangement two ordered series, one from biology and another from culture, that, technically speaking, do not go together. The incrementum of physical evolution above has been made to march in step with the incrementum of technical and scientific "evolution" that lies just beneath it. Consequently, as these two series move toward the present, they also converge; biological evolution ends with Descartes and cultural evolution with the discovery of scientific method. By making this scientific thinker evolution's end, the museum's curators also give pride of place to science in biological history—the march of physical evolution ends with *homo scientificus*.

I am going to argue that this identification of science with natural evolution is an important pattern in science's public life, and I mean to support this claim by tracing the emergence of this pattern in modern science's historical development—the very subject that the curators of the Musée de l'Homme depict. I believe that the inclination to treat science as if it were the very purpose or destiny of natural evolution itself is a symbolic pattern fostered by the social conditions that have allowed science to emerge over the past four centuries. The idea of evolution, in other words, is tied up with the very idea of science, so that in the realm of public communication the promotion of evolutionary ideas often adds up to the promotion of the scientific enterprise as well. This gives evolution special rhetorical importance for the culture of modern science. By "rhetoric" I do not intend to denote some set of genres associated with political communication, but rather, following such theorists as Jeffrey Walker and Dilip Gaonkar, qualities of persuasiveness or "rhetoricality" that any genre of discourse may exhibit.[3] The role of evolutionary symbols in producing this rhetoricality for science is my subject.

The specific category of rhetoricality I am addressing here is *ethos*, a term traditionally associated with Aristotle's treatise on rhetoric and used to name the persuasive effects achieved when the character of a speaker is projected through a message.[4] My concern is with how and why the scientific character should enter into the message of evolution. Unlike the classical rhetoricians, who meant by ethos the character of the particular speaker, I mean to enlarge this term, much as sociologists and cultural anthropologists typically do, to denote the collective identity of a culture—in this instance, the scientific culture. But the traditional Aristotelian principle still applies. The collective scientific ethos abides in scientific messages just as much as that of any individual scientist-speaker would.

It has also been customary within this same social science point of view to recognize that a society's ethos is vitally tied up with its religious symbols, and I believe that this insight has special pertinence to the science-evolution symbolism I explore. Religion, as the sociologist Peter Berger summarizes its main symbolic pattern, always involves some identity between the creations of culture, the human *nomos*, and some reality or *cosmos* lying outside the human world. Because society is a necessity for human well-being but is also subject to dissolution once we recognize its fragility as a human creation, religious symbolism is needed to solidify its reality by making *nomos* and *cosmos* "appear to be co-extensive."[5] Religion is thus the most vital and sustaining component of cultural creativity. Because it provides vital linkages between society and some external and inviolable reality, it also provides a culture with its most potent reason for being. My analysis expands upon this insight by supposing that this general sociological principle also applies to the culture of science. Science is a word derived from *scientia*, the Latin word for knowledge, and in our time it has come to mean something like the systematic pursuit and organization of knowledge. But here I want to think of it as a word that also denotes a particular kind of society—a professional community devoted to such systematized inquiry. As such, science may be different in many respects from the social groups that sociologists and anthropologists have traditionally thought of when developing theories of religion, but what reason have we for supposing that scientific culture would be immune to similar pressures, to pressures of existence that would invite such *nomos-cosmos* identities?

EVOLUTIONARY MYTHOLOGY

If the science-evolution version of this *nomos-cosmos* identity belongs to the same category of symbolization that defines religious traditions, we would also expect this to manifest in that narrative or mythic mode that is the most characteristic vehicle of faith. It is thus when the scientific imagination runs free in science fiction that we most clearly witness its expressions. In October of 1963, just a few weeks before John Kennedy's assassination, an episode of the popular ABC television show *The Outer Limits* aired under the title "The Sixth Finger."[6] This tale is set in Wales, where a scientist works in the isolation of his country manor on an experimental device, a kind of genetic time machine capable of accelerating human evolution. Professor Mathers has already used this machine to advance a chimpanzee to the point where it can perform basic clerical tasks, but he wants to try this experiment on a human subject. Gwyllm Griffiths, a local coal miner played by David McCallum, volunteers to be genetically altered. In

Mathers' machine, Griffiths is advanced 10,000 years into the future, and afterwards his development continues spontaneously, taking him millions of years further. By the end of the story the Welsh lad is hardly recognizable; the megacephalic features that now dramatically set him off from even the brilliant geneticist who has engineered his transformation are the outward signs of an intellect so transformed that Gwyllm now views his human companions as mere apes. What is also apparent is that every step of his evolution is making Gwyllm into a scientist. Even before he steps inside the evolution machine, he has exchanged his miner's clothes for a white lab coat, but afterwards his intellectual tastes grow in accordance with his ever-expanding cranium. At first, Gwyllm's insatiable appetite for knowledge turns him to art. In one scene, Professor Mathers finds him playing Bach preludes on the piano with the skill of an advanced concert performer, but this interest is quickly subsumed by scientific aspirations as he realizes that "playing the piano is only a matter of mathematics with a certain degree of manual dexterity."

The virtue of Gwyllm's scientific evolution is in doubt at first. The young Welshman's smoldering anger has now become so pronounced that his initial contempt for the local mining village now threatens to boil over into a genocidal mania made possible by his enhanced powers. In this regard, the first phase of Gwyllm's evolution is merely a recapitulation of scientific history as it was popularly conceived during the Cold War. As his scientific powers grow, so also does the temptation to destroy the world from which he has arisen. Ultimately, however, just as his wrath is about to fall upon his neighbors, evolution redeems him. He moves "beyond hatred and revenge or even the desire for power," beyond those emotional impulses that formerly empowered science for destruction. Hatred gives way to compassion, and Gwyllm now wishes to fully realize this destiny by returning again to the evolution machine. He recognizes that in the fullness of evolution he will be set free from the corruptions of the body.

> I feel myself reaching that stage in the dim future of mankind when the mind will cast off the hamperings of the flesh and become all thought and no matter—a vortex of pure intelligence in space. It is the goal of evolution; man's final destiny is to become what he imagined in the beginning when he first learned the idea of the angels. But that is far ahead and I am impatient to go the whole way.

This story manifests in narrative form the same linkage between biological evolution and the scientific identity that we witnessed in the Musée de l'Homme, but it also gives this a clear religious meaning, much like George Bernard Shaw's *Back to Methuselah* (1921), from which the above speech was lifted almost verbatim. Not only does evolution make human beings more scientific, it also brings them closer to realizing a gnostic salvation from the slavery of matter. Ultimately Gwyllm's desire to follow its path into the realm of pure spirit is thwarted by his girlfriend Cathy, who takes charge of the genetic time machine and reverses his course, but evolution is by no means impugned by this act. As the story closes, a narrator steps in to explain that humans are merely not ready for this final destiny.

> An experiment too soon, too swift. And yet may we not still hope to discover a method by which within one generation the whole human race could be rendered intelligent, beyond hatred, revenge, or the desire for power? Is that not after all the ultimate goal of evolution?

The "method" that will achieve this ultimate goal is the technological mastery of evolution that this story imagines—science, in other words. In the end, the evolution of science converges with the evolution of nature; they are the same thing.

This theme found perhaps its most poignant statement a few years later in Stanley Kubrick's film *2001: A Space Odyssey* (1968). The mystical union of science and evolution that reaches its climax deep in space, in the then-distant future of the twenty-first century, is anticipated in its opening episode, "The Dawn of Man," where australopithecine tribes battle extinction in the harsh Pliocene deserts of Africa. As yet without tools or speech, they struggle to find food and to avoid becoming food, but their fate takes a hopeful turn with the appearance of a mysterious black monolith, the creation of an extraterrestrial intelligence that has been supervising human evolution for eons. This object triggers a new stage of brain development, and this manifests in the discovery of primitive tools. The spirit of science that hovers over the deep is guiding human evolution toward a scientific future, and Kubrick visually underlines this theme at the close of this act when the story's hominid inventor triumphantly thrusts his bone weapon into the air. As it tumbles above the earth, the club becomes a space station orbiting the moon four million years later, where a second evolutionary epoch is about to begin. A second monolith has now been found at the center of the Moon's Tycho crater, buried deep beneath the meteoric dust that has accumulated since alien scientists deposited it there four million years earlier. As daybreak again falls upon the newly excavated monolith, it emits a powerful radio signal aimed in the direction of Jupiter. Science has again joined in the work of evolution.

In the film's final movement, "Jupiter and Beyond the Infinite," a group of astronauts follows this signal into space only to be sabotaged by their own science, by the deranged rationality of HAL, the artificial intelligence that regulates all the technical operations of the spaceship *Discovery*. This scientific journey recapitulates the evolutionary one witnessed in the first movement, but now it culminates in the final transformation of human nature. In anticipation of this, HAL plays an important role as the story's antagonist. He symbolizes the shortcomings of the merely human science that has not yet completed its odyssey, its full evolutionary convergence with nature. Science can only be complete when it becomes nature, and nature, when it becomes science. And since the merely human science now embodied within HAL falls short, it has turned against nature by attempting to abort *Discovery*'s mission.

Like the antagonists of more conventional romances, HAL's fatal flaw tells us something important about his counterpart, Dave Bowman, the sole surviving astronaut who manages to arrest the computer's rampage. This struggle replays an age-old dialectic: science as power versus science as knowledge. As rivals for control of *Discovery*—and the ship's very name is an allegory for science—both Bowman and HAL are in search of more complete knowledge. But for HAL, whose universe is limited by the ship he was created to regulate, complete knowledge means complete control—science as power. His "psychosis," as noted in Arthur C. Clarke's novel, is the same "xenophobia" that had manifested in pilot studies done on human subjects who were introduced to the prospect of a human encounter with alien science.[7] More specifically, it is a scientific xenophobia. Realizing that the mission's goal will bring him face to face with the fullness of science as knowledge, HAL also realizes that knowledge as mere power will be lost. Thus his madness becomes a thematic representation of limited knowledge turned against the scientific soul of natural evolution, its inability to open itself to the "infinite" that is Bowman's final scientific destiny.

Bowman awakens to this evolutionary *telos* once he has defeated *Discovery*'s supercomputer brain. This dooms the astronaut, as the great deeds of romantic heroes always do—either figuratively or in fact. But it is also this act that brings about the hero's rebirth and the symbolic rebirth of the human world he represents. In the more detailed account given in Clarke's novel, the attentive reader will realize that the mysterious technological monolith toward which Bowman now heads is a perfected version of the artificial intelligence he has just silenced. It performs the perfect unity of body and spirit that was denied to Gwyllm Griffiths. Bowman's final descent into the monolith unites him with pure science, just as Griffiths' descent into the evolution machine had done, and when he ascends from this subterranean journey he has been transfigured as a "star child." Nature is science-like, and thus in the culmination of this evolutionary odyssey Bowman departs the realm of the body for the realm of pure thought. Science is discovered to be nature in its spiritual aspect, and thus when Bowman again encounters the scientific perfection of these same extraterrestrial stewards at the end of the story, humanity's ultimate fate shows forth.

This thematic spiritualizing of science and its identification with natural evolution runs through numerous popular films of the last half century that imagine earthly encounters with benevolent extraterrestrials. The sainted aliens that we find in such films as *E.T.: The Extra-Terrestrial* (1982), *Close Encounters of the Third Kind* (1977), *Starman* (1984), *Cocoon* (1985), *2010* (1984), *Contact* (1997), and in that slightly older forerunner to these, *The Day the Earth Stood Still* (1951), foreshadow some anticipated destiny in which science and its offspring—technology—will transform the human condition. As with the previous examples, the unspoken premise that sustains this theme is the notion that scientific hegemony is not merely a logical outcome of cultural development but a tendency of natural evolution itself. The alien visitors who populate these stories consistently manifest superior powers of knowledge that the viewer will attribute to the far longer time frames in which these civilizations have possessed science. However, these advanced powers also seem to have analogous biological footings that can be accounted for by these alien beings' correspondingly longer exposure to the effects of natural evolution. In several of these stories—*2001*, *Cocoon*, and *Contact*, for instance—the aliens seem to have achieved the same transfigured state that Gwyllm Griffiths had aspired to realize, in which embodied biological life has been gradually changed, presumably by natural evolution, into a disembodied, mind-like life—but a mind-like life still closely identified with nature. Evolution has brought matter and scientific thought together in these characters. The alien in Steven Spielberg's *E.T.*, for instance, has enough scientific knowledge (in the conventional sense) to build a radio telescope from household odds and ends, but similar powers are shown to lie within his bodily organism when he revives a wilted chrysanthemum and later even his own body. He is science incarnate. Similarly, the alien whose natural body is destroyed at the beginning of the film *Starman* spontaneously clones another one to wear during his earthly sojourn. It is as if the same advancements of knowledge that we would expect to witness in a civilization whose science was millions of years in advance of our own had also achieved analogous results in the realm of biological evolution.

The spiritual meaning hinted at in these stories can be traced to the narrative forms they have borrowed from religious traditions. The scientist visitor in *E.T.* comes down from heaven to sojourn briefly among the child-like of this planet. Only certain innocents are able to recognize him, and yet, much as with his New Testament counterpart, we recognize that he is the face of the very ancient of days. All of nature's power is incarnate in him, enabling him to levitate balls, read minds, revive wilted flowers, and ultimately even resurrect himself. But in spite of his manifest benevolence, E.T. is rejected and hunted down by those who are his earthly counterparts, by Pharisaical scientists whose integrity has been compromised by a corrupt alliance with a secretive and paranoid government. But their tomb of glass and steel cannot hold him. Before he ascends back into the heavens, he gathers his friends and promises to be with them always.

One might reasonably object that such messages do not really support my thesis since they are only loosely related to science, that if cinematic and television representations of science derive religious meaning from this nature-science identity, this is only because they reflect the culture of the lay consumers they were created to entertain. But many who have given voice to this science-as-spiritual destiny theme have been respected members of the scientific community. A generation ago this was Jacob Bronowski, whose 1974 BBC series on the history of science, *The Ascent of Man*, later became the inspiration for another program that I will also discuss, Carl Sagan's *Cosmos* (1980).[8] Judging from the similarity that Bronowski's title bears to Darwin's *Descent of Man* (1871), we would be correct in supposing that it was devoted to the subject of human evolution, but it clearly takes liberties with this scientific subject. The "ascent" in its title in fact signals a narrative form that Bronowski could not have derived from evolutionary science. Broadly speaking, the program unfolds as an incrementum, a climactic historical progression in which biological evolution gives rise to civilization, civilization to science, and science now to all of humanity's future hopes. Science, having arisen from biological evolution, has now become nature's mechanism of progress. As such, it has special apocalyptic import for Bronowski; because science alone follows the path of evolution, only science can bring humanity through the travail that had thus far marked the twentieth century. The counterpart to HAL in Bronowski's tale is Nazi Fascism, which, by attempting to fix knowledge as political dogma, arrested the upward flow of natural progress. In this scene he wades ankle-deep into a pond outside the Auschwitz crematorium to make his climactic speech. Standing among the human ashes that were flushed into its waters, Bronowski denounces National Socialism for turning science into a false idol that would "dehumanize people and turn them into numbers," by engendering the belief that people can "have absolute knowledge with no test in reality." This idolatrous science aspired to possess "the knowledge of gods" but only produced "dogma" instead. The corrective for such evils, in fact, is the humility that keeps science in step with nature's movement. As Bronowski explains the redeeming quality that sets science apart, one cannot help but notice how similar this sounds to the trial and error of evolutionary gradualism. "We are always at the brink of the known; we always feel forward for what is to be hoped. Every judgment in science stands on the edge of error and is personal. Science is a tribute to what we can know although we are fallible." Then, as he crouches to scoop up a handful of ash from the pond, he swears an oath as a "survivor and witness" to advance the cause of that science which can forever cure "the itch for absolute knowledge and power."[9]

Bronowski, of course, is narrating a familiar historical dialectic of the Enlightenment that one finds in all of its children: reason advancing against superstition, base against superstructure, fact against faith, matter against ideas, modernity against tradition. But now one particular scientific product, the theory of biological evolution, has become the truth standard against which these evils are contrasted. By framing the antinomy of the real and the unreal in scientific terms, he makes scientific knowledge the standard by which history is to be judged. Understanding of evolutionary biology becomes the qualifying condition that enables us to understand and to participate in history's unfolding course. Bronowski would later encapsulate this idea in another book.

> Something has happened regarding the eruption of science into Western Civilization which is new and yet permanent and irreversible. In the evolution of any animal there come moments when the species takes a radically new step, a mutation is built into the total genetic complex, and from that moment on the species is committed to some new way of life—like coming out of the water onto the land. Now I believe that the scientific revolution has done exactly that kind of thing to our cultural history and we must simply face this fact. It isn't just that science has happened, that if you don't look it might go away. There has been an irreversible step in the cultural evolution of man; it took place at the beginning of the

scientific revolution from, say, 1500 to 1700, and it will never be undone. We are committed to a scientific way of acting, and we cannot go back.[10]

The cultural evolution that is now driven by science is not merely analogous to biological evolution. It is the fact that it is "exactly" like the genetic mutations that drive biological evolution that gives Bronowski's message its authority and moral urgency. The *nomos* of science reflects the *cosmos* of evolutionary biology. To resist the irreversible evolutionary step brought on by the scientific revolution is to go against nature's destiny, and thus the calamities of the twentieth century that figured so prominently in *The Ascent of Man* signify humanity's rejection of both science and evolution.

Created with a budget of 8.2 million dollars and watched by half a billion people in sixty nations, Carl Sagan's *Cosmos* made this millenarian theme the centerpiece of the most ambitious and most widely viewed public television event of its day.[11] Sagan's unprecedented popularity is often attributed to his gift for plainspoken scientific exposition, but one has to wonder if it did not have more to do with his willingness to lift scientific ideas up to higher philosophical and religious elevations. Such metaphysical license is apparent in his introduction to the printed version of this series, where he characterizes the human predicament as a kind of anomie that arises from our having "grown distant from the Cosmos." The remedy for this he calls a "cosmic perspective," the recognition "that we are, in a very real and profound sense, a part of the Cosmos, born from it, our fate deeply connected with it."[12] If we wanted to be literal, we might presume that the connection that Sagan speaks of is merely the pattern of material causation that science specializes in explaining, but the moral significance that he attaches to this makes it fairly clear that he has entered into a mythical mode of symbol construction. To assert that our scientific deficiencies cause us to grow "distant" from nature is to imply that science founds not only an I-It relationship with nature, as Martin Buber famously called this, but also an "I-Thou" or subject-to-subject relationship that sets us in right standing with the sources of our existence.[13] In this regard, *Cosmos* confronts us with the same sort of "scientific mythology" that Stephen Toulmin recognized in Sagan's earlier books, an effort that actively works "to reinsert humanity into nature."[14]

In the end, Sagan's narrative sustains the same vision of human destiny that we witness in extraterrestrial science fiction. The crucial difference is that, as a PBS documentary narrated by a respected astronomer, *Cosmos* wears a scientific mask. Sagan situates his program within the genre of science education, and the scientific subjects it explores receive much the same treatment as one would expect to find in textbooks and university class-rooms. Consequently, when he frames the series thematically by introduc-ing Darwin's theory of evolution in its second episode, viewers have every reason to presume that he is merely talking about biological science, not the mythopoeic evolution of "The Sixth Finger" or Kubrick's film. Sagan goes on to affirm this supposition by insisting that, while his narrative has "the sound of epic myth," it is "simply a description of cosmic evolution as revealed by the science of our time."[15] But what one finds is not "simply" science. Evolution may be an important scientific subject in this series, but more importantly it is also the series' theme. The familiar body of scientific learning that it references simultaneously serves as a metaphor for a histori-cal vision of progress that is imbued with more traditional notions of value, purpose, and even design.

Even before Sagan broaches the topic of biological evolution in his second episode, this double meaning is already at work. The introductory episode opens with the "personal voyage" that is referenced in the series' sub-title, but this is the voyage of *both* cosmic evolution and historical progress. Viewers here accompany Sagan as he pilots an imaginary starship from the farthest reaches of the universe back toward Earth, where the episode's first segment ends, as its title indicates, on the "Shores of the Cosmic Ocean."[16] His ship takes us past quasars, spiral galaxies, black holes, globular clusters, red giants, and then makes a closer approach to examine the geological features of our neighboring planets before Sagan returns to Earth. What is recapitulated in this scientific journey is cosmic evolution. As Sagan travels the universe from the outside in, his voyage retraces the broader evolution-ary "journey" that gave rise to biological evolution here on Earth. But by depicting this also through the symbolism of space travel, the material "voy-age" of evolution has also become the "voyage" of science. The shore of the cosmic ocean where this journey ends is at once both the beginning point of biological evolution and the point of departure from which the future of science now takes leave.

As a teaching device, Sagan's space voyage enables him to offer a quick preview of the astronomical science that is the main subject of these pro-grams, but this "journey" does more than teach science. At the end of this grand tour, with contemporary astronomy firmly in command of their attention, Sagan's viewers will hardly notice that their host has made a quali-tative shift. What began as a scientific survey of our "evolving" universe has now given way to a narrative about an "evolving" human "destiny"—the spe-cies' destined reunion with the cosmos that is being accomplished through science. At this point the story of evolution blends into a historical narrative in which science takes over as the mechanism of the cosmos' development.

In narrative form, Sagan has produced something that bears a notable similarity to the transformation of evolution into science that one witnesses in the Musée de l'Homme, only on a grander scale. The process of biological evolution that began on our planet is now "coming of age" in science, in that "passion for exploring the Cosmos," by which we are "in some pain and with no guarantees, working out our destiny."[17] The aspirations of science by this account are also the aspirations of nature, and we have an obligation to pursue its course back to the outer reaches of the universe where this journey first began. The "matter of the Cosmos has become alive and aware" in human evolution—that is to say, in mystical union with the natural universe—and this makes the pursuit of science a moral responsibility, not only because it honors "the accumulated wisdom of men and women of our species, gathered at great cost over a million years," but more importantly because it is the eternal return called for by our evolutionary heritage. We honor evolution by pursuing science. In science, human beings who were "born ultimately of the stars and now for a while inhabiting a world called Earth, have begun their long voyage home."[18]

EVOLUTIONISM, PATRONAGE, AND THE SCIENTIFIC PRIESTHOOD

I will come back to this *nomos-cosmos* identity, but before I do I would like to give this pattern a name and explain why I think it has significance of the kind I have outlined. I will call this "evolutionism," a term already put into play by the philosopher Michael Ruse to distinguish evolution as worldview from evolution as science. In his *Monad to Man* (1996), Ruse describes evolutionism as any nonscientific application of the ideas of evolutionary science. He reads it, as I also will in part, as a pattern that has descended from the Enlightenment notion of "Progress."[19] Ruse and I also agree that its attraction has not diminished with the maturation of evolutionary studies. He recognizes that evolution still has "the trappings of a religious faith," just as it did for the generation of Thomas Huxley and Herbert Spencer, because scientists continue to confuse it with evolutionism.[20] Ruse substantiates this claim with extensive and detailed evidence gathered from personal interviews and from the writings of evolutionary science's most important contributors of the last two centuries. Almost without exception, Ruse finds that evolutionism has been the rule rather than the exception. It is not a peculiarity of science fiction or of overly zealous documentary hosts.

It correlates in a nearly one-to-one fashion with devotion to evolutionary science. Ruse's interest in its persistence reflects his concern that it is also a cultural phenomenon that in the past has stymied the professional development of this field, preventing it, at least until recent decades, from attaining the kind of professional respectability and robustness it deserves.

Although Ruse concedes at the end of his book that evolutionism remains just as prevalent as ever, he does not believe that it compromises evolutionary science in any significant way.[21] He tends to regard it merely as a personal ideology or worldview, a kind of secular religion that has no significant bearing upon scientific research as such. So far as the closed world of professional scientific communication is concerned, it would seem reasonable to agree with him. Here the rigors of scientific peer review are likely to keep such distortions at bay. But Ruse's conclusion seems to overlook the public significance of evolutionism. He is clearly aware that evolutionism has a public face and that it has been promulgated by notables such as G. Gaylord Simpson, E. O. Wilson, Richard Dawkins, and dozens more like them, but he does not make note of the bearing that this might have on public perceptions of science.[22] But communication of this kind, though commonly bracketed off from serious science under the heading of "popularization," is not mere entertainment. Rather it is an important force for shaping public understanding. Public science may not seem to matter in the thinking of scientists who have been socialized to regard only what is reported in scholarly journals as authentically "scientific," but it is crucial in a way that academic science is not. Since this is where the face of science is shown to the world, its professional interests and integrity are at stake in such messages. When evolutionism is presented as science (which it surely has been), then the rest of us are actively misled about evolution and about the character of science more generally.

Were evolutionism just a personal belief, scientists might be expected to keep it to themselves, lest it be confused with evolutionary science. I will argue, in fact, that it is precisely because evolutionism has rhetorical import that many respected scientists wish to promulgate it. Richard Dawkins is one of these. Oxford University's "Charles Simonyi Professorship of the Public Understanding of Science" was created for him in 1995 so that he might be freed from some of his academic responsibilities to advance his work as a public intellectual.[23] One might think that a great scientist who works under such a title would be especially devoted to a rigorous scientific decorum, but as Davi Johnson has recently shown, what we actually get in his recent *Ancestor's Tale* (2004) is evolutionary science coded as myth.[24]

Superficially, we would expect the very opposite, since myth is the stuff of religion—something Dawkins vehemently dislikes. Indeed, one of his manifest purposes in *Ancestor's Tale* is to repudiate the traditional religious idea that the natural order privileges human beings.[25] But upon closer inspection, it becomes evident that Dawkins undertakes to remove human beings from the top rung of this more traditional Great Chain of Being because he has an alternative natural order in mind. As Johnson points out in her critique, it is not to uphold the value neutrality of science that Dawkins repudiates the privileging of human beings; rather, his goal is to construct an alternative natural order by claiming to reveal an egalitarian meaning in the evolutionary record.[26] While we might agree with Dawkins that the testimony of science could never bear witness to the privileging of human nature, neither could it bear witness to the equality of all living things. Yet this is the overarching theme of Dawkins' book. He trades on the ambiguity that one may find in the notion of "common ancestry" in order to project the value of equality upon the biological world. At first glance, the "Pilgrimage to the Dawn of Evolution" of his subtitle might seem to be a merely playful allusion to Chaucer's *Canterbury Tales*, but in reality he has made the "Dawn of Evolution" a sacred place. As the author introduces us to our various evolutionary ancestors as we journey with him from the present into the deep past, he promises that "we shall inevitably meet these other pilgrims and join forces with them in a definite order, the order in which their lineages rendezvous with ours, the order of ever more inclusive cousinship."[27] Those who make this journey—in other words, those who adopt an evolutionary perspective—will overcome the "speciesism" that plagues the common lot of humanity.[28] But from a truly scientific point of view how could the evolutionary forces that Dawkins has famously called a "blind watchmaker" be more "inclusive"? Dawkins has added his own anthropomorphic meaning to the lesson of evolution. He has made it a sign of the universal democracy of all living things.

Why would a "Professor of the Public Understanding of Science" so freely promulgate confusion about biological history? This should seem especially odd in the face of how often we hear scientists complain about the fact that only roughly half of Americans fully accept what evolutionary science teaches.[29] Why would so many of the very scientists who so strongly criticize lay observers who dismiss the rigorous reasoning and vast stores of evidence that support evolution be so quick to take up a pseudoscientific perspective of their own? Professional concern for evolutionary science would seem to demand the very opposite. We would expect scientists to be as vigilant in warding off evolutionism as they are in repudiating the theistic motives they detect in creationism and intelligent design.

Such inconsistencies make sense once we consider the rhetorical potency of *nomos-cosmos* linkages. By supposing that human values can be read out of nature, evolutionism sustains an ethos that is highly attractive to scientists. I will call this a "priestly" ethos, not only because it arises from evolutionism's capacity to depict scientists as mediators of a reality inaccessible to all others, but also because of its essential religious properties.[30] Cultures elevate certain individuals as priests because they regard them as uniquely equipped to receive and interpret sacred signs, messages thought to emanate from the source of all being and value. For a culture strongly under the spell of naturalism, in which there is no being that is not identical with the reality of the natural universe, science is likely to assume this role simply because it assumes such authority once the natural world has moved into the position vacated by God. This is not to say that science, as science, deals in the sacred. We might safely presume that most of its practitioners are content to be mere plowers and sowers in various fields of material causality. It is only when evolution transmutes into evolutionism that science appropriates this priestly identity. When this occurs, scientific knowledge about the origins and development of life will have transformed into a narrative about life's meaning, value, and purpose, thus transforming the scientific role as well.

To hold the office of priest is to garner tangible rewards. Science, by emulating this social role, is able to siphon off some of the respect traditionally directed at religious authorities, but this is more than merely a shift of subjective allegiances. My focal concern is with the more concrete benefits of patronage that accrue to those who occupy such a role. This is particularly worthy of emphasis simply because the problem of patronage is such an obvious one for the scientific culture. Like others who wish to undertake intellectual pursuits, scientists depend upon the goodwill of strangers, the goodwill of various outside interests that might benefit by sharing with science some part of their expendable wealth.

Patronage is a problem for science simply because there is never enough of it. There always seems to be plenty of public enthusiasm for science—just never enough to keep it fully employed. This is because the return that science pays on such investments is typically only indirect. Industries will support scientific research if they perceive that it might contribute to their profitability or perhaps give a scientific aura to their products, and governments will do so if they perceive that science has bearing on public policy or the public good. But the journey of science does not move in concert with such public motives; it is likely to be derailed when it depends too much on such limited justifications. Ronald Tobey has illustrated this dilemma in a fascinating study of scientific patronage in the decades between the world wars.[31] In spite of their first organized campaign to deepen public support for basic research, U.S. scientists failed, as they consistently had up until this time, simply because the American public was so deeply wedded to pragmatism. Basic science is not pragmatic, and it progresses most effectively when it is free to pursue the sorts of questions that offer the most promise of giving up answers—not when it pursues commercial or military payoffs. Pure research was a hard sell in a country that regarded Thomas Edison as its greatest scientist. Basic research in the world's most affluent nation lagged far behind that in much smaller countries like Germany, France, and England. This changed considerably after the Second World War when the advent of the atom bomb fused basic science with pragmatism in the American consciousness, but science has remained particularly vulnerable to the volatilities of a public mind that still doubts the worth of science for science's sake.

Alexis de Tocqueville had predicted as much when the French government sent him to the United States in 1831 to study the U.S. prison system. Theoretical science required a reflective frame of mind that our democratic culture was unlikely to foster. In a country where everyone "is in motion: some in quest of power, others of gain," there would be little time for contemplation, and little value would be attached to the pursuit of knowledge that was not also the pursuit of power or gain.[32] How Tocqueville explained France's stronger tradition of scientific patronage is particularly notable. He thought that science had continued to prosper in his native country, in the aftermath of its own move toward democracy, because certain residues of the older feudal world still persisted in its cultural psyche. The French historian does not say what aspects of the *ancien régime* these were, but from his emphasis on the value of contemplation as a necessary condition for prospering basic science, we might surmise that he had in mind science's share in the religious ethos of his society.

If science finds a personal motive in its association with things transcendent, it may find an ideal public motive here as well. When science is connected to religion, it also becomes an instrument for the achievement of spiritual purposes, and spiritual purposes supersede the practical and material ones that scientific patronage might otherwise depend upon. When science has religious meaning, it will be valued for its own sake, and I believe this is key to understanding evolutionism as a rhetorical resource. If God commanded his creatures to undertake science, science would have an absolute value. Even better would be a religious worldview in which nature, the very subject matter of science, had taken God's place. This is precisely what evolutionism proposes to do. By suggesting that evolution has absolute meaning as nature's generative principle, evolutionism makes the natural world its God, and science, as nature's priesthood, the only activity capable of interpreting the mind of this deity. Thus it provides an ideal symbolic superstructure for scientific patronage.

In theoretical terms, this claim rests upon the understanding of religion that I invoked at the outset, the description of religion as a *nomos-cosmos* identification that Peter Berger derives from the sociological insights of Émile Durkheim.[33] Durkheim theorized that religion gives "birth to all that is essential in society because the idea of society is the soul of religion."[34] The corporate self that we refer to in speaking of society, though lacking the same properties of realness as any corporeal individual, gains objectivity by being identified with some more stable and transcendent reality, such as the life of God or the unfolding of nature, to which a people can affix the transitory state of their group existence:

> Religion is in a word the system of symbols by means of which society becomes conscious of itself; it is the characteristic way of thinking of collective existence. There then is a great group of states of mind which would not have originated if individual states of consciousness had not been combined, and which result from this union and are superadded to those which derive from individual natures.[35]

In a similar vein, Clifford Geertz describes religious symbolism as the "fusing" of "ethos and world view" that enables social groups to affirm the objectivity and authority of their moral identity.[36] Religion ratifies a group's ethos, "the tone, character, and quality of their life, its moral and aesthetic style and mood . . . the underlying attitude toward themselves and their world that life reflects," by situating it in their "most comprehensive ideas of order," their ontology and cosmology.[37]

The recognition that societies are the tenuous and fragile products of some merely subjective consensus accentuates religion's importance. Without some such extra-human basis, the manifestly constructed character of social order would become apparent and would threaten its dissolution. Religion compensates for this threat (more or less spontaneously) by projecting social identity upon some seemingly more permanent or transcendent reality. In spite of the variable ways in which this has been performed in human history, the general pattern is always the same. In an aboriginal society, a tribe might stabilize its identity by regarding itself as the distinctive model of some more permanent macrocosm, or it might, by regarding its chiefs or priests as both men and gods, imbue the top rung of its social hierarchy with a sacred essence that then seeps down into every subordinate tier. In the bookish religions that have superseded such traditions in the West, sacred revelation provides these linkages. Theistic societies affirm their realness by emulating the social representations encoded in the Gospels, the Torah, or the Qur'an. The sacred substance that many aboriginal cultures attach to natural objects is found by these people of the book in patterns of symbolization breathed into human consciousness by God.

From this theoretical standpoint we may predict that new modes of linking *nomos* with *cosmos* will spontaneously arise, even in secular settings, simply because the necessity of maintaining a volatile social consensus presses in upon every human culture. Because every society is a "precarious symbolic hypostatization," as Berger describes it, "a product of human activity that has attained the status of objective reality," the bases by which such social formations are tied to this reality must be constantly reaffirmed or reinvented.[38] The normative features of a group's social consciousness remain dependent upon belief in the external reality from which it derives its being.[39] Nature and society must reflect each other, so that in every human society, as Geertz puts this, the "powerfully coercive 'ought' is felt to grow out of a comprehensive factual 'is.'"[40]

This also implies that religious ideas will evolve in step with the societies they constitute. It is from this standpoint that I wish to interpret various forms of public communication that sustain evolutionism. Evolutionism is not some mere coincidental adjunct to evolutionary science. So long as the aspiration to possess a priestly social identity remains attractive to scientists as a way to justify their place in the world of their cultural patrons, the scientific identity will depend upon evolution to affirm its extra-human foundation. Evolutionary science has revealed this scientific *cosmos*, and evolutionism, accordingly, sustains a counterpart *nomos*. The "powerfully coercive 'ought'" that would compel the world to cherish scientific learning as an absolute good, is the "comprehensive factual 'is'" of evolution. Evolutionism could never stand entirely apart from evolutionary science for this reason, for to doubt evolution would be to doubt the scientific identity.

This claim is certain to shock some readers, but (if I may be forgiven for introducing something of a paradox) it would be unscientific to suppose that science is somehow exempt from the sociological principle I have out-lined. Some will say that scientific claims are different from others because they are held accountable to the most rigorous factual and rational criteria. I completely agree. But scientific arguments do not by themselves constitute the scientific identity, and so if this ethos is at all like other social identities, we would expect Durkheim's theorem to hold true. At least in the realm of cultural anthropology, according to Geertz, no society has been found that can be exempted:

> Though in theory we might think that a people could construct a wholly autonomous value system independent of any metaphysical referent, an ethics without ontology, we do not in fact seem to have found such a people. The tendency to synthesize world view and ethos at some level, if not logically necessary, is at least empirically coercive; if it is not philo-sophically justified, it is at least pragmatically universal.[41]

Geertz may not have been thinking about science when he wrote this, but Mary Douglas has applied this principle to the worldview of one scien-tist—paradoxically, in fact, to Durkheim himself. Even though he regarded it as law-like that all societies are brought into being by religion, he seems to have exempted his own scientific worldview from this principle. As Doug-las points out, it was in trying to make science the exception to his own rule that Durkheim most aptly illustrated it. The sociologist regarded his findings as true representations of the nature of things and therefore as immune to the sociological reductions he used to account for other groups' constructions of the world. But if Durkheim's theory of social construction was right, this could only mean that he had himself merely hypostatized the scientific consciousness as an expression of nature.[42]

In fact, Durkheim's efforts to work around this problem are suggestive of evolutionism. In a lecture called "Mythology and Truth," he acknowl-edged that myth will continue to hide under the cover of such abstractions as "democracy," "progress," or "the class struggle" even in a secular society, and for this reason he admitted that, for the moment at least, "scientific thought cannot rule alone." In saying this, he expressed the hope that myth would one day be completely superseded by science. "For a long time," he writes, there will be "a tendency towards objective scientific truth and a ten-dency towards subjectively perceived truth, towards mythological truth."[43] However, "a long time" is not forever, and so we can see in this comment a narrative vision akin to the one that turns up in 2001 and "The Sixth Finger," a vision of history as gradually rising toward scientific purity. Superficially, one might suppose that this evolutionary vision is the very opposite of myth since Durkheim asserts it as scientific truth, but by his own admission, science cannot reveal the plan of history that seems to be presupposed in this utterance. What evidence have we that would suggest that human history is tending by some innate dynamic toward the abolition of myth? In principle, Durkheim ought to have thought the opposite, but he was caught in the very mythic web he so brilliantly illuminated. He was trapped by the "ought" of evolutionary myth in appealing to the comprehensive factual "is" of evolutionary gradualism.

This is the marvel of evolutionism. Even as it sets science against myth, the historical vision needed to sustain this faith is itself mythical. This is because, as René Girard has explained it, to "expel religion is, as always, a religious gesture," insofar as such acts themselves always presuppose an alternative grounding for human existence.[44]

Romance and History

Some will doubtless regard this thesis as radical. I will insist that it is not a claim capable of undermining the integrity of evolutionary theory; but I admit that it is one that is certain to trouble it. To argue that the scientific identity has some stake in the believability of evolutionary science will certainly raise questions about the objectivity of what scientists say about it. One way out of this problem would be to turn the tables and contend that I am the one who lacks objectivity, perhaps by supposing that I write as an advocate for an alternative religious perspective or that I lack sufficient respect for science. But if we are to speculate about motives, we should do so on all sides. We all have motives, and so I am not claiming that the public purveyors of evolutionary thought are generally more likely than any others to distort matters. The problem with motives is that they operate upon us differently in different circumstances, and this is all I am saying about the culture of modern science. Motives capable of distorting inquiry and argument are always afoot, and it is precisely for this reason that scientists enforce methodological guidelines. In advancing the claim that evolutionism wears the mask of evolutionary science, I am concerned with scientific discourses that are not regulated by these norms and which take much of their inspiration from the never-ending struggle of scientists to find their place in the world. My subject is not science in what G. Thomas Goodnight has called the "technical sphere," the specialized arenas where experts exchange ideas, but rather science in the "public sphere" where it is mediated to the broader communities in which scientists operate.[45] When scientists step into the public sphere, they certainly do bring much expert knowledge with them, but its treatment is no longer constrained by the same sense of professional etiquette. What I am talking about here is not merely the relaxation of standards that is needed to get difficult ideas across to lay audiences. My concern, rather, is with the competing purposes that are at work in public science. Because the scientific livelihood depends so vitally on the sanction of public patrons, scientists are forever inclined to promote science as a worldview or ideology even as they undertake to inform the public in more straightforward ways. The problem is that one of the most attractive ways to do this is by seeming to give such ideologies a scientific standing.

Because science's public actors are also the architects of its public image, I will insist that their messages have considerable importance. These could never be mere efforts of "popularization"; they carry on the serious work of representing what science is and knows to the world at large. Having become the voice of science for its patrons, these actors are also inclined to assume the responsibility of constructing ideologies or worldviews that advance science's standing in the world. Public actors of all sorts do this, but, as Karl Mannheim pointed out long ago, they will be inclined to do so in some manner reflecting their own unique way of experiencing the world, since collective identities or ideologies are likely to be "associated with a given historical and social situation, and the *Weltanschauung*" and "style of thought" bound up with their situation.[46] For a scientific culture this means that its own methods, assumptions, and even discoveries are likely to provide the symbols from which its ideological systems are built. More specifically, in light of the perennial challenges of sustaining public patronage, we would expect a scientific culture to broaden as much as possible the scope of expertise that makes it attractive to potential patrons. It might be expected to do so by accentuating one or more of the following three interrelated ideas: (1) *naturalism*, the supposition that inquiry cannot reach beyond the bounds of materiality; (2) *scientism*, the assumption that only the techniques of inquiry used within the natural sciences have epistemic worth; and (3) *evolutionism*, the belief that concepts arising from evolutionary science apply to all human affairs. Because each of these ideas at least gives the appearance of arising from scientific inquiry itself, and because each is suggestive of an epistemic hierarchy that gives science the highest position, a society attracted to any one of these three notions may be strongly disposed to patronize science.

It is important to note that, in terms of their rhetorical potential, these three concepts are more or less interchangeable: each idea would seem to entail the other two (figure 3).

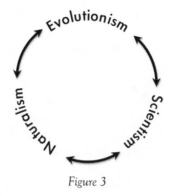

Figure 3

A public made to believe in naturalism will also be inclined to accept the scientistic assumption that all questions fall within the scope of the natural sciences, since this ontological premise will condition them to presume that all meaningful questions are scientific ones. Conversely, a public that believes in scientism will likely share the assumption that nature is all that is or at least all that can be known. Similarly, the doctrine of evolution, once generalized as evolutionism, will also seem to support the other two ideas. Scientific work is thought to occur within the bounds of material nature, and so, for those who already believe that evolutionary science has accounted for the most complex of natural complexities that fall within these limits, both naturalism and scientism will be presumed.

Any culture inclined to embrace naturalism or scientism might also be eager to patronize the natural sciences. But when these notions are expressed through evolutionism, they gain unique rhetorical leverage. Evolutionism rolls scientism and naturalism back into the world of scientific research and thereby promises to broaden the scope of scientific entitlement without endangering its autonomy. Because the doctrines of naturalism and scientism are likely to be defended through abstract examinations of epistemology and ontology, they tend to externalize scientific authority. Scientists will sometimes directly advance these notions, but the most authoritative proponents of naturalism and scientism have been philosophers: John Locke, David Hume, Étienne Condillac, John Stuart Mill, A. J. Ayer, Bertrand Russell, Rudolph Carnap, Daniel Dennett, Jerry Fodor, and many others. Evolutionism's stronger identification with evolutionary science enables it to sustain the impression that naturalism and scientism are mere inductive generalizations arising from the data of nature—from science itself. To stand upon evolutionism is to hold that nature is all that is, that science alone knows nature, and, most importantly, that these two claims have a scientific basis.

In light of this, it is not surprising that we should find in the agnosticism of Thomas Henry Huxley, who I will present later in this book as the first great architect of mature evolutionism, an active campaign to nullify the competing authority of philosophy. One of the curiosities of Huxley's rhetorical career was his inclination to claim that the epistemologies of Kant and Hume were the bases of naturalism and scientism, and then to deny this very thing by loudly insisting that he embraced no philosophy but science.[47] But this inconsistency makes sense once we understand evolutionism's power to subsume philosophy within science. Had Huxley simply grounded science in an epistemology authorized by philosophers, he would have perpetuated its dependency upon external authority. He would have conceded the determination of science's value and authority to outsiders, entitling them to the lion's share of public support he wished to secure for the army of scientific laborers he was mustering. Agnosticism, as a kind of anti-philosophy that denied all philosophical and theological authority, negated this threat. But to do so it needed to sustain the idea that science was capable of providing the kind of knowledge these other fields had formerly authorized, and this is what evolutionism added to agnosticism for Huxley. Evolutionary science became for him a mythical vehicle through which to envision a future in which all knowledge, material as well as moral, would be brought within the compass of science. Thus from the standpoint of evolutionism, Huxley was not bowing to a higher philosophical authority when he invoked the names of Kant and Hume; rather, he was bringing these figures into a scientistic framework in which they were science's evolutionary precursors.

The stories I opened this chapter with reflect a second rhetorical advantage of evolutionism. Because evolutionary science constructs a developmental view of nature, a "natural history," to use its more traditional name, it also taps into the persuasive power of those familiar narrative forms that traditionally give historical accounts their persuasive power. The stuff of evolutionary science is not history per se. As I think Hayden White rightly surmises, history is never a mere chronology of events such as we might expect to find in a *Science* or *Nature* article on the descent of whales from land-dwelling mammals. Such information only becomes history when narrative form is brought into play, a "story type or mythos," as White puts this, "which the historian has chosen to serve as the icon of the structure of the events."[48] Thus, for example, while the scientific materials compiled in Dawkins' *Ancestor's Tale* do not make it a history, the form of the "epic pilgrimage" into which he orders them does.[49] The narrative form of the quest romance that he lays over evolutionary science operates metaphorically, as White would say, to construct "a relation of similitude between such events and processes and the story types that we conventionally use to endow the events of our lives with culturally sanctioned meanings."[50]

Events, in other words, derive historical meaning from the literary forms that order them. Most Americans remember the Vietnam War as a tragedy, not merely because of its terrible human costs and failed objectives, but, more fundamentally, because public memory has fashioned it in imitation of traditional literary tales of moral failure rooted in the overbearing pride that the ancients called hubris. The most familiar versions of this tragedy recount the deeds of a great but flawed hero, an American government so swelled by a sense of invincible power and global destiny that arose from its recent triumphs in World War II that it became blind to the folly of supposing it could win a ground war in the jungles of southeast Asia. Of course, countless variations on this narrative are possible, simply because of the range and diversity of elements a narrator may choose to include or exclude. The tragic hero, for instance, might be an individual like Lyndon Johnson or Richard Nixon in some renderings, in others a faceless Washington bureaucracy or perhaps an American public so softened by postwar affluence that it had lost its nerve. But so long as the form remains more or less stable, it will always be a tragedy, a story about a great protagonist brought low by the insurmountable limitations of human nature.

The factual material incorporated into historical accounts will often cause us to lose sight of their narrative derivations. For this same reason, evolutionism often gives the impression of being scientific. Because credible findings from evolutionary biology and paleontology are included in its narratives, audiences are less likely to notice the vital literary properties of these accounts. Documentary histories, such as those of Bronowski and Sagan, in other words, will always have a sense of scientific authenticity that audiences would never attribute to the two tales of science fiction that I discussed earlier in this chapter. We would categorize "The Sixth Finger" and *2001: A Space Odyssey* as science fiction romances and *The Ascent of Man* and *Cosmos* as documentary histories, but in narrative terms all four are romances. All participate in a similar story line, one that presents science as humanity's natural destiny and the scientist as history's hero.

It is not the facts of evolutionary science that show this but rather the narrative form that orders them. A quick comparison of the plot features of these fictional romances with their documentary counterparts will bear this out. Like the protagonists of tragedy, romantic heroes and heroines are persons of extraordinary but also flawed character; what makes them differ-ent from their tragic counterparts is the fact that they prove able, by various acts of heroism, to overcome these flaws. Thus, just as tragic form works to indict human nature, romantic form works to vindicate it. Northrop Frye uses a classical vocabulary to outline the three stages of form that execute this: "the *agon* or conflict, the *pathos* or death-struggle, and the *anagnorsis* or discovery, the recognition of the hero, who has clearly proved himself to be a hero even if he does not survive the conflict."[51] The *agon* faced by Gwyllm Griffiths in "The Sixth Finger" is the tension between the corrupt human motives that are magnified once he is genetically altered and the motive of knowledge that grows in concert with his physical evolution. We might describe this as a conflict between science as power and science as knowledge. As Gwyllm grows as a scientific being, so also does the temp-tation to turn knowledge against his enemies. In his death-struggle, the merely human resentments he harbors against the townspeople who once held him back and who now regard him as a monster threaten to erupt into a destructive rampage. Science stands in the balance: conjoined with the lust for power, its growth threatens to undo the very humanity that is the vehicle of its evolution. But science as knowledge (because it is revealed to be the more essential property of human evolution) saves this protagonist at the last moment. In the story's *anagnorsis* stage, we come to realize that the decision to pursue science that Gwyllm made when he first volunteered for Mathers' experiment has also put him on an evolutionary course that has ultimately enabled him to transcend his merely human hatreds. A true scientific hero emerges from this death-struggle. Like the beggar of medieval romance who throws back his ragged cloak to reveal the crimson vestments of a prince, we discover beneath the humble human appearance of our pro-tagonist Welshman an evolutionary god.

2001 works out a similar story line upon a more sweeping mythological canvas by first visualizing the dialectic of science as knowledge versus science as power in the primordial setting of the film's first act. Here the scientific purity of the extraterrestrials who are Kubrick's counterparts to the Creator (or at least his angelic emissaries) finds its representation in the monolith they have planted in Eden. The monolith is science completely given over to nature's own ends, an instrument of natural selection placed on earth by a selfless intelligence in order to nudge our ape ancestors toward their scientific destiny. But there is trouble in Kubrick's paradise. This first taste of knowledge also gives rise to evil. Like the fruit that Eve desires because it will make her like God, knowing good and evil, the monolith symbolizes the scientific journey that lies ahead. But in human hands the gift of science is both life (science as knowledge) and death (science as power). Only a scientific god who possessed the fullness of knowledge could resist the temptation to abuse it, and this time had not yet come; as this episode closes, the very bone tool which has enlarged our ancestors' prospects for survival has become a weapon wielded by an ape-Cain against an ape-Abel. This *agon* is later recapitulated in the climactic death-struggle between Bowman and HAL, but with scientific redemption as its outcome. Knowledge as power in this stage of evolution, having found its highest expression in HAL's artificial intelligence, once again threatens to destroy science as knowledge—represented here by the mission of the space ship *Discovery*. In order for science to be purified, it must forsake power, and this is enacted in Bowman's death-struggle. When he surrenders his life by shutting down the ship's computer intelligence, he symbolically completes what was left undone by humanity's ape forebears. While they had merely tasted from the tree of scientific life, Bowman, having now abandoned himself to knowledge, has become one with it. In death he is analogous to the Christian Messiah who undoes the harm introduced by the tree of knowledge by being nailed to its branches. Bowman's ensuing descent into the underworld of the extraterrestrial monolith recapitulates what has occurred in his death-struggle with HAL. Just as the Edenic tree represents the fullness of moral knowledge that only God can possess, the monolith represents the fullness of scientific virtue—science as knowledge purified of all other motives. His death, like Christ's, enacts the perfect moral obedience that alone can open the way to life. All others must enter by the same gate. By disabling HAL, Bowman severs science as knowledge from science as power, but this also cuts off all hope of rescue. Having surrendered himself to pure knowledge, he becomes powerless, yet he is made strong in his weakness. This fatal choice makes possible his entry into evolution's city of God—the heavenly Jerusalem in which science and nature are one.

We would never mistake these two stories for science, but this is precisely what their documentary counterparts make possible. This is because the evolutionary science presented in *The Ascent of Man* and *Cosmos* doubles as thematic material for a historical narrative. Like their fictional counterparts, these documentaries employ biological evolution as a metaphor for the human story writ large. As I noted earlier regarding Bronowski's title, this shift from evolution into evolutionism is reflected in the word "ascent." While the professed subject of the series is the "ascent" of civilization, with all its usual value associations, this term simultaneously denotes the merely biological "ascent" revealed by evolutionary science. Bronowski needed to do this, I would surmise, because science could not be history's hero if the *nomos* at stake was not also identified with something above the merely human— with the evolving *cosmos*, in this instance. Evolution thus is mythologized in the same fashion as it is in the documentary's fictional counterparts.

By mythologizing evolution in his way, Bronowski elevates the scientist as a romantic hero whose sacrificial devotion to learning enacts the rise of civilization in parallel with the unfolding of nature. In Frye's language, we would say that Bronowski has made science "analogous to the mythical Messiah or deliverer who comes from an upper world."[52] Nature, through evolution, has descended upon the world as science. This explains why the opening scene of *The Ascent of Man* bears such a significant resemblance to the first act of *2001*. As birth narratives, both episodes clarify the circumstances that set the scientific hero apart as a god-like actor. In Kubrick's tale, science arises from the very same event of evolution that first set humans apart from apes, and in Bronowski's story, this evolutionary separation is depicted in precisely the same way. He begins his narrative of civilization by returning to the same African scene of hominid evolution where science is born in Kubrick's film. We are taught that progress is rooted in nature because it was at that crucial juncture in human history when biological evolution ramped up the power of the australopithecine brain that science became possible. It was in the ancient savannahs that paleontologists now excavate in eastern Africa that "scientific ideas" found their "origins in the gifts with which nature has endowed man, and which make him unique." Science is the protagonist of civilized history because it alone can "express what is essentially human in his nature," and in this the whole course of Bronowski's drama is foreshadowed.[53] It is to be the story of continuous struggle between those who faithfully pursue science, the "root from which all knowledge grows," and those who resist nature's course. Within science "lies the ability to draw conclusions from what we see to what we do not see, to move our minds through space and time, and to recognize ourselves in the past on the steps to the present."[54] Those who abandon this gift turn from nature and thus from progress as well.

As with *2001*, the symbolic resolution of this tension grows out of a battle to the death between science as knowledge and science as power, but now with Galileo playing Bowman's part and the Catholic Church playing the part of HAL. To sustain this polarity, Bronowski has to tinker with various historical facts.[55] He presents Galileo as the "creator of modern scientific method," something scientific historians have long known to be an exaggeration, and the Catholic Church as science's mortal enemy. The story's death-struggle could not work to reveal science's unique heroism as nature's prophet unless those who opposed it were utterly against nature. This is because the "content of the form," to borrow a phrase from one of White's titles, *is* the form.[56] Bronowski could not make science history's savior without conforming the facts of history to the formal parameters of romance. For this reason, he represents Galileo's condemnation in 1633 as both absolute and inevitable. Having invented science twenty years before, the Italian astronomer's fate was already sealed. There was "never any doubt that Galileo would be silenced, because the division between him and those in authority was absolute." The church believed that "faith should dominate; and Galileo believed that truth should persuade."[57] Only a polarity of this kind could give the romantic hero's scientific stance its redemptive meaning. If the progress of history arose because science had put civilization on the same course as natural evolution, its protagonist would need to have a purely scientific motive and its antagonist a polluted one. And so Bronowski also needed to overlook the church's general friendliness to science, the various Catholic scientists and clergy who by this time had already accepted the Copernican position, the minority of dissenting cardinals who voted against Galileo's condemnation, and the papacy's earlier demonstrations of appreciation for the astronomer's accomplishments.[58]

The biblical model that structures this evolutionary romance, in fact, makes an overt appearance as Bronowski closes this episode of his drama. By reminding his readers that John Milton had visited the blind astronomer as he languished under house arrest during his final years, Bronowski also finds an opportunity to identify Galileo with the hero of Milton's *Samson Agonistes* (1671). Galileo's fatal flaw, as we see throughout the narrative, was a naiveté born from his very greatness as a scientist. Consumed, like Samson, by the splendor of the supernatural gift he was given, he became blind to the mundane political seductions that would betray him into the hands of a Philistine pope. But because Samson's supernatural powers were not his own, they transcended his weakness and were destined to triumph in spite of him. Thus just as the biblical hero "destroyed the Philistine empire at the moment of his death," Bronowski tells us, this is also "what Galileo did, against his own will." Because it is nature that speaks through science, the church could not silence it by destroying Galileo. His death only meant that a new scientific messiah would be reborn in Northern Europe. "Galileo died, still a prisoner in his house, in 1642. On Christmas Day of the same year, in England, Isaac Newton was born."[59] Galileo's folly, no less than that of his biblical counterpart, could not frustrate purposes that were rooted in evolutionary history.

The trajectory of this redemptive growth leads in Bronowski's final episode to a vision of the coming kingdom, in this case the "scientific civilization" for which the "long childhood" of evolution has been inexorably preparing us. Although the narrator expresses misgivings about the West's "retreat" from science, its triumph is assured because science is "nature's unique experiment to make the rational intelligence prove itself sounder than the reflex." Ultimately, science has a transcendent or perhaps immanent basis. Nature is history's Great Experimenter who assures us that "knowledge is our destiny," that "self-knowledge, at last bringing together the experience of the arts and the explanations of science, waits ahead of us."[60]

THE MIMETIC EVOLUTION OF EVOLUTIONISM

What brought us to this examination of the literary form that shapes scientific communication was an effort to understand a persistent thematic identification between science and nature, especially in historical representations depicting science as the human incarnation of natural evolution. I do not doubt that those who advance this identity may also have personal motives, or spiritual ones as Ruse has surmised, but for the main part I mean to argue for a public and thus rhetorical explanation—that evolutionism is most crucially an outgrowth of the scientific culture's patronage interests. Evolutionism is a symbolic construction that is uniquely able to enlarge the authority of science and thus its claim on public sponsorship. Argumentatively speaking, this is because evolutionism entails much of what is advanced by such ideologies as scientism and naturalism, but it brings two other rhetorical advantages to the table as well: first, the appearance of being backed by technical authority that it achieves by drawing upon the language of evolutionary science, even to the point of claiming to be science; and second, the unique persuasive qualities it gains by imitating a literary form already imbued with spiritual meaning.

In the body of this book, I intend to examine these features longitudinally, which is to say by showing why the path of science's historical development as a professional avocation has necessitated their emergence. The scientific identity now tied up with evolutionism began to take shape in the seventeenth century by latching on to a set of explicitly religious ideas, and I intend to follow the process of development which gradually transformed its supporting narrative into one that, by the end of the nineteenth century, had linked the scientific ethos to the doctrines of evolutionary science. My rationale for taking this approach is my belief that, because evolutionism bears the rhetorical marks of these founding discourses from the seventeenth century, it can best be understood by tracing its cultural development. The best way to understand evolutionism, in other words, is by understanding its own evolution, by recognizing that it is a symbolic phenomenon that descends from the vital and explicitly religious rhetoric that first formed the scientific identity.

This is not a new idea. Examinations of early modern science by historians and sociologists have consistently revealed its close alliances with religion.[61] In my interpretation, this relationship developed because the scientific ethos could only be fashioned from cultural materials then available—the established *nomos-cosmos* identity of Christianity. The scientific role began as an extension of the church's role as God's instrument for restoring a fallen world. As I turn in the next chapters to the Baconian rhetoric that first articulated this idea, we will begin to see in outline the narrative that once sustained this identity and also how it anticipates the secular scientific romance I have just sketched.

With cultural no less than with biological notions of evolution, it should be assumed that ancestry is vitally determinative. In the realm of evolutionary biology, though I am mindful of Stephen Jay Gould's well-known reservations on this count, form and function are consistently related through adaptation. If a function persists down through the ages, even as dramatic alterations occur in a species' morphology and natural habitat, we can be fairly certain that the form that originally sustained its life will remain recognizable as well. Although one can only speculate, for instance, about the objects that our Miocene ancestors manipulated once they had acquired the incomparable manual dexterity that we inherit from them, we can be fairly certain that the tasks they put their hands to must have resembled our own. It is an analogous argument that I am making about evolutionism. Because the religious functions of a Baconian science-creation identity enabled early modern science to fit into a social environment dominated by Christianity, the science-evolution identity that I have described so far should be expected to manifest similar narrative forms and to perform similar functions in science's descendent social environment.

Such elements persist in the more Lamarckian way that cultures evolve because the process of descent with modification that shapes cultures occurs through a creative process of imitation or mimesis. In outlining this general principle as it arose out of his own work as an ethnographer, Clifford Geertz also provides a compact summation of my own rationale.

> Human societies never create out of whole cloth but merely choose certain combinations from a repertory of ideas anteriorly available to them. Stock themes are endlessly arranged and rearranged into different patterns: variant expressions of an underlying ideational structure which it should be possible, given enough ingenuity, to reconstitute.[62]

The "ideational structure" that I hope to reconstitute here is a narrative form that found its most poignant early expression in Francis Bacon's religious arguments for science. It has persisted through various stages of secularization leading up to the advent of evolutionism—most vividly and decisively in the rhetorical career of Thomas Henry Huxley. From the time of Bacon roughly until that of Huxley two hundred years later, science had gained its position in the public consciousness by claiming to be a second priesthood. As evolutionism gave rise to a seemingly secular ethos, a new narrative (but one preserving science's priestly status) persisted as an adaptation of the older Baconian one. Although the evolutionary linkages that account for this transformation have largely fallen out of view, a little bit of rhetorical paleontology can quickly recover them.

If cultures never create out of whole cloth, we can be certain that this developmental process did not begin with Bacon. Indeed, it is evident that when the Viscount St. Alban related the scientific role to the historical mission of the church by portraying the godly natural philosopher as a priest mediating the contents of a second revelation to the world, he was reiterating what the church fathers had suggested more than a millennium before. But Bacon's imitation was also a vital adaptation occurring within a fast-changing social environment, and it is for this reason that this study begins with him. Bacon's "two books" trope reconstructed the natural theology tradition to fit the views of the Protestant world that was rising to power during the reign of James I and which would gain even greater ascendancy soon after his death.

The reformers, by standing the hermeneutical idealism of *sola scriptura* against traditional notions of church authority, had committed themselves to an epistemic hierarchy in which the truth value of religious claims seemed to be measured by an impersonal standard—the plain truth of Scripture. The Bible was no longer mediated by tradition or authorized teachers, and certainly not by popes; Christendom's true priests were those who drank only from the pure waters of revelation. To reiterate science's parallel standing as a second divine "book" in such a religious climate was to hitch it to the rising star of Protestantism. This is not what is most often remembered about Francis Bacon, if he is remembered at all. In our fragmentary cultural memory, he is known for his insistence that science should have an empirical and inductive basis and for the aphorism "knowledge is power." But terms like "empiricism" and "inductivism," no less than Bacon's instrumental view of knowledge, are merely the abstract shells that have survived from what was once a vibrant mythological scheme built upon this Protestant vision. Like seekers after scientific patronage today, Bacon needed to relate science to society in some vital way, and he did this by tying it to the larger religious movement that was unfolding around him so that science might share in the ultimate value that the Reformation now assigned to the unmitigated reception of God's revelation. This was an imitation, but a revolutionary one. The church had always respected science, for the same reason that Bacon now gave, because it was an activity of reading the "book of God's works." His rhetorical genius lay in recognizing that this idea could be more specifically allied with the revised notions of Christian priesthood that were emerging within the Protestant Reformation. If nature was indeed God's revelation, and if empirical science offered the only direct path to its truths, then the new natural philosophers were also priests and could lay claim to the same authority that entitled English clergymen to draw from the public treasury. In this way the same ascendant ethos of Protestantism that was on the verge of creating a Puritan revolution in England became tied up with the identity of a scientific culture that was soon to gain unprecedented fame in the generation of Hooke, Boyle, and Newton.

But why should we regard this Baconian rhetoric as the ancestor to evolutionism? Again, I believe that the answer to this question is found in those operations of cultural mimesis that preserve narrative forms. I said earlier that evolutionism gains its rhetorical force from being identified with evolutionary science, by seeming to have the same technical basis, and we should notice that in the scientific vision mediated by Bacon something analogous to this was already in place. At the same time that empiricism was being developed as a technical philosophical rationale, it was also being drawn into the orbit of cultural meanings and values associated with Protestant hermeneutics. What this meant in practical rhetorical terms was that the one always implied the other. In a culture that hallowed as singularly virtuous a fact-based reading of the Bible, attention to the "facts" of nature would have similar sacred meaning. The same dialectic persists now in the same hallowing of "fact" that is so persistent in evolutionism. Fact continues to have technical associations with an epistemology that is the presumed basis of science's distinctive achievements, but it is also the valorizing principle of a historical narrative in which science is set above all other ways of knowing as nature's hero. This accounts for the oddity of statements such as Carl Sagan's assertion in *Cosmos* that "evolution is a fact, not a theory."[63] A general statement about the truth value of evolution that was more attuned to professional scientific standards would not put it this way: to deny the theoretical importance of evolution is to lobotomize it as science, to devalue it as mere data collection. But while Sagan's statement is false to science, it is true to its Baconian cultural legacy. To suggest that those who embrace evolutionary science are true to "fact" is to make them actors in a narrative of progress that has traditionally measured virtue in an analogous way.

If scientific empiricism is thus *homologous* with the Protestant doctrine of *sola scriptura* and with all of that slogan's attendant implications, we should also expect that contemporary notions of science would reflect other features of the Reformation worldview. One feature that will figure prominently in this treatment is the Protestants' gravitation toward a millenarian outlook on history. The reformers needed to forge a break with the past if they were to sustain the idea that their movement represented the living branch of the Christian church. But in trying to achieve this they confronted an obvious problem: if Christ himself had assured his followers that even the gates of hell would not prevail against his church, how could Protestants now reject it as the harlot of Babylon? They overcame this dissonance by insisting that the Reformation represented a new and final revelation. In other words, they accentuated what R. G. Collingwood called the "periodized" feature of the Christian historical consciousness, its theologically based assumption that new revelations launch new epochs and that from the standpoint of such new ages, all previous history needs to be understood differently.[64] The reformers applied this principle in supposing that their break with Catholicism marked the onset of the millennium, the culminating stage of divine history already anticipated in Scripture. This enabled them to dismiss the age of Catholic hegemony as belonging to a prior epoch that had now run its course.

Bacon appealed to an analogous notion of historical periodization in order to affirm the idea that the new science was genuinely new and that within it, as much as in the new Protestant epoch, the bride of Christ was being purified in preparation for her wedding feast. Since the new empiricism was the secular counterpart to the Bible-based theology of the reformers, it also occasioned a new beginning. A multitude of biblical references that were featured prominently in Bacon's writings kept this idea before his readers, but this notion found its full-fledged dramatic enactment in his *New Atlantis* (1627)—a fictional recapitulation of Christian history that imagines the purified church of the future as one fundamentally devoted to science.

The parallels that Bacon forged between Protestant conceptions of the millennium and the scientific paradise envisioned in *New Atlantis* continue to be found in the analogous connection that persists between modernism (as an epochal construction especially) and science's widening dominance. We have seen this already in the more perfect civilizations envisioned in the science fiction narratives and historical documentaries I surveyed earlier. The future hopes imagined by Bronowski and Sagan turn upon the more wholesale commitment to science that they demand from their audiences. Science is declared to represent the underlying principle of historical renewal, and so to realize the aspirations of modernism, the world must truly embrace and in fact fully universalize its principles. Conversely, the apocalyptic forebodings that both programs invoke in their closing episodes highlight the same idea. Both speakers believe that while the course of history leads inexorably toward scientific predominance, misguided choices may yet interrupt this destiny. Clearly alluding to the rising counterculture movement of the 1960s, Bronowski decries the "loss of nerve," signaled by popular inquiries into "Zen Buddhism . . . into falsely profound questions . . . into extra-sensory perception and mystery," that threaten to detour evolution's course. These developments "do not lie along the line of what we are able to know if we devote ourselves to it: to an understanding of man himself," and thus, while the "ascent of man will go on," we cannot "assume that it will go on carried by western civilization as we know it. We are being weighed in the balance at this moment."[65] Sagan ends *Cosmos* with the similar warning that any "turning away from the Cosmos" could spell doom. Our destiny is "the universe or nothing," and to choose nature is to choose science wholeheartedly. "If we survive, our time will be famous for two reasons: that at this dangerous moment of technological adolescence we managed to avoid self-destruction; and because this is the epoch in which we began our journey to the stars."[66] The future now turns upon the embrace of science because history, ever since the revelation of evolution, has been conflated with the passage of natural time.

A familiar analysis of this pattern can be found in Richard Weaver's well-known observation that the "god term" of "science" has become a synonym for "progress." A god term is an "expression about which all other expressions are ranked as subordinate and serving dominations and powers," a term that "imparts to the others their lesser degree of force, and fixes the scale by which degrees of comparison are understood."[67] Weaver recognizes that the term "progress" now stands atop such a verbal hierarchy because it has stepped in to play the part formerly enacted by the theologically charged notion of "providence." I would refine this somewhat by adding that "progress," more specifically, has descended from "providence" in its millenarian aspect. Providence, as generally conceived in Western theological traditions, does not necessarily privilege the future as modern notions of progress so clearly do. It might just as easily prefer things of the past, were they judged to accord with God's divine orchestration of history. But as a secular substitute for this religious conception of history, progress reflects a specifically Protestant turn toward the future that, as we will see in the next chapter, is rooted in certain theological pressures that coincided with the Reformation. Because the reformers needed to cast off the authority of the Catholic tradition, they were strongly disposed to contend that revelation was coming into sharper focus in the present and that it would achieve even greater clarity in the future. The millenarian expectations of the Bible provided a necessary sanction for this belief, and it is this perspective on providence that seems to anticipate the scientistic notions of evolutionary progress that I will deal with here.

Because "progress" descends from "providence," it also continues to reflect the personal attributes of the latter, a sense of willfulness and benevolence embedded in the fabric of history. Weaver recognized that this was why the alternative god term of "science" is so often "hypostatized" in phrases like "science says." Another similar abstraction that is personified in this way is "history," and this is precisely for the same reason—because both terms descend from the more traditional notion that the passage of time is the revelation of a transcendent design. What made the god term "science" slightly subordinate to "progress" in Weaver's mind was the greater scope of the latter term, and in this regard we might say that the rhetorical campaigns of evolutionism are an effort to remedy this. Evolutionism is an effort to identify modern historical understanding so closely with evolution-ary science as to collapse "progress" into "science" entirely.[68]

My job in the next two chapters will be to describe the Christian base-line from which these features of evolutionism developed. However, I do not expect the reader to simply believe that the similarities I have outlined thus far establish such a cultural ancestry. For this reason, the middle chapters of this book examine the transitional rhetorical adaptations that bridge the Baconian revolution with nineteenth-century evolutionism. This transition did not begin within scientific circles so much as in the broader efforts of Enlightenment thinkers and their positivist successors to rebuild European society in science's image. Bacon's rhetoric, by contrast, was more closely tied to the concerns of scientific patronage than were these later forms, and the momentum he gave to English science sustained it well into the nine-teenth century. It was not until the middle of that century, when scientific practitioners (who were not even yet called "scientists") faced a patronage crisis brought on by their own intellectual prosperity, that these Enlighten-ment adaptations of the Baconian narrative begin to become relevant in the world of science as such. At this time they provided for advocates like Huxley the kind of material that the Reformation had provided for Bacon—a scientized narrative into which the scientific role could be written.

To look at the Enlightenment idea of history as a secularization of the Baconian one is to accentuate change; but in light of our guiding premise that cultural evolution is necessarily a mimetic process, we should expect to find that this process of secularization will be marked by continuity as well. What complicates this in considering the transition from a Baconian scientific ethos to one based in evolutionism is the fact that such modernist ideologies are disposed to deny the very continuity that cultural evolution would seem to necessitate. We would predict, in light of this, that the rheto-ric that negotiated this transition would be characterized by forms of inven-tion that maintain existent cultural patterns while also managing to make them appear altogether novel. They will involve mimesis (remembering by imitation) but also a kind of learned forgetfulness that is needed to sustain the appearance of modernity.

Patterns of this kind are all around simply because modernism is all around. One example is the persistent habit in commercial marketing of declaring products to be forever new, as if they had no past. So long as I can remember, Tide laundry detergent has always been the "New Tide," even though it has always been basically the same thing since its debut in 1946. The marketers at Procter & Gamble want people to attend to the impression of discontinuity between the new and the old that this creates, of course, because they know that consumers associate "new" with "better." Many consumer products are aligned with progress in this fashion, but this backfires sometimes (remember the "New Coke"?) simply because the value of newness never completely overcomes the value of continuity. No matter how powerful the spell of newness, it is always tied up with some sense of historical continuity that must also value what is old. The newness of the "all-new Toyota Camry of 2011" for buyers is only meaningful because it is *still* a "Camry," a car with a history of reliability. This is the pattern that we need to understand in order to recognize why Enlightenment writers would have advanced a version of the Baconian narrative while being utterly opposed to its religious viewpoint. Only a seemingly secular and thus *new* story could succeed in accomplishing what the Enlightenment was about, the complete undermining of Europe's traditional power structures; but there were attractions in the *old* story that a genuinely new one could not reproduce. To unseat powers predicated upon the assumption that God and king were destined to rule by providence required that their replacements should also have providence-like authority.

I believe that the learned forgetfulness that resolved this double bind for Enlightenment writers may be explained in terms of what Northrop Frye has called "displacement," a literary pattern that is in fact much older than the Enlightenment. A displaced narrative is one that typically treats some contemporary or at least secular subject matter but orders it in accordance with a narrative form that descends from myth. Because narrative form (plot or *mythos*) is itself a conveyance of meaning (*dianoia* or theme), such impersonations also bring into secular narratives some of the religious meaning that one would find in their sacred antecedents.[69] Frye believed that the displacement executed through romance, the narrative genre most evident in evolutionism, is the most potent conveyance of this kind. "In every age," he wrote in his classic survey of Western literature, "the ruling social or intellectual class tends to project its ideals in some form of romance, where the virtuous heroes and beautiful heroines represent the ideals and the villains the threats to their ascendancy."[70] The ability of romance to situate traditional notions of the sacred in some present social order, of course, accounts for this pattern. Romance seems not to belong to the older world from which its religious meanings are drawn, and yet it draws upon them nonetheless.

In terms of Durkheim's thesis introduced earlier, we might say that displacement is the mechanism by which more traditional *nomos-cosmos* relationships migrate into secular narratives. Anyone who has ever noticed that Western romances are typically populated by Christ figures is already partially attuned to this notion. Such stories center around heroic figures who are merely human rather than divine protagonists, but the quests they undertake are nevertheless patterned after the life, death, and resurrection of their biblical counterpart. The frontier hero of the American Western is such a character, a mysterious figure who emerges out of the wilderness to perform sacrificial deeds for a community that is likely to be ambivalent or even hostile to him. Even so, he suffers death (at least symbolically) for this community by personally facing down its greatest evil: the outlaw. When he rises up from his near death, we find that his sacrifices have brought rebirth to the people, but he must depart from them into the west—into this secular narrative's displaced version of the upper world of heaven. The recognition of such associations, according to Frye, indicates that some aspect of the biblical *dianoia*, namely its theme of divine redemption, has been transferred from one realm into another. The perfect *nomos*, the "obedience" of the Son of God which overcomes sin, has been displaced as "liberty," a value that now seems to arise from the *cosmos* of America's frontier landscape and to assure us that the *nomos* of American democracy can overcome the temptations of lawlessness.[71]

The secularization of biblical themes that we detect in American Westerns indicates that, like the narratives of evolutionism, they descend from the Enlightenment. Both are exercises of displacement in which the notion of providence has been naturalized to denote the design of a seemingly immanent destiny associated now with the term progress. In applying this concept to the rhetoric of the Enlightenment, I am overstepping the reach of Frye's theory somewhat by applying his notion of displacement to the realm of history. But here I again take my cue from the related work of Hayden White, who has already bridged this gap by showing that every genuine history is also a narrative. Without a narrative form, a historical account is without human meaning. It becomes merely a "list of events" that has no "social center" by which to locate events "with respect to one another and to charge them with ethical or moral significance."[72]

I believe that evolutionism is a displacement of a displacement. It is an effort to scientize a familiar Enlightenment narrative of historical progress which was already a displaced version of the Baconian narrative. While several Enlightenment texts might illuminate the middle phase of this process, the example I have chosen is the Marquis de Condorcet's influential *Esquisse d'un Tableau historique des progrès de l'esprit humain* ("Sketch for a historical picture of the progress of the human mind"). Because this work appeared in 1795, just as the Enlightenment was about to give way to various descendent movements in post-revolutionary France, its compact narrative provides a helpful retrospective on this secularizing pattern. By highlighting its employment of a narrative structure similar to that found in Bacon's *Works*, I will show that it applied to society at large a displaced version of a narrative that already featured scientific actors as history's protagonists. This Enlightenment transposition, in other words, while designed to craft a vision for the renewal of European civilization, imitated the millenarian features of the Baconian model. Condorcet's *Esquisse* continued to make the scientific revelations of the present the interpretive center from which to comprehend the entire course of history.

In the next stage of evolutionism's evolution, the era of classical positivism in the first half of the nineteenth century, this view of history began to be theorized, to be treated as a form of scientific knowledge. Condorcet had only claimed that the historical plan of progress had come clear in the progress of science; Henri de Saint-Simon took this one step further by claiming that he had discovered a scientific explanation of history's scientific progression. This notion was subsequently systematized and popularized by his onetime disciple, Auguste Comte, who also proposed to substitute positive science for the Catholic worldview that the revolution had torn down. Such scientistic aspirations show positivist philosophy to be a version of evolutionism, and it is certainly not an extinct variety. (If we have forgotten Saint-Simon and Comte for the most part, this is only because of the greater success that Karl Marx's similar philosophy came to enjoy.) But this is not the category of evolutionism that was illustrated in the opening pages of this chapter. In Comte's vision of the evolution of knowledge, each individual academic field was destined to achieve its final positive state on its own terms. The end of the process he envisioned was not a world in which natural science would subsume all other fields, but a world in which every field would become a positive science in its own right. All sciences would remain equal, each performing its own function within a natural division of labor. But Comte's own field of sociology, since it was the positive science of history, was clearly (in an Orwellian sense) more equal than others. Because it took command of historical knowledge, it was the master science, the field that was to usher in a new European civilization. For this reason, positivism had little rhetorical value as a platform for establishing patronage for the natural sciences. Its importance for my thesis is found in the creative inspiration and competition its writers offered for the natural scientific evolutionism that was soon to emerge.

The competitive influence and inspiration of positivism will become especially apparent once we consider Thomas Huxley's role as evolutionism's chief architect. One of the lesser-known hallmarks of Huxley's rhetorical career was his perennial jousting with English positivists, a group of prominent intellectuals who coveted his endorsement. The positivists had good reason to regard Huxley as one of their own. His scientific oratory rang with similar ideals of scientism and naturalism, and he was a close friend and intellectual ally of Herbert Spencer—who came as close as any British writer to inventing an indigenous version of French positivism. But what drove Huxley as a public actor was his keen sensitivity to science's deficient patronage, and while positivism had drawn much of its ideological inspiration from the natural sciences, it also threatened to replace England's older clerical hierarchy with a new one governed by sociological priests. Huxley recognized that to embrace positivism was to perpetuate science's subservience. I believe that this competitive threat was the crucible in which evolutionism took form. If the positivists were poised to set themselves atop a new spiritual hierarchy by claiming to have attained a scientific mastery of history, Huxley needed a science of history that would do the same for the army of professional scientists he was raising up. Suitable material from which to build this was being made available in the evolutionary science that was emerging around the time he entered public life.

The fact that Huxley recognized in Darwin's achievement an opportunity to advance evolutionism is supported by the consistent way in which he drew these subjects together in his public treatments of evolutionary science. In *Man's Place in Nature* (1863), for instance, we find him making a scientific case for human evolution, but this was simultaneously an effort to advance evolutionism. Huxley set his scientific expositions within a narrative that collapsed the history of civilization back into natural history. Evolution thus took on the same kind of double signification frequently given to natural objects in myth; his evolutionary language retained its scientific meaning by referencing the empirical data of natural history, but it also symbolized the scientific character of human progress. The latter of these two features is especially evident in the notable way that Huxley draws upon the familiar vocabulary of Baconian myth—much as John Angus Campbell has recognized in Darwin's own appropriations of England's natural theology tradition.[73]

Huxley's role in the development of evolutionism explains an interesting anomaly of historical memory—the fact that the scientist everywhere remembered as "Darwin's bulldog" was at best a pseudo-Darwinist. Huxley certainly did subscribe to the doctrine of biological evolution on empirical and philosophical grounds, but he was never able to accept the explanatory sufficiency of the mechanism proposed by Darwin. So why has this been lost in public memory? An answer to this question emerges once we recognize evolutionism's dependency upon evolutionary science. Because mythical treatments of evolution take their authority from the truth value that evolutionary theory has earned in the professional scientific realm, their authenticity is called into question once evolutionary science is subject to doubt of any kind. This has made the firmly Darwinian Huxley of legend more attractive than the doubting Huxley of history. To remember him as a rhetorical actor who exploited the mythical potency of evolutionary concepts in order to advance scientific patronage would draw attention to the fact that the symbolic creations that sustain the scientific ethos do not come from science.

My purpose in following the path of evolutionism's historical development is to provide an account that explains why it has remained a vital feature of scientific life, and I will explore the implications of this argument in closing the book. Because science is an institutional culture as well as an enterprise of inquiry, it has always depended upon symbolic resources of a nonscientific kind to maintain its public ethos. This fundamental reality did not change as it divorced itself from its former institutional and ideological connections to religion in the nineteenth century. What happened at that crucial moment was that the content of science itself began to perform this duty. Conventional views of scientific history treat the appearance of Darwinian science as an event marking the final emancipation of scientific theorizing from the theological world picture that had dominated up until that time. My argument is that evolution provided the scientific culture with symbolic materials that enabled it to subsume rather than eradicate theology. Such a rhetorical move was demanded by the growing patronage needs of the scientific culture, the greater need for institutional autonomy that was achieved through the secularization of higher education, and the professionalization of scientific vocations. It is not a coincidence that these profound institutional changes were happening at the same time that evolutionary ideas were gaining scientific credibility. Neither were they a direct consequence of Darwin's achievement. Rather, the new evolutionary science was incorporated into a preexistent ideological framework, one that already had an evolutionary character but not a scientific ethos. As I have suggested already, it is this aspect of evolutionism that Michael Ruse did not consider in his important study. Ruse and I agree that evolutionism draws from evolutionary science; what I am unable to accept is his supposition that it is merely a personal belief. Once we recognize that evolutionism is vitally a public phenomenon, it becomes a matter of far greater seriousness than even Ruse seems to suppose. My claim that evolutionary myth and evolutionary science coincide is certainly not likely to ease public skepticism about evolutionary science, but I do believe that it is in the interest of evolutionary science to recognize this tendency. Scrutiny of these mythic temptations is consistent with the spirit of scientific inquiry and is likely to make public consumers better able to discern where science leaves off and ideology begins.

2

FRANCIS BACON AND THE SCIENTIFIC IDENTITY

Thus, if there is any secret to reading Bacon's Essays or almost anything else Bacon wrote, it lies in this sense of performative art whose assurance in performance rose from controlled language. For Bacon, soteriological purpose for a text demands a soteriological style and language.

–W. A. Sessions

If it may be supposed that the pervasive evolutionism now so recognizable in our scientific culture is a function of identity needs that have remained constant during the past four centuries, then we might fairly ask what a reasonable baseline would be from which to begin to examine its origins. If such a baseline antecedent can be identified, then we might also want to consider why it expressed the scientific ethos as it did and why the properties of this identity have both endured and changed.

To answer these questions we need to consider again the social and institutional conditions that make science possible on any large scale. The transformations of thought that science makes possible, as Benjamin Nelson has noted, always follow upon previous breakthroughs "at the social relations level and the social organization level."[1] Individuals who pursue scientific careers make vocational choices that, while certain to express their own scholarly predilections and aptitudes of mind, could never be realized on these grounds alone. Because individuals are also social beings, they are unlikely to choose any vocation unless it also enjoys the sanction of the larger social groups they belong to. The meaning of what we do as individuals, in other words, is never entirely personal; we are likely to value a career because it provides pleasure or monetary rewards, but we are also likely to value it because it enacts a role capable of earning us the approval of relevant groups. Social approval is a vital human need, and its importance for something like science becomes even more apparent once we recognize that it is also likely to express itself in social organization. While it might be possible to imagine individuals pursuing science in a social vacuum, as a mere intellectual striving, it is rather impossible to imagine them doing so within an organizational vacuum. Without institutional support, systems of reward, and networks of communication and collaboration, the individual in pursuit of natural knowledge would be mostly helpless. Science does not live by science alone; it depends on certain social structures that science itself cannot provide or sustain.

If scientific work depends upon social organization, now most notably in the form of colleges, fields, labs, granting institutions, scientific societies, and journals, and if these social structures depend, in turn, upon the existence of more rudimentary social values and roles, how then did these relationships arise? The thesis of this book is that evolutionism now works to sustain these relationships, but where did evolutionism come from? Some vital social mechanism of support must have arisen in the sixteenth and seventeenth centuries when modern science first began to prosper, and if we can presume, as historians typically have, that the scientific culture of our own time is a continuation of that one, it should also be safe to presume that the rhetorical creations that first gave such social meaning to science would have evolved along with it. Who then were the architects who first linked social values to science in such a dynamic fashion?

SCIENTIFIC CITIZENSHIP

If we could poll all the scholars who have given thought to the ideological origins of modernism and modern science, it is likely that René Descartes (1596–1650) would be named more frequently than Francis Bacon as the figure most responsible for setting modernity on its current course. This judgment is certainly defensible, but it may also be slightly Whiggish. The modern consciousness, as witnessed by its strong emphasis upon the individual, wishes to presume that the prosperity of science can be accounted for on technical grounds alone and is therefore not tied up with the social motives more typically associated with public life. Descartes depicted the scientific thinker in this way, as one who worked in dispassionate solitude, perhaps symbolized by the physical isolation Descartes reputedly put himself in to write his *Meditationes de prima philosophia* (1641). For Descartes it was a personal attitude of skepticism that set the scientific thinker apart, an attitude operationalized in the French philosopher's famous method of doubt. By accentuating the individualism that sustains scientific objectivity, this enduring view of science has also tended to draw attention away from science's public needs. It upholds belief in science's unique epistemic status, but it is hard to imagine how it could uphold public patronage. Evolutionism, by contrast, is a historical vision that draws *all* human beings into an understanding of the world that stands upon scientific authority, and nothing in Descartes' writing directly expresses this. The scientific identity now advanced by evolutionism could only be of use to scientific practitioners if it also meant something in the broader world in which science seeks patronage, and no active attempt seems to be made either in the *Meditationes* or in Descartes' earlier *Discours de la méthode* (1637) to establish a scientific role that could integrate it into existing societal roles. The view of the natural philosopher that Descartes gives us would be of little use to scientific practitioners if their patrons did not also esteem such an ethos on other grounds.

For this reason, Descartes' slightly older English contemporary seems a more likely source of the ideological materials that endure within evolutionism. I argued in the previous chapter that evolutionism gains much of its rhetorical force from religious patterns of meaning, and so to find a starting point from which to trace its development, we should expect to find a more explicit identification between science and faith in earlier centuries. We happen to find just such an identification in the English society that emerged after Bacon's death. Here the numerous advocates, patrons, and practitioners who openly identified with the new science also tended to link it to the sorts of religious themes that Francis Bacon had accentuated in his scientific advocacy. In posterity, both Descartes and Bacon would be remembered as pioneers of the new science, but Bacon provided a model more capable of sustaining a stable relationship between science and society. Descartes' influence undoubtedly endures in the global aspirations of modern science, in its characteristic posture of skepticism, and in its modernism, but Bacon's influence lives on in those specific categories of historical consciousness that continue to define the scientific ethos.

This can be explained by Bacon's more active efforts to relate the scientific enterprise to his own religious culture, and through this to the social world already emerging in his lifetime. While Descartes' *Discours* also addressed religious concerns, these came in, seemingly, only as efforts to offset the atheistic implications of the mechanistic world he was envisioning.[2] But Bacon went on the offensive. He invoked religion more actively and pervasively to create an ideological architecture capable of providing a level of social and political support unlike any that natural philosophy had ever enjoyed. Of course he had set out to do much more than this. He also aspired to construct a new *Organon,* a body of principles to guide scientific investigation that would replace Aristotle's outmoded system. Bacon's contributions to the philosophy of science are still being debated, but a majority of interpreters seem to regard this aspect of his work as a failure.[3] Intellectually, he was too far removed from scientific problems and practices to appreciate their complexity or to formalize their operations as philosophy.

Bacon's greater concern with the problems associated with relating the scientific enterprise to the worldviews of its prospective patrons can be understood only by first recognizing the aspect of his public self that was most contrary to the modern spirit, namely his abiding commitment to a humanistic tradition that championed the rhetorical arts.[4] Bacon belonged to an English culture that regarded eloquence as the highest refinement of learning, and he was born into a family that had built much of its fame and position by its exercise. The groundwork of the rhetoric education that Bacon was exposed to when he went up to Trinity College, Cambridge, in 1573 had been laid down by a classical civilization that regarded productive citizenship as the ultimate goal of education, and this principle was impressively manifest in his family lineage. His maternal grandfather, the eminent classicist Sir Anthony Cooke, believed that each of his five daughters should receive the same education as England's most privileged young men. One of these daughters, Lady Anne Cooke (1528–1610), became not only Bacon's mother, but also, in the judgment of C. S. Lewis, the greatest translator of her generation.[5] But rhetoric's call to action in civic life found its highest attainments on his father's side. That which came forward from the lips of Bacon's father, Sir Nicholas Bacon, who was "Lord Keeper of the great Seale," and from those of his uncle Lord Burghley, who was Lord Treasurer of England, was described by George Puttenham, author of one contemporary work on rhetoric and poetics, as a "more grave and naturall eloquence, than from all the Oratours of Oxford and Cambridge."[6]

While we do not have space here to give a fair summary of all that such a pedigree would have meant so far as Bacon was concerned with the scientific cause, we can be certain of one thing: Bacon would not have regarded science as something that was likely to prosper merely because its epistemic potential had been laid bare. The substance of rhetoric as understood within this humanistic culture, that is to say, was social integration. Science for science's sake is an ideal contrary to the sensibilities that an education in the rhetorical arts (to say nothing of the example of his parents) would have planted in his mind. Rhetorical learning fulfilled this goal by enabling those equipped with the broad range of knowledge required for wise political leadership also to integrate this knowledge into public life. As suggested by the icon of the "open hand" that commonly represented rhetoric in the Middle Ages, we might say that a rhetorical philosophy prizes the social qualities of messages as much as it prizes their truth value. Thus conceived, science's promotion required that it should be couched in symbols already meaningful to the polity.

Once we understand the influence that a rhetorical perspective might have had in shaping Bacon's approach to the advancement of science, we also gain a more mature understanding of the importance attributed to him a generation after his death when he was celebrated as one of the visionaries responsible for the formal charting of the Royal Society of London. Bacon's connection to this institutional triumph is signaled by the inclusion of his image, among those of Charles II and William Brouckner, the society's first president, on the cover of its official history, Thomas Sprat's *History of the Royal Society* (1667) (figure 4).

Figure 4

But it is the poetic inscription offered in this book's introduction by Abraham Cowley that gives us a more specific clue regarding the character of the contribution that had earned him this honor. Bacon, like Moses, "Did on the very Border Stand of the best promis'd Land," and from there he saw science—but only "from the Mountain's Top of his Exalted wit."[7] Like the Bible's lawgiver, Bacon had provided a vital part of science's revelation, but not the essential part. The new natural philosophers, though undoubtedly inspired by Bacon's idealizations of induction and empiricism, did not follow the specific methodological course that he had charted.[8] It was not Moses but Joshua, the Old Testament namesake of Jesus, who led the Hebrews into Israel, and thus by Cowley's analogy Bacon was not a scientist. His role was one of preparation, and the "law" that he gave in performing this duty was his understanding of the conditions under which true learning might advance. As St. Paul had written of the law in that pivotal text of the Reformation, his Letter to the Galatians (3:24), Bacon's writings had not fully revealed the ways of science; they were only its "custodian."

But Cowley's poem tells us something even more significant. In aligning the scientific role with this prophetic one, he was in fact imitating Bacon's mode of argument. The guiding premise behind Bacon's advocacy had been the supposition that science deserves a more central place because it gave distinct expression to England's faith commitments. Cowley's analogy reiterated the essence of this argument. Even if Bacon's notions of scientific method were ignored by scientific practitioners, his formula for situating science within English society remained relevant. This becomes especially evident once we recognize that science's place in the world still remained unsettled, and that it was Bishop Sprat's purpose in writing this history to continue pursuing the goals he attributes to Bacon—the "defence of Experimental Philosophy; and the best directions, that are needful to promote it."[9] From our standpoint, the defense and promotion of science might seem to demand only a philosophy of science, but in a world where science had no established place in the order of things, it meant more fundamentally the integration of science into the structures of meaning that constituted its social being.

In his own introduction, Sprat explains that Bacon deserved this special place of honor because he "had the true Imagination of the whole extent of this Enterprize."[10] Certainly this "whole extent" encompassed those technical applications that Bacon envisioned for science, but these were only occasional subjects of his writings. The more meaningful "whole" in which the growth of learning was destined to be realized was the drama of Christian history in which Bacon actively situated the new science when he used the kind of religious language that Cowley was now echoing. Science could not have universal meaning except by being fashioned as acting within a narrative that encompassed the whole of history.

This is the direction that Bacon's arguments took from the very beginning. His *Advancement of Learning* (1605) opens, following its dedication to James I, with an effort to acquit science of various "tacit objections," and this depiction of the character of religious resistance sets the stage for science's reintegration into the broader scope of religious history.[11] To say that these sources of resistance were "tacit" was to say that, while they arose from the existing religious worldview, they did so spontaneously and without conscious reflection. This made it possible for Bacon to present his own view of religion's relationship to science as the more orthodox one. What was thought to be a fundamental tension between science and religion was in fact a distortion that could be put down to moral failing, an example of what Bacon would go on to call "idols" in his *Novum Organum*. Religionists had thought that Scripture discouraged natural inquiry, but this was only a facile judgment drawn out of focus by the "zeal and jealousy of divines."[12]

In this way Bacon managed to condemn religionists but not religion, and this is the step that enabled him to go on the offensive. As he proceeds to argue against religious objections in the first part of the *Advancement*, he is not content merely to show that science is compatible with religion. He instead argues that science has a positive religious value all its own, that a true understanding of the Bible would in fact show that the Christian faith mandates science. What makes this especially significant for us is the fact that it is also a performance of the emerging Protestant take on Christian reform. His method of argument is to show that religious resistance to learning stems from an errant understanding of Scripture, and thus his defense of science enacts a version of the Protestant corrective for this by counterpoising the plain meaning of the Bible against such false interpretations. Bacon may be speaking in behalf of science, but he is doing so in the role of Protestant reformer. Thus in his response to the "tacit objections" of divines he just as *tacitly* aligns his own campaign for science with the reformers' campaign for the restoration of Christian purity.

Bacon begins this process by addressing the first and most rudimentary objection that "knowledge was the original temptation and sin, whereupon ensued the fall of man." He approaches this challenge by first citing various passages of Scripture that might appear to support this objection, such as Solomon's cautions in Ecclesiastes against the vanity of learning and St.

Paul's warning (Col 2:8) to "be not spoiled through vain philosophy." But as he goes on to work to "discover then the ignorance and error of this opinion and the misunderstanding in the grounds thereof," he does so through a more complete assessment of Scripture. That which Adam coveted when he disobeyed God's commandment regarding the tree in the garden, he points out, could not have been the sort of knowledge sought by natural philosophers. The larger context of the Bible's primordial history indicates that Adam was created to undertake science, to discover the "pure knowledge of nature and universality," when God commanded him to "give names unto other creatures in Paradise." The idolatrous knowledge that tempted Adam, by contrast, was not science at all, but rather "the proud knowledge of good and evil, with an intent in man to give law unto himself and to depend no more upon God's commandments, which was the form of the temptation."[13]

Bacon, in other words, was not content just to refute biblical interpretations that seemed to oppose science; his tactic was to answer these with more faithful readings. He does this by shifting the center of attention, so far as the Bible speaks to natural wisdom, onto other passages, such as this one that affirms the religious substance of the scientific act:

> God hath made all things beautiful, or decent in the true return of their seasons: Also he hath placed the world in man's heart, yet cannot man find out the work which God worketh from the beginning to the end: declaring not obscurely that God hath framed the mind of man as a mirror or glass capable of the image of the universal world, and joyful to receive the impression thereof, as the eye joyeth to receive light.[14]

Natural philosophy was not merely vindicated by the Bible; it was mandated by it. Because the "spirit of man is as the lamp of God, wherewith he searcheth the inwardness of all secrets," it is also God's work.[15]

In the process of defending science against tacit objections, Bacon was also tacitly writing science into Christian history. The natural philosopher who speaks in the *Advancement* speaks as a Christian, as if to assume that the scientific ethos, once fully realized, was also the Christian ethos and thus one bent on acting out the human destiny envisioned in the New Testament. This aspect of his "style and language," to go back to the quote from W. A. Sessions that opened this chapter, reflects the "soteriological purpose" that is everywhere recognizable in his philosophical works—and everywhere the theological fashion in his day. By making use of the openness to radical historical revision that the Protestant movement had required, he could also bring science into the Christian story of salvation as one of its actors.

The basis of this identity can be found in the two books metaphor that Bacon features in the *Advancement* and in several of his other philosophical writings. A commonplace justification for secular learning dating back at least to the church fathers and, in Bacon's interpretation, to the Bible itself, this trope expands upon what the doctrine of creation implies—namely, that since God is the author of nature, natural philosophy is likewise a form of theological inquiry.[16] Thus conceived, the Bible is the "book of God's word" pertaining to spiritual matters and to salvation in particular, but nature is the "book of God's works," the great tome that science has been commanded to probe and ponder in order to illuminate God's creative rationality.[17]

While the notion of nature as a second revelation was not new, it seems fairly certain that Bacon's pervasive and emphatic appeal to this idea was designed to accentuate the specifically Protestant character of the new science. The reformers' insistence upon the solitary witness of the Bible as the corrective needed to overcome the unsavory excesses of Catholic exegetes also gave Bacon's fact-centered science a similar role once the book of nature was recognized as a parallel source of revelation. If the Protestant slogan of *sola scriptura* represented a kind of "received view" in theology, the demand for an empiricist approach to natural philosophy was likely to have similar meaning for this movement. In the decades immediately after Bacon's death in 1626, this manifested in the inspiration he gave to the Pansophist movement. The leaders of this amalgam movement of Continental Pietists and English Puritans recognized in Bacon's scientific proposals the basic premise of their own reforms. The Pansophists had endeavored to complete the work of the Reformation by expanding its implications into every arena of learning and social reform—into secular as well as sacred realms. These humble scholars and itinerant clergymen (many of them refugees of the religious wars unfolding on the Continent) were certainly not the aristocratic patrons that Bacon had hoped to win over, but in England at least they represented views that were destined, in consequence of the Puritan Revolution, to come into the mainstream.

Bacon became a hero of religious reform because his decidedly Protestant spin on the two books idea also situated the science he was advocating within the Christian historical narrative as understood by the reformers. Although it would make sense to suppose that Bacon was drawn to this traditional convention merely because it could protect science from theological encroachments, this was clearly not merely a *pax Baconia*, as Thomas Huxley would later call it—that is, a convenient temporary division of the world into two states, one scientific and one religious. It did differentiate these realms, but the price that Bacon paid to purchase this separation of powers was a closer identification of the empiricist ideal of *sola natura* with the Protestant ideal of *sola scriptura*. In a cultural milieu in which exacting scrutiny of the Bible was regarded as a life and death matter, to assert that science was a humble recipient of God's revelation was to draw it into an intimate bond with this religious worldview. Science recognizably gave expression to the same principle that had brought about this new birth of the faith, and thus it was not merely made compatible with faith: it was being made an actor in the Christian drama. Bacon solidifies this idea in his *Valerius Terminus* by representing Christ himself as a proponent of the second book. Science is valued, says Bacon, for two reasons. The first is the traditional medieval notion that it "leadeth to the greater exaltation of the glory of God," but the second is more distinctly Protestant. Reading the book of God's works is also "a singular help and preservative against unbelief and error, for saith our Saviour,"

> *You err, not knowing the Scriptures nor the power of God;* laying before us two books or volumes to study if we will be secured from error; first the Scriptures revealing the will of God, and then the creatures expressing his power; for that latter book will certify us that nothing which the first teacheth shall be thought impossible.[18]

In quoting Christ's reprimand to the Sadducees who doubted those biblical prophesies relating to the resurrection of the body, Bacon was undoubtedly aligning the errors of these Jewish teachers with Catholic corruptions thought to arise from disregarding Scripture. But by identifying the text of nature with the *power of God* in this retort, Bacon also had made scientific knowledge an indispensable actor within the larger narrative of the Bible. Christ's rebuke implies that knowledge of Scripture was incomplete unless God's revelations were also made known within nature, and so science was not a mere additive to the Bible but its necessary fulfillment. The reformed natural philosopher was a religious actor singularly devoted to God's revelation and thus also to the new epoch of Christian history that Protestants were ushering in.

To conceptualize the relationship between natural and theological inquiry in this way was to insinuate that science was entitled to the same privileges of authority customarily assigned to the clergy. But with all the prudence one would expect from a career politician who had once served as Counsel, Extraordinary to Elizabeth I, Bacon is careful to recognize the priority that special revelation would still need to retain in the judgment of the constituents he appealed to. Religion would need to continue to impose limits on science, for it would be unwise, he warns in the *Advancement*, to "so place our felicity in knowledge, as we forget our mortality," or to "presume by the contemplation of nature to attain to the mysteries of God."[19] But this did not change the fundamental fact that, so far as science was also God's revelation, it would be "a weak conceit of sobriety or an ill-applied moderation, to think or maintain that a man can search too far or be too well studied in the book of God's word or in the book of God's works; divinity or philosophy." Rather the faithful should "endeavour an endless progress or proficience in both," being careful only to "apply both to charity, and not to swelling; to use, and not to ostentation; and again, that they do not unwisely mingle or confound these learnings together."[20]

That which offered food for the spirit and guidance toward salvation was indisputably more important than natural philosophy, but Bacon is careful to stay clear of language that would invite his readers to think that science should merely be an underling. Science was obligated to recognize the supremacy of sacred revelation, but it was only obliged to remain within its jurisdiction so far as its ethical commandments were concerned. Science was subject to Christ's great commandment of "charity," but since it also read a different book than the one studied by divines, it could not be asked to subject its findings to the theological authority of the church. Science, Bacon reminds his readers, moves only in the realm of "second causes," wherein theologians have no more authority than Job's friends (Job 13:7) who held that his physical maladies were a divine punishment. It therefore remained at liberty to read and interpret nature on its own terms. As such, science could not possibly threaten God's truth. Since it dealt in revelation itself, Bacon could assure his readers that while "a little or superficial knowledge of philosophy may incline the mind of man to atheism . . . a farther proceeding therein doth bring the mind back again to religion."[21]

In light of the enlarged liberty that this reasoning won for science, it is not surprising that another traditional metaphor of medieval science, its placement among an assortment of subjects that were the "handmaids" of theology, seldom appears in Bacon's rhetorical lexicon.[22] Science still ranked beneath theology as a merely temporal form of revelation, but the independence it now gained by identifying its empirical methodology with the same plain reading of Scripture also meant that traditional religious authority had no direct jurisdiction over its inquiries. Science was a fellow laborer in the field of revelation, just not the same revelation. To make a play upon the language of the Supreme Court ruling in *Plessy v. Ferguson,* we might say that Bacon had declared science and theology "separate but equal." Science and religion were equal to the extent that both realms had revelation as their subject matter, but they were separate because the new science could have no bearing upon the metaphysical concerns of theology. As a distinct revelation coming only from natural facts, science could in principle pose no threat to religion, and therefore theology had no reason to interfere with it.

Given the facility of the two books metaphor in negotiating this balanced alliance, it is not surprising that Galileo should have latched onto it as well, though without the same success. The Italian astronomer invoked this commonplace in his famous *Letter to the Grand Duchess Christina* of 1615, on the eve of his first failed effort to secure the blessings of the church for Copernican science.[23] Galileo had a more specific aim for this trope, a desire to reaffirm the traditional Catholic position that the Bible's authors used the common idioms of their day in speaking of nature and were not concerned about scientific precision. But while the Catholic exegetical tradition was clearly on his side, as William E. Carroll has shown, the times were not.[24] A conservative backlash prompted by the Reformation had pushed the church toward a more general literalism. Galileo's division of hermeneutical domains suggested that those scriptures dealing with natural questions were not subject to the exclusive interpretive authority that the church had reasserted at the Council of Trent. If it had conceded independent authority to astronomers and mathematicians to interpret the book of nature, as Richard Blackwell interprets this complex event, it would also have had to grant them authority to decipher those passages of Scripture which seemed to fall within the scope of science. By failing to perceive this implication of the two books argument, Galileo had unwittingly embroiled himself in the reactionary politics of the Counter-Reformation. His depiction of natural philosophy as an exegetical activity aroused fears in the Catholic hierarchy that science might usurp the church's already besieged authority.[25]

The same implication of the two books argument that helped to derail Galileo's cause in Catholic Italy helped to advance Bacon's in Northern Europe, where the Protestant movement was taking a firm hold. Even if Protestants felt similar fears, these were likely to be allayed by the metaphor's suggestion that science participated in the spirit of religious reform. In throwing aside—after the fashion of the reformers—the secondary influences of tradition, ancient authority, and textual disputation in favor of the direct examination of nature's revelation, Bacon's empirical science put on the Protestant ethos as its mantle. He dramatized this by even insinuating that the scholastic natural philosophy that this new science was about to replace had been party to the errors of Catholicism. Having been similarly dependent upon the traditions of "received authors," the Aristotelian natural philosophers were not merely wrong. Like their papist sponsors, they were unregenerate scientists:

> But as they are, they are great undertakers indeed, and fierce with dark keeping; but as in the inquiry of the divine truth their pride inclined to leave the oracle of God's word and to vanish in the mixture of their own inventions, so in the inquisition of nature they ever left the oracle of God's works and adored the deceiving and deformed images which the unequal mirror of their own minds or a few received authors or principles did represent unto them.[26]

The significance of Bacon's eagerness to contrast the new science with all things Catholic is highlighted by the fact that this polarity was clearly a historical contrivance. Opposition to science had not typically come from the religious sector. If the emergence of modern science was a reactionary event, as Stephen Toulmin points out, it "was a reaction against a reaction against the Middle Ages," one that "originated not from any direct opposition to medieval thought" but instead "from a secondary reaction against the secular and literary skepticism of the humanists."[27] But Bacon would have gained little by making Renaissance humanists the enemies of science. Only by having a Catholic scholastic enemy could it become an actor in the Protestant drama that was reshaping England.

BACON AND THE PURITAN MOVEMENT

By linking science with purified Christianity, Bacon gave it a decisive role in the new social order that the Reformation was bringing to power in England. If science was doing the true work of the church by opening up the book of God's work, then its practitioners were fellow laborers in the church's ministry and in the revitalization of civilization that the Protestant movement envisioned. This has prompted the sociologist Joseph Ben-David to argue that it was the crafting of this distinctive role for science that put England on the leading edge of the broader scientific movement that was already unfolding in Europe.[28] In saying this, Ben-David summarizes a main conclusion drawn from a vast scholarly enterprise devoted to understanding the distinct causes of science's sudden prosperity in seventeenth-century England. Bacon's importance in this view comes from the leading role his messages

played in providing a unifying point of reference for this emerging consciousness.[29] While at a technical level England's scientific revolution followed on
the heels of the same new emphases and methods—those of Descartes and
Gassendi especially—that were becoming prominent in Continental centers
of scientific inquiry, it was Bacon's dramatic reimagining of science's social
meaning, a reimagining that had special resonance for Puritans, that moved
this small country into its front ranks. Although Bacon may have fashioned
himself as a philosopher of science, it was his "fundamentally religious and
poetical view of the world," as Harold Fisch summarizes this, his "transference of the energies of Faith into the region of technology," that made him
the symbol of the new science in the next generation.[30]

As was true for science in its other European centers, it had been developing by fits and starts in England at least since the century and a half
leading up to the generation of Boyle and Newton, but after the middle
of the seventeenth century it was all starts. Charles II's chartering of the
Royal Society of London in 1662 was the obvious watershed moment in
this process. But as is always true of such triumphs of institutionalization,
this was the outcome of a process of social construction that had been afoot
for several decades, a process that, initially at least, was carried on by the
Puritan faction rather than the Royalist one that was now regaining some
of its power alongside the restored monarchy. This religious constituency
had been closely associated with those who had beheaded Charles' father
in 1649, but by the time the new king presented the Royal Society with his
mace, the symbolic associations that had allied the new science with Calvinist reforms had lost some of their radical edge. As a new religious and social
establishment was emerging (a kind of Hegelian synthesis of Anglicanism
and Puritanism), Bacon's rationale had begun to symbolize a new Protestant
unity. For these more moderate heirs of Puritanism, as Margaret Jacob has
interpreted this, the new science still remained "an alternative to the old
Aristotelian philosophy taught in established universities under the sponsorship of the British throne and a corrupt religious establishment," but it
also inspired hope as an alternative religious avenue for mediating the sort
of sectarian disputes that had brought political instability to the country in
the middle decades of the century.[31] Ideas that had at first set the English
Parliament against the throne were fast being integrated in a new compromise, so that by the end of the century the Baconian scientific ideology had
become a fixture of the emerging social order and would remain in place, as
we will see at the end of this story, until subsequent social upheavals of the
nineteenth century conspired to unsettle it.

This is a familiar pattern for social movements. As radical ideas succeed, they are integrated into social establishments not entirely unlike those they once hoped to bring down. In the middle decades of this century of revolution, Baconian reforms were taken up by a political and religious faction that was willing to commit regicide in order to realize its vision of a Christian commonwealth. But a generation later, as Sir Isaac Newton's remains were interred alongside those of England's kings in Westminster Abbey, Britain was giving the scientific figure who epitomized this Puritan vision the most conspicuous place among its most conspicuous dead. Of course if the thesis of this book has any merit, we should expect to find reversals of this sort. If scientistic ideologies are inspired by the patronage needs of scientific practitioners, they are likely to have deep-seated societal bases that their radical appearances might seem to be belie. The justifications for change offered up by social movements are never so completely different from the establishment notions they target as to be incapable of being integrated into them. The notions of black power enunciated by Stokely Carmichael and Malcolm X that shocked white Americans in the 1960s hardly get a rise out of my students now. For those who have grown up in a society now more likely to champion the ideals of racial "diversity" than the ideals of "integration," the resentments of these civil rights leaders will seem instantly compelling. But diversity was no less valued when their parents were in college; it was merely couched in different terms like "independence" or "liberty" and dramatized in narratives that worked to exonerate established interests. Something analogous to this was true of the Puritanism that came to be linked with science after Bacon's death. The already widespread belief of Protestants that the Bible was the sole basis of religious authority could certainly validate a shift toward patronage of a radical empiricism that insisted on the solitary witness of natural fact, but the deeper Protestant bases of this association ensured that it would persist even as moderate groups once again gained an upper hand.

What this says is that a change in any subculture, such as the scientific one that found its ideals expressed in Bacon's philosophical works, must occur in step with whatever developments are occurring in the general culture it depends upon for support. The bonds between science and society that secure both the symbolic and material support that makes scientific inquiry possible could not be broken during this process. They needed to evolve in tandem. In supposing that the Puritan-Baconian ideology was the ancestor to evolutionism in such a process, I am merely stretching the scope of this claim by applying it to a longer (but still relatively short) period of scientific history. The symbolic role played by evolutionism now represents the endpoint of what has been a continuous effort to adapt scientific interests to the evolving historical consciousness of its patron societies. Evolutionism is certainly a radical notion, no less than Puritanism was for seventeenth-century Anglicans, but like this ancestral rationalization for science, it represents a process of symbolic conservation. It may at first seem to champion a scientistic ideal that would seem to have little currency for most Americans; nevertheless, it grounds its scientism in notions of historical progress that remain as mainstream as ever—postmodernism notwithstanding.

Taken in their original context, Bacon's messages clearly represent one of the conservative moments in this ongoing dialectic. Despite the anti-establishment themes that later generations would draw from his writings, his books were originally addressed to a series of reigning monarchs who were notorious for their resistance to the religious reforms favored by Calvinists. But writers do not have the power to choose their audiences. Seemingly already aware of the divergent constituencies that were destined to take up his cause, Bacon opens the fourth book of his *Advancement* by taking a posture of neutrality. He declares himself a "trumpeter, not a combatant," an intermediary such as "might go to and fro everywhere unhurt, between the fiercest and bitterest enemies."[32] The Lord Chancellor was not so naive as to suppose that his ideas would come to fruition in any of the specific ways he envisioned. He confesses in his *Novum Organum* that he is only "sowing in the meantime for future ages the seeds of a purer truth, and performing . . . towards the commencement of the great undertaking," and he acknowledges in the dedication to his *Instauratio Magna* that "there is something of accident (as we call it) and luck as well in what men think as in what they do or say."[33] And he was right. Bacon had sought the patronage of kings, but the most significant result of his efforts was the embrace of his message by a powerful offshoot movement of the Reformation that was destined to eclipse the monarchy. Eventually, this amalgam of pious reformers, utopian visionaries, political radicals, and scientific practitioners would in fact draw in the kind of mainstream patronage that Bacon had envisioned, but initially it achieved this in the more informal way that movements so often do, by building a broad network of social alliances. What Charles Webster describes as the "evolving complex of scientific 'societies,' 'colleges' or 'clubs' which emerged in England between 1640 and 1660," created an informal infrastructure without which the great successes of the Newtonian era would have been impossible.[34] This was not patronage in its conventional sense as monetary support; indeed, even the formal sponsorship of

Charles II had not opened the royal treasury to science. This was patronage built with symbols, a network of social relations that prospered scientific work by situating it within an emerging historical consciousness.

As I noted earlier, those who took up this cause in the middle decades of the century were certainly in tune with Bacon's philosophical program, but their preeminent loyalties lay with the broader cause of the Reformation. Although this movement developed a more decidedly scientific focus after 1660, it had a decidedly Protestant one during the decade of the interregnum. It would even be fair to describe this as a Protestant rather than a scientific movement. This contention gains much ammunition from the fact that its central figure was a clergyman, the Czech divine Jan Amos Komenský (1592–1670)—Comenius in Latin. A figure certainly as renowned in his own day as Bacon had been, Comenius had visited England in 1641 at the invitation of Parliament's Puritan faction, which held out some promise of sponsoring the refugee minister's "Pansophic" schemes, his sweeping vision for the universal reform of education.[35] By the time of his arrival, these political patrons were too distracted by an impending civil war to attend to such matters, but the sponsors of his visit, most notably the Prussian expatriate and gifted intelligencer Samuel Hartlib (1600–1662) and the Scottish social reformer and ecumenist, John Dury (1596–1680), put this cause in motion in a local reform movement.[36] This small band of followers, remembered now as the "Hartlib circle," developed during the interregnum into a national network that joined together a broad and diverse array of Puritan intellectuals who had taken common inspiration from Comenius' vision. It seems doubtful that anyone observing this movement during these crucial decades could have supposed that the Pansophists were destined to shape English science. Scientific reform was certainly a part of this movement but just as certainly not its main theme. However, various concrete links can be found that tie the Hartlib circle to the development of the Royal Society. The various intellectual hubs that developed within this social network, which Robert Boyle famously called "invisible colleges," clearly were antecedent to the emergence of this revolutionary scientific institution.[37] Several founding members of the Royal Society, including its chief architect, the German Calvinist Theodore Haak, as well as its first secretaries, Henry Oldenburg and John Wilkins, and the mathematicians John Pell and William Petty, had first belonged to Comenius' broader movement.[38]

That Comenius would have had a prominent role in setting English science in motion makes sense once we recognize that any effort to identify science with a particular societal pattern cuts both ways. A clergyman interested in building a reformed religious community would have as much to gain by such an identification as natural philosophers did. Once Bacon had succeeded in showing that the new experimental philosophy was an offshoot of Protestant reform, the growth of science came to signify the merits of the broader educational and social reforms that clergymen such as Comenius wished to advance. The growing popularity of the Pansophic movement in turn worked to reinforce the earlier Baconian connection between science and religious reform. When Comenius credited Bacon in his *Way of Light* with the "first suggestion and opportunity for common counsel with regard to the universal reform of the sciences," he was asserting that science coincided with Protestant ideals but also the inverse of this—that the Reformation was validated by the success of science.[39] This implication also surfaced in the first chapter of the Moravian clergyman's visionary *Panorthosia*, his treatise on "universal reform," where he reasoned that just as human beings needed to restore their true relationship "with God through true Religion," they also needed "a true relationship with Nature through true Philosophy" and "with each other through true Politics."[40] If the success of the new science reflected its unique fidelity to the revelation of the first book, these triumphs of natural philosophy also bore witness to the triumphs of Protestantism as "true Religion" and its potential to found a "true Politics."

THE PURITAN SPUR IN RHETORICAL PERSPECTIVE

The emergence of the Hartlib circle as both an offshoot of Comenius' Pansophic movement and an antecedent of the Royal Society exemplifies that general pattern which the sociologist Robert K. Merton dubbed the "Puritan spur," the sometimes controversial notion that the variety of dissenting sectarian groups now remembered (though perhaps with insufficient rigor) as "Puritans" played a vital part in creating England's scientific revolution.[41] Merton argued in his 1938 monograph *Science, Technology and Society in Seventeenth-Century England* that this occurred because Calvinist theology had "transfused ascetic vigor into activities which, in their own right, could not as yet achieve self-sufficiency. It so redefined the relations between the divine and the mundane as to move science to the front rank of social values."[42]

Although scholars continue to quibble about the precise character of this association and the specific way that Merton instrumentalized the Puritan demographic, the general linkage between science and various dissenting

Protestant groups (among whom the Puritans were especially visible) has held up well during the last seventy years.[43] Merton's thesis is affirmed, as we have just seen, by the unprecedented significance that Comenius and his English followers assigned to the new experimental science. They resonated to Bacon's notion that secular inquiry of this kind was in keeping with the same purity of heart which had restored doctrinal integrity in the theological realm, and they expected, as Bacon had also argued, that the worldly benefits of a science so practiced signified its importance as an instrument by which providence was making all things new.

In this regard, Merton's thesis is certainly commensurate with the significance I have attached to Bacon's crafting of the scientific identity, but my greater accentuation of his role also represents a refinement of this position. Merton seems to have assumed that the theological affinities that connected science with Calvinism arose more or less spontaneously, but the rhetorical interpretation I am advancing would suppose that this was only a latent connection, one that needed to be actively engaged before it could have any effect. If Puritanism facilitated science's integration into the English consciousness, it was because a gifted architect made this linkage salient. Bacon, in other words, gave what Chaim Perelman has called *effective presence* to this association.[44] A pattern of association was established in England between the radical exclusion of Catholic teaching traditions from Christian theology and the radical empiricism idealized in the new natural philosophy because one towering public figure had actively drawn attention to this idea. This interpretation is supported by the fact that, while Calvinism was also prevalent elsewhere in Europe, it was only its English wing that produced such institutional results. Another explanation for this difference might be, as S. F. Mason has thought, that subtle variations in the English interpretation of Calvin's theology invited greater emphasis upon the good works that science was thought to advance and gave greater presumption to natural causes.[45] But it seems unrealistic to suppose that subtle shadings in English theology should have made more difference than an aggressive rhetorical campaign launched by the century's most visible public personality. Like Merton, the numerous historians and sociologists who have advanced and developed his thesis have recognized the important role that Bacon played in establishing this religious identity for science, but they have not recognized his rhetoric as a vital factor. The primacy of his inspiration is sometimes strongly suggested, as when the historian Charles Webster chose Bacon's phrase "Great Instauration" as the title of his detailed history of the Puritanism-science relationship, but like other scholars Webster treats the presence of such arguments for science as just one manifestation of a broader Puritan spur.

Rhetoric is something that will be prevalent in any society that provides some measure of tolerance for public expression, and in this regard Bacon's was only one among many voices who spoke on science's behalf. However, in every age there are rhetorical figures whose creative choices are especially fateful. For instance, while many Americans wrote about the separation of church and state in the eighteenth and nineteenth centuries, Thomas Jefferson's advocacy of a "wall of separation" in his 1802 letter to the Danbury Baptist Association continues to dominate such discussions. One phrase in one letter by a single individual in one particular political moment (when that individual happens to be a person with Jeffersonian gifts and stature) can successfully infuse the public consciousness for centuries. This is rhetoric's power of "selection," as Kenneth Burke famously described it.[46] Out of a perhaps unlimited array of metaphors that could have been used to characterize the relationship between religion and government, Jefferson's creative choice predominates for two reasons. The first of these is the writer's commanding position in cultural memory. The second is the fact that this selection was made at a pivotal time, a moment of opportunity—*kairos* as the Greeks called it—in which a formulation of this kind was especially in demand and therefore especially likely to gain widespread influence. Both of these conditions hold in Bacon's case as well. His visibility in English life was unparalleled when he began his campaign for science at age thirty, and he undertook this just as growing social instabilities were creating an opening for such reforms.

What I am suggesting here should not be mistaken for an effort to revitalize an obsolete "great man" theory of history. I do not mean to suggest that science would not have taken off in the seventeenth century without Bacon any more than I would suggest that the American policy barring the establishment of state religions would not have come into place without Jefferson's input. What I am saying is that prominent voices acting at pivotal historical moments are likely to determine *how* such ideas are rendered in subsequent generations. Such expressions become definitive in directing the course of cultural evolution, and thus the fact that the issue of science's relationship to religion was taken up by a figure of Bacon's magnitude at such a critical moment in scientific history was in some sense fateful.

In terms of the cultural evolutionary model that shapes this study, we might say that, had science been successfully promoted in the seventeenth century through a different configuration of symbols, its public ethos might look quite different today. Key rhetorical choices determine key trajectories of thought. Had Jefferson opted to use a metaphor suggesting a more permeable barrier between church and state, say a "fence of separation" rather than a "wall," the language and arguments appearing in public debates on this subject today would likely be somewhat different. In the same way, we might have reason to think that Bacon's decision to harmonize the new science with a specific set of Protestant values has been similarly determinative—though by no means absolutely so.

One sign of this, as I said in the previous chapter, is the scientific culture's tendency to depict what it does in purely empiricist and inductivist terms, even though scholarly examinations consistently show scientific work to have a thoroughly rationalistic and deductive side as well. I believe that this one-sided view descends from Bacon's fateful identification of science with a Protestant shift away from the inward authority of theological reason toward the outward testimony of the Bible.

A second way in which Bacon specifically anticipates evolutionism, which I will take up in the next chapter, is in his persistent tendency to identify scientific knowledge with the notion of historical progress. In the rhetoric of evolutionism, this now manifests in the supposition that because science alone "reads" nature strictly on its own terms, the historical understanding that arises from tracking the course of natural time has distinctive relevance for humans. Science's devotion to empiricism, in other words, gives it prophetic historical authority as well. Evolutionism in this regard descends from the prophetic vision that Bacon dramatized in his *New Atlantis*. The imaginary Christian civilization depicted in this tale had remained true to the book of God's word since its conversion in the first century, and for this reason it had likewise remained true to the book of God's works. In consequence, the lost European seafarers who stumble upon Bacon's island Christendom discover a civilization on the brink of realizing the millenarian expectations that had been forestalled in real Christian history by the corruptions of Catholicism. Science and historical destiny are drawn together on this island utopia because Bacon's story draws upon the underlying assumption that natural time and historical time have the same divine author. And thus to be true to God's revelation in nature is to be in tune with history's unfolding plan. The historical narrative voiced in contemporary forms of evolutionism continues to reflect this legacy of scientific millenarianism whenever it depicts the arrival of evolutionary science as a sign marking the dawn of history's final epoch.

Without the further evidence that I will examine in the remaining chap-ters of this book, the reader may (not undeservedly) be quite skeptical of the supposition that the historical reach of one individual, such as Bacon, could be this long. At this point I can only ask for patience as I continue to make my case. But while our attention is still focused on the seventeenth century, I would like to mention some support that my position finds, not only in its agreement with the Merton thesis, but also in the clarity it brings to some of the debate that has surrounded the interpretation of this sociologist's work.

Critics of Merton's theory reject a premise that rhetoricians are inclined to share with sociologists, the supposition that career choices, though seem-ingly having to do merely with technical or private concerns, cannot realis-tically be divorced from public ones. Like most others who have forcefully opposed Merton's position, Hugh Kearney misses this problem when he objects to the pragmatic character of the scientific reforms endorsed by figures like Comenius and Hartlib.[47] Since the distinctive attribute of the new science was its theoretical power, Kearney argues that the promise of applicability that figured so prominently in the religious rationale offered by Bacon, Comenius, Sir Thomas Gresham, and Hartlib could not have pro-vided a workable "blueprint" for the kind of science undertaken by Newton and Boyle. Similar arguments have been made by James Carroll, T. K. Rabb, A. Rupert Hall, and Richard Westfall.[48] Uniformly, these scholars assume that a Puritan motive would matter only if it were somehow a proximate cause of scientific work. But proximate causes are not the only necessary causes, and so the rise of the scientific enterprise cannot be accounted for, as John Henry argues, on such strictly "internalist" grounds; external social factors are equally vital.[49] The specific intellectual motives that give rise to scientific outcomes can only operate upon persons who have first been drawn into some social circle in which such activities are occurring, and what draws them are values that link science with broader societal concerns.

The premise behind Merton's thesis, we might say, was that social motives are logically prior to and distinct from personal and intellectual ones, that the passageway that leads into the technical sphere must also pass through the public sphere. This principle is illustrated by one dramatic change in the demographics of science that came somewhat later in its history, the explosion of Jewish representation in scientific vocations that occurred late in the nineteenth century. So long as Jewish communities had remained closed to the Gentile world, the intellectual talent that might have been channeled into science was consistently directed into other pur-suits, rabbinical studies more often than not. But as secularization brought

Jews into contact with the framework of values in place within the more general public sphere, they began to pour into the scientific professions.[50] We would not presume that this process of secularization provided the specific intellectual attractions that drew Jews to scientific work any more than Puritanism did for their Gentile counterparts in earlier centuries. But it was needed in order to bring public motives into accord with personal vocational ones.

What made the mass migration of Jews into science different from the earlier Protestant migration was the fact that in the secular world they were now entering, the value of the scientific role was already well established. Jewish intellectuals only awaited a sea change in the orientation of their own public culture to open this door. But prior to the seventeenth century, there simply was no clearly established societal role that even Gentiles who wished to practice scientific research could step into. Such an identity needed to be created, but it could only be fashioned from symbolic materials already available in the public sphere. This of course would seem to make a religious rationale for science inevitable. In a society where political and sacred space so consistently overlapped, the politics of science were also the politics of the church. If English men and women were willing to enter into a civil war because changing assumptions about the character of religious life could no longer be reconciled with traditional conceptions of kingly power, it is hardly surprising that science's public legitimacy should have been won on religious grounds as well.

In this regard, perhaps greater clarity may be achieved by substituting for Merton's "spur" metaphor the language of "roles" employed by Ben-David.[51] The notion of a Puritan spur has tended to suggest that Merton was claiming a direct and personal correspondence between Puritan theology and scientific work. This confusion has been compounded by the fact that an important part of his argument consisted of demographic evidence showing that English Puritans had a much larger representation in the Royal Society than other religious groups—as if to suggest that Puritan beliefs simply "caused" individuals to take up science. But this was not what Merton was really arguing, and so critics miss the point of this "spur" when they object to the fact, for instance, that prominent scientific figures such as William Harvey, Robert Boyle, John Wilkins, and Seth Ward were not Puritans per se.[52] Even when not derived from the individual worldview of the persons who enact it, a role remains attractive by virtue of the place it gives individuals in some larger social realm. From such a viewpoint, the efficacy of science's alignment with such a Puritan role did not depend on the theological preferences of individual scientific practitioners so much as on the attractiveness of this theology in the broader society. Thus even if we agree with Henry that there is no "really convincing reason why Puritans should have been more concerned about, more successful or more productive in science than any other religious group," we cannot conclude that Puritanism therefore did not advance science in an important way.[53]

Certainly it makes sense to suppose that, since Puritan theology had become a defining part of the English public identity by the mid-seventeenth century, individual pursuits thought to enact its beliefs would have also attained special value. What I am asking readers to consider as I bring rhetoric into this equation is whether something more was needed. Even though such a society might identify Protestant redefinitions of the Christian role with the scientific role, would those individuals possessed of intellectual interests conducive to scientific activity care about this linkage? And what would make the Puritan version of this theology especially capable of spurring such choices? The conventional answer to such questions is found in a subsidiary supposition that Merton derived from Max Weber's notion of the Protestant work ethic. Puritanism relied upon outward signs of spiritual fruit as evidence of the believer's inward state of grace, and this made the instrumental outcomes associated with science especially attractive.[54] By this reasoning, the utility promised by empirical science filled a need for spiritual assurance that was no longer satisfied through the sacramental religious performances now rejected by radical Calvinists. But while this is broadly consistent with an increased interest in scientific activity, it cannot explain why this particular vocation should have suddenly prospered over other professions more obviously tied to practical life and charitable good works.

A rhetorical understanding of the Puritan spur resolves this problem by bringing in once again Burke's notion of language's special powers of selection. Even before the Puritan movement had achieved its social ascendancy, Bacon had specifically crafted linkages between empirical science and Reformation values. For the Puritan intellectuals who were making vocational choices later in the century, these connections had already been made available and salient (if the reader will pardon my anachronism) by the "Jeffersonian" reach of Bacon's art.

Without recognizing the selective power of particular messages, we could still say with Merton that specific religious beliefs spurred interest in natural philosophy, but this would be a bit like saying that it was the establishment clause that caused Madalyn Murray O'Hair to sue Baltimore's public schools in an effort to ban Bible reading. The legal backdrop for this certainly was the establishment clause, but only a reading of this clause driven by a metaphor of *separation* could give rise to such an interpretation of the law. Similarly, while Merton was certainly right to recognize a general symmetry between Calvinist thought and empirical science, this relationship was put into effect because a rhetorical figure of enormous influence selected the specific symbolic lines of association that would guide its interpretation in the next generation.

Bacon was able to catalyze this relationship because, like Jefferson, his distinctive prominence in public life and distinctive discursive talents were exercised at an opportune moment. In Bacon we find a person who was at once a dominant political figure, a formidable late-Renaissance writer, an interested follower of the new science at the time of its rising, and a person imbued with sympathy, both by his mother and his Cambridge professors, for Calvinism.[55] In this regard, when his personal physician, William Harvey, wrote that Bacon "writes Philosophy like a Lord Chancellor," he was perhaps saying more than he meant.[56] With one foot in the broader realm of public life and the other in the technical realm, Bacon was more capable than any of his contemporaries of doing what rhetoric does best, of "adjusting ideas to people and people to ideas," to use Donald C. Bryant's well-worn definition of this activity.[57]

Even if we were to suppose that there was some latent potency within English Calvinism that would have inevitably established science's place in this changing society, how this was activated would still depend upon how it was expressed. As Bacon formulated this relationship, it was the value Protestantism shared with science by virtue of its disciplined devotion to reading the plain meaning of revelation that drew it into this religious orbit. There is nothing in Bacon's scientific advocacy that explicitly sustains Merton's speculation that scientific work satisfied the Puritan believers' need for signs of their predestined place in the covenant of grace. What we do find is something even more enduring: the idea that there is an inherent moral fidelity in what science does that sets it apart from other forms of secular inquiry. Notably, as we continue to move along the symbolic trajectory that will lead up to evolutionism two centuries later, we will see that this apparently secular ideology still appeals to similar moral justifications when it seeks to place science at the vanguard of historical progress. The radical empiricism that is still held up as a warrant for science's special role in history continues to be tied, much as Bacon's Protestant version of this was, to the belief that this movement has ushered in the final phase of history.

Just as the ideology of empiricism continues to reflect Bacon's shaping influence, though having dropped the "book" metaphor that once tied it to the Bible, the historical consciousness in evolutionism's visions of progress continues to reflect a specific pattern of providential meaning that Bacon had also accentuated.

3

SCIENCE IN GOD'S BOSOM

Bacon tells us that human existence is radical discovery and transformation; classical and biblical prophetic contexts provide him with a framework for understanding and engendering historical change, and therefore for conceiving of man as an innovative master of change. Further, the oppositions in biblical prophecy between fulfillment and new beginning, and between piety and iconoclasm, provide a precedent for the productive and dangerous discontinuity between two visions of change that characterize Bacon's modernity.

—Charles Whitney

It seemed to us that we had before us a picture of our salvation in heaven; for we that were awhile since in the jaws of death, were now brought into a place where we found nothing but consolations.

—Francis Bacon, New Atlantis

In the previous chapter, I proposed that the two books argument, by identifying science's empiricist ethic with the hermeneutic idealism of the reformers, established a rhetorical formula for public patronage that has had enduring qualities. Once such a vital link was found that was capable of tying scientific inquiry to such a widely sanctioned public value, it was likely to persist even as the gradual secularization of the English-speaking world made any explicit identification with traditional religious beliefs untenable. A version of this hermeneutic rationale lives on, I will argue, in the persistent inclination to argue that science gains its unique public authority from its empiricist devotion. Science continues to have a priestly ethos because it continues to be regarded as selfless, an undertaking that is distinctly virtuous because it blocks out those deceptions ("idols," as Bacon would call them) that the fallen self mistakes for reality. Science may also draw much public favor from the instrumental potential that Bacon promoted, but as I have pointed out already, this could have only limited effectiveness as a public rationale. A scientific enterprise justified by its applications stands or falls with promises that are for the most part unlikely to be fulfilled, but one that stands on some moral or transcendent principle will remain compulsory regardless of its practical merits. The value that continues to reside in the perception of science's special and unwavering devotion to the text of nature explains why we can always expect odd declarations like Carl Sagan's assertion that "evolution is a fact, not a theory." Science's empiricist side tends to be magnified and its rationalistic side diminished because the creative human contributions to knowledge denoted by the word "theory" draw attention away from the distinctive natural bases of its priestly ethos.

I turn now to the historical consciousness that also infused the scientific ethos of the seventeenth century. By bringing a specifically Protestant meaning to scientific empiricism, Bacon also gave science a place in the new understanding of providential history that was arising within the Reformation. My purpose in illustrating how the historical aspect of the Protestant consciousness was dramatized in Bacon's *New Atlantis* is to show how his message anticipates a pattern of historical thinking that continues to be integral to evolutionism, namely the doctrine of progress.

Of course Bacon's *New Atlantis* is not a work of history per se; it is only a work of fiction that happens to incorporate familiar historical themes of Christianity. It does so by imagining an ancient Christian civilization that was able to remain true to the revelation of the Bible because it arose in isolation from Catholic Europe on a distant Pacific island. Having remained true to the Christ's original message, it has also developed a robust scientific culture. In this regard it is an example of what Bacon had earlier called "feigned history," an exercise of literary imagination that is better able than actual historical exposition to reveal those patterns of divine action that are the genuine bases of historical meaning. Understood in this way, *New Atlantis* spoke historical truth, not because Christianity had ever produced a great scientific civilization, but because the truth of providence, once made clear by the imagination's power to see past the corruptions of fallen human nature that clouded actual history, showed that science was Christendom's ordained destiny. Bacon's imaginary history possessed this prophetic authority because it modeled historical premises that the Reformation had brought to the fore. The reformers needed such a revised understanding of Christian history because they were breaking with a tradition grounded in alternative historical conceptions, and Bacon's tale enabled science to piggyback on this effort. Protestants could not insist that Christian teaching ought to be circumscribed by the Bible without also proposing a revised understanding of church history. Having rejected the centuries-old tradition which regarded the church itself as the ultimate arbiter of religious truth, they also needed to regard the entire epoch of Catholic dominance as a detour from providential history and the advent of the Reformation as the restoration of the course that God had truly ordained. Bacon jumped on board in his *New Atlantis* by projecting these historical conceptions upon an imaginary past. His is a "what if" tale. It imagines an isolated Christian world that had not followed the Catholic Church into its Babylonian exile, and through this it models science's place in the different course of historical development that Protestants were now envisioning.

In this regard Bacon's fable fleshes out the historical implications of the two books doctrine. If faithfulness to the book of God's word was needed to keep the church on the course of providence, then faithfulness to the book of God's works was necessary as well. And this meant that a truly reformed church was destined for science.

If we go back for a moment to the beginning of the Reformation early in the previous century, we can locate the logical inertia that leads from Protestantism's renewed emphasis on the Bible to the new historical consciousness that Bacon had now tapped into. Martin Luther had objected to the sale of indulgences in 1517 because this practice was at odds with the plain reading of Scripture, which showed that salvation was by faith alone and not by works of any kind. The local theologians who were soon called upon to refute this renegade monk countered with a different reading of St. Paul that had the backing of the church's interpretive traditions. This turned the debate into a contest about interpretive authority and implicitly suggested Luther's rejection of Catholic authority. This had not been his intention when he posted his Ninety-Five Theses, and the radical implications of his Bible-only stance might have just as easily been overlooked. But the heavy-handed response of the Dominican John Eck, professor at Ingolstadt in Bavaria, who charged this lowly Augustinian with heresy, forced him to enlarge the argumentative scope of this premise. Luther now proposed that the dictates of individual conscience alone should arbitrate such interpretive differences and that the proposals of religious authorities that violated such convictions (even those of popes) must be rejected.[1]

On this principle, when Leo X formally declared him a heretic in the bull *Exsurge Domine* of 1520, Luther merely reversed the accusation. But

Catholic authority was also grounded in a traditional understanding of providential history, and so Luther needed to find an alternative historical basis for his own doctrinal pronouncements. The title of one of Luther's great treatises from that year, *The Babylonish Captivity of the Church*, anticipates this change. While his subject was doctrinal, the biblical grounding of the sacraments which Luther was now paring down from seven to two, his title reflects the altered historical thinking that such a sweeping doctrinal change demanded. If the Catholic Church had erred so fundamentally, the traditional assumption that its teaching authority was validated by the historical continuity of apostolic succession also had to be rejected. Such a reconfiguration, no less than Luther's doctrinal alterations, needed a biblical grounding, and his title indicates where this was to be found. Luther had identified the errors of the Roman Church with the apostasies that had once caused God to abandon ancient Israel to its Babylonian conquerors. The period of Catholic dominance was now being interpreted as a recapitulation of ancient Israel's idolatry, with European kings now playing the part of Nebuchadnezzar and the dawning reform movement representing the faithful remnant of Israel that made a second exodus back into Palestine.

Validation for this historical analogy came from the fact that the same comparison was already found in New Testament eschatology, where Israel's Babylonian exile and restoration were used to symbolize a similar scenario of the end times. This way of situating the Protestant movement in history had the important effect of reorienting historical thinking from the past to the future. The Babylonian exile had already been appropriated in John's Apocalypse (Rev 17–18) as the model for that future epoch in which the greater portion of Christ's followers would be led astray by a second Nebuchadnezzar, the antichrist of the end times. Once Protestants adopted this visionary narrative as a prophetic template for their own struggles, the Catholic Church became the "Harlot of Babylon" which had abetted these worldly temptations. Protestants, by contrast, were the faithful remnant destined to return to the heavenly Jerusalem of this future cycle as the purified bride made ready for the "marriage of the Lamb" (Rev 19:7).

Appeals to this prophesied future undermined the historical authority of the Catholic past, but their more important effect was a vital shift in temporal orientations. Providential history could no longer afford to find its point of reference in the past, since this was what sustained Catholic authority. It needed to find its main point of historical reference in the future, and millenarian prophecy enabled Protestants to do this without abandoning their self-imposed requirement that all teachings have a biblical grounding.

Once we recognize how vital this millenarian pattern was in the Protestant world in which Bacon situated the new science, we can better understand why he was destined to become one of the chief forebears of modernism. As Bacon strove to conflate the scientific ethos into the Protestant ethos, he was also compelled to work within the new historical framework that the reformers had brought into play. If science was to have some share in the true priesthood of God's revelation, it also needed to represent itself as an instrument of providence that played some part in bringing the remnant church into the millennium. Thus, the emerging scientific movement, just like the Protestant one in whose image Bacon was creating it, found its primary historical reference point in the future.

By the time Bacon published his *Instauratio Magna* (1620) exactly a century after Luther's first intimations of this historical shift, the identification of Rome with Babylon had become a Protestant commonplace. Thus it is not surprising that the title of Bacon's great effort to systematize the new science (in tacit and sometimes explicit opposition to the Aristotelian natural philosophy of the Catholic universities) would also reference this Old Testament episode. The word *instauratio* in Bacon's title, meaning restoration or re-edification, was the same Latin word used in Jerome's translations to depict the Old Testament reforms that Luther had invoked as the model for his second exodus.[2] This connection was an obvious one for Protestants. The restoration of true worship that was enacted when the high priest Ezra commanded that the Mosaic law should be read before a remnant congregation of Israel that was struggling to rediscover its truths (Nehemiah 9) anticipated the Protestants' own rediscovery of the text of the Bible.

Science's typological connection with this Old Testament episode was the rebuilding of Solomon's temple. As a material act of reconstruction corresponding to this larger program of reform, the temple's instauration, as Charles Whitney has so ably shown, made science its millennial counterpart.[3] Just as the temple had been an earthly representation of heaven, Bacon now declared that the record of natural history was a "second Scripture" that needed to be "compiled with a most religious care, as if every particular were stated upon oath; seeing that it is the book of God's works."[4]

The oath-like fidelity that Bacon demanded for science reiterated the biblical basis of his doctrine of empiricism. Because nature was a second revelation, its reading was sacramental. But its linkage to the rebuilding of the temple reiterated its historical significance. Since it was the prophetic fulfillment anticipated by this ancient undertaking, it was also its antitype and therefore, like the Reformation itself, one of the final truths of revelation history.

What is of interest to us now is the cultural evolutionary course on which Bacon was putting science through this undertaking. If his efforts to situate the scientific ethos within Christian history set in motion a pattern that now finds expression in evolutionism's similar efforts to situate this ethos in natural history, we might also expect to find that the particular creative choices that shaped this effort will have left their mark upon evolutionism. My argument goes like this: just as Baconian science was linked to the Protestant ethos through the two books doctrine, and through this to subsequent forms of empiricism that now sustain science's priestly ethos, so did his alignment of science with this Protestant reconfiguration of sacred history put it on the path that now aligns it with progress.

To understand why the mimetic habits that drive cultural evolution would have forged such a connection, we will first need to understand what Bacon achieved for the scientific ethos by depicting natural philosophy as a sign of the millennium. The Bible is filled with new beginnings, but the millennium, since it is history's final epoch, provides unique rhetorical pull. As a new and definitive beginning that had not yet manifested, it made available to Bacon the kind of creative freedom that could anticipate a future dominated by science—even though the Christian past seemed not to be. Millenarianism's futuristic orientation in this regard is both iconoclastic and conservative, and this is why, as Charles Webster has noted, millenarian thinking has usually become pronounced in periods of religious crisis. In particular, during the period of the Puritan Revolution when Baconianism was also in ascendancy, it "emancipated reformers from any obligation of respect for the long-established institutions or of operation within the boundaries imposed by current intellectual values."[5] It was able to do this, just as the modernist doctrine of progress continues to do, by treating the future rather than the past as the historical standpoint from which to judge the present. In modernism the push of the past is always weaker than the pull of the future. To common sense reasoning this might seem absurd, since knowledge of the past is always more certain, but common sense was superseded by prophetic authority. Millenarian conceptions of history may be iconoclastic, but they still bear the authority of revelation, and this enables their prophets to engage in free speculation even while professing exegetical moderation.

The Gospel of Science

The potency of this speculative freedom is perhaps borne out by the fact that *New Atlantis*, though a work of fiction, came to be closely associated with science's most significant institutional achievement in the seventeenth century—the establishment of the Royal Society of London. Salomon's House, the scientific college that dominates the imaginary Christian civilization of this tale, was destined to become, as the clergyman and philosopher Joseph Glanvill (1636–1680) declared in his *Scepsis Scientifica* (1665), "a Prophetick Scheam of the ROYAL SOCIETY."[6] A decade earlier Samuel Hartlib had said that the similar institute he had hoped to establish at Lambeth Marsh had likewise been "designed for the execution of my Lord Verulam's *New Atlantis*."[7] The story's influence in linking the new natural philosophy with the prophetic fervor of this age may likewise be measured by the extraordinary popularity it enjoyed during this period. Written in 1624 and published posthumously in 1627 along with Bacon's *Sylva Sylvarum*, a treatise on natural history, his *New Atlantis* would appear in seventeen editions before the century was out.[8]

This "fable," as Bacon's secretary and chaplain William Rawley called it, has features that may reflect some debt to Plato and to the utopian tale of one earlier Lord Chancellor, Sir Thomas More, just as its setting on an island in the South Pacific marks the influence of those fashionable tales of exploration and new-world adventure then being circulated by Hakluyt, Raleigh, and Harriot.[9] But its explicit use of Old Testament types also made it a work of millenarian prophecy. By giving a dramatic form to the theological reasoning elsewhere outlined in Bacon's works of scientific advocacy, it anchored what it imagined in providential history. This enabled his auditors to visualize a partnership between science and religion that brought scientific work into concert with that of the church, thereby making it an expression of that same obedience to revelation by which, in the reformers' view, a once prodigal flock was now turning back to Christ.

Bacon's contribution to what we would now call science fiction is a mariner's story about a ship blown off its course in the South Pacific, somewhere out beyond the shores of Peru. Having exhausted the provisions meant to sustain their journey to China and Japan, the mariners find themselves lost "in the midst of the greatest wilderness of waters in the world."[10] They are saved, however, when an unexpected wind carries them northward to the previously undiscovered island of Bensalem. Here, as we are told by the voyager who narrates the tale, they are greeted by an entourage of officials bearing a Christian cross and reading proclamations from scrolls written in various familiar languages. The island's inhabitants treat their European visitors with great courtesy, but in accordance with laws restricting the entry of aliens due to the fear that they might bring disease to the island, the visitors are only allowed to come ashore under quarantine and only after they have avowed their Christian faith and good behavior. There they reside in the island's "Strangers' House," a medical facility where they are treated for their various ailments, and they begin to learn about Bensalem's history, laws, and culture. What unfolds before them is a society brimming with hospitality and goodwill, one superior to European Christendom in its charity and beneficent government but most especially in its natural philosophy.

Bensalem's dominant institution is its "College of the Six Days" or "Salomon's House," the scientific institute described at the climax of the story in a private audience granted to the narrator by its "Father." Salomon's House is the "greatest jewel" of the island, and its scientific directors, as Bacon makes clear in an elaborate description of their regal entourage, bejeweled garments, and blue turbans, enjoy a position of honor like that accorded to Europe's highest clergy and nobility. Their rank is commensurate with their role as the guardians of a scientific tradition that was already sixteen hundred years old and the unmistakable wellspring of the island's prosperity. "The end of our Foundation," the Father tells our narrator, "is the Knowledge of Causes, and secret motions of things; and the enlarging of the bounds of Human Empire, to the effecting of all things possible." These ends are detailed in the narrative's closing pages as the narrator catalogues the many undertakings that bring science to bear upon the island's industry and economy. The priest tells of caves used for "all coagulations, indurations, refrigerations, and conservations of bodies"; towers for meteorological study and astronomical observations; lakes, artificial wells, and fountains made for "health" and for "the prolongation of life"; propagation and dietary horticulture being undertaken in "orchards and gardens"; breeding "parks and inclosures"; "shops of medicines"; "diverse mechanical arts"; and "brew-houses, bake-houses, and kitchens, where are made divers drinks, breads, and meats, rare and of special effects."[11]

Up until this time, the Bensalemites had carefully guarded all these accomplishments. Although they had periodically sent scientific emissaries out into the world as "Merchants of Light" commissioned to scour the world for the "books, and abstracts, and patterns of experiment of all other parts," they had done so discretely so as not to be discovered. All scientific laborers are under an "oath of secrecy," the Father says, "for the concealing of those which we think fit to keep secret." But as the story draws to a close, so also does the isolationist policy which had governed Bensalem since its Christianization. The scientific high priest who has related all these things rises to his feet as the story's narrator kneels before him to receive his blessing:

> God bless thee, my son, and God bless this relation which I have made. I give thee leave to publish it for the good of other nations; for we here are in God's bosom, a land unknown.[12]

The story ends as the European visitors are assigned "a value of about two thousand ducats" for the propagation of this scientific gospel. If we believe Rawley's note added at the end of the text that "the rest was not perfected," we might surmise that Bacon had intended to add more. But the narrative strikes a telling allusive pose by closing at this point. By ending on this note, in other words, this great scientific commission is brought into parallel with the closing passage of Matthew's gospel in which Christ commands his apostles to "go therefore and make disciples of all nations" (Matthew 28:19). Just as Christ's coming had filled out the revelation of the Old Testament and thus marked the beginning of a new and final epoch, so now with science. The full vision of science's possibilities that Bacon's fable dramatizes represents an analogous endpoint in the realm of natural philosophy. Since the fullness of the scientific gospel was manifest in Bensalem, it could no longer remain hidden. Like the truths stored up by Israel until the coming of the Messiah, Bacon's scientific Israel had remained in "God's bosom, a land unknown." But Israel had been given this revelation, as we see again and again in both the Hebrew and Christian Scriptures, not for its own sake but so that the revelation it was given might benefit all the nations of the earth (Genesis 18:19, 22:18; Acts 3:25; Galatians 3:8). Applied now to the revelation of God's works in Bensalem's cultivation of scientific technique, Bacon was dramatizing a corresponding historical meaning. The new science was not a deviation from the continuity of Christian history; it was as old as providence itself, and its manifestation now at the end of the age simply marked the epoch of its universal propagation.

The historical continuity that *New Atlantis* achieves by presenting the age of science as a new revelatory dispensation also sanctioned the radical new beginning Bacon was calling for. What might have otherwise seemed unorthodox in substance—the notion that the church was destined to bring in a kingdom of works in addition to the kingdom of the word—was made orthodox by being represented through a sacred narrative form. The reformers had done much the same when confronted by a similar need to validate a new historical beginning, and for this reason their example provided a compelling precedent for Bacon. The success of Protestant leaders in portraying their movement as the "new Jerusalem" of John's Apocalypse (Revelation 21:2) made it that much easier for Bacon to use a conjugate term, "Bensalem" or "son of Salem," to name the holy city of his scientific millennium. Like the other prophets who had announced new dispensations in Scripture, Bacon was anchoring the new scientific age in the orthodoxies of the past, and this was precisely how he purchased the liberty to call for something radically new. When he aligned his new age of science with the beginning of church history in Christ's Great Commission, he enabled what he was envisioning to appeal to conservatives and radicals alike. Once having identified the advent of science with the advent of the gospel, science was assured of finding favor with the guardians of tradition. But by also insinuating that this new Great Commission represented the millennial fulfillment that, like every past moment of prophetic disclosure, necessitated the rewriting of historical understanding, the same principle of interpretation that made this narrative conservative also lent itself to the historical radicalism that was destined to infuse modernism.

THE REVOLT OF IMAGINATION AS LEARNED FORGETFULNESS

The religious features of Bacon's *New Atlantis* are unmistakable. Still, it is not at all uncommon for interpreters to pay them little mind. To our eyes, as I believe the bulk of Bacon scholarship bears witness, this historical vision may seem thoroughly modern, but this is because we selectively attend only to those symbolic road signs that point forward into a seemingly secularized future and just as selectively overlook the ones that point back into the Christian past. In large part this interpretive habit is a product of Bacon's own legacy. The millenarian turn that we find in his writing, despite its obvious religiosity, puts into play the learned forgetfulness that is so characteristic of modernism even now. Although millenarian rhetoric is tied to the past by prophetic authority, it also liberates itself from tradition by locating the principle of historical interpretation in the future. Scholars who pass over the religious language in Bacon's writing conform their thinking to a secular variation of the same logic. They are inclined to suppose that his ubiquitous religious references have no particular importance because their interpretations operate out of a conception of history that is grounded in their own time rather than the author's.

My own position is that these religious features still matter because they continue to be present in evolutionism through its grammatical descent. Rhetorical Darwinists still suppose that the revelations of science ought to define historical understanding. They may be oblivious to the religious ancestry of this idea, but theirs nevertheless is a form of historical consciousness that derives from the same millenarian logic that Bacon appropriated from Christianity. Our interest in looking at Bacon's historical vision as an antecedent to evolutionism stems from the supposition that it will uncover some clues that may explain how and why such religious patterns of signification continue to abide. The question driving this analysis, therefore, is why those patterns would be able to persist even while modernist ideologies such as evolutionism deny their validity. From whence comes the learned forgetfulness that enables evolutionism to sustain a religious view of history even while defending scientism and naturalism?

The basis of my answer can be found simply by considering how rhetoric works in its longitudinal aspect. The enduring effects of old messages are the end products of specific acts of mediation, each having occurred in accordance with the circumstances of its own successive moment and audience. Contemporary messages will seem to have no relationship to the counterpart ones of centuries past until we take into consideration the succession of mediating messages that lead from one antipode of cultural evolution to another. This is because change and conservation work dialectically. The chain of thought that links Bacon's messages to the scientific rhetoric of today would have been broken if seventeenth-century audiences had not been able to reconcile such novelties with the established truths of their own time. The same principle carries down to the present. Any novelty that arises within such a larger historical continuum must be capable of being integrated with the established truths of its own milieu. The needs of conservation that arise at each juncture in this process ensure that some abiding continuity of meaning will persist even over the long term.

The principle of language that accounts for the operation of this dialectic of change and conservation is narrative form. Northrop Frye's theory of displacement, which will become the driving force of this argument in my next chapter, supposes that narrative plot structures or forms (which I will apply to historical accounts as well as fictional ones) are vehicles capable of mediating an enduring thematic substance in messages that will otherwise seem quite different. Form and substance, this is to say, are somewhat interchangeable. What this means in practical terms is that when a narrative form that originally expressed religious meaning becomes detached from its sacred moorings and reattached to secular ones, its thematic substance will nevertheless abide because that substance has been impressed into the narrative form. In our case this means that the seemingly secular visions of scientific history that began to manifest in the Enlightenment (though then still consciously credited to Bacon) continued to employ a millenarian form like the one I have just described in Bacon's *New Atlantis*. Because form is a conveyor of theme (being consubstantial with theme in some sense), such secular imitations of Bacon's scientific history brought over from it the thematic substance of "providence"—albeit now under the heading of the different term "progress."

Although Charles Whitney has applied the concept of displacement to Bacon's messages themselves (with insightful effect), my interpretation is that this kind of literary expression is only anticipated in his messages—in Bacon's case, this is biblical recursion but not yet displacement.[13] For seventeenth-century readers, at least, the biblical narrative would have remained fully present in Bacon's applications. However, the novelty of his interpretations of the biblical narrative represents a step in this direction, and this accounts for the odd fact that he could so easily become as much a hero for eighteenth-century skeptics as he had been for the Puritan intellectuals of his own century. His *New Atlantis* in particular foreshadows the more genuine displacement of the next century to the extent that, as an exercise of literary imagination, it had already loosened its traditional Christian elements from the realm of real history by setting them in a fictional one.

Bacon's exercise of imagination in his *New Atlantis* anticipates the forgetfulness that genuine displacement fosters. In part we can understand why this would be by considering what Bacon himself had to say about the rhetorical role of imagination. Every student of rhetoric is familiar with Bacon's belief that reason could win out in persuasive communication only if it also operated upon the auditor's imagination in appropriate ways. Reason would become "captive and servile," he argued in his *Advancement of Learning*, "if Eloquence of Persuasions did not practice and win the Imagination from the Affections's part, and contract a confederacy between the Reason and Imagination against the Affections."[14] As applied to history, this was necessary because, while "reason beholdeth the future and sum of time," human emotions, which "beholdeth merely the present," obscure the better future that reason might win. Thus it was the office of rhetoric to encourage a "revolt of the imagination" against the emotional ties that bind readers to present experience so as to make "things future and remote appear as present."[15]

Imagination thus employed also served the interests of prophecy by enabling auditors to see "more according to revealed providence," which was constantly obscured by the effects of human sinfulness in real history.[16] Since providence could only be imperfectly shown in real experience, Bacon judged that "feigned histories" better satisfy the "mind of man" by constructing "acts and events greater and more heroical" than what "true history propoundeth." Prophetic reason unassisted by imagination "doth buckle and bow the mind unto the nature of things," but poetic imagination brings together "magnanimity, morality and . . . delectation." This explained why imagination was in ancient times "ever thought to have some participation of divineness" by virtue of its capacity to "raise and erect the mind, by submitting the shews of things to the desires of the mind."[17]

Here we find an explanation for Bacon's attraction to fable and, more importantly, an object lesson that anticipates how the persuasive scope of prophecy won by its exercise would be further extended once it was displaced by the secular authors of later generations. By imagining such pure operations of providence in the fictional history of Bensalem, Bacon could envision what Christendom might have looked like had it never wandered from the path of true faith. As one might expect, the perfected church of Bacon's imagining looks a lot like the Protestant Christianity of his contemporaries, and this is precisely what also makes Bensalem's scientific preoccupations so compelling. By also writing science into this reimagined Christian history, Bacon made it that much easier to imagine a Protestant future dominated by science. But what would happen if subsequent imitations of this imaginary excursion further distanced it from its biblical model? I will suggest that the more genuine displacement that eventually gave rise to evolutionism represents an extension of this imaginative principle. In the secular milieu, Bacon's narrative was pushed to the breaking point of forgetfulness. The religious bases of this story were destined to be forgotten, but its religious meaning would endure through the conveyance of its form.

In the cultural evolutionary terms that I laid out at the onset of this project, we might say that Bacon is a transitional figure. When Robert Faulkner describes Bacon's *New Atlantis* as "conversion poetry," he makes note of the ways in which this message points back to the sacred source from which the historical consciousness of science comes but also forward toward its secularization. Bacon wrote science into a traditional notion of Christian history as an instance of conversion or reform, a new beginning, but he adapted it for secular use by doing so through poetry, by exercising the freedom that is afforded once the powers of literary imagination come into play. In this way his effort to "meld his scientific project with the reinterpreted hopes of the religious" also enabled him to put "the fabulous in the service of worldly progress."[18]

If narrative form is a carrier of religious meaning, what are the theological principles that we find in Bacon's *New Atlantis* that we should expect to endure in its secular displacement? My concern in the remainder of this chapter will be with three thematic pairings that persist in evolutionism via displacement: sin and redemption; separation and election; and revelation and millennium. By considering how these ideas advanced the scientific cause through this explicitly Christian view of history, we can foresee the rhetorical attractions that have tended to ensure their enduring presence in the secular narratives that will be the subject of my remaining chapters.

Sin and Redemption

Bacon's determination to set the struggle for science within the moral drama of the Bible accounts for the novel's long delay in getting to the scientific subject for which it is most remembered. Thus it is only in the last eleven pages (out of thirty-seven in the Spedding edition) that Bensalem's scientific essence comes into focus. The early part needed to bring the Christian concept of sin into the open, something it does through various biblical and historical allusions, in order to ensure that readers will recognize science as one of its correctives. The idea of sin is frequently expressed in the Bible through metaphors of wandering and lostness, and so the plight of Bacon's mariners instantly brings the moral deficiencies of their European culture into play. Allegorically, they are prodigal humanity fleeing from God but brought to repentance through a life-threatening disaster. The implication that these travelers are also Catholic (since they communicate with the Bensalemites in Spanish) likewise identifies their plight with the "lostness" of unreformed Christendom. Allegorically we might say that theirs is the misguided voyage of the Catholic Church adrift from Scripture on the chaotic sea of human opinion and doomed to die of spiritual hunger and thirst.

One biblical type for this kind of religious person is the prophet Jonah, and so it is no surprise that the first part of Bacon's narrative is rife with allusions to this character. A figure whose behavior suggests the turbulent history that Protestants saw in the Catholic Church, Jonah is God's disobedient ambassador. Though commanded to carry God's word eastward to the lost Ninevites of Assyria, the rebellious prophet has instead set his face toward the Mediterranean where he is found "fleeing from the presence of the LORD." Once Jonah's apostasy is discovered amidst a terrible storm, he is thrown overboard by his Gentile shipmates and swallowed up by a great fish. But God does not abandon his chosen messenger. In response to the prayer of repentance that wells up from the prophet's underwater tomb, God commands the great leviathan to spew him out upon the dry land, whence he returns to his ordained work.

What makes the Jonah narrative especially attractive as a model for Bacon's scientized reimagining of Christian history is the fact that its imagery brings the Bible's drama of spiritual salvation into close association with parallel notions of a restored creation and thus with the scientific role that Bacon wished to link to this sacred resource. Jonah's westward flight across the Mediterranean is manifestly an act of spiritual rebellion that recapitulates Adam's primordial disobedience, but the story's corresponding shift of scenes from solid land out into the chaos of the sea also recapitulates the natural fall that coincided with this. By drawing the natural and spiritual aspects of this drama together in a similar way, Bacon was setting his *New Atlantis* against a similar theological backdrop. He draws attention to this by bringing the language of the primordial creation and fall into the prayer of desperation offered up in the story's opening scene. Bereft of provisions and hope, Bacon's narrator tells us, "we gave ourselves for lost men, and prepared for death."

> Yet we did lift up our hearts and voices to God above, who *showeth his wonders in the deep*; beseeching him of his mercy, that as in the beginning he discovered the face of the deep, and brought forth dry land, so he would now discover land to us, that we might not perish.[19]

Like the allusions to God's original separation of land and sea that one finds in the Jonah narrative (Jonah 1:9-10, 2:3-5; Gen 1:6), the narrator's prayer reminds Bacon's readers that the human story of salvation recapitulates this primordial drama, and in doing so it also reminds them that, since sin always has natural as well as spiritual implications, so also does its opposite. The story of redemption may be about fallen spirits restored to life, but it is also about the reversal of nature's descent into chaos. This sets the scene for the story's introduction of a Bensalemite Christendom that is devoted to God's natural works in the same measure as it is to the word of God. Bensalem is providence imagined in both its spiritual and material aspects, and thus the Europeans who escape the chaos of the sea by stepping upon this scientific paradise are symbolically returning to the original order of the creation before its fall.

The notion that science participates in God's redemptive work was already implicit in Bacon's two books doctrine. Because science represented obedience to a parallel revelation, Bacon wrote in his *Instauratio Magna*, it was "content to wait upon nature instead of vainly affecting to overrule her" and thus enacted the most fundamental condition of salvation. It was an effort to return the creation, "to its perfect and original condition" and therefore participated in God's most essential and eternal work.[20] Science was a means by which to regain paradise, to reenact the pursuit of pure and uncorrupted natural knowledge that Adam first undertook when he "gave names to the creatures according to their property" (Gen 2:19-20). In the primordial disaster, as Bacon explains in his *Novum Organum*, Adam had fallen "from his state of innocency," but also from his "dominion over creation," but God's creative purposes were not to be forever frustrated. Both of these consequences of original sin could "even in this life be in some part repaired; the former by religion and faith, the latter by arts and science."[21] Human beings were God's instruments of creation; and though temporarily exiled, they were destined to enter an Eden they would participate in remaking.

As Bacon's mariners enter Bensalem, this theme finds expression in the story's various allusions to the creation and its undoing in the great flood. Just as the fallen condition symbolized by the impending death of Bacon's mariners had called to mind the collapse of cosmos back into chaos that one finds in the primordial flood, their return to the dry land anticipates the reversal of this fall, the restoration of creation, and by extension, science's creative participation in this millennial task. The undoing of God's work that had occurred in the deluge was brought about by human disobedience, and so the sailors' initial plight underlines, in its negative aspect, the natural destructiveness of human evil. All sin, we might say, is a rejection of God's creative work, but this also implies that science is sin's inverse. Consequently, the resurgent chaos in which Bacon's protagonists are trapped symbolizes both the religious apostasy of the European culture they represent and the scientific inadequacy that follows from such spiritual defects. For this same reason, it follows that the dry land upon which they have now set their feet should also be a place of science. Just as both Noah and Jonah are returned to the cosmos of the dry land in response to their obedience, thus causing these stories to recapitulate the creation narrative, the landing of Bacon's Europeans upon Bensalem represents a third such cycle of human reform, one now having to do with science explicitly.

As we press on, we will see that Bacon's effort to depict scientific work as redemptive action manifests the fundamental mechanism of cultural conservation that, as it continued to be plied, was destined to ensure that this Baconian theme would be imitated by the figures who gave us evolutionism. His new ideas could only take hold by being tied to existing ones, and this limitation would also hold for those who would carry these ideas forward in later generations. Thus, even though the story's imaginative aspect strives to bring about a novel turn in Christian thinking by introducing science into the trajectory of history, its traditional form—the story of sin and redemption which was already a reworking of the Bible's most ancient themes of chaos and creation—anchored it to mainstream religious ideas and ensured that these would continue to abide. This could hardly have been otherwise. Had Bacon been the purely modern thinker he is now often mistaken for, he could not have hoped to win over an audience that by all appearances remained firmly committed to the traditional premises of religion. The conservation of form is the price by which public acceptance of his scientific vision was purchased, and since this constraint has operated upon similar efforts of scientific advocacy in every subsequent moment of the scientific culture's development, we have every reason to expect that something akin to this earlier theme would persist. Thus when Carl Sagan declared several centuries later that the rejection of science was a "turning away from the Cosmos," he was invoking a secularized redaction of Bacon's theological drama.[22] Certainly the Cornell astronomer did not see his message in this way, since he clearly regarded theistic beliefs of this kind as fundamentally anti-scientific, but this was only because he could not see the longer reach of the rhetorical pattern that had descended upon his mind. Like other voices of evolutionism, Sagan was reworking a thematic pattern that an unbroken chain of public advocates going all the way back to the seventeenth century had imitated.

SEPARATION AND ELECTION

If human beings are alienated from God by sin, the elect can return to God only by separating themselves from a fallen world—from the cultural matrix that perpetuates evil. In every biblical narrative that expresses this, separation is enacted through some act of obedience to God's revelation, and the natural consequences of this obedience, such as the physical redemption that occurs in the Noah and Jonah stories, are reminders of the fact that nature has analogous revelatory significance. To obey God is to honor his creation, and thus the elect are the friends of nature. In the narratives of evolutionism that we will examine in later chapters, we will see that the revelatory obedience that distinguishes science from other enterprises of inquiry as nature's elect is its unwavering adherence to the empiricist doctrine. Faithfulness to fact now enacts separation—the forsaking of "cherished beliefs," those polluting idols that arise within human subjectivity. Separation is the necessary moral condition that enables science to perform its heroic mediation of the book of nature.

Such hints of election, of course, draw our attention to the fact that this scientific exceptionalism could have no scientific basis in evolution. E. O. Wilson, for instance, who has built his fame as a public scientist upon the assumption that natural evolution is all-encompassing, seems oblivious to the fact that he contradicts this premise when he insists that "the human mind evolved to believe in the gods," but it "did not evolve to believe in biology." Science alone stands with history because it alone transcends natural determinism, and Wilson therefore surmises that religion must be thrown off. The "uncomfortable truth" that only the scientific elect are capable of facing is that "those who hunger for both intellectual and religious truth will never acquire both in full measure."[23] Such expressions remind us that evolutionism's basis only appears to be scientific. Rhetorical Darwinism's supposition that science's historical election comes from its unique power to transcend material determination reflects its dependency upon a story form capable of making science the sole inhabitant of an upper world of spiritual freedom and the one agent of historical destiny capable of willingly separating itself from a lower one of brute causality.

Bacon's *New Atlantis* also anticipates the broader drama of election that now sets science against religion. Set within Bacon's own time, however, this is an extension of the conflict between Protestants and Catholics. In this drama, science derives special virtue because it participates in the same act of spiritual separation that the Protestant movement was thought to enact. Protestants were God's elect because, in their singular devotion to revelation, they rejected all the worldly impurities that had infected the Catholic faith, and the new science enacted the natural scientific counterpart to this. This background drama is brought into Bacon's fable by various symbols associating his lost European voyagers with Catholicism and their Bensalemite saviors with Protestantism, and also through its allusions to the Jonah narrative. We might say that the story's lost European mariners replay the Mediterranean journey of this rebellious prophet and thereby align the errors of Catholicism with both the spiritual and material aspects of Jonah's sin. Jonah's return to his prophetic calling is carried over into *New Atlantis* in the Protestant restoration that Bacon's Bensalem envisions. Just as Jonah's spiritual repentance led to his physical resurrection, the penitence of Bacon's voyagers likewise leads to their physical restoration as they are integrated into this new Christendom.

This interpretation of Bacon's creative intent finds support in the fact that it so clearly comports with his theory of feigned history. The theological sanction that Bacon ascribed to such exercises of historical imagination came from their power to make God's providential orchestrations of history visible. Imagination enabled the believer to see through the dark cloud of sin behind which providence was veiled in real history. However, such exercises could only reveal this higher truth if they also conformed to the matter of providence as it was already revealed—that is to say, in the Bible. Bacon could not make plausible the public expectation that the future Christendom was destined to be dominated by science without also showing that his narrative was consistent with Scripture, and it was this need that made the story of Jonah's rebellion and restoration such an attractive model. The story's two phases—the prophet's initial rejection of his sacred calling followed by his subsequent obedience—made it useful as a biblical example capable of authorizing the Protestant supposition that the Reformation now carried forward the gospel mission formerly abdicated by the Catholic Church. Moreover, the natural symbolism that coincides with these two phases—the prophet's descent into the chaos of the sea and his restoration to the dry land—also gave plausibility to Bacon's effort to imagine the reform of science as one realization of this rediscovered election.

These scientific implications find an even deeper biblical resonance in Bacon's similar allusions to the flood narrative, since the Noah story follows so closely upon the primordial story of creation in Genesis. While Noah's saving work presages all those other acts of prophetic intercession in the Bible that became models for Christian ministry, symbolically it is more closely aligned with God's first work of creation than is any subsequent recursion of this narrative cycle. Thus, as we find the ark that Noah has fashioned floating between the waters pouring up from "the fountains of the great deep" and those descending from "the windows of heaven" (Gen 7:11), we are witness to what is recognizably a recapitulation of God's separation of the waters on the second day of creation (Gen 1:6-8). Noah performs the work of a prophet when he saves a remnant of life, but his role in perpetuating life is also the work of scientific invention. In this post-Edenic world, human culture (represented especially by Noah's technical labor in fashioning the ark and his subsequent agricultural endeavors) participates in the creative work of God.

For the same reason that Noah's obedience results in the saving of some remnant of nature, Jonah's abandonment of his prophetic election threatens to end in natural calamity. The physical destruction of Nineveh that was sure to follow if Jonah did not bring God's corrective revelation to that city is this story's correlative to the great flood. Prophecy coincides with God's creative work in nature, and this means that prophetic obedience and disobedience have natural consequences. Just as the story of Noah enacts the positive side of this relationship, Jonah's westward flight across the Mediterranean, away from "the presence of the LORD," enacts its inverse. Having refused God's call to enlighten the Ninevite Gentiles, Jonah (by a telling ironic stroke) finds himself among Gentiles nonetheless, but now as a kind of antiprophet who, by abandoning God's word, has brought death rather than life. Jonah and his Gentile shipmates can be saved from the tempest only if he separates himself from them by again reclaiming his prophetic office, and this occurs when he professes his identity as a Hebrew and makes the prophetic disclosure that it is his own disobedience that threatens their destruction. The priestly separation that Jonah acknowledges in this speech is then ritually enacted as he commands the crew to throw him into the sea (Jonah 1:9-15). Now dead to the world, Jonah again is made alive to God, and the consequences of his reclaimed election are then played out in the story's final scene. Having arisen from the depths of the sea, the repentant prophet is restored to the solid ground of the ordered creation. God's primordial separation of the land from the sea is once again replayed. For a second time Jonah finds himself among the Gentiles, but now he has reclaimed his prophetic election. Separated from them by his obedience to God's revelation, Jonah's message is heeded and the destruction of Nineveh averted.

If the Catholic past found its biblical touchstone in the rebellious phase of Jonah's prophetic ministry, the Protestant world to come is anticipated by the prophet's rebirth and also in Noah, that other flood survivor of the Bible whose priestly heroics are similarly aligned with the theme of nature's instauration. Bacon draws out this second linkage by making Bensalem's isolation from the world the consequence of a second great flood. We are told by one of the island's governors that the first Atlantis of legend was in fact an ancient confederation of civilizations in the Americas that was later destroyed, not by an earthquake as Plato had surmised, but by a "deluge or innundation," an act of "Divine Revenge" brought against it because of its aggressive overtures toward Bensalem.[24] The old Atlantis, like the worldly civilization destroyed in the flood, was now buried beneath the sea, while Bensalem remained. Thus, just as Noah was set apart to save a remnant of nature by heeding God's command to build the ark, this island's isolation signals an analogous correlation between Protestant obedience to God's word and scientific salvation.

This connection between Bensalem's scientific achievements and the post-diluvian work of Noah also drew science into alliance with the primordial command to Adam that he "bring forth abundantly on the earth and multiply in it" (Gen 1:28). In this regard, the scope of this scientific work is no less universal than the mission of the church. This is underlined when the Bensalemites inform their visitors that the island's scientific institute, Salomon's House, is also called the "College of the Six Days Work." It is, we are told by one of Bensalem's governors, the "noblest foundation (as we think) that was ever upon the earth; and the lanthorn [lantern] of this kingdom." The island's ancient patriarch, the wise King Salomona, having learned "from the Hebrews that God had created the world and all that therein is within six days," gave the college this second name, since it was instituted "for the finding out of the true nature of all things, (whereby God might have the more glory in the workmanship of them, and men the more fruit in the use of them)."[25] Like the great temple of Solomon from which it derives its other name, Salomon's House is an abode of the living God, and it is thus, in accordance with Mircea Eliade's reading of temple symbolism, also a prophetic symbol of the earth itself.[26] Just as God's presence in the inner sanctuary of Solomon's temple signaled Israel's role in making the word of God universally known, Salomon's House signaled the analogous destiny of God's works.

Divine election necessarily involves separation from the world, and this accounts for the self-imposed isolation that was first ordained by Bensalem's ancestral king and lawgiver in various "interdicts and prohibitions . . . touching the entrance of strangers." Bacon makes sure to remind his readers that this was not a merely political caution to ensure that no future attempts were made to invade the island; more fundamentally it reflects the island civilization's divine calling. Bacon is careful to point out that the policy did not arise from the kind of xenophobia which had made China "a curious, ignorant, fearful, foolish nation."[27] Bensalem's isolation in fact has the opposite meaning. It has a universal meaning similar to that performed when God calls Abram out of pagan Chaldea. The great patriarch's separation, like Noah's before him and like God's isolated presence within the holy of holies, was ordained so that by his offspring "all the nations of the earth shall bless themselves" (Genesis 18:18). Bensalem's separation, as we soon discover, has prepared the world for a similar universal blessing. Just as Israel was set apart as a spiritual preparation for its universal mission, Bensalem was isolated, not to maintain the secrecy of its accomplishments, but to make science ready for its global mission. Bensalem had been set apart from the world for the same reason that the church was "betrothed" to Christ as a "pure bride to her one husband" (2 Corinthians 11:2), so that it could prepare for his final revelation. It is notable in this regard that Bacon's climactic survey of the scientific achievements that have been wrought within Salomon's House is immediately preceded by a discussion of the island's marriage customs. The fact that there is "not under the heavens so chaste a nation as this of Bensalem," which is "the virgin of the world," also tells us, by way of a familiar pattern of biblical allegory, something vital about its scientific purity. Just as the Bensalemites look with "wonder" and "detestation" upon the widespread "concupiscence" that undermined marriage and the propagation of children in Europe, their own intellectual chasteness, which has protected their science from the distractions of worldly lust, was also the condition that had made possible that fecundity which was soon to bless the world.[28]

The scientific secrecy depicted in New Atlantis has puzzled many readers, especially since it seems to violate the norm of open communication that was soon to become vital for the emerging scientific culture.[29] This is compounded by the fact that Bacon elsewhere indicts Catholic natural philosophers for precisely this error. They were "shut up in the cells of a few authors (chiefly Aristotle their dictator)," he writes in his Advancement of Learning, just "as their persons were shut up in the cells of monasteries and colleges." This had made the scholastic doctors "fierce with dark keeping," as if their work had been touched by the madness that afflicts animals left too long in darkened cages.[30] Such statements might seem to be contradicted by the secrecy imposed by Bensalemite law, but this problem evaporates once we recognize the author's allegorical purposes. Bacon was not laying out a technical blueprint for institutional science; he was trying to integrate its identity into an established pattern of spiritual and historical understanding. If natural philosophers were to be seen as God's elect, it was also necessary that they should manifest all the traditional signs associated with the prophetic office. To the extent that separation from the world always coincided with the obedience required of those human actors who aspired to fulfill their elected role as partners in God's redemptive work, Bacon needed to dramatize science's separation in some similar way.

Bensalem's isolation is thus the Baconian antecedent to that preference for the "uncomfortable truth" of natural fact that E. O. Wilson now lauds as science's defining virtue. I am not saying that the empiricist ethic invoked in such catchphrases has no importance in upholding science's distinctive rigors; I am only saying that it does something more that only becomes evident once we take note of how empiricism coincides with the progressive meanings that evolutionism promotes. Having inherited from Bacon the supposition that science manifests a historical destiny closed off to most people, the scientific culture needs to uphold some similar historical rationale that demonstrates what exempts it from the common errors of humanity. Empiricism, as a key expression of that exempting separation, is thus as much a historical ideal as it is an epistemic one.

REVELATION AND MILLENNIUM

This third pairing has to do with the thematic association between new revelations and new beginnings that was so vital to the emerging historical consciousness of Protestants. I draw attention to it here for two reasons. The first and most immediate reason is that it illustrates how Bacon reconciled his prognostications with the difficult historical fact that science had never been particularly prominent in Christianity. As I noted earlier in this chapter, by linking science to a prophesied millennium, Bacon worked with an orthodox historical conception, but one that also lent itself to novelty. The second reason is that millenarian reasoning of this kind clearly anticipates the future-centered consciousness of modernism and in this regard is the likely antecedent from which evolutionism's modernist themes descend. When Bacon identified the rise of science with the millennium, he was also linking it to a notion of history which supposed that the revelations of the present and future supersede those of the past. In this regard, science was taking an important first step in linking itself to that pattern of epochal thinking that now makes the scientific revelations of the present the standard for all historical interpretation. New historical epochs in the Bible are always initiated and defined by sacred disclosures, since it is prophecy that reveals the providential order of history. As I noted earlier, the rising interest in millenarian prophesies within the Protestant movement signals its efforts to rationalize sweeping reforms by mainstreaming them. This likewise gave Bacon an opportunity to create a central role for science by putting it on the same bandwagon. The millenarian turn had created a pretext for novelty—that most fundamental value of modernist ideology—that the emerging scientific movement could exploit.

Bacon's efforts to situate science in prophetic history may at first appear to be a mere anomaly having nothing to do with the scientific identity in our time. But if we attend to what these messages suggest in the abstract, apart from the concrete religious referents that made them compelling for his immediate audiences, we can recognize a pattern that clearly persists within evolutionism. Perpetuated now in the notion that the discoveries of contemporary science (and of evolution especially) have fundamentally redefined our historical situation is something akin to the traditional millenarian idea that history has an ordained structure and that it is only in the final stage of human life that its true character has been discovered. To be modern (or even postmodern, since that term expresses the same epochal reasoning) is to be uniquely attuned to the sanctioning significance of the disclosures that define the present epoch. Although this now manifests in manifold ways, evolutionism stands apart as the effort to suggest that the disclosures of evolutionary science have some supremacy of place in this process. We can trace this theme, for instance, in a recent guidebook for science educators published by the National Academy of Sciences. The book's introductory chapter, "Why Teach Evolution?" is mainly an effort to outline the educational importance of its subject, but in its closing paragraph it also invokes the broader epochal notion that evolutionary knowledge in particular gives the present age its distinctive meaning. Evolutionary knowledge is needed to enable today's children to adapt to modern life.

> All of us live in a world where the pace of change is accelerating. Today's children will face more new experiences and different conditions than their parents or teachers have had to face in their lives.

> The story of evolution is one chapter—perhaps the most important one—in a scientific revolution that has occupied much of the past four centuries. The central feature of this revolution has been the abandonment of one notion about stability after another: that the earth was the center of the universe, that the world's living things are unchangeable, that the continents of the earth are held rigidly in place, and so on. Fluidity and change have become central to our understanding of the world around us. To accept the probability of change—and to see change as an agent of opportunity rather than a threat—is a silent message and challenge in the lesson of evolution.[31]

This is a classic expression of the more general *nomos-cosmos* pattern discussed already, but it is one expressed in terms that distinctively reflect a millenarian legacy. We should teach evolution, these writers surmise, because it enables students to integrate their lives into the modern age. Their *nomos*, the rapidly changing society in which they live, finds its ordering principle in a volatile *cosmos* that only evolutionary constructs can account for. By supposing that evolutionary science has so redefined history as to mark our time as such a new beginning, the committee of scientists and educators who authored this guidebook have set the present apart from the past as a new epoch which is also the vantage point by which all of history is defined. Science is the key to this new age, and only the new revelations of evolutionary science can understand it. This also explains why the effort to combat creationism is such an important purpose of the NAS book. The stability of life forms that is traditionally associated with the assumption of biological design is not just wrong; it is also a sin against the order of history. To oppose science's evolutionary revelations is to be out of tune with progress.

Bacon's attraction to an analogous argument reflects the fact that the Reformation with which he wanted to identify science was in some sense modern already. To shake up Christianity while also remaining true to its essentials required a powerful but also malleable historical rationale, and millenarian reasoning provided this. The historical "periodization" that we find in the Christian concept of the millennium, as R. G. Collingwood names the concept behind such new beginnings, supposed a final stage of history that balanced the movement's conservative and radical tendencies.[32] It was conservative in that the very idea of Christianity is founded on the notion of a new beginning, since time had begun anew with Christ's coming, but it was open to novelty for the same reason. Just as the incarnation had dramatically altered traditional Jewish conceptions of prophecy's meaning, subsequent revelations (which for Bacon now included scientific revelations of God's works) could likewise rewrite the meaning of the past and future.

If the revelations of science were to be regarded as capable of founding a new age, it would be necessary to show that they were compatible with traditional understandings of revelation, and Bacon demonstrates this by appropriating the seasonal metaphors that biblical authors had used to depict pivotal epochal changes. Just as Christ's coming had been associated with the cycle of seasons, he depicts science in his *Valerius Terminus* as a latent development whose fruition was "appointed to this autumn of the world."[33] Like the seemingly dead branch of Jesse that had borne Christ as its fruit,

Christianity's scientific limb had likewise seemed barren. But it had in fact been growing all along in preparation for its modern fruition. The novelty of science was thus a fulfillment, not a break with, the past. Bacon compares it in his *Novum Organum* to the inconspicuous work of building God's kingdom that had been carried on by the prophets who, though unrecognized and rejected by Israel's elites, were destined to see the fruit of their labor realized in Christ.

> Now in divine operations even the smallest beginnings lead of a certainty to their end. And as it was said of spiritual things, "The Kingdom of God cometh not with observations," so is it in all the greater works of Divine Providence; everything glides on smoothly and noiselessly, and the work is fairly going on before men are aware that it has begun.[34]

This interpretation was also affirmed by the evident virtue of scientific knowledge. Since Christ taught that "fruits" are the signs of God's providence in history (Matt 7:16), Bacon assured his readers that science's "beginning is from God" because "the character of good is so strongly impressed upon it."[35]

If it had not previously been apparent that science was part of salvation history, this was only because the workings of providence are inscrutable. Prophecy was only to be fully understood in its fulfillment, and science's place in sacred history was now recognizable as having been anticipated quite explicitly in the eschatological vision of Daniel (12:4).

> Nor should the prophecy of Daniel be forgotten, touching the last ages of the world—"Many shall go to and fro, and knowledge shall be increased;" clearly indicating that the thorough passage of the world (which now by so many distant voyages seems to be accomplished, or in course of accomplishment), and the advancement of the sciences, are destined by fate, that is, by Divine Providence, to meet in the same age.[36]

Similar invocations of this passage in his *Advancement of Learning* and *Valerius Terminus* give indication of its special significance.[37] In an age dominated by the literal reading of biblical eschatology, Bacon could dare to link the advent of science to prophecy, and thus a Latin inscription of Daniel's words also made its way onto the frontispiece of his *Instauratio Magna*, where the fulfillment of this prophecy is visualized through an illustration of ships sailing "to and fro" upon the Atlantic, out beyond the pillars of Hercules (the classical symbol of human limitations), in defiance of past expectations (figure 5).

Figure 5

The fact that both the science and exploration that Bacon thought were foretold in Daniel figure prominently in his *New Atlantis* supports my argument that Bacon's story belongs to the genre of "feigned history" rather than to that of utopian literature. Quite unlike the "nowhere" world imagined by Thomas More, writes W. A. Sessions, Bacon's is "a 'model' of a higher reality that is being presented as truth, not a choice of options."[38] Bacon does not bracket Bensalem off from history as More had when he called his imaginary civilization "nowhere." The Christian civilization he depicts is certainly a product of imagination, but it is one that is also created in the image of established theological truths. As a version of the "New Jerusalem" of the Apocalypse, Bensalem represents something clearly envisioned in the eschatology of the Bible. As a city that lies in "God's bosom," it is an imaginative representation of what was for his readers a sanctioned trajectory, that future city of God whose coming was certified by Scripture.

To make such an imaginary trajectory plausible, its narrative representation in the *New Atlantis* needed to be theologically coherent. This meant that the narrative would need to be a dramatic reenactment of Christian history—but on Protestant grounds. This explains why Bacon is so careful to lay out the story of Bensalem's conversion to Christianity before he gets around to his famous catalogue of its scientific accomplishments. His conversion narrative recapitulates Christian history by imagining the course it might have followed had it remained true to those primitive truths that the Catholic Church had failed to honor. By doing so, Bacon made it easier for his readers to envision the historical steps by which an unimpeded providence would spontaneously give rise to science. We discover that the island's conversion was realized, much as the reformers thought the conversion of the primitive church had been, solely through the revelation of the written Bible, without any assistance from tradition or teaching. But unlike the Christian church of real history, Bacon's feigned Christendom had remained on the path of providence by virtue of its unwavering faithfulness to God's first book, and this (narratively speaking) accounted for its spontaneous devotion to God's second book. In this way, Bacon's feigned history gives "some shadow of satisfaction to the mind of man in those points wherein the nature of things doth deny it," and it does so in a way that is calculated to bring science into accord with the specific theological expectations of his readers.[39]

The story of Bensalem's conversion is told by one of its governors. The islanders became Christians in the middle of the first century after there appeared off Bensalem's eastern shore a miraculous sign, a great pillar of light rising up from the sea into the heavens with "a large cross of light" at its top. Floating at the pillar's base was a small "ark of cedar." But when the island's inhabitants went out in their boats to approach this holy of holies, a mysterious force blocked their way. The only Bensalemite who is found to have sufficient purity of heart to pass through this barrier is one of "the wise men of the society of Salomon's House," the scientific "eye of this kingdom." Having "awhile attentively and devoutly viewed and contemplated this pillar and cross," this man of science "fell down upon his face; and then raised himself upon his knees, and lifting his hands to heaven, made his prayers in this manner:"

> "Lord God of Heaven and earth, thou hast vouchsafed of thy grace to those of our order, to know thy works of creation, and the secrets of them; and to discern (as far as apperaineth to the generations of men) between divine miracles, works of nature, works of art, and impostures and illusions of all sorts. I do here acknowledge and testify before this people,

that the thing which we now see before our eyes is thy Finger and a true Miracle; and forasmuch as we learn in our books that thou never workest miracles but to a divine and excellent end, (for the laws of nature are thine own laws, and thou exceedest them not but upon great cause,) we most humbly beseech thee to prosper this great sight, and to give us the interpretation and use of it in mercy; which thou dost in some part secretly promise by sending it unto us."[40]

At the end of his prayer, the wise man's boat was unbound, though all the rest "remained still fast," and taking this as a summons, he rowed toward the pillar, which now dissolved back into the heavens, leaving only the ark of cedar upon the water. This ark, an allusion to the Noah narrative and, by virtue of its cedar construction, to the house and temple built by the wise Solomon, is found to contain both Testaments of the Bible and a letter from the Apostle Bartholomew, a favorite of Protestants, explaining how an angel had instructed him to "commit this ark to the floods of the sea" for the purpose of delivering "salvation and peace and goodwill" to "that people where God shall ordain this ark to come to land."[41]

The intercessory role played by this scientific actor in bringing Christianity to the island dramatizes the familiar Baconian notion that the scientific motive, once rightly conceived, is the same motive that opens God's revelation to all believers. By selecting one of the men of Salomon's house to break through the supernatural barrier that kept the Bensalemites from God's revelation, Bacon has merely applied to science St. Paul's admonition not to "despise prophesying" but to "test everything" (1 Thessalonians 5:21-22). But what was in this regard an effort to affirm science's orthodoxy also attained radical implications once science's revelatory powers were specifically associated with the millennium. Every biblical epoch is defined by some new revelation, and thus by making science the prophetic ingredient that made Bensalem a picture of the purified church to come, Bacon also insinuated that science was destined to attain new regulatory authority. As Bacon's history progresses from Bensalem's Christian beginnings in the first century to its present-day prosperity, we discover that its scientific institution has become the "very eye of this kingdom."[42] It was the continuous presence of that same natural revelation that certified the truth of the biblical revelation upon its initial reception that ensured that this imaginary Christendom was not beguiled into following those detours which had led to the real church into its Babylonian exile. It had been this complementary revelation that Christendom previously lacked that was destined to make it complete in its final rebirth.

THE SCIENTIFIC MILLENNIUM IN ITS MODERN ASPECT

My interest in the Protestant narrative that structures Bacon's tale is tied up with the same interest of many others in deciphering how his *New Atlantis* foreshadows modernist culture. What makes my approach different (though certainly not unique) is my presumption that such influences need to be understood in their immediate religious context before their long-term progenitive role can be understood. In other words, unless we first understand what Bacon was preserving, we cannot understand the changes he made possible. But when Bacon is presented to us now in various retrospectives on the origins of modernism, we typically get depictions of his futuristic prognostications that have been divorced from the religious context that shaped their original meaning.[43] These religious meanings seem to have no place in the rhetorical progeny of modernism, and so they are passed over in this parent discourse as well. For instance, Margarita Mathiopoulos in her book *History and Progress* gives this characteristic summation:

> The idea of a total mastery of nature by the human being and science as one of the modern principles of secularized change of the world in the sense of a forward-moving linear improvement, was first propounded by Francis Bacon in his utopian essay "Nova Atlantis" (1627) and remained influential well into the second half of the twentieth century.[44]

Certainly the notion that Bacon envisioned progress as an enterprise empowered by technical rationality is consistent in a loose sort of way with what one finds in his *New Atlantis*, and I also agree that Baconian rhetoric was a vital precursor to the Enlightenment view of science's historical role— and thus to such visions of historical progress as predominate now. But it is not the "newness" of modernism that one finds in Bacon's discourses. Since the theological backdrop to his argument for the "newness" of science is "instauration"—God's work to restore a fallen nature through an obedient remnant of humanity—it is implausible to say that he envisioned a "total mastery of nature by the human being and science." Human action in the historical vision promulgated by Bacon is always God's action.

The impossibility of finding in *New Atlantis* anything exactly resembling contemporary notions of technical rationality can be put down to inviolable principles of audience adaptation. The fact that the persuasiveness of these messages for seventeenth-century readers depended upon their theological coherency would require that they at least be perceived as religiously sincere. To the extent that Bacon worked in a cultural milieu preoccupied with religious questions, it is difficult to imagine how the kind of undisguised technological imperialism described in the above excerpt could have won much sympathy for science. Auditors belonging to a culture that regarded the sovereignty of God and the governance of providence as unassailable premises could not have supposed that human beings had any unilateral right to master nature. We might suppose, as the Encyclopedists certainly would in the next century, that Bacon's religious arguments were insincere, that they merely masked a worldview that was in its essence much more similar to their own secular one. To the extent that it is audiences as much as authors who ultimately determine the success and meaning of messages, however, such speculations lose much of their plausibility. In the generation immediately following Bacon's death, it was clearly those who took the religious themes of his rhetoric most seriously who also resonated to its scientific advocacy. A prophetic vision that did not relate science to faith simply could not have sustained the English scientific revolution.

My point here is not merely revisionist. It is an expression of the working assumption of this book that the *mimesis* that drives cultural evolution involves *descent* as well as *modification*. Whiggish readers who treat Bacon's religious arguments as mere filigree may be able to recognize the modifications he foreshadows but not the religious patterns that persist in evolutionism—its own notions of redemption, election, and millenarian expectation. In chapter 1, I explored the sociological insight that messages constituting social identities are characteristically infused with religious meaning. If this is also true of messages constituting science's social identity (as clearly was the case for Bacon), this would imply that subsequent generations would find it difficult to separate science from the sacred, even if they were intent on undermining established religious authority. The religious ideas that sanctioned seventeenth-century social reality were more likely to be integrated into secular ideas than to be blotted out once their theological content was called into question, and this makes secularization more evolutionary than revolutionary. If the original morphology of these religious ideas is not understood, we cannot easily follow their transformation though subsequent cultural mimesis.

The pattern that most clearly signals such continuity is the manifest similarity that the religious concept of *providence* articulated by Bacon bears to the seemingly secular notion of *progress* championed in the Enlightenment. Historians who turn Bacon into a mere modernist, of course, bear witness to this connection, since they recognize that elements of his rhetoric denote something similar to progress. Were there not some conceptual similarity between these two ideas, such interpretations would be impossible. In fact, the plausibility of such later readings reflects a real genealogical connection. There is something progress-like in Bacon's interpretations of providence, but this is only because the modernist ideas that contemporary readers recognize in his works have descended from Bacon's works themselves.

In chapter 1, while treating the feigned histories that now convey evolutionism in contemporary science fiction, I noted the extent to which they recapitulate narrative structures of salvation found in the Bible. The quests undertaken by human characters like Dave Bowman and Gwyllm Griffiths, and by alien ones like E.T., reenact the saving heroics of Christ. This is because while these are stories about an imagined future, they take their plot structures from the past. In general, this occurs because the mechanism of descent in cultural evolution is imitation, or mimesis. But one reason why mimesis is so attractive is that it maintains at every moment of this evolutionary process a sense of coherence that enables the future to be reconciled with the past. The long-term consequence of this is that past story forms abide all through the course of such evolutionary change. The evolution of literature may represent the constant search for new stories, but the necessities of audience adaptation (cultural integration) will always guarantee that old structures endure.

4

FROM TWO BOOKS TO ONE

*Nature and reason are thus the two gods of modern man, and sometimes
the two are one.*

—*Reinhold Niebuhr*

Bacon's religious conceptualization of the scientific role will surprise readers
not directly acquainted with his writing. Perhaps more surprising is my own
claim that his efforts to visualize a scientific civilization are the antecedents
to evolutionism. How could a radically materialistic ideology rooted in evolutionary science descend from one rooted in Protestant Christianity? My
belief that this is indeed the case stands upon the recognition that cultures
unfold in accordance with something like the gradualism and uniformitarianism that account for the evolution of biological organisms. To understand
how we get from the Christianized proto-scientism of Bacon to the genuine
evolutionism of the present, we need to recognize that large cultural changes
occur by increments and in accordance with abiding (uniform) principles of
language use. Turning now to an Enlightenment text that appears to be
intermediary between Bacon's vision of the scientific identity and the one
we now see in evolutionism, my chief purpose will be to elucidate the pattern that accounts for this cultural change.

    If Baconian proto-scientism is the trunk from which evolutionism arose,
one of its main branches must certainly be the ideology of progress that
began to emerge a century later in the French Enlightenment. To suppose
so, one would have to account for the fact that the rhetoric of progress that
took form in the eighteenth century stood in militant opposition to the very
religiosity that was its antecedent. How could an ideology of progress grow

out of the very thing it rejected? The answer to this question, again, lies in an appreciation of the evolutionary gradualism by which cultural variations unfold. Although Bacon's ideology of science was clearly rooted in traditional Christian ideas, his two books doctrine had already conceded some autonomy to natural revelation. Once enlarged by Enlightenment writers, this liberty would eventually enable natural revelation to compete with and even supersede special revelation as a basis for cultural authority. Bacon had sanctioned natural inquiry by accentuating its status as a parallel revelation, but he had also created a historical rationale for its rising importance by linking it to the millenarian reasoning that was sustaining the historical novelty of the Reformation. The reformers' compelling need to justify a new beginning for Christian history provided the same potent formula for rejecting tradition that Bacon so clearly exploited in his *New Atlantis*. This millenarian shift anticipates the doctrine of progress and modernism more generally in its tendency to value the concrete realities of the present as the privileged vantage point for historical thinking. All that was needed to transform Bacon's providential vision of the history of learning into a progressivist one would be an expurgation of its apparent ties to traditional religious thought.

PROVIDENCE AND PROGRESS IN THE FRENCH ENLIGHTENMENT

The continuing separation by which progress eventually became distinct from the idea of providence occurred along a fault line stretching from Edinburgh down through London and across the English Channel toward its Parisian epicenter. Certainly this process could be productively studied by examining the spiritual tremors that were shaking Great Britain in the eighteenth century, just as it could by following the branch of this fault line that turned eastward toward Königsberg. But it was at its Parisian epicenter that the pressures building up as reason pushed against revelation produced the most violent cataclysms. For this reason, the rhetoric of the French Enlightenment provides the best opportunity for considering how the idea of progress began to become viable apart from the idea of providence.

I believe that the rhetorical mechanism that accounts for cultural evolution of this kind is the process of displacement that I briefly introduced in the last chapter. As applied to expressions of the progress doctrine, Frye's theory presupposes that similarities of narrative form are analogous to what comparative anatomists call "homologies," formal and functional similarities that signal common descent. As such, the detection of displacement reveals a continuity of thematic substance that persists as cultures evolve. When we follow the transition from Bacon's scientific narrative in which the church scientific played the role of hero to one in which this part was played by science alone, we will begin to recognize that the idea of providence was not lost but only reinvented under the rubric of progress. Because the theory of displacement also shows that form and meaning are interchangeable, the finding that Enlightenment narratives of progress have borrowed narrative forms from recognizably religious antecedents indicates that they are not entirely secular.

The text I will use to examine this transformation is the Marquis de Condorcet's (1743–1794) *Esquisse d'un Tableau historique des progrès de l'esprit humain* (*Sketch for a Historical Picture of the Progress of the Human Mind*) (1795). Superficially, this brief history of reason's evolution might seem to have nothing in common with the providential narrative given by Bacon since its attitude toward religion is so patently hostile. Like his teacher, Voltaire, Condorcet rejected Europe's religious traditions as mere superstition and as the cardinal obstacle to civilized advancement. But despite this, the *Esquisse* reveals an undercurrent of historical thinking that is homologous with what one finds in Bacon. Just as Bacon's *New Atlantis* was an effort to imagine how the history of learning might have unfolded if the church had remained faithful to revelation, Condorcet laid a similarly preestablished narrative over European history. Bacon's story is constructed as a theology of history, an effort to account for the past shortcomings of learning by appealing to the Protestant doctrine of *sola scriptura*. In Bensalem, Bacon imagines a civilization that was unwavering in its faithfulness to the book of God's word and consequently was also steadfast in its devotion to the book of God's works. This was explicitly a fictional history, but it was one that unfolded in accordance with theological reality. Condorcet's *Esquisse* is not feigned history in the same overt sense since its ten chapters (nine summing up past progress and one projecting its future course) deal with a familiar historical record, but like Bacon's work it does fictionalize the past by conforming it to a similar theory of historical development. Condorcet's sketch imposes a philosophical model upon the past that is designed to bring to light an imagined pattern of continuous progress that would otherwise be invisible. Bacon had been able to make history accord with the purity of providence by a free play of imagination; Condorcet brings his story into accordance with a derivative notion of progress by shaping the historical record into a romantic narrative that both appropriates and obscures this theological model of history.

The rational integrity of Bacon's imaginary history was purchased by its conformity to established theological principles. Since these principles had constituted the cultural ethos of Europeans for centuries, they could not easily be thrown off by either author or audience. For the same reason, the most direct route toward revolution for one such as Condorcet was a path of symbolic accommodation such as one finds in narrative displacement. Rather than surrendering the assumption that history had a preordained meaning and purpose that science could discover, Condorcet follows Bacon's lead by supposing that time is governed by an overarching purpose, though one now identified more completely with nature as detected through reason and experience alone. Louis de Bonald, a prominent reactionary against the excesses of the Enlightenment and French Revolution, had sensed this even at the time of its first appearance, dubbing it the "apocalypse of the new gospel."[1] As one whose mind was still firmly planted in a more traditional theological view of history, Bonald was especially attuned to the biblical patterns that had passed into the *Esquisse*. In more recent times, Carl Becker has claimed that similar religious markers continued to dot the whole landscape of Enlightenment thought. Enlightenment thinkers, no less than "the medieval scholastics, held fast to a revealed body of knowledge, and they were unwilling or unable to learn anything from history which could not, by some ingenious trick played on the dead, be reconciled with their faith."[2] Despite their forceful opposition to the Christian tradition, to abandon its historical assumptions was not in their interest and likewise beyond the reach even of their secular imagining. Thus while Condorcet formally rejected religion, its symbolic patterns nevertheless provided his narrative form. Once having displaced God into nature, he was bound to produce a view of history that was analogous to the older religious one.

In advancing this interpretation of Condorcet's visionary text, this chapter will unfold in four stages. It will begin with a brief discussion of the historical and ideological setting in which his *Esquisse* was composed. The second section will step back momentarily from this subject in order to more fully outline the rhetorical features of displacement. As applied here, Frye's theory will be used to explain how certain explicitly metaphysical notions that were evident in Bacon's self-conscious appropriation of the Christian narrative could make their way undetected into Condorcet's account of the rise of scientific rationality. Frye's theory was developed in an effort to explain the mythical residues that are always detectible in secular literature. In extending his insights into the realm of historical writing, I draw upon Hayden White's important insights into the "narrativity" of history, his recognition that histories likewise appropriate their forms from literary tradition. The displaced character of the *Esquisse* is then illustrated in the third and main part of this chapter, where I trace out these enduring providential themes in Condorcet's historical sketch. The final section considers the social knowledge created by this literary move and how its capacity to create a new secular constituency for science anticipates evolutionism.

The *Esquisse* in Its Historical Setting

Condorcet wrote the *Esquisse* as an apology for the Enlightenment in the face of the dissonance brought on by the reactionary excesses of the Terror—excesses that then threatened to bring him face to face with that notorious instrument of death that now awaited every enemy of the revolution in the Place du Trône-Renversé. Denounced as a traitor late in 1793 for his opposition to the constitution proposed by Marie-Jean Hérault de Séchelles, Condorcet was in hiding when he began this brief history. He had intended to compose an apology for his actions in the revolution during the last months of his seclusion but was persuaded by his wife to abandon this fragment. He instead undertook what J. Salwyn Schapiro describes as an effort to "justify mankind itself."[3] The *Esquisse* was only a preliminary sketch. Had he escaped capture, his intention was to expand this outline, but this was not fated to be. Fearing the retribution that would fall upon the house of Mme Vernet, who had given him asylum, Condorcet set out from Rue Servandoni to wander the streets of Paris. He was soon imprisoned and died just a few days later under mysterious circumstances.

Despite the political circumstances that inspired it, the *Esquisse* also reflects the deeply scientistic thinking of its author. As a mathematician and political scientist who had gained election to France's *Académie Royale des Sciences* at age twenty-six, Condorcet was perhaps more closely tied to the work of science than any other Enlightenment figure save his early mentor, Jean le Rond d'Alembert. We would expect Condorcet to construct a vision of history more like what we now find in evolutionism, and indeed this is true. But it is not this similarity that concerns us just yet. At present I want to understand how it mediated some of the religious meaning that was so crucial to Bacon's effort to give science a socially compelling ethos. Bacon had constructed a constituency for science by fusing the scientific ethos with a Protestant one. Empirical science, in Bacon's view, was the natural ally of true Christianity because it arose from the same ethical posture that Protestants regarded as the entry way to conversion, an obedient receptivity to revelation. What I mean to show now is that Condorcet maintained this theme of scientific obedience while also obscuring its religious bases by collapsing Bacon's two books into the one book of nature.

Condorcet's historical sketch was not directly aimed at the promotion of science, as Bacon's *New Atlantis* had been, but it has its own share in the latter's imaginative supposition that the meaning of history is revealed in the evolution of science. Moreover, it is particularly significant that the *Esquisse* is a rendition of that more general narrative upon which the Enlightenment and the political rhetoric of the French Revolution were founded. As a political story that justified liberation from the impostures of monarchy and church by appealing to the solitary authority of reason and nature, the Enlightenment narrative was itself a displacement grounded in the deism of its chief philosophers. The deists no longer had any use for special revelation, but this only meant that the work of natural revelation had entirely appropriated this role. To the extent that science was seen as the office most capable of reading the book of nature, it had in some sense become the central actor in the historical drama imagined by that cluster of philosophers and social reformers that gathered around Voltaire and the *Encyclopédie*. This implied that the very existence of the new civilization envisioned by this movement would depend upon the enlargement of scientific knowledge.

For this reason, the rationale for scientific patronage suggested by Condorcet's narrative had greater long-term potential than the one Bacon had envisioned. In a worldview such as Bacon's, where there were two books and thus two distinct avenues to truth, the best that science could hope for was a seat alongside the clerical priesthood at the table of public patronage. But in the world envisioned by Condorcet and various other *philosophes*, there was only one book and one priesthood. Their "book" was not yet one that could be read only by scientists. The republic of reason envisioned in the Enlightenment was, as Steve Fuller has called it, a "big democracy," a broad confederation of intellectual pursuits united by the inspiration it took from the example of science. But to the extent that it was science that now epitomized this potential, we can easily see the inspiration that later advocates of a specifically professional ideology of scientism would take from this vision as they strove to build the more exclusive "small democracy" of positivism that anticipates the elitism of evolutionism.[4]

Two things begin to come clear once we recognize the thematic continuity that Condorcet's vision shares with Bacon's. The first is that rhetorical constructions employed to secure science's epistemological autonomy must rely upon narrative constructions that themselves range outside the scope of scientific knowledge, drawing upon the same spiritual legacy these constructions purport to subvert. The second point, in looking ahead to the second half of this book, will be that evolutionary science is something especially likely to be drawn within the orbit of such narratives. Scientism without evolutionism is unthinkable. A scientific ideology wishing to establish ontological boundaries based in naturalism but also needing to construct a historical rationale to justify this claim will need to make natural history its subject, and this leads inevitably to the special sanctioning of evolutionary assumptions. For this reason we should not be surprised to find that while Condorcet remained silent on the question of biological evolution, the more general assumption of evolution lies in the background of his historical sketch.

Although Condorcet's short book was written against the backdrop of the French Revolution, it was also the final act of a career that had earlier been devoted to the work of securing science's institutional status in France—particularly through wide-scale educational reforms.[5] A nobleman by birth who was educated in mathematics and philosophy, Condorcet abandoned the traditional expectation of his family that he make his career in the clergy or military so that he could pursue his scientific aspirations. It was his early entry into the *Académie des Sciences* that brought him into the circle of the *philosophes*. As one of the youngest of these Enlightenment philosophers who lived to participate in the revolution, Condorcet stands apart from his more reactionary older colleagues as one more concerned, much like the positivists of the next generation, with planning the construction of a new society.

Probably for the same reason, Condorcet also stands apart from the older *philosophes* as one who more actively promoted the doctrine of historical progress. Although it is often assumed that this new faith was broadly rooted in the secular Enlightenment of the eighteenth century, such ideas were in fact not as pronounced in the thinking of its earlier figures as one might think.[6] The rudiments of this doctrine can be found in what might be called the *philosophes'* ideology of liberation, especially in their belief that the human condition would be improved once the Christian doctrine of original sin was rejected, but this was progress mainly in a negative sense—a movement away from the oppression thought to arise from the false consciousness of superstition. Once humanity could be made to recognize that there was no inherent disposition toward evil in human nature, then the true sources of our self-inflicted misery—now identified with the tyrannies of illegitimate government and priestcraft—would become visible. "Man is born free; and everywhere he is in chains," Rousseau famously wrote, and if society was ever to be brought into conformity with humanity's true nature, it was necessary first to recognize the conditions of its bondage.[7] But the phase of the Enlightenment with which he is associated was dominated by a rhetoric of critique rather than a rhetoric of world-building.

In his effort to illuminate the pessimistic tendencies of the earlier *philosophes*, Henry Vyverberg has also tended to soften Condorcet's progressive philosophy, calling it a "doctrine of regeneration" that "includes a Rousseauistic protest against the denaturing of man and demands the reestablishment and extension of man's natural faculties." Condorcet certainly participated in this protest, but he did not hold that progress occurs, as Vyverberg asserts, only as people "break free from institutional restraints."[8] This is evident in Condorcet's many efforts to build new social institutions. Most notable in this campaign was his *Bibliothèque de l'homme public* (1790), a series of five memoirs written during the revolution as a blueprint for erecting a state system of public education to replace that of the Catholic Church.[9] Work of this kind seemed to call for a visionary historical framework, and so even as he joined the prophetic chorus of the older *philosophes* in denouncing the evils of the monarchy and the church, he was also critical of their inability or unwillingness to strategize a better world. Condorcet thus shunned Montesquieu's influential and pessimistic history, *Considérations sur les causes de la grandeur des Romains et de leur décadence* (*Considerations on the Causes of the Grandeur and Decadence of the Romans*) (1734), arguing that it would have been of more use if it had been less preoccupied with "finding the reasons for that which is than with seeking that which ought to be."[10] The *Esquisse* appears to have been inspired by Condorcet's recognition that the crafting of a doctrine of historical progress was a necessary step toward building a new France.

The *Esquisse*, though the work of an outcast Girondist, soon became the official philosophical manifesto of post-Thermidorian reconstruction and was distributed throughout France by the National Convention—perhaps as penance for having persecuted a sainted author who was destined for symbolic burial (his remains having been lost) in France's Panthéon along with Rousseau and Voltaire. The enduring influence of his new apocalypse is perhaps best shown by what it anticipates, namely the utopian turn that would gain prominence in various secular ideologies of the next century— the worldviews of the ideologues, Saint-Simonians, positivists, Marxists, and finally, that of the rhetorical Darwinists. These systems of thought would carry forward Condorcet's attitude of scientism, and with it his urgent demand that all epistemic appeals find their grounding in nature. But, more importantly, they also followed him in appealing to notions of history that imitated the more traditional narrative that organized Bacon's efforts to situate science in the Christian story. The historical consciousness of this older religious worldview persisted even amidst the anticlericalism of these scientistic movements because it continued to play a key role in sustaining a public rationale for constituents whose worldviews also had an important share in enlightenment.

To use Geertz' language again, we might say that in the historical thinking that carried over from Bacon's thought into Condorcet's, the powerfully coercive "ought" of science continued to grow out of some comprehensive factual "is." For Bacon this "is" had been the providential certainty established by revelation that history was orchestrated by a transcendent Creator. By continuously accentuating the fact that the knowledge of nature was also the knowledge of God, science became an "ought," a Christian vocation made virtuous by its participation in the broader drama of salvation history. Once written into this historical narrative, the advent of science also took on apocalyptic significance as a prophetic moment. The analogizing power of this displaced "ought" persisted in Condorcet's *Esquisse* in a notion of progress that now attributed the earlier religious faith in history to nature or reason—or perhaps to a natural world that had become incarnate in the realm of thought. By taking over this older role, progress also took over its meaning as a transcendent good, and by this same analogy science continued to enjoy a similar priestly and prophetic role as the agent of progress.

This interplay of religious and secularist ideas reflects Condorcet's debts to one of the more moderate philosophers of the Enlightenment, the economist and onetime candidate for holy orders, Anne Robert Jacques Turgot (1727-1781), whose own progressivist theory of history was explicitly tied to Christianity.[11] Although Turgot was no less committed than his younger protégé to building a scientific society based on secular principles, his friendly attitude toward Christianity brought "Progress and Providence" so close together in his writing as to inspire the historian Charles Frankel to suggest that he should perhaps be regarded as "a rebel against the dominant empiricism, the growing naturalism, and the struggling secularism of his age." Turgot is for Frankel a transitional figure like Bacon, whose "philosophy marks a stage in the secularization of the idea of Providence."[12] This feature of Turgot's contribution to the Enlightenment has prompted Frank Manuel to regard him as the "true initiator of the rationalist prophetic tradition," who did more than the "wit of Voltaire" or the "mechanistic materialism of La Mettrie in deflecting Western consciousness from a religious to a utilitarian earthly morality."[13]

Outwardly at least, Condorcet shared none of his older colleague's lingering affection for Europe's faith traditions; nevertheless he adopted the basic outline of Turgot's Baconian vision of historical progress.[14] It was Bacon, Turgot professed, who had "traced out for posterity the road" that enlightenment must follow, and the *philosophe* mapped this road in his 1750 lecture at the Sorbonne, "On the Advantages that the Establishment of Christianity Has Brought for the Human Race."[15] Here Turgot argued that progress could not have come to European civilization without the transcendent moral influence of religion: "What else could have been able to combat and vanquish the alliance of interest and prejudice? The Christian religion alone has succeeded. It alone has brought to light the rights of humanity."[16] Since religion rooted human rights in the eternal rather than the temporal, Turgot believed that the powers ruling over human affairs could never have just a secular legitimation. The vices of prejudice and self-interest could only have a temporary hold, whereas the power of moral improvement was unstoppable because it had a teleological basis:

> Universal history embraces the consideration of the successive stages in the progress of the human species, and the specific causes that have contributed to it; the formation and mixing of nations; the origins, the revolutions of governments; the progress of languages, of physics, of morals, of manners, of the sciences and arts; the revolutions which have made Empires succeed Empires, nations follow on nations, religions on religions; the human species, always the same through these upheavals, and constantly advancing towards its perfection.[17]

The role of Christianity in ensuring progress was destined to disappear in Condorcet's appropriation of this historical vision, but not the Christian meaning that Turgot had given it. Even though Condorcet would denounce religion as the very essence of "interest and prejudice" responsible for social inequality and for blocking the way of progress, he continued to follow Turgot in assuming that a transcendent (or perhaps now immanent) moral imperative was at work in universal history to gradually and imperceptibly subvert evil. Whereas Turgot still pointed heavenward to providence as the cause accounting for history's upward march, Condorcet merely credited progress more entirely to nature.

DISPLACEMENT AND THE NARRATIVITY OF HISTORY

It seems quite evident that the explicitly providential orientation of Bacon and Turgot was transformed into the progressive orientation of Condorcet and his successors, but how did this happen? The theory of displacement that I will use to answer this question is an effort to give account for that ubiquitous literary pattern by which, as Frye puts it, "mythology merges insensibly into, and with, literature."[18] Displacement explains the persistence of sacred meaning in secular imitations of myth by positing a necessary relationship between *dianoia* (theme) and *mythos* (plot). Because the thematic elements of a literary work arise from *mythos*, that is to say, from the sequence of actions which comprise the whole of a narrative, plot and theme may be recognized as commensurable literary features. *Dianoia*, in other words, denotes the "larger pattern of simultaneous significance" that arises when a reader follows the plot of a story.[19] The sequence of events that the reader traces out in following a story can be expected to solidify into a thematic whole. Readers may not remember, for instance, the detailed way in which the plot of *Robinson Crusoe* moves from one event to the next in the course of reading it, but they will likely understand that it is "a story about the intolerableness of isolation." A story's *mythos*, in other words, is ephemeral, but its *theme* is enduring. We remember its theme, what "the work of fiction was all *about*," rather than the precise sequence of actions that produced that meaning. Thus Frye notes that "as we go on to study and reread the work of fiction, we tend, not to reconstruct the plot, but to become more conscious of the theme, and to see all incidents as manifestations of it."[20] "We *listen* to the poem," Frye observes,

> as it moves from beginning to end, but as soon as the whole of it is in our minds at once we "see" what it means. More exactly, this response is not simply to *the* whole of it, but to *a* whole in it: we have a vision of meaning or *dianoia* whenever any simultaneous apprehension is possible.[21]

Because theme arises from plot in this gestalt fashion, the displacement of a sacred plot into a secular narrative will also preserve the original's *dianoia*, whether or not this theme is recognized. This transference of meaning may be detected, especially in secular romance, by notable vestiges of religious language or symbolism that carry over in "some form of simile: analogy, significant association, incidental accompanying imagery, and the like."[22] The divinity of the Christian protagonist which is signaled by the fact that he has no earthly father in this fashion carries over symbolically in the parentless orphans of romance, in figures like David Copperfield, Harry Potter, Dorothy Gale, and Frodo Baggins, who carry out some redacted version of the Bible's sacred quest. Because these parallel elements are likewise ordered into a parallel *mythos*, the thematic features of myth persist in these secular spin-offs.

An illustration of this may be found in Isak Dinesen's brief comic romance, "Babette's Feast."[23] Two of the story's main characters, Philippa and Martine, are the devoted daughters of a stoic and somewhat controlling Lutheran minister who presides over a small flock of believers who occupy a remote fishing village that lies along the grey and frigid coastline of Norway. At the time in which the main part of the story unfolds, their father has been dead many years, and the two elderly daughters carry on their father's work by attending to the remnant of his declining congregation. In their youth, their beauty and talent had drawn the attention of suitors of considerable worldly promise. A young officer exiled by his father to this rural village as punishment for his dissolute excesses finds himself roused from his despondency by the supernatural beauty of Martine. Philippa receives vocal training under the disapproving eye of her Puritanical father from Achille Papin, the director of the Paris opera. Papin's discovery of Philippa's talent revives him from the depression of a mid-life crisis, causing him to become entirely consumed with the hope of transforming her into a great diva. But the sisters refuse these suitors. Bowing to their father's opinion that "earthly love and marriage are of scant worth and merely empty illusion," they remain with him in obscurity and poverty.

Many years later, and long after the death of their father, Papin solicits the sisters' help as he tries to find a home for Babette Hersant, a Parisian refugee whose husband and son have become the victims of brutal political reprisals against the Paris Commune. An important element of irony enters the story at this point. Although Philippa and Martine offer asylum to this woman, they have no idea of her true stature. Once the greatest chef in all of France, Babette now spends her years in exile cooking for the elderly residents of this faraway fishing community. In addition to the austerity of their living conditions, relationships among the villagers have been strained by years of bickering and accumulated resentments. But Babette seems to revitalize them in both body and soul. The servant seems almost the master. In the hands of this artist, the villagers' bland diet of cod and ale-and-bread soup becomes palatable, and her service frees the two sisters to again perform various charitable works.

The crisis in the story occurs when Babette learns that she has won 10,000 francs in the French lottery. Her hosts assume that their mysterious guest will now leave them, and when Babette announces her intention to prepare a "real French meal" for the villagers as they commemorate the centennial of the founder's birth, all believe that this is her parting gift. When the day of the great banquet arrives after many weeks of preparation, one of the guests is General Lorens Lowenhielm, Martine's former suitor. This outsider is the only guest who truly recognizes what kind of feast has been set before him, for he is a man of the world who had once tasted of Babette's art when she was head chef at Paris' *Café Anglais*. The other unenlightened guests enjoy the meal, but they approach it with great trepidation, fearing that these exotic delicacies are part of a witches' Sabbath. But they cannot resist its transformative powers. As these simple fisher folk eat and drink, the seven-course meal becomes a love feast. Bitterness and rancor give way to blessings and forgiveness. The elderly Lutherans become childlike and mirthful, as if transformed by some divine power.

Afterwards, when Phillipa and Martine approach their servant to express their thanks and regret over her impending departure, they are greeted by a great surprise. Babette has spent her entire fortune on the feast, telling the sisters that "a dinner for twelve at the *Café Anglais* would cost ten thousand francs."[24] Having forfeited her only means of escaping servitude, she has given herself to her friends in perpetuity.

"Babette's Feast" is not a religious story per se. Despite its setting in a Lutheran community, the saving act of its protagonist is secular. It is the high Parisian culture that has descended upon coastal Norway that redeems this pietistic sect. But in taking its narrative form from the New Testament story of Christ's last supper, this narrative has also borrowed its themes. Upon close inspection, we notice that Babette is related to the Christ of the Gospels, as Frye would say, by "simile." In the New Testament we have Jesus of Nazareth, a person of obscure origins who, like Babette, takes up with a lowly band of fishermen. Although he is the anointed Son of God, in taking a servant's role his true identity has been hidden. Even his inner circle of disciples do not seem to fully understand who he is. As his departure approaches, Jesus likewise hosts a banquet for twelve that commemorates the founding of his own religious community, and this is greeted with similar misunderstandings and trepidations. It is in this final feast that his role as servant finds its epitome as he lowers himself to wash the feet of his guests—even though he, like Babette, is clearly the one in charge. The true meaning of this last supper is lost on his guests—even though certain out-siders, a variety of Gentile characters introduced elsewhere in the Gospels, seem to fully understand his identity. It is only in its aftermath that his dis-ciples finally realize what the dinner had signified. It turns out to have been more than just a meal; it was also a dramatic representation of Jesus' love for them, a dramatic enactment of a greater sacrifice as yet unknown to them.

When we reflect back upon this New Testament narrative, it becomes evident that it has "merged insensibly" into Dinesen's story. "Babette's Feast" is an instance of what Mircea Eliade described when he wrote that "myth never quite disappears from the present world of the psyche," but "only changes its aspect and disguises its operations."[25] But why would the creator of this story do this? The answer that Frye proposes, and which I will adopt here, is that such "indirect mythologizing" makes stories both credible and morally acceptable.[26] By borrowing its *mythos* from the Bible, the story also achieves a thematic resonance with Scripture, surrounding in a holy aura Dinesen's tale about the sacrificial significance of art. Those who enter into her story experience the super-rational evocations of the sacred, even while their minds are focused on its nonreligious subject. Similarly, and more vital to our present purposes, the preordained logic of its plot enables the moral significance of the original religious source to be carried over into the author's world. A vision emerges of the artist (Dinesen's own vocation) as a suffering servant who provides a covering for the sins of the people. Art, we learn, is not only morally pure but also redemptive, the vehicle by which the transformative power of love is poured out upon the earth.

In order to recognize the relationship between the *mythos* of the New Testament and that of "Babette's Feast," one must consciously employ an exegesis by analogy, and so the similarity of plot shared by the two stories might not be noticed by those who are not actively looking for such connec-tions. Literary displacement, in other words, never draws attention to itself as such, and this is precisely what makes it a subject of special rhetorical interest. The fact that the mythical basis of a secular narrative's plot is not instantly recognizable means that the derivative character of its thematic meaning may go unrecognized as well. Thematic outcomes that are still saturated with religious meaning can persist with impunity in a secular story, leaving it substantially like its source in certain of its spiritual prin-ciples. At this level, in other words, "Babette's Feast" declares the redemp-tive power of sacrificial love no less than does the passion story of the New Testament, but it also maintains a sense of separation that enables it to substitute a merely human figure for a divine one. The rhetorical potency of these thematic parallels depends on their not being noticed. To recognize their mythical origins would suggest a dependency upon borrowed premises that Dinesen probably did not wish to acknowledge, and so "Babette's Feast" remains a narrative not about God but merely about God-like deeds. Borrowed plots can take from a myth what the storyteller wants, while leaving all else behind.

In supposing that Condorcet's *Esquisse* also displaces the more traditional story of providence into something like natural history, I presume upon the rationale that Hayden White has given for regarding history as a category of discourse that is structured by narrative forms and thus equally subject to such interpretation.[27] History, White has argued, only becomes meaningful when it has the property of "narrativity," because "a refusal of narrative indicates an absence or refusal of meaning itself."[28] Never merely attempting to model the past in symbol, histories are also, says White,

> metaphorical statements which suggest a relation of similitude between such events and processes and the story types that we conventionally use to endow the events of our lives with culturally sanctioned meanings. Viewed in a purely formal way, a historical narrative is not only a *reproduction* of the events reported in it, but also a *complex of symbols* which gives us direction for finding an *icon* of the structure of those events in our literary traditions.[29]

Because narrative forms are projected onto other categories of discourse, no complete distinction between fiction and historical nonfiction is possible—and just as often, this is true between sacred and secular discourses. For White, the irresistible impulse to imitate sacred narratives in particular arises from the "moral meaning" that myths encode, their "motive" force, as we would say in Kenneth Burke's parlance.[30]

From Providence to Progress

What does the theory of displacement then tell us about historical narratives which have been structured by the Christian worldview? If secular histories such as Condorcet's take their form from the Christian view of history, what Christian themes are likely to persist? In his classic examination of the Christian idea of history, the philosopher R. G. Collingwood indicates that there are four such themes: Christian histories (or in our case displaced Christian histories) will be providential, universal, apocalyptic, and periodized.[31] Once it is supposed that history is *providential*—that it is governed by a divine plan rather than by the merely human interests of powerful individuals or nations—then any appropriate perspective on history must likewise be *universal*. Since providence has given history a transcendent basis and thus no center within itself, historical perspectives cannot privilege the point of view of any one culture or society. All people and all societies will seem to move along a common trajectory. Since the meaning of history comes from without, it can only be made intelligible from an *apocalyptic* standpoint, from the transcendent perspective that has made its way into the historical consciousness through various defining revelatory events. New revelations make previously hidden features of this transcendent plan known, and for this reason Christian histories are also *periodized*. Successive revelations divide time into distinct epochs, each qualitatively set off from a previous period by some new prophetic disclosure that has reconfigured the understanding of providence. The Christian division of history into old and new covenants, which turns upon the revelation of the incarnation, is the most familiar and definitive manifestation of this principle, but the millenarian turn that we examined in the last chapter is the biblical model most pertinent to our understanding of a modernist history such as Condorcet's. Christian periodizations, such as Bacon's, sanction the novelty of new epochs, but they also represent the fruition of something manifest in the previous epochs they supersede. In interpreting the modernism on display in the *Esquisse*, I will argue that it was this conserving tendency in the millenarianism that Condorcet borrowed from the Christian model that enabled him to posit a seemingly secular history without actually abandoning those sacred meanings that formerly integrated life in the Christian epoch.

These four features of Christian history are evident in Bacon's *New Atlantis*. When Bacon brought the emergence of science into accord with the Bible's drama of sin and redemption, he was interpreting its advent in accordance with the providential supposition that a destined salvation is the backdrop against which human history must be understood. As applied to natural revelation, this meant that science could only be harmonized with Christian history by having some share in the church's redemptive work. Bacon's similar concern with science's priestly election and separation from worldly affairs manifested both its apocalyptic (revelatory) and universal qualities. Once scientific discovery was recognized as manifesting the gospel, it necessarily had a universal scope as well. Since revelation was God's work, it transcended the particulars of national or personal interest and thus had application to the whole of humanity that God was working to redeem. Bacon needed to appeal to the concept of periodization in order to make the novelty of the scientific role consistent with this idea. Science's sudden appearance could not represent a discontinuity within providential history. Rather, it needed to represent a new understanding of history's continuity, in this case the idea that science represented the "autumn" fruition of a prolonged seasonal cycle.

Providence

We are unlikely to recognize the continued presence of these themes in Condorcet's history without also taking into account the operations of displacement. The absence of any explicit links to the Christian story, as well as the general academic tone that we witness in the following paragraph that opens the *Esquisse*, will hardly suggest that it could have any share in Bacon's more traditional account.

> Man is born with the ability to receive sensations; to perceive them and to distinguish between the various simple sensations of which they are composed; to remember, recognize and combine them; to compare these combinations, to apprehend what they have in common and the ways in which they differ; to attach signs to them all in order to recognize them more easily and to allow for the ready production of new combinations.[32]

Continuing in this vein as he seems to ground his arguments in the associationist psychology of Locke and Condillac, Condorcet then goes on to chronicle the evolving complexity that arose from these rudimentary principles of inquiry as "composite sensations," and the various "artificial methods which these first developments have led" human beings "to invent." This scientific-sounding process then gave rise to the evolution of moral consciousness by virtue of the fact that such sensations were "attended by pleasure or pain."

In invoking the fashionable sensationalist epistemology of his day, we can see that Condorcet is attempting something quite uncharacteristic of traditional historical treatments—to say nothing of Christian ones. He proposes to build up a vision of history not so much from the evidences of the past as from a scientific explanation of the mind's development. Certainly this is an approach that anticipates what evolutionism now attempts to do, but its scientism also makes it seem unlikely that Condorcet's approach could reflect the traditional thematic elements found in Bacon's Christianized history. Condorcet seems to strive for pure naturalism as he explains the inevitable advance of learning, whereas Bacon had openly attributed this to God's superintendence of history. But Frye's theory of displacement would ask us to consider whether there lies beneath even such marked differences some continuity of form. It asks us to do this by searching for figurative language (simile, metaphor, analogy) that points back to a religious prototype, and once looked at in this fashion, Condorcet's history begins to take on a quite different appearance.

One subtlety in the previous passage that suggests an analogy to this more traditional form is Condorcet's use of a now-familiar convention of scientific writing, the passive voice. We might think of this as a stylistic accentuation of the objectivity that inductivist and experimentalist epistemologies attribute to science, but passive constructions also accord with a particular narrative structure. By writing human agency out of what it describes, the scientific passive also invites readers to assign agency to nature. Syntactically the passive puts the scientist in a receptive pose, as a kind of listener who is acted upon by nature, and by doing so it always implies that nature is the real actor in the drama of scientific advancement. Thus when Condorcet depicts human beings less as actors than as creatures being acted upon, he is also setting up the plot of a historical narrative which makes nature analogous to God and the role of science analogous to that of God's elect. This pivotal displacement becomes more manifest at the close of this opening passage. The evolving complex of mental associations that we receive at birth find their culmination in the harmony of societal bonds, those "ties of interest and duty" to which

> nature herself has wished to attach the most precious portion of our happiness and the most painful of our ills.[33]

It would be easy to wave off this momentary personification of nature as a mere poetic embellishment, but the theistic analogy it invokes is also consistent with the entire narrative of the *Esquisse*. If we are "born with" science, then science represents what the human psyche does once it is fully in touch with its native operations, and science is likewise the obedient servant of nature that is working to expedite her "wish" for our happiness. In this regard, Condorcet's passive construction of the scientific condition is the exact corollary to Bacon's notion that the work of science is obedience to providence.

As Condorcet goes on to discuss the "aim of the work," he continues to sustain a narrative form that is analogous to Bacon's. His language denotes a larger context of purpose and virtuous inevitability within which to position the scientific evolution he is about to chronicle. His goal is to show that

> nature has set no term to the perfection of human faculties; that the perfectibility of man is truly indefinite; and that the progress of this perfectibility, from now onwards independent of any power that might wish to halt it, has no other limit than the duration of the globe upon which nature has cast us.[34]

As traditionally constructed, perfection implies intent and foresight. And so, while Condorcet's claim that "nature has set no term" to progress might mean that there is nothing in its known laws that would seem to preclude perpetual advancement, grammatically he has planted the seeds of teleological intentionality by depicting nature as a volitional agent. His readers, as members of a culture already steeped in that drama of historical perfection in which God is the protagonist and his obedient servants are his instruments, are likely to read this narrative in an analogous way. This clearly works to the author's rhetorical advantage. Were Condorcet merely willing to say that the power to achieve continuous improvement lay at the command of human nature, progress would be tainted by the appearance of self interest. But by aligning progress with the transcendent purposes of a selfless providence, he could do much more to sustain the special heroism of science.

Just as Isak Dinesen's heroine did not need to be explicitly identified with the Christ of the Bible in order to speak for the messianic promise of art, Condorcet's did not need to be directly identified with God in order to achieve a similar outcome. Babette's messianic significance arises from the similarity her great sacrifice bears to that of Christ. To make science history's protagonist in the *Esquisse*, its author did not need to say this in any explicit way; he only needed to plot its relationship to nature by analogy to a sacred narrative that already communicated a similar meaning.

Universalism

If the providential features of Condorcet's narrative work to relate the quest for scientific knowledge to a transcendent purpose, its universal features signify the eternal scope of such labors. In the explicitly Christian view of history that Collingwood discusses, universalism means that the historical process is "everywhere and always of the same kind, and every part of it is a part of the same whole."[35] Since history's unity of purpose manifests the transcendence of an omnipotent and omnipresent architect, parochial views of history must be rejected as spiritually out of touch. On the flip side, this means that the humble are exalted. The meek shall inherit the earth precisely because their self-effacement opens them to the fullness of this universal purpose and enables them to participate in its realization. In his 1791 essay on "The Nature and Purpose of Public Instruction," Condorcet had already declared his faith in a similar immortal destiny.

> If this indefinite improvement of our species is a general law of nature, as I believe, man must no longer consider himself as a being bound to a fleeting and isolated existence, destined to vanish after an alteration of happiness and sorrow for himself, of good and evil for those whom chance has made his neighbors. He becomes an active part of a great whole, a co-worker in an eternal creation. In a momentary existence on this speck in space, he can by his efforts encompass all places, bind himself to all centuries, and still act long after his memory has disappeared from the earth.[36]

Condorcet's universalism has the same equalizing value as its Christian counterpart. Every servant of science is a citizen of the world. But while a history that finds unity of meaning outside human volition may erase conventional social stratifications, it could not do this without positing a hierarchy all its own. This is what critics tune into when they recognize the Eurocentric and imperialistic tendencies in modernism's various forms. While the secularization of such universalist ideals undoubtedly contributed to the rise of democracy, the fact that this was undertaken by appropriating a Christian universalism that was also tied up with the notion of divine election made it inevitable that modernism would harbor its own formula for constructing hierarchies. The generic "man" that Condorcet speaks of, much like the "proletariat man" of Marx and Engels, may belong to nature in principle, but he clearly believes that such universal citizenship could only be realized by the scientific elect. Because it is a "general law of nature" that enables individuals to transcend their finite existence and to realize their common human destiny, only those who come to grips with nature through science (whose business it is to discover such laws of nature) actually contribute to this historical purpose.

Just as Bensalem's separation from the world symbolized its role in working out the same universal history advanced by prophets and priests, the separation from worldly ways of conceptualization enacted now by empiricism becomes the basis for scientific election. The world Condorcet envisions is destined, with the help of a beneficiary priestly culture set apart by its scientific discipline, for the promised land of positive knowledge. Science's mediation is necessary because "the picture of the progress of the human mind" can only be realized if one "confines oneself to the study and observation of the general facts and laws about the development of these faculties" as they manifest in the individual human subject.[37] Without science to speak the language of nature, the world cannot realize this universal destiny.

The "symbol of this universalism," Collingwood tells us, "is the adoption of a single chronological framework for all historical events," and in displaced representations, this manifests when the hero's actions are symbolically related to the whole of history.[38] In the science fiction examples that I introduced in chapter 1, this is achieved through those plot features that tip viewers off to the fact that the struggles of Gwyllm Griffiths and Dave Bowman represent the human struggle writ large. In the first case, we learn this when we are told that the genetic manipulation that Griffiths has subjected himself to recapitulates the process of biological evolution that has brought humanity into its present state of being. In Bowman's case, this is symbolized by the fact that his quest replays the primordial drama of evolution that opened the film.

Condorcet's historical drama relies upon similar devices. His effort to make the operations of science and nature one and the same ensures that the individual scientific acts he recounts will have a microcosmic significance similar to the import that the acts of Griffith and Bowman had in their own narratives. More specifically, since the *Esquisse* depicts a historical quest spanning all human generations, its prescientific heroes enact universal meaning by being situated within recursive cycles that anticipate the arrival of modern science. This is more in line with how Christian universalism integrates the various epochs making up its history. It is by representing Old Testament characters as prophetic types who find their fulfillment in Christ that the continuity of Christian universalism is upheld. The various actions of Old Testament characters like Moses, Elijah, Jonah, and Joshua that are replayed in Christ's life enable the Christian reader to tie the two Testaments together into a single narrative that stretches from the first act of creation to God's final redemption.

The universalism at work in Condorcet's doctrine of unending progress demands something similar, and the heroes found in each of his historical stages prefigure in some way the apocalypse of seventeenth-century science. The more that past heroes of learning can be shown to be types for scientific figures like Galileo and Descartes, the more that the historical progress now associated with science will seem to manifest such a unified perspective. This explains why Condorcet treats so many figures from the past in such a curiously unhistorical way. If the Socrates of the *Esquisse* sounds more like Descartes than like the character depicted in Plato's dialogues, it is because Condorcet has made him into a type for those present champions of progress who advance humanity's continuous effort to "perfect its own powers of reasoning and to trace everything back to origins."[39] He does something similar with the Stoics and Epicureans. In many respects the Stoics are the familiar philosophers of old, who "saw virtue and happiness as consisting in the possession of a soul that was equally insensible to joy and pain, that was freed from every passion, that was superior to all fears and weaknesses and that knew no true good but virtue and no real evil but remorse." But Condorcet's Stoics also manifest a rather modern-sounding will to power in their belief "that Man had the power to raise himself to this height if he had a strong and inflexible will to do so, and that then, independent of fate, always master of himself, he would be equally impervious to vice and misery."[40] What is lost here is what Reinhold Niebuhr describes as the "air of melancholy" that hung over Greek life.[41] This is because Stoic resignation has become something else, an ethic of epistemic naturalism more like the disciplining skepticism of Descartes that was now seen, not as mere fidelity to reason, but also as fidelity to history—a purposeful and ever-expanding directive for the future. Likewise, the Epicurean virtue which "consists in following one's natural inclinations" by "knowing how to purify them and direct them," becomes in Condorcet's hands the manifestation of a generalized moral posture that was putting humanity on "the road that leads to both happiness and virtue." Like modern natural philosophers, the Stoics and Epicureans had rejected "philosophy that claimed to rise above nature" in favor of one "that only wished to obey her." And this shared receptiveness to nature led both philosophies, despite their "contrary principles," to the singular truth that the "resemblance between the moral precepts of all religions and all philosophical sects suffices to prove that their truth is something independent of the dogmas of these various religions and the principles of these different sects; that it is to the moral constitution of man that we must look for the foundations of his duties and the origins of his ideas of justice and virtue."[42]

A vital complement to this unified view of history is sustained by what Frye calls the "dialectical structure" of character development in such romantic narratives. Every character in such a story will be either for or against the quest, "idealized as simply gallant or pure" if they support it and "caricatured as simply villainous or cowardly" if they do not.[43] Without such consistency of action and clarity of motive, the reader would likely lose sight of the transcendent singularity of purpose that romance associates with the various cultural values its heroes enact. This accounts for another interesting oddity of the *Esquisse*. When Condorcet treats the history of global exploration and colonization, he protects the viability of this universal reference point by forging a stark moral divide between the explorers and those who patronized their ventures. Seafarers like da Gama and Columbus were drawn by a "noble curiosity" to investigate the world, but "the kings and ruffians who were to profit from their labours" were motivated by "base, pitiless greed" and "stupid, fierce fanaticism." Although it would seem implausible to suppose that these adventurers (who risked much more than their patrons) were any less culpable, such moral ambiguity would not sustain the singularity of historical purpose that Condorcet wished to illustrate. If the path marked by the march of progress could not be clearly traced out, the scientific ends of history would lose their sense of preordination. Thus the scientific motive needs to be clearly set apart from its opposite, just as its ancestral manifestations need to anticipate its modern ones. Thus in exonerating these explorers of responsibility for the evils of colonialism, Condorcet also shapes their motives into scientific ones, making their inspiration a desire to attain "a knowledge of the natural world that can furnish new truths and destroy accredited errors in the sciences." As reason's servants, they were agents of a scientific destiny not of their own making. By increasing activities of trade, these explorers had "given new wings to industry and navigation," and these benefits were in turn destined to be extended "by a necessary chain of influence, to all the sciences and to all the arts," enabling "free nations to resist tyrants" and "enslaved people to break their chains or at least to relax the chains of feudalism."[44]

Not so the wicked. The parochial interests of the European powers that sponsored these voyages put them on the outside of reason's destiny. It is not the global character of the colonizing motive itself that is evil; rather, it is the fact these European powers acted in accordance with the inverse of natural universalism—the false universalism of Christianity.

> The unfortunate creatures who lived in these new lands were treated as though they were not human beings because they were not Christians. This prejudice, which had an even more degrading effect on the tyrants than on their victims, smothered any feeling of remorse that might have touched these greedy and barbarous men, spewed up from the depths

of Europe, and they abandoned themselves to their insatiable thirst for blood and gold. The bones of five million men covered those unfortunate lands where the Portuguese and the Spaniards brought their greed, their superstitions and their wrath. They will lie there to the end of time as a mute witness against the doctrine of the political utility of religion; a doctrine which even to this day finds its apologists among us.

The undoing of these evils will not come though a cessation of Europe's global aspirations, but rather by bringing the colonizing motive into harmony with the universal aspirations of nature itself. These "discoveries will have repaid humanity what they have cost it," Condorcet goes on to say, only when

> Europe renounces her oppressive and avaricious system of monopoly; only when she remembers that men of all races are equally brothers by the wish of nature and have not been created to feed the vanity and greed of a few privileged nations; only when she calls upon all people to share her independence, freedom and knowledge, which she will do once she is alive to her own true interests.[45]

The fact that the evils brought on by colonization are to be corrected by a global crusade of a different kind signals the extent to which Condorcet's historical narrative imitates the Christian one he impugns in these passages. As an attribute of history created in the image of a religious universalism that assumed the benevolence of those who acted in harmony with the purposes of a transcendent Creator, the historical reasoning at work in this secular analogue necessarily involves similar missionary expectations. Reason so conceived could never be a mere instrument of knowledge; its realization in human affairs must also destine the welfare of all peoples.

Apocalypse

Condorcet's confidence that science was the revelation of a universal pattern also meant that the advent of modern science represented a fundamental rebirth of history, the onset of its final epoch. This new age had begun with science in the same sense in which its sacred model had begun with Christ, and this meant that all of previous history had been an age of darkness. Prior to modernity, events had unfolded according to the pattern that became known with science's full flowering, but it was a pattern that had remained unseen and unrecognized.

The Christs of this new covenant are the three founders of modern science, Bacon, Galileo, and Descartes. Bacon had "revealed the true method of studying nature and of using the three instruments that she has given us for penetrating her secrets; observation, experience and calculation." In doing so he also launched history's rebirth. Now that the path to knowledge had been made plain, the philosopher was obliged to renounce all the "beliefs that he had received and even all notions he had formed," to make way for "a new understanding admitting only of precise ideas, accurate notions and truths whose degree of certainty or probability had been strictly weighed." Galileo likewise showed "by example how to arrive at a knowledge of the laws of nature by a sure and fruitful method," when he "founded the first school in which the sciences were studied without any admixture of superstition in favour of either popular prejudices or authority, and where all methods other than experiment and calculation were rejected with philosophical severity." But the most significant revelation came not from Bacon, who "possessed the genius of philosophy in the highest degree" but "without the genius of science," nor from Galileo, who by "limiting himself exclusively to the mathematical and physical sciences . . . could not afford mankind that general guidance of which it seemed to stand in need."[46] The full incarnation of reason would have to be fully universal, and thus it is found in the thoroughgoing scientism of France's own Descartes. Even though his "philosophy was less wise than Bacon's" and "his progress in the physical sciences was less certain than Galileo's," Descartes stands above them because he extended "his method to all the subjects of human thought; God, man and the universe were in turn the objects of his meditations." With this full recognition of reason's unlimited scope and power, he "stimulated men's minds" and spoke as a prophet, commanding all to "shake off the yoke of authority, to recognize none save that which was avowed by reason; and he was obeyed, because he won men by his boldness and led them by his enthusiasm."[47]

This great apocalypse, by making known the sure method and unlimited scope of science, also brought to conscious awareness the principles upon which the course of human history had been unfolding since the beginning of time. This meant that one could now compose "the picture of its progress" simply by reading the "uninterrupted chain of facts and observations" left since the invention of alphabetical writing. As we now reflect upon our past as it has been recorded since the invention of writing, the picture of the march and progress of the human mind becomes truly historical. Philosophy has nothing more to guess, no more hypothetical surmises to make; it is enough to assemble and order the facts and to show the useful truths that can be derived from their connections and from their totality.[48]

If science had decoded the mechanism of progress so as to explain its past course, this meant that it could likewise foresee history's ultimate consummation. With the advent of science, the "human mind was not yet free but it knew that it was formed to be so," and the enemies of progress who "dared to insist that it should be kept in its old chains or to try and impose new ones upon it, were forced to show why it should submit to them; and from that day onwards it was certain that they would soon be broken."[49]

Had Condorcet developed a new calendar to go with the *Esquisse*, it might have emulated the one he helped to redesign in 1793 as a member of the National Convention. The Christian calendar began with the birth of its founder because all of history found its meaning in that revelation, and thus the scientific apocalypse that had inspired the French Revolution required a new beginning. Now the first day of history was September 22, 1792, the day the republic was declared. Had Condorcet had his way, history might have begun with the birth of Descartes, but the Convention's thinking was nevertheless very much like his own: since the French Revolution was born from humanity's first full awakening to the ways of universal reason, it likewise represented the birth of an age utterly different from all that had preceded it. Condorcet's sympathy for this alternative dating of history's apocalypse can be seen in the title of the ninth and climactic chapter of his *Esquisse*: "From Descartes to the Foundation of the French Republic." If science was the revelation of this new gospel, the Christmas of the modern age, then the founding of the French Republic was the Pentecost that had established the universal church of reason, that human instrument by which nature would now propagate the message of science to the whole world. The French Revolution followed from science's full entry into human consciousness, and therefore its liberating influence was certain to become a global phenomenon. This was shown by the fact that "in Europe the principles of the French constitution are already those of all enlightened men."[50]

Such an apocalyptic view also implied that the previous age of darkness had been mere prehistory, an age worthy of examination only to the extent that it further illuminated modernity and its future course. The premodern age, in other words, had a relationship to the age of modern science that is analogous to that traditionally given by Christians to the history recorded in the Hebrew Scriptures. Just as Christians read the Old Testament from the standpoint of the incarnation, and thus would not characteristically regard as particularly relevant the vast rabbinical commentaries that came into existence in coincidence with the formation of this canon, Condorcet has little use for interpretations provided by any of the historians who may have lived in the periods he discusses. Thus, despite his professed devotion to empiricism, his mind is not particularly exercised by factual concerns. He makes no effort, for instance, to reconcile his interpretations of Greco-Roman history with the testimony of contemporaneous historians like Herodotus, Tacitus, or Livy. In fact, he freely contradicts them. Their testimony has been rendered irrelevant by the scientific apocalypse. The advent of science had made known the true structure of history, the fact that history was forever progressing toward science, and so the perspective of the Enlightenment superseded every past understanding of human affairs.

As scientific thought now began to take hold as the governing principle by which social relationships were being reinvented in accordance with the ideals of the French Revolution, Europe was merely bringing into this societal arena the natural principles of development that accounted for the growth of the individual. If "progress is subject to the same general laws that can be observed in the development of the faculties of the individual," then the higher development of scientific figures like Galileo and Descartes anticipates the future of human development and recapitulates its past. The phylogenesis of global liberty and prosperity was destined to recapitulate the scientific ontogenesis of the individual person. Condorcet acknowledges that this sounds like mere "metaphysics," but he escapes this problem by promising his readers that this relationship will be fully borne out by a scientific examination of the "record of change . . . based on the observation of human societies throughout different stages of their development."[51]

In supposing to describe the laws governing history, Condorcet's *Esquisse* is clearly a precursor to the better-known philosophies of history that would soon appear in the systems of Comte, Hegel, and Marx—what Karl Popper would later call "historicism."[52] For each of these scientific historicists, the pattern of history was found in some principle or law revealed only in modernity. If this pattern was faithfully followed, it would lead from the present dawn of enlightenment into the full daylight of reason. Like these other modern historicists, Condorcet is thus more concerned with teleology than with factual fidelity. The purpose of his "observations upon what man has been and what he is today," is not to understand the past but rather to "instruct us about the means we should employ to make certain and rapid the further progress that his nature allows him still to hope for."[53] In one sense, this might be said to be historiography aspiring to become science. Scientific theories have predictive power, and so if history could genuinely gain such theoretical standing it might have some share in this. This undoubtedly was what Condorcet thought he was doing. But because he also belonged to a culture long accustomed to making similar suppositions on revelatory grounds, he could not help but do more than this.

Periodization

This supposition that the advent of science was history's apocalypse is borne out in particular by the periodizations that follow once Condorcet has set forth this premise. Were we to take seriously his claim that his subdivisions of the past derive from a scientific theory of history, we would expect treatments that were more faithful to the historical record. But usual scientific concerns about evidentiary fidelity are superseded by what is demanded once it is supposed that history's immanent purpose was the advent of science. If it was "nature's wish" to achieve scientific enlightenment, then the prescientific world would need to be interpreted, not in accordance with the testimony of past witnesses, but in light of the theory of history revealed in the scientific apocalypse of the present. A corollary to this can be found in the different historical interpretation that Christianity brought to the period of Jewish history inaugurated by the delivery of God's law to Moses on Mount Sinai. While Christians continued to attribute a similar moral value to the law, it no longer had the same constitutive significance that it had for Jews since its meaning was now subservient to a more significant apocalypse. Thus for Paul the Mosaic epoch became a period of preparation during which the law had acted as "custodian until Christ came" (Gal 3:24). The law's meaning was no longer found in its content (thus the effectual suspension of its various dietary and ritual prescriptions) so much as in what it pointed to, namely the satisfaction of its demands in the sacrifice of Christ. The revelation of Christ similarly redefined the period of the prophets. Their more immediate contextual role as God's messengers to an ever-errant Israel was not rejected; rather, the reference point of interpretation had changed. All prophecy in the historical consciousness of Christianity is in some sense messianic prophecy, so that the age beginning with Samuel now found its end in the New Testament in the character of John the Baptist, thus assuring that the earlier period of revelation could be fully brought into accordance with the master revelation of Christ.

It was by appealing to this periodizing consciousness that Bacon had been able to identify the coming age of science with a millenarian epoch already anticipated in the Christian historical consciousness. The general assumption that providence extended beyond the pages of the Bible created the expectation that new revelations might require new interpretations of past and future periods. Novelty could have a culturally sanctioned value for serious Protestant thinkers so long as they could assure themselves that it was anchored in eternal truths. Writing for such an audience, it is hard to imagine how Bacon could have differently imagined a future dominated by science.

Having displaced God into nature, Condorcet was confronted with an analogous problem—how to explain the late arrival of a scientific millennium destined by reason and nature. In part, at least, Condorcet accounts for the apparent novelty of science's late coming on evolutionary grounds. Knowledge could only unfold through an ordered series of steps. Certain kinds of advancement would have been impossible prior to the invention of phonetic writing or the development of moveable type. But the full blossoming of science was still, in principle, too slow. Condorcet accounts for this problem, much as Bacon had done, by constructing a historical periodization which supposed that the natural progress of learning had been derailed by something like a scientific fall. Like the Catholic priests, who Protestants blamed for forestalling providence by refusing to obey the prophetic knowledge entrusted to them, Condorcet's history follows from an analogous assumption applied to priestcraft more generally. The emergence of priestcraft in antiquity *was* the unfolding of natural reason working out its historical destiny. Reason had always been present and moving along its destined scientific course, but the learned priests who had come to understand its ways had perverted them. What made priestcraft evil was not ignorance. To deny that they possessed the full powers of reason would be to deny the fundamental premise of historical providence that Condorcet wished to preserve (now as progress). Priestcraft, instead, was an idolatry of reason—reason that had become an instrument of personal advancement and power rather than truth.

Since Condorcet was now working within a displaced narrative in which the counterpart to the biblical fall was the exile of natural reason, he no longer needed to work within the parameters of Christian history. But a similar periodic contrast remained. Thus his dark age begins, not with the Catholic

Church's errant wanderings, but with reason's exile into priestcraft in classical antiquity. By positing this early onset for reason's abandonment of nature
for metaphysical speculation, he could account for the failure of ancient
Greek rationalism to found the scientific revolution it should have brought
about. Condorcet makes this periodization seem plausible by interpreting
the martyrdom of Socrates as the key manifestation of this fateful turn.
"The death of Socrates is an important event in human history," he writes,
because, as the "first crime that marked the beginning of the war between
philosophy and superstition," it also brought the very principle of historical
evil into focus. As a vignette that captured in this negative fashion his theory
of historical development, it would also "occupy one of the most important
places in the picture that it still remains for us to trace."[54] It accounted for
the struggles against superstition yet to come because, much like the various
biblical episodes of rebellion that Bacon had alluded to in his New Atlantis, it
revealed a principle of historical evil that was perennially relevant because it
reflected (as a kind of inverse image) the eternal principle of progress.

Once we understand the persuasive role played by Condorcet's historical displacement, we can also begin to understand why his explanation of
Socrates' demise has such a weak historical grounding. Condorcet's explanation of Socrates' condemnation also works to constitute the past as a dark
age, and, by contrast, to make the present one an age of light. His modern
theory of history required a decisive break with the past, a periodization
that would be true to the historical principle set out in his Esquisse. Now
that the ways of reason had fully come into the human consciousness, the
evils of the past were destined to fade away, but a progressive apocalypse,
no less than a providential one, must also explain why the revelations of
the present have made possible what the past could not. Bacon achieved
this by bringing the story of science into alignment with the new Protestant
periodization that had made the epoch of Catholicism a dark age and that
of the reformers an age of light. The rediscovery of God's word was ushering in the final millennium, and the kindred progress of science, as the
ordained reader of the book of nature, was advancing toward paradise along
the same road. Condorcet's Esquisse is a version of the same story. Socrates,
though one of reason's faithful in the past age, could not advance the cause
of science because its power had been seized by a priestly caste that was powerful enough to mask its revelatory truth behind a façade of superstition.
But things were different now. The philosopher's modern counterparts had
fully made the ways of reason known, and now it was impossible for the old
alliance of superstition and tyranny to obscure it again.

This story form requires the reconstruction of Socrates as science's suffering servant. By more rigorous accounts, science seems to have had little importance in this philosopher's life. Although it is believed that Socrates was interested in scientific pursuits in his youth, these were abandoned in favor of his philosophical quest for self-understanding and moral purpose. The scientific disillusionment of the mature Socrates, as W. K. C. Guthrie interprets the accounts left by his disciples Xenophon and Plato, grew from his recognition of "its irrelevance to human problems and its neglect of final causes."[55] Philosophy, not science, had proved to be the higher path. But the epochal principle that Condorcet wished to put in place could not abide this more mainstream view. Once it was supposed that the rationality that had surfaced in Socrates' philosophy was the very same principle of progress that was destined to give way to scientific dominance, the continuity of the story would be undermined if Socrates was not driven by scientific aspirations. Fact needed to follow form. Thus it is not surprising that Condorcet's martyr would seem more like the imaginary Socrates of Aristophanes' comic farce, The Clouds, than like the philosopher we see in Plato's Apology. But even Aristophanes' depiction is at odds with Condorcet's. The Esquisse follows the playwright in making Socrates out to be a religious skeptic whose school was a center for geophysics, astronomy, geometry, and geography, but not in throwing him in with the Sophists—Condorcet had already aligned these ancient skeptics with the priests as fellow dissemblers and enemies of science.[56]

The view of this Greek philosopher taken by a majority of philosophers and historians, the Socrates who articulated the broader philosophical principles of induction and definition, simply would not do. Condorcet needed him to be a kind of proto-positivist who eschewed philosophical and religious speculation in order to follow the straight and narrow path of a more grounded truth. "All that Socrates wanted to do," Condorcet asserts—undoubtedly giving ancient meanings of the term "nature" a Whiggishly modern spin—"was to warn men to confine themselves to those things that nature has placed within their reach, to make sure of every step before attempting a new one, and to study what lay around them before embarking for strange and unfamiliar lands."[57]

If this summary of Socrates' philosophy sounds more like a description of the Cartesian worldview, this is because modern science is the apocalypse of Condorcet's history. If it was modern science that made manifest the true principle of historical evolution, Condorcet needed to suppose that its spirit had been present all through the past. Its modern appearance was merely the fruition of what had been driving progress all along, the operations of reason in nature.

More specifically, Socrates' transformation into a man of science is made necessary by the fact that the dark age inaugurated by his martyrdom functions as a historical theodicy. In it, Condorcet seeks to explain how a rationality embedded in history and inclined by nature toward progress could have been so long delayed in reaching its full scientific maturation. The distractions of ordinary human ignorance and passion could not account for this, since the doctrine of progress would be weakened once it was supposed that such merely venial foibles had forestalled its march. Learning's derailment would have to find its cause in the perversion of reason itself, in this case in an idolatrous rationality that arose in coincidence with priestly institutions. If the full revelation of reason was natural and inevitable, the actions which delayed it for so long would need to have roughly similar power, and so to round out his drama, Condorcet presents priestcraft as scientific rationality turned against itself—and thus against the ancient philosopher who had been its prophet.

Priests such as those blamed for Socrates' fate had been around since the earliest period of civilization. Long before the Greek Enlightenment, they had established themselves as "the depositaries of the principles of the sciences or the procedures of the arts, the mysteries or ceremonies of religion, of the practices of superstition, and often even of the secrets of legislation and politics." By using reason to build institutional monopolies, the priests also engineered the

> separation of the human race into two parts; the one destined to teach, the other made to believe; the one jealously hiding what it boasts of knowing, the other receiving with respect whatever is condescendingly revealed to it; the one wishing to place itself above reason, the other humbly renouncing its own reason and abasing itself to less than human stature by acknowledging in others prerogatives that would place them above their common nature.[58]

Religious authority for Condorcet thus remains an exercise of rationality, but one now divorced from nature so as to sustain social privilege. These priests had not discarded so much as misapplied and monopolized reason. In doing so, they had abandoned reason as knowledge for the sake of reason as power. This explains how priestcraft could have "accelerated the progress of reason at the same time as it has propagated error, which has enriched science with new truths whilst it has plunged the people into religious servitude, and which has brought transitory benefits at the price of a long and degrading tyranny."[59] In this regard, Condorcet's understanding of religion's historical role anticipates Marx's materialistic dictum that the "criticism of religion" should be the "premise of all criticism." Once reason was closely identified with nature, the root of all evil became any form of reason that failed to reference the natural world, and this made supernatural religion, more than any other such rational perversion, as Marx would later say, the "inverted consciousness of the world."[60] This is why priestcraft always supersedes political ambition as the root cause of tyranny for Condorcet. To be sure, political motives always lurk within religious actors, but only a perversion of reason could in theory have sufficient power to overcome natural reason. Thus it was when the priests became the "depositaries" of science that they were able to monopolize its power and thereby prevent the rest of humanity from enjoying its benefits. Political privileges followed. It was only by first perverting reason that priests emerged as a "class of individuals who affected insolent prerogatives, who separated themselves from the common mass of mankind so that they might dominate them more effectively."[61]

The priestly castes had put such controls in place long before Socrates' time, but the emerging Greek Enlightenment threatened to expose them, thus prompting his martyrdom and the onset of a prolonged dark age.

> It was with a heavy heart that the priests observed how mankind in its efforts to perfect its own powers of reasoning and to trace everything back to origins, discovered the full absurdity of their dogmas, the full extravagance of their ceremonies, the full imposture of their oracles and miracles. They were afraid that these philosophers would unmask them before the pupils who attended their schools; that such knowledge would then be transmitted to anyone who, in pursuit of authority or prestige for himself, felt the necessity to cultivate his mind; that as a result priestly dominion would soon hold sway only over the most vulgar of the people, and that in the end even they would be undeceived. Hypocrisy in terror hastened to accuse the philosophers of impiety towards the gods so that they would be unable to teach the people that these gods were the work of the priests.[62]

Close study of Greek religion makes it seem improbable that ancient Athens' priests would have had the power or inclination to persecute Socrates.[63] But the thematic continuity that Condorcet sustains by inventing a centralized and powerful Hellenistic priesthood in the image of the medieval Catholic one to come is vital to his ability to theorize progress. Condorcet's historical thinking was driven by a compulsion to conform fact to form, and this form demanded an array of facts that would sustain the supposition of a decisive historical divide, a millenarian division capable of sustaining faith in progress.

DISPLACEMENT AND THE NEW SCIENTIFIC CONSTITUENCY

If Condorcet was displacing the same narrative into which Bacon had already written the history of science, then it might be safe to predict that he was supporting rhetorical outcomes similar to those that Bacon manifestly sought to realize through his *Advancement of Learning* and *New Atlantis*, namely the public patronage of science. I say outcomes rather than purposes because, as I pointed out at the onset of this chapter, scientific patronage was not Condorcet's explicit aim. The *Esquisse* was intended as a theodicy of progress, a historical treatise that would affirm the advancement of liberty in the face of the irrational turn that now seemed to diminish such hopes. If progress was rooted in the very notion of historical being, then the new despotism that was seeking to devour our author was merely a momentary interruption. Science was making the voice of nature audible, and this assured that convulsive relapses such as those brought on by the ascendancy of Marat, Robespierre, and Hébert were merely ephemeral. The world could look beyond the Terror to a future time when

> the sun will shine only on free men who know no other master but their reason; when tyrants and slaves, priests and their stupid or hypocritical instruments will exist only in works of history and on the stage; and when we shall think of them only to pity their victims and their dupes; to maintain ourselves in a state of vigilance by thinking on their excesses; and to learn how to recognize and so to destroy, by force of reason, the first seeds of tyranny and superstition, should they ever dare to reappear amongst us.[64]

This was certainly not an explicit push for scientific patronage, but it clearly anticipated what evolutionism now advances. A society that looked for human emancipation in natural understanding would be greatly disposed to patronize science. Since history arose from nature itself, and since the natural sciences alone knew how to read it, science was certain to assume a prophetic role in any liberal democracy that embraced such a narrative. To attain freedom was to conform to nature. Liberation, Condorcet declared, began and ended with science:

From the moment when the genius of Descartes gave men's minds that general impetus which is the first principle of a revolution in the destinies of the human race, to the happy time of complete and pure social liberty when man was able to regain his natural independence only after having lived through a long series of centuries of slavery and misery, the picture of the progress of the mathematical and physical sciences reveals an immense horizon whose different parts must be distributed and ordered if we wish to grasp the significance of the whole and properly observe its relations.[65]

This is a statement that captures the very essence of scientism as a category of social knowledge. By linking the evolution of liberty to the evolution of science, Condorcet had made scientific knowledge something that had a social as well as a natural substance; thus it came to define the whole framework of human experience. A polity inspired by such an understanding of history would certainly wish to make itself in the image of science. It would be inclined to regard its way of life as an extension of the scientific way of life.

My story cannot end with Condorcet for one simple reason. While the potential of such thinking for building scientific patronage is obvious, there is no direct line of causality leading from scientism to public support for the natural sciences. A society or movement steeped in scientism can always be counted on to support science in general ways, as Joseph Ben-David has so ably illustrated, but not necessarily in ways conducive to the interests of its professional practitioners.[66] In this regard, while Condorcet's vision anticipates the kind of scientific self-validation that now makes evolutionism attractive, it also illustrates the rhetorical shortcomings of such a generalized scientism that would soon make evolutionism an attractive alternative. In making Descartes' mapping of the ways of reason the event which had founded this new world, Condorcet constructed a version of scientism that took the authority of scientific method as its ground. It was the certainty of knowing how to find nature's truth that guaranteed social progress. In this view, the natural sciences did not directly drive evolution. Scientific achievements were historical signs that certified the applicability of its methods to all human endeavors, but this did not necessarily suggest that the advancement of the physical sciences assured progress. This distinction may seem subtle, but in the decades following Condorcet's death, its concrete implications would become manifest in France as social science began to usurp the place of the natural sciences. In the end, the society brought to life by the French Enlightenment, in spite of its creative leadership in establishing scientific institutions, was more likely to pour its rhetorical energies into social, political, technological, and educational pursuits rather than scientific ones.[67]

In this regard, Condorcet's Enlightenment narrative had some of the same liabilities that Bacon's had as a rhetorical resource. The gains that Bacon made by giving scientific practitioners a share in the ethos of the clergy came at the price of continued dependence upon forms of social authority not of their making. Condorcet's more thoroughly scientistic ideology partially corrected for this by fashioning the emerging French Republic in the image of science, but, implicitly at least, this made something more like political science the center of scientific authority. Certainly the scientized polity he envisioned was one that might be expected to support science, but in such an imagined world, the state itself was regarded as a scientific authority. Followed through to its logical ends, a scientistic ideology such as Condorcet's, much like the Marxist one I have also touched on in this chapter, might easily give rise to a pattern like the one manifested in the Soviet Union during the Lysenko affair in which the dictates of dialectical materialism could freely override the intellectual autonomy of geneticists.

Societies like those of France, the Soviet Union, and the United States that have taken up some version of Enlightenment scientism have often shown themselves to be great patrons of science. But this support has also been uneven. What is always wanted, more ideally, is an ideology that can sustain faith in science's general social applicability, and thus a general sense of indebtedness to science that will sustain its patronage, but which accomplishes this while maintaining the assumption that this authority is fundamentally rooted in the natural sciences. Ultimately the field best equipped to sustain this would be evolutionary science. Because evolutionary science purports to bring every subject within the purview of the natural sciences, it has the capacity to universalize scientific authority without also distributing that authority into other fields, such as sociology or political science. Classical positivism, as we will see in the next chapter, took an important step in this direction by making the evolutionary aspects of Enlightenment scientism more apparent. But by virtue of its social scientific origins, it was itself only a transitional form.

5

THE NEW CHRISTIANITY

Descend, O Liberty, daughter of Nature;
The people, recovering thy immortal power,
Upon the stately ruins of old imposture,
Raise once again thy altar!

Come, conqueror of kinds, Europe's example;
Come, over false Gods complete thy success!
Thou, Saint Liberty, inhabit this temple,
Be of our nation the Goddess!

—Marie-Joseph Chénier

Commissioned for the November 1793 "Festival of Reason and Liberty"
orchestrated by various members of the Convention, this hymn was chanted
as a Paris actress, playing the part of the goddess Reason who was serving,
for the moment at least, as the new sacred emblem of the French Republic,
was carried into the cathedral of Notre Dame de Paris. As poem and rite
all too clearly evince, while these acts were certainly part of a revolutionary
effort to undermine the hold of Catholicism, they could not help but also
emulate it. The festival was the ceremonial climax of a process that had
begun four years earlier with the seizing of church property. The prohibi-
tion of monastic vows soon followed in 1790 when the National Assembly's
Civil Constitution of the Clergy gave it administrative control of all religious
institutions. Now, on the eve of the festival, the republic was in the process
of *becoming* the church. Only a month before it had replaced the Gregorian
calendar with one that substituted the birth of the French Republic for the

139

nativity of Christ as the event marking history's beginning. Shortly afterward all of Paris' churches were closed.

Although Condorcet had participated in this process, he was not present for the drama that brought it to this ironic climax. Denounced as an enemy of the National Convention because of his opposition to the Jacobin Constitution, he was in hiding just a short distance away, holed up across the Seine in the house of the Paris landlady, Mme Vernet. Many of his Girondist friends were already among the human cargo being loaded onto death carts as part of the daily blood offering demanded by this goddess.[1] As a faithful disciple of Voltaire, Condorcet was certainly in favor of crushing l'infâme, but he would have winced at the obvious impersonation of religion put on display by those who now wished to mingle his blood with their sacrifices. Nevertheless, the historical sketch he was writing as he distracted himself from these horrors celebrated in its own fashion the arrival of this new deity. Condorcet's pageant may have played out in a less ostentatious medium, one more worthy of a philosophe's reserve, but it too imitated what it thought to attack. He possessed a genuinely visceral hatred of religion, and in his thinking about how to remedy the world of this nuisance he stood, at least in spirit, with the Jacobins. But in his own way he was no less prone to imitate this enemy even as he actively reproached it. We need only to translate the historical plot of his Esquisse into its thematic corollaries to recognize how much of the substance of Chénier's poem it contains.

This bears witness to the guiding principle I have taken from Durkheim. His theory proposes that religious meaning is the only kind of meaning that can sustain social authority. Social authority is as abstract as it is vital, and because abstractions are always susceptible of appearing to be mere assertions of imagination or will, the greater stake individuals have in them, the more they will strive to link these mental constructions to things eternal and inviolable. As the merely verbal anticlericalism of the Enlightenment gave way to the revolution's dismantling of the church, the vulnerability of the emerging order became more apparent. The Enlightenment, we might say, had been an effort to audition nature (now closely identified with reason) for the role formerly played by God, and the revolutionary success of this movement now required even stronger demonstrations of its adequacy for this part. This, of course, accounts for the odd irony of the 1793 festival. The best way to prove reason's fitness to perform the society-building work formerly done by God was to demonstrate just how much like the church its human representatives were.

So far as the more specific subject matter of this book is concerned, this would also mean that coinciding efforts to win scientific patronage during this and later periods would reflect the same pattern. To the extent that the scientific ethos is always a kind of microcosmic reflection of the social macrocosm, scientistic movements will always evolve in concert with the societies they aspire to influence, and in the *Esquisse* we gain a glimpse of this co-evolution. Condorcet's main subject was the revolutionary movement from which he had been exiled, but as an author who had another foot firmly planted in the world of science, the affairs of science were especially likely to be drawn into this picture. If a religious rationale was needed to sustain the public authority of the new republic, it was needed to sustain the scientific ethos as well. Such imitations were likely to occur, not merely because the mimetic impulse is the foundational element of human creativity, but also because they were ideologically attractive. Science already had sacred import, and so to ground it in anything less than eternal truth would be to demote its significance. Once having been elevated as a full partner with theology by the end of the seventeenth century, it seems unlikely that the culture of science would willingly surrender the status it had come to share with theology as a second "queen of the sciences." To step back upon any lower rung of the social order would be to sacrifice its public visibility, presence, and sense of higher purpose, to turn science back into what it had been before the modern era—a minor tributary running out of lesser waterways of the medieval intellect such as mathematics, logic, and medicine. In this regard, mimesis of the kind chronicled in the last chapter is not particularly surprising, even if it is often unnoticed. The spiritualization of science persists because it builds upon the cultural success of a public identity that the scientific culture first found in orthodoxy.

The religious trappings of the French Revolution depict this pattern from the outside in, that is to say, by showing the complementary work of religious invention that was occurring in the ideologies of the secular nation-states in which science would henceforth need to implant its ethos. Just as Bacon's religious narrative could have had little rhetorical efficacy without linking science to the Protestant world that was then gaining ascendancy, Condorcet's naturalized one would have had no comparable significance as a resource for scientific patronage unless analogous religious sentiments were arising within France's new secular order. The scientistic potential of a text like the *Esquisse* could only be realized if something like the transformation of the Christian narrative was also going on in French society and in Europe more broadly. And this certainly was the case. For the civilization emerging out of the Enlightenment, as Eric Voegelin observes, the *"corpus mysticum Christi* has given way to the *corpus mysticum humanitatis."* The meaning of history on this "intramundane level" was being constructed as "an analogue to Christian meaning so closely that we can trace the parallelism step by step."[2] As Reinhold Niebuhr has put this, despite much talk about nature and reason, the dominant note in modern culture continued to be the faith in history it had inherited from previous generations.

> The conception of redemptive history informs the most diverse forms of modern culture. . . . Though there are minor dissonances the whole chorus of modern culture learned to sing the new song of hope in a remarkable harmony. The redemption of mankind by whatever means, was assured for the future. It was, in fact, assured by the future.[3]

In the end it was much easier for Western cultures to close down churches than to extinguish the desires that had built them, and these same desires had also been responsible for fashioning the architecture in which science found its home in society.

The continued evolution of this pattern in the positivist messages of Henri de Saint-Simon (1760–1825) and his onetime disciple August Comte (1798–1857) that I turn to now will bring us to the doorstep of evolutionism. As one of the most influential offshoots of the Enlightenment, the positivist movement was still mainly concerned with the larger problem of building a new European civilization. But as a rhetorical resource that later came to be closely associated with the scientific worldview, it is recognizably, if not the immediate ancestor of evolutionism, at least its evolutionary cousin. As such it represents a symbol system even more conducive to scientific patronage than the one erected in the Enlightenment. The crucial development within classical positivism that makes it a key stopping point in this evolutionary journey was its effort to envision a *history of science that was also a science of history.* Saint-Simon and Comte continued to stand with Condorcet in holding that the structure of history could be decoded in the evolution of modern science, but they also went one step further by actively claiming that they had brought the knowledge of these historical structures within the compass of scientific analysis. Condorcet had also asserted that science, as the epitome of progress, was the inevitable outcome of an ever-expanding human consciousness set free from brutality and superstition as humanity increasingly came into contact with nature and reason. He had also asserted that history could be theorized as science but without ever really saying how. It was left to the positivists to make this effort explicit and programmatic. Enlightenment philosophies of history bore witness to science's universalism; positivist ones asserted this as a scientific doctrine.

Another way to explain this difference would be to say that in positivism scientism reached its completion. In order for the scientific life to become the only life, it was necessary that the whole text of history should be understood in scientific terms and that each part of that history, especially the part accounting for the rise of scientific interpretation itself, should be understood in terms of the whole. In this regard we might say that positivism represents the apparent closing of a kind of hermeneutic circle. The interpretive work of science was folded back into the text of natural history, and natural history—like a great Ouroboros—was enfolded back into science. The advent of evolutionary biology at midcentury, just as positivism was also approaching the peak of its influence, would solidify this identity. "With Darwin," Collingwood writes,

> the scientific point of view capitulated to the historical, and both now agreed in conceiving their subject-matter as progressive. Evolution could now be used as a generic term covering both historical progress and natural progress. The victory of evolution in scientific circles meant that the positivistic reduction of history to nature was qualified by a partial reduction of nature to history.[4]

Of course this reduction could only be "partial." Because this progressive notion of history only seemed to have a scientific basis, this hermeneutic circle only seemed to have been closed. In this sense science was harmed by this identification, since, as Collingwood goes on to note, it sustained the false "assumption that natural evolution was automatically progressive, creative by its own law of better and better forms of life."[5] But whatever this may have cost the biological sciences in technical clarity was more than made up for by the dividends it paid to scientism. By giving the notion of progress scientific credentials, the roots of this idea in literary or mythical displacement were further obscured, thus enabling the scientific ethos to retain the sacred aura in which Bacon had first enveloped it even as it was becoming more secular and professionalized.

In mentioning Collingwood's observations on Darwinism, I am getting ahead of myself. Positivism is similar enough to evolutionism to be classified as a first cousin, and so our main objective, which is to understand the latter, might easily be accomplished without dwelling extensively on the former. But when we turn to Thomas Huxley in the next chapter as the principle architect of evolutionism, it will be crucial to understand what differentiates positivism from its more prosperous successor. This difference has chiefly to do with the role of scientism in efforts to establish scientific patronage. Positivism is no less scientistic than evolutionism, but when it becomes part of the public ideology of a society it does not necessarily produce the kind of ideological framework that translates into material support for the natural sciences. Evolutionism I believe does.

For the moment, my aim is to discuss three features of positivism that anticipate but which also provide helpful contrasts to evolutionism. The first, which I have already mentioned, is the positivists' explicit claim that they had reduced history to science even as they continued to advance historical ideas that were derived from the Christian tradition. Once enfolded into science, the speculative and mythologized features of this history became less subject to critical inspection and could more effectively sustain the emerging ethos of scientism. The second feature is positivism's tendency to merge decisively these enduring religious themes into the notion of evolution. This pattern stands out even more sharply in classical positivism than it does in evolutionism proper, simply because of this earlier movement's explicit efforts to establish itself as a scientific alternative to Europe's religious traditions. As the architects of a movement concerned with social science, the positivists theorized that religion was a necessary mechanism of social stability and prosperity. Consequently, they actively and self-consciously articulated what evolutionism continues to advance in more indirect ways: an evolutionary scheme in which science is presented as religion's natural descendent. The third feature of positivism, which I will consider at the conclusion of this chapter, is its potential as a rhetorical resource for scientific patronage. By insisting that science was destined to inherit the offices of religion, the positivists were also making it the transcendent authority destined to oversee the revitalization of European civilization, and the rhetorical outcome of this was the construction of a new secular constituency for science. Any view of history is also a picture of the society that is its product, and the social world envisioned in the positivist historical narrative was one created in the image of science.

THE HISTORY OF SCIENCE AS THE SCIENCE OF HISTORY

Although a discussion of these developments might just as easily begin with Auguste Comte, who is the figure most closely associated with classical positivism, I want to begin by looking at some of the scattered ideas of his early mentor and collaborator, Henri de Saint-Simon. Although the main ideas outlined in Saint-Simon's *Introduction aux travaux scientifiques du xixe siècle* (*Introduction to the Scientific Studies of the Nineteenth Century*) (1807–1808), *Mémoire sur la science de l'homme* (*Memoire on the Science of Man*) (1813), and his millenarian *Nouveau Christianisme* (*New Christianity*) (1825) would find their more influential expression in Comte's *Cours de philosophie positive* (*Course of Positive Philosophy*) (1830–1842) and *Systéme de politique positive* (*System of Positive Polity*) (1875), Saint-Simon's words were spoken into the hurricane winds of crisis that still raged as the revolution gave way to the Napoleonic period and Bourbon restoration. For this reason they give us a clearer picture of the rhetorical pressures that were then working to condense the loose speculations of Enlightenment philosophers into a harder scientific substance. Saint-Simon's writings may be only the disorganized outpourings, as Frank Manuel describes them, "of a man who suffered from intermittent fits of mental disorder," yet "for all their exasperating confusion they constitute the first version of a socio-philosophical system which gained broad acceptance on the European continent."[6] Indeed, Saint-Simon's creative genius would cause Durkheim to give him greater primacy than even Marx in the development of those positivist notions of society that were beginning to give rise to socialism.[7]

Like other heirs of the Enlightenment, Saint-Simon found himself enthralled with the visionary implications of Condorcet's *Esquisse*, and this gives us good reason for supposing that he absorbed into his own historical worldview the displaced narrative already at work in this outline. There were, no doubt, some personal reasons for this attraction. Like Condorcet, Saint-Simon was a liberal aristocrat and had nearly become a victim of the Terror himself. He responded to the disillusionments he shared with the elder *philosophe* by pressing harder to justify the intellectual currents that had given rise to the revolution. By the time this former soldier and veteran of the American War of Independence had begun his second career as a social theorist and pamphleteer at the turn of the nineteenth century, Condorcet's *Esquisse* had been enshrined by a new generation of liberal thinkers as its manifesto of progress. For these writers and political activists, it was no longer merely an apology for the Enlightenment project but rather a roadmap capable of righting the course of the ongoing movement it celebrated. Those of Saint-Simon's generation were not inclined to doubt Condorcet's rationalization for the Terror as the inevitable counteraction of tyranny and "its faithful companion superstition" seeking to take hold of the gains made by reason. Nor did they challenge his optimistic expectation that progress was assured by reason's immanence within nature and only slowed by certain interests of power that tempted some to turn reason against itself. Taking their inspiration from this hope even as they criticized the merely reactionary posture taken by many of its elder prophets, they aspired now to make straight the course of progress by codifying it as science.

It was, no doubt, the fact that Condorcet's *Esquisse* already hinted at a science of history that inspired Saint-Simon to declare it "one of the most beautiful productions of the human mind."[8] But he also wished to overcome its fatalistic tendency to foresee a perennial warfare between reason and superstition, and he did this by instead interpreting this apparent polarity in dialectical terms. The mechanism of historical progress he theorized in his 1813 *Mémoire sur la science de l'homme* had advanced through two alternating modes of scientific rationality, a synthetic or *a priori* mode now fully understood in the scientific philosophy of Descartes, and an analytical or *a posteriori* one associated with Locke and Newton.[9] The Enlightenment had been unable to achieve the liberation it promised because it was preoccupied too exclusively with science's analytical side, and now it was time for a balancing response. Earlier setbacks only indicated that the "critical and revolutionary" stage of the *philosophes* was passed, that it had given way to a new period of "inventive and organizing" work that would bring new order to civilization.[10] The revolution had remained incomplete only because the attack on the *ancien régime* had not been complemented by this offsetting synthesis. This work of construction would arise when the "system" of scientific principles that governed social nature was discovered, thereby enabling philosophers to predict and regulate history's course.[11]

Saint-Simon's unwavering belief that these scientific laws were soon to be found explains the often rash urgency of his political appeals. Although he remained unknown and unread until the last fifteen years of his life, this did not deter him from soliciting the attention of kings, emperors, or anyone else who might listen, always with the confident expectation that the world should instantly recognize the scientific character of his visions. The manifesto that he wrote with Augustin Thierry to the delegates of the 1814–1815 Congress of Vienna, *De la réorganisation de la société Européenne* (*The Reorganization of European Society*) reflects this certainty. With neither any hint of diffidence nor scholarly sobriety, the unknown philosopher asserted that Europe's only hope of political stability in the aftermath of the Napoleonic wars was to be found in the implementation of his own theories.[12] Speaking *ex cathedra* as an oracle of natural law, Saint-Simon presented himself as the prophet of a new epoch. The "philosophy of revolution" had run its course in the previous century and was now giving way to the "constructive" course he promised to chart.[13] To realize its promise, the Congress needed only to abandon its old-fashioned diplomatic approach of negotiation and compromise and instead adopt principles of social organization laid out in accordance with discoverable laws.[14] All that was needed was a scientific architect capable of producing the appropriate theorems, and this duty Saint-Simon now offered to perform.

Believing that the European destiny he plotted had this scientific basis, the variant political ideologies of the patrons Saint-Simon sought for his plans did not matter. Natural truths were universal truths that transcended such differences, and so he was just as happy to pitch his schemes to Bonaparte as to Louis XVIII.[15] He had also hoped that the *industriels*, the emerging class of scientists, artists, and technicians, would rise spontaneously to his prophetic directives and seize the reins of government. They were nature's constituency and ought to instantly recognize the voice of its prophet. But as he waited in vain for this group to rally behind his genius, whatever other powers seemed to be in ascent would have to do.[16] Even as he was making his appeal to the Vienna Congress as it worked to undo Bonaparte's destruction, simultaneous overtures were also going out during the "Hundred-Days" to Napoleon through his minister of the interior.[17] The future he envisioned for the Vienna Congress was to be a loose confederation.[18] The same "general reorganization" of Europe that he proposed to this democratic body as the instrument that would establish peace among autonomous nations by "adjusting the claims of each and conciliating the interests of all," simply took on a more decidedly Francocentric and imperialistic flavor in the letter he sent to Napoleon.

Saint-Simon was not the only French intellectual on this quest. His search for a science of history that would guide the reconstitution of European society by "certain, absolute, universal principles, independent of time and place," took much of its inspiration from the social theorizing of the ideologues.[19] This collection of philosophers, publicists, physicians, and scientists had been influential during the revolution and continued to carry forward its aims in the early part of the nineteenth century before falling out of Napoleon's favor. *Idéologie* was their word for the generalized science of society, a precursor to what the positivists under Comte's influence would first call "social physics" and later "sociology." Destutt de Tracy defined it as a "science of ideas," and Saint-Simon's friend Pierre-Jean-George Cabanis as "the science of methods."[20]

But despite these aspirations to technicality, the general science of everything envisioned by the ideologues was also meant to fill France's widening spiritual vacuum. These heirs of the Enlightenment approached political reform with a new caution borne out of their memory of the Terror, and this inspired many liberal thinkers to reconsider the spiritual destruction it had wrought. The opinion now percolating through the liberal mind was that it had been futile to tear down the old religion if there was no new spiritual order to take its place, and thus a true science of society would also need to build a new religion. One early contributor to this line of thought was Madame Germaine de Staël (1766–1817), the great *femme lettrées* of the age, who Saint-Simon is thought to have visited in 1802 during her political exile in Geneva. While there is no concrete evidence that this audience also occasioned Saint-Simon's failed effort to win de Staël's hand in marriage, as his disciples would later claim, the philosopher certainly did share her expectation that science and religion would soon be joined in a conjugal union.[21] Europe's emerging civilization was to be grounded in the certainty of what she now, after Georges-Louis Leclerc, comte de Buffon, called "positive" knowledge, and thus its moral authority would have to be scientific as well. This meant that the social scientists who were destined to rule over this new universe of knowledge would also need to be a spiritual body, a scientized version of the Catholic Church. Like many kindred thinkers of her generation, de Staël had begun to abandon the Encyclopedists' rash disdain for medieval culture and to suppose instead that the old Catholic order provided the appropriate historical model upon which to construct this new scientific Christendom.[22]

The ideologues, having at first won Napoleon's favor, envisioned themselves becoming the priesthood of this new order, only to have these hopes crushed by the emperor's 1801 Concordat with the Catholic Church. In restoring the church, the First Consul had found a more expedient shortcut by which to restore the spiritual bearings of a French public wearied by the constant erosion of traditional certainties. Robbed of this destiny, the ideologues would soon have to endure further indignity as enemies of the state.

Saint-Simon's belief that the new social order could not exist in a religious vacuum also brought him into intellectual communion with conservative counterrevolutionaries of this period such as Chateaubriand, Bonald, and Maistre who saw this spiritual crisis as a pretext for restoring some nominal form of Catholic authority. Saint-Simon agreed with such conservatives in principle, and for a time had even hoped that France's clergy could play this part once they came around to the positivist point of view. But in the end he judged that the Catholic Church was no longer up to the job. Spiritual order needed to be restored, but only a more evolved religious authority would be capable of providing the vital checks on temporal power that the medieval church had formerly instituted.[23] The unified technical class he would later describe in his *Nouveau Christianisme* was destined to become this new Roman Curia, a spiritual buffer against the destructive tendencies of political ambition in the emerging secular state. In its earliest incarnation, this was to be a "council of Newton" explicitly modeled after the scientific theocracy of Bacon's *New Atlantis*.[24] In it, the role played in the old Europe by the Catholic Church was to be filled by a parliamentary body of scientific priests—with mathematicians holding the highest ecclesiastical rank.[25]

Seen now from our more distant perspective, Saint-Simon's preoccupation with religion might seem to signal only the nostalgia of a thinker disposed to venerate the ways of an older culture from which he did not have the emotional fortitude to break free. But we dare not lose sight of the fact that this religious enthusiasm was also thought to have a religious basis. It signaled the author's conviction that the scientific explanation of history he had discovered also demonstrated an evolutionary linkage between science and the older faith. So long as positivism seemed to descend from religion, it would also seem to retain religious meanings that it might have formally denied. This evolutionary thesis was first formulated by the ideologue Charles Dupuis (1742–1809) in his *De l'origine de tous les cultes ou religion universelle* (*The Origin of All Religious Worship, or Universal Religion*) (1795). Dupuis contended that the religious conceptions of past ages represented scientific thought in an immature phase of its development.[26] What religion had conceptualized through the dark glass of anthropomorphism were in fact positive truths that modernity was now beginning to look in the face and to render in mathematical language.[27] Regarded in any straightforward manner, Dupuis' explanation was merely reductive, one that evaporated the essence of religious thought and experience into merely sociological mists. But to the extent that Saint-Simon's incorporation of this thesis into his own vision of history continued to involve the nonreductive element of displacement (as signaled by its explicit modeling after Bacon's *New Atlantis*), it also retained traditional elements of religious meaning. No less than the Enlightenment philosophers whose work he carried forward, Saint-Simon was still transposing, as Voegelin describes this, the story of scientific progress onto a preexistent narrative of providence.[28] Whatever the sociological merits of this new explanation of religion, it was being advanced in company with notions of religion's historical role that it did not theorize so much as imitate.

Dupuis' thesis was attractive to opponents of the Bourbon Restoration because its reduction of religion to science armed secularist arguments against the reestablishment of Catholic authority.[29] But it also suggested that science was being elevated to take its place, that science could provide what conservative reactionaries sought by restoring some part of the church's power, and this was the opportunity that Saint-Simon ran with. If the philosophers of the Enlightenment had been influenced by the instinctive fear, as Carl Becker puts it, "that to profess atheism would be no less a confession of failure than to return like lost sheep to the Christian fold," this had become a manifest concern for their successors.[30] Saint-Simon seems to have recognized in Dupuis' scheme how an explicitly evolutionary view might enable one, in some sense, to make the first of these options mean the same thing as the second. If the past religions of a given culture represented scientific thinking at some stage of its social evolution, then one could embrace the past without abandoning one's commitment to the purity of the new scientific way. The new age of science, he declared in his 1813 *Mémoire sur la science de l'homme*, was thus a continuation of the age of Catholicism since "every organization of the scientific system leads to the reorganization and improvement of the religious system."[31] Formally, traditional religious beliefs may have remained what they were for the *philosophes*, the empty productions of alienated reason, but informally their older meanings tended to abide, especially because they were now linked to scientific conceptions by an evolutionary premise. Because religious ideas were also the steps by which nature was leading humanity toward the positive science of society that was destined to fulfill all the same functions, formal distinctions were in effect muddled. Dupuis' evolutionary viewpoint had made a precise distinction impossible, and this enabled his successors to perpetuate religious ideas even while insisting that they were advancing a scientific perspective.

PROTO-EVOLUTIONISM

This pattern is the pivotal element of evolutionism put in place by the positivists. To reduce religion to science was to enlarge the scope of scientific authority, but it also naturalized the deeper spiritual associations that science had already achieved in the Baconian era. As an effort to reconstruct the scientific ethos, we might say that positivism enjoyed the best of both worlds. It maintained the Enlightenment view that science was, epistemically speaking, religion's superior, but by doing this on evolutionary grounds it sustained a historical linkage that enabled science to retain some of the meaning it had formerly gained through its identification with religion. Now regarded as mere developmental steps, traditional religious viewpoints remained in check since they could no longer claim to exercise any influence in the coming enlightened age. But while traditional religion was thus disarmed, science could also present itself as its rightful heir. As we will also see when we turn to evolutionism proper in the next two chapters, this was achieved by scientizing progress—by contending that a view that was in fact the product of narrative displacement had resulted from the scientific discovery of history's evolutionary structure.

It was such a vision of history that enabled Saint-Simon to speak of positivism as a *Nouveau Christianisme*,. Like every other kind of prescientific thought, religion had been scientific rationality in the process of becoming. In its former life, it had been a merely immature attempt to achieve the same goal that a grown-up humanity now pursued more self-consciously— the "progress of the universal idea."[32] In science, he declared in his *Mémoire sur la science de l'homme*, the key had been found that would decode every other system of thought:

> Systems of religion, politics, ethics, and education, are simply applications of the system of ideas, or, in other words, of the system of thought, considered under different aspects. Thus it is obvious that when the new scientific system has been constructed, a reorganization of the religious, political, ethical, and educational system will take place; and consequently a reorganization of the church.[33]

The reconstitution of the Catholic Church on positivist grounds was for Saint-Simon the endpoint of evolutionary history. The church had been the most universal of those systems of thought that had formerly encompassed all other systems, and so it represented the clearest historical antecedent and type for positivism—the science of sciences that was destined to take charge of history and to draw every other realm of inquiry into itself. Positivism, in other words, was providing the historical framework for the entire project of modernity.

The historical form that Saint-Simon gave to this scientific claim reflects that same pattern of displacement that we have seen already in the messages of his forebears. This evolutionary view of history related science to religion on naturalistic grounds by reducing the latter to its merely sociological elements, but it also did so, no less than the similar schemes of Bacon and

Condorcet, by appealing to the habitual assumption that history had a pre-ordained purpose and direction. The positivist notion of progress, in other words, remained an article of faith, the unexamined background assumption against which Saint-Simon and Comte would plot their evolutionary visions.

If history was innately progressive, this meant that positive science was its apocalypse, the same awakening to scientific self-consciousness that Condorcet had projected. The difference was that Galileo, Descartes, and Bacon were no longer the chief prophets of this new epoch. Saint-Simon and Comte claimed this role for themselves. This was because the substance of that revelation was no longer the formal mapping of scientific reasoning, such as we associate with these seventeenth-century figures; the new apocalypse was the discovery of a science of history that integrated and subsumed all other endeavors of inquiry.

The mimetic bases of this science of history become especially apparent, just as with Condorcet, in the necessary deviations from the historical record that were necessary to make this account consistent with a pre-established narrative form. Condorcet needed to force fit the past into a structure dominated by a perennial war between reason and superstition in order to explain why the tide of inevitable progress had been held back for so long. Saint-Simon's evolutionary periodizations grew out of a different thesis, but one no less likely to reinvent the past in the image of an imagined positivist future. Since positive science was the natural end of religious evolution, he needed to make the great age of monotheism look much more science-like than it in fact had been. This accounts for the different scientific role given to Socrates in Saint-Simon's *Introduction aux travaux scientifiques* as compared with Condorcet's *Esquisse*. As we saw in the previous chapter, Condorcet fashioned Socrates as a full-blown man of science whose martyrdom had forestalled the revolutionary age of science. Once having claimed that nature's great apocalypse was on the verge of erupting through Socrates' genius, Condorcet needed to posit an opposing priesthood possessed by such malice and genius as could frustrate it. But Socrates' untimely death is not even mentioned in Saint-Simon's account, let alone treated as an instance of religious persecution. In fact, Socrates is championed much more for his theological genius than for his philosophical wisdom. Having taken his inspiration for this historical narrative from Dupuis, Saint-Simon identified science with religion as two manifestations of a single historical process at different stages of its evolution. No less than the Socrates of the *Esquisse*, Saint-Simon's hero remained a scientific figure by virtue of his discovery of the synthetic or *a priori* mode of reasoning, but he had done this as the inventor of monotheism. Socrates had made a great scientific discovery when he first "conceived the idea of confiding the power of Olympus in a single being." He had "proclaimed that there was one God, and that this God ruled everything, both as a whole and in its separate parts."[34]

> Until the age of Socrates none of the four peoples descended from the plateau of Tartary achieved any great superiority over the others. Each of them made similar progress. Each used its own powers to rise to the conception of divinity, but none conceived this idea very clearly. Socrates was the first to proclaim that the idea of God should be regarded as an instrument of scientific calculation. He was the founder of general science. Before Socrates ideas were only bundled together. He was the first to begin to link them systematically.[35]

Because of this, Socrates' advent was the apocalyptic event responsible for the epochal divide separating *histoire ancienne* from *histoire moderne*.[36] The discovery of monotheism had brought into operation the dialectical machinery of history that would thereafter accelerate the course of progress toward its culmination in positivism.

When Saint-Simon goes on to say that it had been Socrates who "invented God," and that he is therefore the true author of Christianity (its more familiar founder escapes mention altogether), he is by no means saying that the God of monotheism exists.[37] No less than would be true of the latter-day positivists of the Vienna Circle, the stated principle of Saint-Simon's philosophy is a radical nominalism that nullified theological speculation of any traditional sort. His God is a phenomenological deity, and the traditional terms he uses to denote it are merely placeholders. Saint-Simon continues to speak of "God" in this metonymic fashion, we might say, simply because such traditional language sustains the sense of historical universalism. The supreme being of monotheism may have been a merely unreal or at best unknowable expression of the synthetic reasoning that was at work in intellectual and social evolution, but to call reason by this traditional name ensured the preordained continuity and purposeful character of the historical progression that was leading toward positivism. The positivist apocalypse that was destined to bring all the world into its compass at the end of history would need to make sense of the past as well. Even the older paganism was now a stage in this scientific progression. The knowledge that the older pagan rationality had merely "bundled together," provided a necessary step toward the "unitary" science of Socrates.[38] Positivism now recapitulated this synthetic turn, even as it advanced this historical progression by finally stripping the notion of "God" of its supernatural content.

In the hands of Saint-Simon's onetime secretary and disciple, Auguste Comte, this philosophy of history was formalized in the better-known doctrine of the three laws. The study of "the progressive course of the human mind," Comte wrote in the introduction to his *Cours de philosophie positive*, reveals the "great fundamental law, to which it is necessarily subject, and which has a solid foundation of proof both in the facts of our organization and in our historical experience." This law showed that "each of our leading conceptions—each branch of our knowledge—passes through three different theoretical conditions: the Theological, or fictitious; the Metaphysical, or abstract; and the Scientific, or positive."[39] The theological stage of intellectual evolution, in which natural events were attributed to the agency of supernatural beings, represented the limitations of a youthful species striving for knowledge beyond its reach. In this early stage, it was inevitable that reason should interpret the natural world as the product of beings imagined to be like ourselves. Just as Saint-Simon had argued concerning the monotheism of Socrates, Comte recognized that the "Theological system arrived at the highest perfection of which it is capable when it substituted the providential action of a single Being for the varied operations of the numerous divinities which had been before imagined."[40] This showed that theological inquiry was driven by reason, even though it was misdirected by its pursuit of an unattainable "Absolute knowledge," and therefore it had at least formal scientific import. In spite of monotheism's misguided search for "the essential nature of beings, the first and final causes (the origin and purpose) of all effects," it had all the while been guided by that innate principle of historical development that was destined to lead to its positive culmination in a grand sociological theory that would encompass and direct all subordinate knowledge. Reason's tendency to move in this direction was shown by the inclination of each branch of inquiry to pass through a middle or metaphysical period, a transitional stage between the theological and positive in which "abstract forces, and veritable entities" took the place of the supernatural beings of theology. Metaphysical knowledge was no less illusory than that constructed in the theological stage, but by substituting abstract representations for the anthropomorphic ones of the theological stage, it detached reason from these false substances and freed it to discover its appropriate natural referents. Once so liberated from this vain search for absolutes, reason attaining to this middle stage would be inclined to seek understanding of "the causes of phenomena, and apply itself to the study of their laws." As each science moved toward its positivist culmination, its explanations would arise solely from the application of reason and observation to establish a simple "connection between single phenomena and some general facts, the number of which continually diminishes with the progress of science."[41]

The fact that Saint-Simon and Comte regarded this synthetic rationality as the real substance of religion never stopped them from adopting many of the traditional symbols of Christianity. Even as he attacked the Catholic Church in his *Nouveau Christianisme*, Saint-Simon made bold to assert that this was because he spoke for the true church. He dramatized this by using the device of *prosopopoeia*, by bringing Martin Luther up from the grave to speak on his behalf, as if to show that this great reformer, were he alive, would be certain to take his side. Speaking through Luther, Saint-Simon warned the bishop of Rome that if he continued "to put forward mystical ideas," a new priesthood of "artists, scientists and industrialists" would rise up against him, a new Reformation that would "open the eyes of the common people to the absurdity of your doctrines, to the monstrous abuse of your power, and you will then have no resource to maintain your place in society except to become the instruments of the temporal power."[42] Such a manner of speech might seem contrary to the epistemic ideals of positivism, but it is quite consistent with the historical dimension of this philosophy. By putting his own renunciation of mysticism in Luther's mouth and Luther's language, Saint-Simon reinforced the premise of evolutionary continuity. Although we can be sure that Luther would have meant something else had he in fact spoken these words, the formal similarity they bear to the language of Protestant reform sustains the impression that it shared a common substance of meaning with positivism.

The attraction of this religiosity for the classical positivists is also witnessed by the greater prevalence and urgency it achieved in the most mature writings of both Saint-Simon and Comte. In the final paragraph of Saint-Simon's final work, his *Nouveau Christianisme*, he even goes so far as to present himself as God's oracle.

> Hearken to the voice of God which speaks through me. Return to the path of Christianity; no longer regard mercenary armies, the nobility, the heretical priests and perverse judges, as your principle support, but, united in the name of Christianity, understand how to carry out the duties which Christianity imposes on those who possess power. Remember that Christianity commands you to use all your powers to increase as rapidly as possible the social welfare of the poor![43]

As his disciples later gathered around his deathbed, he again sounded this theme by reminding them of the evolutionary basis upon which positivism stood. "The attack on the religious system of the Middle Ages has really proved only this, that it was no longer in harmony with the positive sciences. It would be wrong to conclude from this that religion tends to disappear; only that it should adjust itself to scientific progress."[44] Religion lived on in science because science, as the voice of nature, represented its true essence.

It would be tempting to regard such utterances as mere anomalies, perhaps as the aberrations of an author known to have been subject to periodic bouts of mental illness and megalomania. But the fact that this feature of positivism would become just as central in the more mature and more influential writings of Comte—who suffered from no similar psychiatric disorders—belies any easy dismissal.[45] Like the Saint-Simonians who interpreted their teacher's words as an explicit command to spread this pantheistic gospel across Europe, Comte likewise saw himself as the prophet of a new "religion of humanity" that was the predestined end of positivism's evolution.[46] His habit of searching out analogies between the offices and doctrines of this new scientific priesthood and its Catholic antecedent would become one of the hallmarks of both his second magnum opus, *Systéme de politique positive* (*System of Positive Polity*) (1875), and its accompanying handbook for the masses, the *Catéchisme positiviste* (*Positivist Catechism*) (1852).

As Comte made free to propose positivist sacraments and prayers, a clergy over which he would reign as pope, a liturgical calendar, a positivist hagiography, and even hymns to the *Grande Être*, it is not surprising that some of his disciples grew uneasy. They sometimes sensed that he was merely dressing up traditional religious ideas in scientific clothing, but there was always an escape clause in positivism's evolutionary premise. So long as it could be presumed that this enduring religious language referenced the natural underpinnings of the old faith and not its supernatural aspects, one could always suppose that it therefore was science. In other words, Comte makes free use of a persistent ambiguity that always abides within evolutionary thinking. Whatever is understood to be a product of evolutionary descent is necessarily both associated with and dissociated from what came before. Technically speaking, for instance, explorations of human descent (in the biological sense) are primarily concerned with the dissociative side of evolution. To understand the developmental mechanisms that have made us different from our ape ancestors is to attend primarily to the discontinuities of evolution. But while it would thus be fair to interpret the theory of human evolution as saying, no less than any doctrine of creation, that we are unlike any other animal, difference by descent always leaves open the recognition that we are related to apes. To accentuate our ape connections is certainly scientifically meaningful, but it is also an interpretive choice, and one, I might add, that loses sight of the fact that the same premise of evolutionary descent also entails dissociation—that we are apes no longer.

In the evolutionary arguments of Comte and Saint-Simon we find an analogous ambiguity but also a rhetorical opportunity. These writers appealed to an evolutionary dissociation when they asserted that modern science alone had realized the fullness of knowledge that ancestral religious forms had only falsely claimed to possess. But an association between positivism and theism abides here as well. Even if one regarded science as religion's replacement, this evolutionary framework also implies a more substantial connection. So does the religiosity that persists in the language of these two positivist thinkers indicate the endurance of religious content or just the supposition that religion had been a kind of false science? My answer to this question, of course, is that it indicates both of these things. But a more important point has to do with the very ambiguity that enables us to raise this question. So long as it remains possible to think that this can be all one thing or the other, science but not religion, there also remains the possibility that a genuinely religious viewpoint could be advanced unnoticed in the guise of science.

This interpretation of positivist religiosity seems to reflect Leah Ceccarelli's observation that polysemy—that is, the presence within some messages of "determinate but nonsingular denotational meaning"—may reflect an underlying unity that becomes apparent once the "hermeneutical depths" of a message are explored.[47] Messages appearing to be *contradictory* when viewed superficially become recognizably *complementary* once considered at some deeper level. In the case of positivism, this would mean that the apparent contradiction between its epistemological skepticism and its manifest religiosity disappears once we recognize that its historical aspect draws these realms of meaning together. Saint-Simon and Comte could easily deny that any traditional truth claims were being advanced when they appropriated religious language, but would this strip away the traditional meaning that inhered within it? What suggests that they did not escape from these undercurrents is the abiding premise of historical purpose that always lurks within the idea of progress. The unwillingness of these writers to expunge such historical meaning from their writings, even though they propose no scientific basis for this notion, indicates that their prediction that religious meanings were destined to give way to merely naturalistic ones was in fact

grounded in one of those religious meanings. They had appropriated a narrative form that assumed a preordained purpose in the passage of time,
and the evolutionary perfection of religious meaning through science now
enacted that purpose. Here is one of the great paradoxes of modernism: the
very possibility of such a reduction that could strip history of spiritual meaning depended upon the spiritualization of history. For the positivists, everything had a natural or scientific explanation, but the historical framework
in which this unfolding naturalism was envisioned was itself not subject to
this reduction. It could not be. Were history to be rendered merely in terms
of some deterministic model in which blind causation rather than purpose
accounted for its course, positivism would lose its gravitational center.

An alternate way to explain the unity that underlies this polysemy
might be to consider the blurred signification that inclines the "reduction"
expressed through metonymy, as Kenneth Burke describes it, to shade into
the kind of "representation" that manifests in the closely related trope of
synecdoche.[48] Metonymy, for instance, when it references articles of clothing to signify the people inside them—"shirts" for business executives,
"blue collars" or "cloth caps" (as the English say) for laborers—it reduces
one category of meaning to another related to it in some fashion, in these
instances by denoting categories of persons as categories of clothing. Comte
and Saint-Simon attempt something like this when they use the language
of religion to reference what they regard as natural phenomena. It is their
way of saying that religion had merely been science in some evolutionary
stage of becoming. When Saint-Simon declared in his *Lettres d'un habitant
de Genève à ses contemporains* (*Letters from an Inhabitant of Geneva to His Contemporaries*) (1802–1803) that it was "God who had spoken to me" to reveal
this "superior religion," the "God" he was talking about was nature and
his "religion" was science.[49] This is roughly analogous to what speakers are
getting at when they describe men who "chase skirts," namely that while
women seem to be involved, it is really not women that they are after. Correspondingly, for the positivists, the "content" of religion could be reduced to
its "container," to the natural system of ideas with which religion was once
associated. The religionists of old had been in pursuit of a natural world
they had mistaken for God.

But metonymy, as Burke also notes, is inherently ambiguous and "may
be treated as a special application of synecdoche."[50] Language that reduces
some content to its container will work as metonymy so long as we remain
mindful of the assumption that content and container are separate entities, but that assumption can easily drift out of thought. When it does,

the option of treating containers as extensions of the contained opens up. This is shown by how frequently in ordinary speech we are prone to use the same word in one context as metonym and in another as synecdoche. The word "body" is an example. Only the most insensitive person would fail to recognize something demeaning in a factory foreman's declaration that he does not "have enough bodies to staff the graveyard shift." The "body" metonym diminishes personhood by reducing it to mere biology, and it turns upon a traditional dualism that enables us to think of a person as being contained within the physical organism. But the alternative possibility of treating the "body" metaphor as synecdoche always lies close at hand. If the container-contained relationship is read as a part-whole relationship instead, the demeaning of "person" as mere "body" becomes the ennobling of "body" as "person" that we detect in the title of the feminist classic, *Our Bodies, Ourselves*. Once thought of as a symbol of the whole person, the body finds itself elevated to a position of greater honor.

The inherent ambiguity within metonymy that enables it to shift into synecdoche also enabled Comte and Saint-Simon to preserve a more substantial identity between science and religion. Just as the body might be regarded as metonym in a dualistic understanding of human nature and as synecdoche in a monistic one, the evolutionary reduction of religion to science that would strip religion of its traditional public authority could just as easily transform into synecdoche and become an identity capable of sustaining the priesthood of science. In this regard, Comte's claim that every science first passes through a theological stage might mean that scientific rationality had merely been *contained* within religious beliefs of the past that were utterly distinct from science, *or* it could mean that science *coincided* with religion and that religious concepts therefore persisted as scientific rationality gained ascendency.

Polysemy of this kind ensures that the aromas of pantheism that always seem to arise from positivist discourses for some readers will go undetected by others. It enables one to suppose, as Saint-Simon's chief biographer Frank Manuel has done, that the philosopher's religiosity was strictly tactical, while overlooking the fact that authorial intentions are never fully determinative of meaning. Even if Saint-Simon meant something reductive when he claimed, as Manuel puts it, that "History was God and God was History," what was to prevent his followers from treating this as a genuine identity—as they in fact did?[51] Durkheim's answer to this question was to acknowledge these pantheistic significations, but to do so only in passing so as to make them merely so much background noise that had for a time diminished the clarity of this scientific performance.[52] But Durkheim's failure to look this in the face seems to violate the very sociological principle he had absorbed from positivism, the recognition that religion could not sustain social order if it was truly reduced to something else. It is for this reason that Voegelin parts ways with other interpreters and regards the "intramundane eschatology" of positivism, rather than its scientific claims, as its key feature.[53] The very motive force of this religiosity would have been rendered impotent if Comte and Saint-Simon had genuinely enforced the reductive interpretations they posited. Thus it was Comte's "pseudo-prophetic charisma" that enlarged positivism's fortunes in Europe. In spite of the "dubious scientific value" of his ideas, they were endowed "with the glow of revelation on whose acceptance depends the salvation of mankind."[54]

These different interpretations are made possible by the notable fact that neither Saint-Simon nor Comte makes any concerted effort to qualify his use of religious references so as to ensure that readers will consistently understand these utterances within the framework of positivist epistemology. This is to say that the scientific, or metonymic, meanings of religious language are never carefully distinguished from pantheistic, or synecdochic, ones. Instead, we find these writers continuously shifting back and forth across an invisible but vital line that segregates these two realms of meaning.

We see this, for instance, in the analogies that Comte forges in his *Systéme de politique positive* between the Catholicism of the previous age and the positivist world to come. On the reductive side of our imaginary line, this manifests in the theory developed in his earlier *Cours* which proposed that sociology was the full realization of a scientific consciousness that formerly resided in the theological worldview. Formally, the "Catholic" thought that was evolving into scientific knowledge was destined to shed all of its original religious meaning, but Comte makes no real effort to discourage readers from thinking otherwise. His active appropriation of the language of Christianity gives readers the liberty to cross back and forth between the reductive scientific and religious sides of this invisible divide. He in fact encourages this by continuously insisting that his positivist doctrines have "spiritual" import.[55] Readers are free to suppose that this term is a mere metonym acknowledging the naturalistic content presumed to lie inside the mere container of theology, but they also remain free to spiritualize nature by identifying content with container. Comte's formal stance absolves him of any obligation to resolve this ambivalence, since it technically endorses a reductive interpretation, but this does not silence the suggestive power of his religious references.

The invisibility and informality of this dividing line also makes it possible for Comte to advance a form of evolutionary determinism even as he inspires his readers to imagine a world governed by a kind of providential pantheism. As the new social order emerged, it would again bring "feeling" and "intellect" into harmony, just as medieval Catholicism had done, because it was bringing to light the unifying materiality that undergirded them. He could be confident in this because he was sure that this movement of historical evolution "rests at every point upon the unchangeable order of the world" that science was increasingly forcing upon the human consciousness. But while these statements seem to stand him on the side of scientific naturalism, he does not hesitate to personify this unchangeable order. This same nature "*teaches* us that the object to be aimed at in the economy devised by man is wise development of the irresistible economy of nature which cannot be amended till it is first studied and *obeyed*."[56] The naturalistic determinism that he offers with one hand when he speaks of the "irresistible economy of nature," he takes back with the other by simultaneously imagining nature as a teacher who demands human obedience.

The same ambiguity abides in Comte's descriptions of the scientific role in society. He makes no secret of his expectation that the goal of the scientific enterprise was "to construct upon the firm basis this raised, the new faith of Western Europe, and to institute the priesthood of the future." Scientists were these new priests, of course, because positivism was a "philosophy capable of supplying the foundation of true religion."[57] On the official and reductive side of our imaginary line, this "priesthood" simply referenced the capacity of social science to ground the emerging social order in natural law, but Comte could not command this term to shed its more traditional significance simply because it formally purported to have no such meaning.

Nor did he likely want to. To consistently pen up meaning on the metonymic side of this divide would have deprived Comte of the ability to sustain his own prophetic identity. The picture we get as he recounts his discovery of the scientific truths that were about to revitalize religion is that of a man who regards himself as history's chosen instrument. His belief that he had found the "sociological laws" that explained the entire course of cultural history was itself an event of eschatological importance. Sociology was destined to bring to an end the "vast revolution of the West," because his own "work on the spiritual power" would "superintend the entire reconstruction of principle and practice, assuming in fact the function exercised by monotheism before its decay."[58] In this role Comte was the discoverer of a new gospel that was about to replace Christianity. He was uniquely ordained to lead the world into its final age because his work had been inspired by "the rare moral renovation wrought at the right moment by a purified passion." "Emancipated from theology before the end of child-hood, and trained betimes in positive studies," and having also passed "rapidly though the metaphysical period," Comte was history's pioneer. The "true cerebral unity" that he had realized personally at the age of twenty-four was a prophetic anticipation of the whole process of social evolution.[59] This made it "essential that both stages of this exceptional career should be elaborated by the same organ of humanity; otherwise their adaptation would have been imperfect."[60]

POSITIVISM AND THE SYMBOLIC STRUCTURES OF SCIENTIFIC PATRONAGE

Superficially, these last messianic professions might seem to be mere anoma-lies when we look back upon them from this historical distance. They might seem, at best, expressions of egoistic self-indulgence—perhaps even megalo-mania. The casual reader is now likely to laugh at Saint-Simon's claim that he was Charlemagne reincarnated and will perhaps pull back in revulsion, as even some of Comte's disciples did, at their teacher's wish to be recog-nized as pope over a new religion that worshiped humanity as its *Grand Être*.[61] But if we consider the practical rhetorical purposes that such eccen-tricities were capable of supporting, they will not seem nearly so mysterious. These writers were conserving a version of the scientific ethos that by this time had been in place for two centuries. The modern scientific ethos that arose within a theological framework could not persist in a new secularized one except by imitating this older worldview.

What we have not yet seen, except in general outline, is the relevance of these theological imitations for those specifically trying to build scientific patronage. The prospering of the natural sciences was not the direct concern of the positivist movement, but it had analogous aspirations for the social scientific field it was founding. The assumption of the positivists that reason applied to nature was giving rise to meanings such as were formerly sus-tained by sacred history made its philosophers spiritual authorities, the high priests of an emerging secular culture. Recognizably, this descends from the Baconian view of science, but it does not represent the genealogical branch that gave rise to evolutionism. Positivism had carried on the older tradition of regarding science in millenarian terms, but because it envisioned this, not as a historical culmination in which the broadening scope of physics, chemistry, and biology would encompass politics and commerce, but as one in which sociology would appear as history's scientific capstone, it could not sustain the patronage needs of natural scientists.

Thus while evolutionism has similar cultural roots, it represents a different evolutionary branch of the displacement that began in the Enlightenment and came to fruition in positivism. Positivism and evolutionism are only cultural evolutionary cousins—similar enough to warrant comparison but different enough to produce distinctive rhetorical outcomes. The positivist branch that sprang up in the writings of Comte and Saint-Simon was destined to mature in the social theories of Karl Marx and various kindred thinkers. Like Marxism, classical positivism appealed to the epistemic authority of science in an effort to uphold world-building aspirations on the broadest possible scale, but when carried forward to its logical conclusion, it did not elevate natural scientists as its heroes but rather political figures like Lenin and Mao Zedong, latter-day Comtes who derived their charisma from their apparent embodiment of a social scientific philosophy. The natural sciences have often prospered in societies dominated by positivism, but positivist symbol systems nest the natural sciences within some larger constellation of scientistic ideas that may just as easily smother them. Aspects of this pattern certainly manifested in the suppression of "Jewish science" by the National Socialists, who believed that their political ideology was informed by a higher racial science, and something analogous transpired in the Soviet Union when Mendelian genetics was outlawed in favor of the more socialist-friendly science of Trofim Lysenko.

6

POSITIVISM IN THE WORLD OF THOMAS HUXLEY

This increasing consolidation and prevalence of the scientific spirit represents the dominant form of modern consciousness whether we regard it in its theoretical configurations or in its popular or commonsense forms. Viewed historically, it represents the ultimate realization of the spirit of modern positivism, which in turn is closely related to the spirit of capitalism.

Once successfully established on such a basis and elaborated along such lines, modern philosophy and the social sciences tended increasingly to cut themselves loose from history in general and from their immediate roots in the nineteenth century in particular.

—Gertrud Lenzer

What Lenzer offers here is a summation of the general pattern I have been trying to outline in my discussion of positivism. But my own interpretation of her observation that philosophy and the social sciences have tended to cut themselves off from history is somewhat different. I would characterize the declining historical awareness of those most influenced by positivism as a development reflecting the sublimation of history *into* science—more specifically, into natural history. Having staked my position on the theoretical insights of Northrop Frye and Hayden White regarding the transmutability of historical conceptions, I judge that the scientific "consolidation" referenced by Lenzer involved the transference of historical meaning into nature. In positivism, the scientific justification that Bacon had drawn from a traditional historical narrative and which was then displaced into secular history in the Enlightenment was beginning to be transposed once again onto evolutionary history. History was not yet being represented as biological evolution; the positivists had only created a social evolutionary picture.

It would remain for various British proponents of evolutionism to first take this final step.

To the extent that the embodiment of history within scientific concepts was also being carried over into more general patterns of political thought in post-revolutionary Europe—that is to say, becoming a marked attribute of the modern consciousness more broadly—this pattern also had important implications for the public fortunes of science. If we assume that public identities abide within historical narratives, then the rendering of history as scientific theory also meant that the public ethos was now linked to science. In such a world, the scientific *nomos* overlaps with the public *nomos*, and the naturalized *cosmos* in which this public identity is grounded becomes an important resource of scientific authority. World-building of this kind, of course, had been the explicit aim of the classical positivists, and this was also the basis of their grandiose priestly aspirations. Having openly declared that their social theories now assumed the authority formerly given to theology in the interpretation of historical meaning, Comte and Saint-Simon also aspired to command proportionate political power as the high priests of this emerging secular culture.

In the closing pages of the last chapter, I argued that this new microcosm/macrocosm identity had the potential to provide a symbolic structure capable of supporting scientific patronage and that its features are key to understanding the offspring ideology of evolutionism. As we return now across the English Channel to consider the revised positivism of Thomas Henry Huxley, these patronage concerns become crucial—most specifically in accounting for the ways in which evolutionism differentiated itself from classical positivism. While Huxley shared the positivist ambition to remake European civilization in the image of science, his formulations of this idea were constrained by his all-consuming drive to professionalize English science. In this role, Huxley could not vouchsafe a form of positivism that threatened to elevate the social sciences above the natural sciences. To concede the scientific priesthood to Comte's English disciples would have been tantamount to surrendering the terms upon which scientific patronage would henceforth be negotiated.

This practical danger explains why Huxley would continuously rebuff the efforts of Comte's English disciples to align him with their cause. His obstinate unwillingness to acknowledge his own ideological kinship with the English positivists reflects his understanding of the practical rhetorical conditions under which this new professional identity needed to take form. More importantly, this conflict illuminates the ideological needs that account for the emergence of evolutionism as a main feature of Huxley's rhetorical career. The adaptive pressures that would inspire positivism's transformation into evolutionism, in other words, were tied up with his perception of the kind of social patronage that was most likely to advance the scientific cause. French positivism might have boosted science's public prestige by creating the world in its image, but to create the world in the image of the *natural* sciences more specifically, as Huxleyan evolutionism would do, would go much further toward securing the position of the natural sciences in this emerging social order.

It will become apparent, once we look more closely at this controversy, that Huxley attacked positivism by exposing its displaced religious meanings. He charged that positivism lacked scientific substance, that it was, as he famously said, merely "Catholicism minus Christianity."[1] This signaled his awareness of the very thing I argued in the last chapter—that a form of the Christian historical consciousness persisted in the French movement. But could Huxley escape similar enticements? If we are right to suppose that these religious residues signified an inescapable need to displace sacred narratives into secular histories, we should expect the same from Huxley. Indeed, what we will find is that Huxley's public opposition to positivism proves this rule. What we find him creating, even as he purported to expose the unscientific character of classical positivism, was merely a Protestantized displacement that was better adapted to his English audiences. Huxley would discredit positivism by saying that it was instead the "agnostic" thinker whose approach to inquiry represented "the essence of science," but a closer inspection will show that agnosticism was merely positivism under a different heading and that this concept was likewise shaped by narrative displacement.[2] If Comte's philosophy was "Catholicism minus Christianity," Huxley's agnosticism, we might say, was "Protestantism minus Christianity." Like his Continental forebears, Huxley continued to treat science as history's apocalypse. He too claimed that modern science was the end and meaning of history, but he adapted this claim to fit a spiritualized empiricism already deeply worked into England's cultural soil. Since an influential Baconian rhetoric had already drawn empiricism into alliance with English Protestantism by regarding the reading of natural facts as a basis for social and religious authority analogous to revelation, the idea of agnosticism already lurked within this culture's religious consciousness—even before Huxley coined this term. English followers of science were already accustomed to regarding the limits to knowledge honored by true science as analogous to the religious limits imposed by the ideal of *sola scriptura*, and this had already made science an actor within the revised historical narrative that Bacon had outlined in his *New Atlantis*. Thus when Huxley now reiterated these traditional epistemological virtues under the heading of agnosticism, he was also sustaining a version of this more traditional historical narrative. To argue for faithfulness to the text of nature was merely a more circumspect way of saying what the British had traditionally believed—that science gave expression to something akin to providence and that it worked to bring about something like the kingdom of God.

This interpretation will set the stage for my argument in the next chapter that the Protestant character of this displaced narrative also coincided with the enlarged symbolic role that evolutionary constructs played in Huxley's worldview. Huxley's more circumspect narrative of history *was* evolution. The most direct way to bring history within the compass of the natural sciences was to make it a product of nature, as evolution. The positivists were on the track of this idea already. In Huxley's able hands evolutionary science became a rhetorical resource—rhetorical Darwinism, an effort to conflate history with science and thereby to give scientists a more complete command of the very symbolic resources by which they had traditionally secured their patronage.

THOMAS HUXLEY AND THE ARCHITECTURE OF ENGLISH SCIENCE

It would be impossible to fully appreciate Huxley's role in the development of evolutionism without first appreciating certain particulars of his personality and life situation. Although he was an important scientist in his own right, he is best remembered by those of us born in the century after his death for his public advocacy of Darwin's theory. However, historians now agree that the popular assumption that his chief significance came from his role as "Darwin's bulldog" is the product of selective memory and a sometimes distorted view of the role he played in the advancement of evolutionary science.[3] Still, the broader picture suggested by this famous sobriquet of a man much consumed by zeal for science is meaningful. Huxley was in some sense the firstborn of a species of scientists that continues to play a recognizable role in formulating science's public self. Like such twentieth-century counterparts as Jacob Bronowski, Carl Sagan, Richard Dawkins, Stephen Jay Gould, and his own grandson, Julian Huxley, to name just a few, he exercised rhetorical talents that were especially suited to the needs of a newly powerful but perennially vulnerable profession. His native literary gifts, evident to anyone who has read even a single page of his prose, were matched only by his enormous appetite for argumentative display.[4] These discursive powers came to the avail of science at an opportune moment in its history, the middle of the nineteenth century, when science had a compelling need to find a new and dynamic public identity.

The picture given by Huxley's biographer, Adrian Desmond, shows a personality constantly given over to these broader ambitions.

> In the Victorian high noon science *was* Professor Huxley. He was its greatest proselytizer; he made it adventurous and dangerous. Nobody held an audience as he did. He tweaked posh lecture-goers with his stiletto stabs at the clergy; he roused plebeian ones with his sea slang and profusion of "paddyisms." He popularized fossils and morals and the meaning of evolution. He became the high priest of a new secular faith.[5]

Some of our more legendary images of Huxley remain in Desmond's depiction of him as an anticlerical warrior and popular interpreter of evolution, but the loftier aspirations that come at the beginning and end of this summation are most critical. Huxley was above all else the great architect of a new scientific identity, and he intended to project this identity upon the world as a "secular faith."

It is the breadth of this ambition that gets lost in folk tales that seem to fence this bulldog up in Darwin's back yard. Huxley's doggish tenacity was more likely to flare up against those who dared trespass upon science's place in English society than against those who called Darwin's work into question—though these were sometimes the same people. For reasons that will become clear in the next chapter, although Huxley had been an evolutionist even before Darwin's *Origin of Species*, he was *never* a Darwinist after it. If it is meaningful to associate him with the theory of natural selection, it is only because Darwin's great achievement symbolizes the scientistic prospects that were so crucial to his perennial campaign to broaden and deepen scientific patronage. Huxley was a rhetorical Darwinist, not a scientific one; he was evolutionism's bulldog rather than Darwin's.

Even before Huxley's career was fully in motion, we are witness to certain inklings of this work of scientific world-building. As he endured a long and painful search for academic employment in his mid-twenties, he signed on as a scientific columnist for the radical weekly *Westminster Review*, where he was positioned to play the role of John the Baptist to the publication of Darwin's *Origin of Species*.[6] Once his discursive genius had been put on display in prominent reviews of Darwin's book, which were published in *Macmillan's* and the *Times* late in 1859 and then in the *Westminster* in the spring of 1860, he had in some sense crossed his own professional Rubicon.[7] Huxley the public voice of science was destined from that time forward to become greater, and Huxley the scientific practitioner less. By middle age he had largely abandoned the laboratory for the scientific pulpit and a crushing weight of administrative duties. Huxley the scientific rhetorician and leader was found to be so much in demand that Huxley the scientist was always in danger of being put out of business.

In the end, despite the precocious beginning of his scientific career—his first publication at age twenty and election to the Royal Society just a few years later—the number of his nontechnical publications would far exceed the number of his scientific ones. Being drawn away from scientific work was something Huxley particularly regretted, but the enormity of his rhetorical talents in this period of enormous need made it inevitable that he would be pressed into service to carry forth the discursive and administrative work that was transforming British science. He came with a mind hardwired for public communication, an astute talent for negotiating difficult and complex problems of adaptation, and the ability to bring every available means of persuasion to bear upon a multitude of tasks and audiences.

The robust richness of Huxley's rhetorical career is easy to miss, especially for those who have been exposed only to those pervasive historical glosses that sum up his career by referencing just a handful of his most agonistic moments in defense of Darwin's work. Such treatments falsely narrow the scope of his public career. Huxley indeed was a controversialist. He entered public life as an angry young man, and this fire burned even in the elder statesman's declining years. But his bottom line was the welfare of science, and this made him wary even of his own disposition to verbal aggression, lest it derail this greater good. His correspondence is dotted with testimony to this struggle, acknowledgments of his love for battle but also of the urgency of a countervailing diplomacy. When the editor John Morley wrote him in 1878, for instance, once again trying to draw him into some unnamed fight, undoubtedly with an eye on profits such as he had reaped from some of Huxley's earlier polemics in the *Fortnightly Review*, the scientist recoiled, declaring that "controversy is as abhorrent to me as gin to a reclaimed drunkard; but oh dear! It would be so nice to squelch that pompous impostor."[8] A decade later, in a feigned rebuke thrown in the direction of Herbert Spencer after a similar effort to stir up his polemical bloodlust, we find Huxley's abiding sense of the overriding public concerns that always stood guard.

Your stimulation of my combative instincts is downright wicked. I will not look at the *Fortnightly* article lest I succumb to temptation. At least not yet. The truth is that these cursed irons of mine, that have always given me so much trouble, will put themselves in the fire, when I am not thinking about them. There are three or four already.[9]

Like addicts of other sorts, Huxley was on and off this wagon, but he was forever cognizant of the dangers of any merely militant approach to the campaign for science. "Battles, like hypotheses, are not to be multiplied beyond necessity," he wrote to the Oxford scientist Ray Lankester, whom he thought needed some "stirring down."[10] And "necessity" for Huxley meant the cause of science.

Even when he did press the attack for the sake of the emerging evolutionary paradigm, this was something done for calculated reasons—with an eye on the larger scientific cause. In one piece of correspondence, we find him offering to fight some public battle over evolution in Darwin's stead so that the shedding of blood would not soil the sainted ethos of the elder scientist. He warned Darwin that, while it would be a small matter for Huxley himself to say "a savage thing," were this great scientist to behave in an ungentlemanly fashion, it would not likely be forgotten.[11] Bare-knuckled brawling had its place, of course, but diplomacy was often more effective than bloodletting. After reviewing some of the work of the German biologist Ernst Haeckel, a radical materialist and vocal proponent of Darwin's work, Huxley cautioned that it would perhaps not be wise to characterize God as mere "gas."

> With respect to the polemic *excursus*, of course, I chuckle over them most sympathetically, and then say how naughty they are! I have done too much of the same sort of thing not to sympathize entirely with you; and I am much inclined to think that it is a good thing for a man, once at any rate in his life, to perform a public war-dance against all sorts of humbug and imposture.
>
> But having satisfied one's love of freedom in this way, perhaps the sooner the war-paint is off the better. It has no virtue except as a sign of one's own frame of mind and determination, and when that is once known, is little better than a distraction.[12]

The higher "virtue" that Huxley had in mind was restraint. His own views were no less radical than Haeckel's, but his abiding desire to see science win out required a measured response to opponents. What will strike any reader who has sampled the whole of his rhetorical output or who has read commentary on this aspect of his public life as it can be traced through his personal correspondence and the reflections of his contemporaries, is his remarkable willingness, one might even say his principled determination, to make his naturalistic positions palatable to the most unlikely audiences. The controversialist merely tries to best opponents in public debate, and this was often Huxley's aim as well, but as we look in on his day-to-day activities of writing and speaking, we are more likely to find gentlemanly engagement, than we are to find antagonistic debate.

Contentious moments often brought out Huxley's rhetorical brilliance, and this provided fodder for the tabloid journalism of his day. Desmond is certainly right to say that he drew blood with "serrated teeth" and that he "harassed" and "harangued" England's elites as he paraded the most radical implications of evolution before popular audiences.[13] But it is in consideration of the more staid aspects of his public personality that we can begin to appreciate the true significance of his career as a rhetorical Darwinist. The visiting American historian, John Fiske, found him to be a man of "tenderness and exquisite delicacy." "I never saw such magnificent eyes in my life. His eyes are black, and his face expresses an eager burning intensity. And by Jove, what pleasure it is to meet such a clean-cut mind. It is like Saladin's sword which cut through the cushion."[14]

Darwin recognized how superbly equipped Huxley was to face down the storms that greeted his book, but those who actually read what Huxley had to say about Darwin's theory itself will be surprised by how tepid his responses are. It was his desire to win a fair hearing for *Darwin* (not *Darwinism*) that put Huxley in motion. As a scientific practitioner, Darwin symbolized something of greater importance than the mechanism of evolution he had proposed. His effort to account for life's origins and development on strictly naturalistic grounds signaled the universal reach that science was destined to achieve once free to follow its own course.

To stand up for Darwin was to advance the same cause that Huxley was undertaking in his extensive efforts to design the institutional and curricular reforms that were breaking down the fortress doors of the Oxbridge establishment and also putting science in on the ground floor of the new redbrick universities that were fast springing up to cater to the needs of England's exploding middle class—Huxley's middle class. It would be fair to say, as Cyril Bibby does, that Huxley had the opportunity in the course of his career "to inquire into and recommend upon the organisation of almost every university and college in the country."[15] Even the ancient institutions at Cambridge and Oxford, under the intellectual and social governance of what Robert Lowe once called a "clerical gerontocracy," were seeking the "plebian" Huxley's council by the time he reached middle age.[16] Huxley's pivotal role in such reforms is evidenced by the fact that one whole volume of the nine books making up his *Selected Works* is comprised of essays on education. Indirectly, at least, this is also a concern of the two volumes in this set devoted to religious topics. Huxley's assaults against orthodoxy never represented an antireligious campaign so much as an anti-institutional one, his unceasing protest against the powerful hold of the English clergy on British education.

His devotion to this broader cause undoubtedly reflected the frustrations of his own youth. When he sailed into Devonport in October of 1850, returning from a four-year tour of duty in the British navy as assistant surgeon and naturalist, he discovered that he had already earned scientific fame in absentia. This was for a paper on sea medusae and polyps mailed to the Royal Society from his cramped quarters aboard the HMS *Rattlesnake* as it surveyed the coasts of Australia and New Guinea. Before another year was out, the society had elected him a fellow at merely twenty-six years of age. But he could find no work. Huxley had in some sense committed himself to a profession that did not yet exist—or at least one that was slowly passing from one life into the next. He had come of age at the tail end of a period when science was still dominated by clergymen and gentleman amateurs and still sanctioned by the worldviews and normative frameworks these privileged groups upheld. This was an intellectual culture that had been able to sustain scientific inquiry for two hundred years, and it had functioned well enough for Huxley's seniors, men like Richard Owen with Tory patronage, and gentlemen scientists like Darwin who drew upon a substantial inheritance. But it made almost no room for middle-class aspirants lacking similar connections or financial means.

By midcentury new resources were becoming available that would broaden and deepen scientific activity in England as power and money rapidly shifted out of the pockets of the upper classes and into the hands of capitalists and industrialists, but science had not yet positioned itself to benefit from this transformation. In 1850, Huxley found himself lost in the shuffle and was forced to suffer through four exasperating years before securing a scientific position. Seized by desperation and depression, he had even contemplated abandoning science for a naval career. "To attempt to live by any scientific pursuit is a farce," he complained in 1851 to the fiancée he had left behind in Sydney.

> Nothing but what is absolutely practical will go down in England. A man of science may earn great distinction, but not bread. He will get invitations to all sorts of dinners and conversaziones, but not enough for income to pay his cab fare. A man of science in these times is like an Esau who sells his birthright for a mess of pottage.[17]

But the same determination that kept him from succumbing to despair also inspired the lifelong vigilance of his efforts to reconstruct English society in the image of science. Not content with the personal success he finally achieved by his appointment to the Royal School of Mines in 1854, Huxley labored without ceasing to secure the creation of scientific institutions that could control their own destiny, that would neither play handmaid to noblemen and clergy, nor sign on as the technological underlings of the emerging industrial class.

CATHOLICISM MINUS CHRISTIANITY

The English emphasis on "what is absolutely practical" brings us closer to the kind of threat Huxley saw in positivism. In 1851 he would have blamed this attitude on an old guard that was intellectually removed from science and still drew what inspiration they had for it from the surviving vestiges of a Baconian instrumentalism. But to emphasize again a point made by Joseph Ben-David, the tendency to identify science with its real-world applications is a disposition that arises from scientism in all its forms.[18] The enlarged value that scientism attributes to the scientific enterprise typically arises from faith in its possibilities of application, and this remained true for positivists as much as for those who had once found inspiration in Bacon's *New Atlantis*. Comte had preached a form of scientism that coincided with the general interests of the new scientific professionals, but its sociological blueprint threatened to perpetuate science's servitude. Indeed, in one respect the social order envisioned in positivism was a greater threat to science's prospects than the old clerical and aristocratic order. The classical model of education that was still held in place by England's elites at least did not claim to have the authority of science at its back. Positivism did. Comte regarded himself as a scientific reader and interpreter of the text of human evolution (in a broadly historical sense), and he claimed that the science of sociology he was ushering in would soon order (and therefore regulate) all knowledge. Sociology was to become the science of sciences, and therefore, in Huxley's view, a generalized science poised to devour its own children.

Notably, it was during his bitter struggle to find scientific employment that Huxley first became intimate with England's leading positivists and first recognized the threat that lay in certain tendencies of their thought. He was drawn into this circle by Herbert Spencer and the physician turned radical publisher, John Chapman, who was scouting out talent for the *Westminster Review*. Huxley was quite willing to enlist his gift for letters, at a return of nearly a guinea per page, by writing reviews that would aid Chapman's campaign to "sap and undermine" the reigning orthodoxy, but he quickly came to blows with G. H. Lewes, whose book promoting Comte's philosophy he smashed for its many scientific errors.[19] Lewes, a playwright, actor, and journalist then on the verge of eloping with Chapman's close associate, Mary Ann Evans (George Eliot), shared Huxley's zeal for popularizing science and for asserting its authority above all other enterprises. What he could not appreciate was Huxley's sensitivity to the ways in which public conceptions of science also tended to shape the fate of scientific practice. Like other English followers of Comte, Lewes was an amateur interested in science largely as a weapon in the arsenal of political radicalism. Huxley was certainly sympathetic to such uses of scientific authority, but not if they threatened to compromise the interests of the scientific professionals he was sworn to defend. His ambition was to make the voice of scientism the voice of the natural scientist and to do this by his own example and on his own terms, as a scientific man of letters. Moving in the same elite literary circles as people like Spencer, Eliot, Lewes, and Chapman was attractive to him because these associations gave science an aura of the avant-garde, but this was a means for the advancement of science, not an end.[20]

In one sense, the English positivists were Huxley's peer group. In spite of some very public squabbles, he always remained at home with them in society. They were, after all, fellow despisers of the established interests that had once locked him out, London's radical young Turks who imbibed similar expectant dreams of a new world and a new religion soon to arise above the rubble of a crumbling Anglican edifice. But Huxley always remained noncommittal and aloof. In part this may be put down to his natively adversarial bent of mind, one sometimes tempted, as George Eliot described it, "to prefer *paradox* and *antagonism* to the truth" in spite of its "conscious and ultimate" scientific aims.[21] Huxley would have accounted for this as a matter of personal devotion to Goethe's principle of active doubt, "*Thätige skepsis*."[22] Nothing was immune, not even the doctrine of evolution with which he was destined to be so closely linked in posterity, and so it is not difficult to comprehend his cautious disdain for the positivist ideology.

Huxley's active displays against positivism were always prompted by the efforts of its leaders to link their views with his, and it is this perceived ideological kinship that also makes these clashes so illuminating. Comte's philosophy was, for Huxley, a scientific heresy, and as writers such as Lester Kurtz and Kai Erickson have shown, the institutional attraction of campaigns launched against internal deviance of this kind lies in their ability to achieve subtle differentiations.[23] A clash of similar worldviews is an opportunity for ideological clarification, and this makes Huxley's efforts to symbolically divorce science from positivism particularly illuminating. These attacks, we might say, provide an inverted reflection of evolutionism.

What this will also show is that evolutionism represents a return to the more indigenous historical consciousness of the Protestant movement that Bacon had already mapped onto science. Of course it was this same Baconian ideology that Huxley was combating on another front, in his many attacks on the clergy and the educational structure they upheld. It was this traditional proto-scientism that had kept this establishment in place as science's overseer, but its deep roots in the British consciousness also made it a rhetorical resource that Huxley could ill afford to pass over. This meant that what he would soon be calling agnosticism was in fact a more indigenous version of positivism that proposed, in contrast with that of Saint-Simon and Comte, a historical vision that had special appeal for England's predominantly Protestant culture.

While it would be fair to say that the controversy over positivism pitted one recondite circle of intellectuals against another, the recognizable breadth of public interest in this French movement certainly enlarged the stakes for Huxley. In the introduction to his history of English positivism, *The Religion of Humanity*, T. R. Wright acknowledges that his project became a "massive undertaking" once he discovered that "nearly all the major British thinkers of the second half of the nineteenth century" had studied Comte. But in spite of the breadth of this fashionable interest, England failed to sustain a developed positivist movement.[24] If this failure reflected any effort of active opposition, Huxley certainly would have been the figure blamed by positivists. Having delved into Comte's work in the early 1850s after discovering John Stuart Mill's discussions of Comte's philosophy in his *Logic*, he had come away with an unfavorable impression. The "mine of wisdom" he had been promised by his friend Mr. Henfry, he would later say, turned up "veins of ore few and far between, and the rock so apt to run to mud, that one incurred the risk of being intellectually smothered in the working."[25] Although he did confess some interest in Comte's sociological speculations, Huxley rejected the positivist's take on the philosophy of the physical sciences and his apparently weak understanding of current scientific knowledge.

By some time around 1868, Huxley seems to have realized that a more deliberate effort to divorce himself from the Comtians was needed. His objections of fifteen years before had been occasioned only by the amateurism of Lewes' book. Pained by Huxley's criticism of him as a mere "book man," Lewes thought to mend the rift by brushing up on his zoology, but this was not the real crux of the problem.[26] Even if the positivists had fully comprehended what was going on in the biological field, their center of gravity was social science, and this made them competitors. Now at the height of his career and bearing much of the weight of the scientific cause on his shoulders, Huxley was actively determined to drive every dilettante from the field of battle. But he was also no less determined than the positivists to situate science in the public mind as the true engine of civilized progress, and this made Comte's personal moral failings an issue for the Victorian constituents he hoped to win over. Émile Littré's biography of his mentor had filled Huxley with "a feeling of sheer disgust and contempt for the man who could treat a noble-hearted woman who had saved his life and his reason, as Comte treated his wife."[27] Had his own friendships not been at stake, Huxley undoubtedly would have also cited Lewes' adulterous relationship with George Eliot as evidence of positivism's moral depravity. Such objections were more than just personal. If he hoped to get English society to recognize that science embodied those ideals that had formerly clustered around the term "providence" but were now being transferred over to "progress," he would also need to create science in the image of English society and to distance it form the more relaxed mores of the French.[28]

Such fears were accentuated by the fact that positivism seemed to be gaining position in the public arena. Around this time, Charles Kingsley complained as he wrote to fellow Broad Churchman F. D. Maurice that the "very air seems full of Comtism. Certainly the press is."[29] "It is Positivism— of a loose maundering kind," he wrote concerning a book on pantheism by the head of a Wesleyan training college in 1871, "which is really growing among our young men. When Huxley proclaims himself a disciple of Kant and Berkeley, they think in their hearts, then he is a retrograde dreamer— 'almost as bad as that fool of a Christian, Kingsley.' "[30]

To make matters worse, Huxley had learned while dining at George Eliot's house with the positivist historians Frederic Harrison and Edward Beesly that these followers of Comte measured the worth of all scientific research in terms of its social outcomes.[31] Should the positivist program gain public support and patronage, he could well imagine theoretical and empirical research programs falling subject to the whims of a new oligarchy of sociologists and historians. There were already signs that these amateur overlords were beginning to mobilize. Richard Congreve, destined to become one of positivism's high priests, had resigned his tutorship at Oxford's Wadham College in 1854 so that he could prepare for these holy orders by studying medicine. Twelve years later he founded the London Positivist Society, and in 1870, a Positivist school.[32]

It is impossible to gauge how seriously Huxley may have taken the prospects of the positivist movement itself, but it was certainly clear to him that its ascendancy threatened the autonomy of the scientific enterprise. This is a concern reflected in his treatments of other competing enterprises of inquiry as well. Although he was happy to give a dedication speech in 1880 in support of a new technical college being opened in Birmingham by the industrialist Josiah Mason, he also used this occasion to reiterate the primacy of "pure" over applied science—lest the new industrialist powerbrokers should become errant scientific policymakers.

> What people call applied science is nothing but the application of pure science to particular classes of problems. It consists of deductions from those general principles, established by reasoning and observation, which constitute pure science. No one can safely make these deductions until he has a firm grasp of the principles; and he can obtain that grasp only by personal experience of the operations of observation and of reasoning on which they are founded.[33]

This characterization of technical application's dependency upon "pure" science is a bit overdrawn. Technological advances, in fact, typically had not followed from basic research, as Robert Gilpin has pointed out. They had emerged in parallel with theoretical science, and had only begun to become dependent upon it in the nineteenth century with the rise of the German system of scientific research and education.[34] Huxley undoubtedly knew this as well, but such "boundary-work," as Thomas Gieryn has called the social construction of such distinctions as this, could also secure the position of basic research atop an epistemic hierarchy.[35]

All threats to the autonomy of the natural sciences had to be kept in check. From 1864 until 1892, much of this was managed from the inside through an informal interest group whose members called themselves the "X-Club." Along with Huxley, the other eight members, all prominent figures in some realm of the new science, were concerned, as Ruth Barton describes it, with the whole "infrastructure of research—that is with libraries, journals, indexes to the literature, equipment, collection and publication of systematic data—and with the status and dignity of science."[36] They conspired to situate their own in the various presidencies of scientific societies and vital government committees that determined science's fate. None from the applied sciences were included in the X-Club, and Huxley and friends fought especially hard to ensure that the Royal Society would not be "exploited by enterprising commercial gents who make their profit out of the application of science."[37] The technical professional class that was also on the rise was trying to help itself by making applicability the criterion by which patronage would be doled out, and this was merely a different version of the same threat that Huxley had recognized in positivist social science.

Huxley could never dare to budge from the inflexible principle that pure science must never take a secondary position behind the technical knowledge that was driving industrialization, behind the supreme science of sociology that the positivists sought to elevate, and certainly not in subordination to the traditions of classical education—an issue over which he would cross swords with Matthew Arnold.[38] In spite of his private sympathy for all of these enterprises and his willingness to let science feed upon industrial wealth, no compromise of scientific independence could ever be vouchsafed. The danger of scientific servitude was too well known to him from the earliest stage of his career, from his fitful struggles for position within a scientific establishment that had purchased its power in collusion with nobles and Anglican elites.

Because of this, and in spite of obvious points in favor of the positivist position, Huxley stuck to his policy of public denial with unwavering constancy, upholding his claim that positivism was a scientific pretender and completely unrelated to the movement he led. Such vociferous efforts of demarcation freed him to advance similar ideas without putting himself in any danger of creating an apparent alliance. Having fixed in the public consciousness the understanding that his own version of scientific naturalism was the one true basis of science, Huxley could advance scientism on his own terms.

This work of rhetorical demarcation began in earnest late in 1868 when Huxley was invited by an Edinburgh clergyman to give a Sunday evening address on a non-theological topic. The main purpose of this lecture, which he entitled "The Physical Basis of Life," was to declare victory for philosophical naturalism in the arena of biology, and in doing so to envision materialism's destined victories to come. In essence, in other words, he was making a positivist argument. But on the eve of this lecture—at least as he sets the scene in the text of that speech—Huxley ran across a newspaper report on a recent address by William Thomson, the archbishop of York, "On the Limits of Physical Inquiry." Recognizing this as a likely attack on his own naturalistic stance, he was even more dismayed to discover that the distinguished cleric had identified Auguste Comte as the "founder" of this "New Philosophy." Huxley saw fit, as an aside to the main subject of the next day's lecture, to challenge this part of the archbishop's address.

> Now, so far as I am concerned, the most reverend prelate might dialecti- cally hew M. Comte in pieces, as a modern Agag, and I should not attempt to stay his hand. In so far as my study of what specially characterises the Positive Philosophy has led me, I find therein little or nothing of any sci- entific value, and a great deal which is as thoroughly antagonistic to the very essence of science as anything in ultramontane Catholicism. In fact, M. Comte's philosophy, in practice, might be compendiously described as Catholicism *minus* Christianity.[39]

It is easy to imagine Huxley's motive for interjecting this attack into a speech that was mainly intended to advance a materialistic assault on the last remnants of vitalism in natural philosophy. The physicalism that he himself was preaching was already widely associated with positivism, as the archbishop had suggested, and so to let those comments stand would have been to concede such an alliance. Positivism, of course, was *not* "thoroughly antagonistic to the very essence of science," in the methodological sense in which Huxley would elsewhere define that essence. It was hostile only to the rival social philosophy that Huxley regarded as better disposed than Comte's "ultramontane Catholicism" to dictate what scientists could and could not do at the parish level.

The good archbishop had made no apparent mention of these applied aspects of positive social philosophy nor of any of its other notorious pecu- liarities; his apparent purpose had merely been to discuss the general meta- physical skepticism of the emerging scientific culture, a skepticism that just happened to have its most familiar representation in the popular positivism of his day. His had been no more than factual observations, with which Huxley should have had little cause to disagree. Huxley's scientific natural- ism, after all, was virtually indistinguishable from the epistemology of the positivists, and thus, superficially at least, his response was a bit of a red herring. But by drawing the attention of his Scottish Presbyterian audience to those papist features of positivism it was sure to find repellant, he also drew attention away from what he shared with Comte's disciples. By attending only to the "Catholic" residues of positivism while remaining silent on his more essential agreement with its core epistemological stance, Huxley could maintain at least the appearance that his own view of the limits of knowledge did not place him in the same ideological enclosure.

The "Catholicism *minus* Christianity" charge was particularly effective, "a *mot*," as Sydney Eisen has described it, "which would forever haunt the English positivists."[40] The February 1869 publication of Huxley's speech in the *Fortnightly Review* put the periodical into seven editions, though probably because of the radical materialistic stance the speech gave voice to rather than because of these comments about positivism.[41] Nevertheless, its wide distribution publicized Huxley's opposition to Comte's philosophy. This was a hard knock for a group that saw itself as the new voice of science. Edward Beesly, complaining that positivism was already "struggling against heavy odds to obtain a fair hearing," bemoaned the fact that this criticism came from a man of such high scientific standing. "From almost everyone else this would not matter. But from a man of your eminence and known emancipation it amounts to something like putting Comte on the *Index Expurgatorius*."[42]

Richard Congreve, the Oxford don recently turned positivist high priest, rang in with a similar protest. In an article-length response in the *Fortnightly Review*, he complained that Huxley's comments "are hardly worthy of their place, and would have come better from one of our débonnaire literary oracles than from a high scientific authority on whom rests a certain responsibility." Congreve offered various speculations that might account for Huxley's dismissive attitude, including the charge that he simply had not read Comte and that the Edinburgh barb was nothing more than "an impatient utterance based on a wholly imperfect and insufficient acquaintance with the subject of which Mr. Huxley is speaking."[43] This was an unwise accusation to raise against a voracious reader like Huxley, who quickly put it to rest in a published response heavily lathered with long quotations from Comte in the original French.[44]

But Congreve was probably closer to the truth when he called Huxley's response "the judgment of a biologist penetrated with the importance of his own subject, and full of respect for the preliminary sciences, but bounding his horizon with his own science; either not allowing that there are higher sciences, or not caring for them."[45] This touched the sore spot. If sociology was indeed a science, it would be "higher" than biology, a science that, by rendering a comprehensive understanding of human nature, could be expected to rule over all human affairs—including the activities of a "preliminary" science like biology. Huxley was ready to admit that a science of human nature would have such a hierarchical position, but he was unwilling to relinquish this domain to powers outside the control of the corps of professionalized laborers he was raising up. His personal reflections show that he in fact shared the positivists' evolutionary view of history as something destined to "organize itself into a coherent system, embracing human life and the world as one harmonious whole."[46] But to allow an outside movement to theorize this evolutionary mechanism would also allow it to determine the place of the natural sciences within this emerging world order—and that he could not countenance.

In 1861 he had already outlined a similar social evolutionary vision in a lecture, "On the Study of Biology," given on his home turf at the South Kensington Museum. The social sciences in this historical scheme were merely immature sciences that were destined to come of age only in the future, when they would be "merged into natural history."

> In strict logic it may be hard to object to this course, because no one can doubt that the rudiments and outlines of our own mental phenomena are traceable among the lower animals. They have their economy and their polity, and if, as is always admitted, the polity of bees and the commonwealth of wolves fall within the purview of the biologist proper, it becomes hard to say why we should not include therein human affairs, which in so many cases resemble those of the bees in zealous getting, and are not without a certain parity in the proceedings of the wolves.

Clearly already aware of the threat posed by the positivists' alternative narrative, Huxley went on to remind his audience that biologists have thus far merely "allowed that province of biology to become autonomous" which "has constituted itself under the head of Sociology." But naturalism dictates that the social sciences should ultimately fall within the compass of biology. The social realm is the scientist's "kingdom which he has only voluntarily forsaken" and would one day fully reclaim.[47]

Protestantism minus Christianity

In light of the universal claims that Huxley was making in speeches like this, it is not surprising that the English positivists would have coveted his blessing. This emerging figurehead of science shared their vision of a future in which the scope of science would expand without ceasing until it encompassed even the human world. Comte, of course, would have rejected Huxley's supposition that the social sciences were destined to be subsumed within the natural sciences since he believed that each stage in the growth of science was distinct from preceding ones and that the methods of the social sciences were therefore destined to be qualitatively different from those of their natural-scientific forebears. But in the aftermath of Comte's death, as Ernst Cassirer has noted, many of his disciples had fallen back into the kind of reductionism that we see in Huxley, and this made Huxley a more sympathetic figure.[48] In the end, it was only Huxley's zeal for the professional fortunes of the natural sciences that stood between him and this group.

Even in his retirement, the positivists were still trying to call him out on this count, and he even managed to acknowledge his agreement with the movement's most fundamental premises as he opened his "Apologetic Irenicon" of 1889. But a writer as clever as Huxley could easily diffuse the significance of such a concession. He did this from the beginning of the essay simply through the distraction of sarcasm. "I hasten to stretch forth my hand for the olive-branch which my courteous opponent holds out," he asserted, referring to the positivist leader Frederic Harrison, "and I assure him of my readiness to 'kiss and be friends,' at least in that symbolic fashion which is alone possible to male Britons." This mocking agreement set the stage for an essay that buried whatever peace it proposed to make in calling itself an irenicon beneath a strident scientific apologetic. The terms of peace offered by Harrison demanded an untenable "cession of territory" that Huxley "considered to form part of the general domain of scientific thought." What positivists regarded as the realm of natural science was in fact "nothing but a sort of Hinterland to the settlement founded by Auguste Comte."[49] Once having brought Comte back into the forefront, Huxley could go back to his old tricks, accentuating the Catholic trappings of the movement by playing up its "resemblance to the Papistical model," which had worked to such great effect for him two decades before. Huxley would miss no opportunity to draw this connection. What he gives with one hand as praise for Harrison's "missionary zeal" he takes back with language that simultaneously draws attention to the movement's religious undercurrents. Ignoring Harrison's assurances that the movement had disavowed the explicitly Catholic linkages in Comte's later works, Huxley made sure his readers would not forget them when he described his positivist friend as a "catechist" addressing the "professed catechumen."[50] The many paragraphs carried forth through satirical play are punctuated by others that manifest another trademark of Huxleyan eloquence, flourishes of righteous indignation so poignant in imagery and phraseology that the breathtaken reader is given no opportunity to reflect upon Huxley's own clerical posturing.

> It is this monstrous religious abortion, with its adoration of an animistic idol, nowise more respectable for being the work of man's brain instead of his hands; with all its baleful consequences of spiritual tyranny and slavish social "organization," which I have done my best, at intervals, during the last quarter of a century, to separate from everything that has a right to the name of scientific thought or of wholesome ethical aspiration; and it would appear that even the epigoni of Comte have, at last, come round to my side.[51]

Were we to lift this last passage from its context and alter the language that specifically signals its Comtian subject matter, it might easily be mistaken for a theological attack upon that other threat to the Victorian establishment, the rising Catholicism of the Oxford movement. Huxley's attack purports to contrast science against pseudoscience, but by comparing the latter to Catholicism he inevitably aligns the former with Protestantism. The same parallel between false science and Catholic idolatry that Bacon once exploited to such great effect is very much alive here. So also is the old alliance between empirical science and Christian virtue. It is positivism's blind imitation of Catholicism that Huxley strikes at most forcefully, but he could not merely by virtue of superior wit or righteous abhorrence escape the Protestant orbit of his native culture. In terms of the Geertzian premise that I invoked in chapter 1, we would put this down to a merely imitative constraint. If cultures can develop only by reworking the materials they inherit from their forebears, we would expect something similar from Huxley. A rhetorical perspective supports a similar view. In principle, those who give voice to scientism will assert that progress moves in a rectilinear fashion within the vacuum of scientific objectivity, uninfluenced except by the inertia of reason and fact, but if scientism is to have public support it must always bend, wittingly or unwittingly, to the gravitational pull of culture. In Huxley's case, we have reason to suppose that some intentionality was also involved. His preoccupation with the concrete work of establishing science's position within the new institutional and social order that was arising in Victorian England made him mindful of what successful rhetorical actors always recognize, namely that such ends can only be achieved, as Donald C. Bryant famously described this art, by "adjusting ideas to people and people to ideas."[52] Even if Huxley had not been inclined to imitate the themes of England's Protestant culture simply because he swam in its waters, his desire to adapt his messages to an audience of potential patrons (many of whom were still believing Christians) invited conscious deliberation and strategizing of this sort.

A contemporaneous rhetorical pattern is the one observed in John Angus Campbell's elucidations of the similar generic ancestry that Darwin's writing finds in the traditions of British natural theology.[53] In spite of the revolutionary character of Darwin's position, its presentation manifested a similar conservation of cultural energy and mass by drawing from the "specific heritage" of natural theology, the "language, *topoi*, maxims, problems, and conventions of reasoning" that this great scientist shared with his readers. Darwin transformed this rhetorical tradition by "reinventing it."[54] Huxley was doing much the same, not only in the discursive arena of scientific writing per se, but also in the broader arena of public discourse in which science was reinventing its cultural identity. If Darwin was the new Bishop Paley of the evolutionary age, Huxley was its new Bacon.

As I suggested earlier, one act of rhetorical invention that manifests this was Huxley's coining of the term "agnostic" in 1869. When Huxley declared himself to be one who does not know, in contradistinction to the many "gnostics" around him who thought they did, he was invoking one side of a dialectical pattern already favorable to the Protestant mind. The Protestant exclusion of all that lies outside the limits of revelation had been a move of the same kind, a decision to err on the side of caution lest the complex multivocality of an alternative authority based in Catholic tradition should undermine orthodoxy. The reformers had thought that theological minimalism of this kind would keep the church from sliding back into its old errors, and Bacon's application of this principle to empirical science promised the same benefit. True empiricism would ensure that science remained true to revelation. So long as inquiry remained within the text of nature, the old Baconian doctrine had supposed, it was not possible for it to overstep its reach. Of course, it was Huxley's precise intention to undermine the religious orthodoxy that this principle once promised to sustain; even as he was appealing to this traditional religious premise in an effort to enlarge public support for science, he was also working to pin the Protestant establishment in a corner of its own making.

My supposition that the limits of knowledge proposed by the term agnostic would have resonated with the Baconian consciousness of science's traditional patrons is corroborated by Bernard Lightman's argument that the model for Huxley's agnostic position was the influential 1858 Bampton lecture of the high churchman Henry Mansel, *The Limits of Religious*

Thought.[55] Drawing from the Kantian epistemology that had made its way into England via the Scottish philosopher Sir William Hamilton, Mansel concluded that knowledge of God was impossible through natural means and could only come through the direct revelation of sacred Scripture. Huxley, who had also himself been under Hamilton's spell since his youth, instantly recognized a form of philosophical skepticism similar to his own, one that promised to forever bar clergymen from speculating about nature. He joked in a letter to Charles Lyell that the churchman's position reminded him of the drunken character in William Hogarth's painting, "Canvassing for Votes," "who is sawing through the signpost at the other party's public-house, forgetting he is sitting at the other end of it."[56] But the fact that this rendering of Huxley's own position appealed to a conservative Anglican like Mansel signaled the rhetorical potential that agnosticism might have as a demarcating strategy. Despite Huxley's belief that Mansel had sawed off the very branch that supported the weight of Christian truth, the fact that the churchman had so successfully aligned his philosophical skepticism with orthodoxy suggested how scientific naturalism might appeal to the same flock. As Lightman puts this, agnosticism was not the opposite, but rather the "mirror image" of the theological rationale that had formerly sustained science.[57] The Baconian scientific ideology had already established the scrupulous reading of nature's text as a form of Christian obedience. Interpreted now in this Kantian framework, the reading of nature's text was no longer capable of producing theological insights, but cultural habit ensured that its scientific interpretation would continue to resonate with traditional notions of epistemic morality.

Shortly after the death of his firstborn son Noel in 1860, Huxley offered up one of his most poignant representations of this Protestant ethic in a letter to Charles Kingsley. The grieving father rejected his clergyman friend's hope of an afterlife reunion with this lost child on the grounds that such prospects lay beyond the reach of knowledge, but he advanced this point by invoking another premise of Christian faith.

> Science seems to me to teach in the highest and strongest manner the great truth which is embodied in the Christian conception of entire surrender to the will of God. Sit down before fact as a little child, be prepared to give up every preconceived notion, follow humbly wherever and to whatever abysses nature leads, or you shall learn nothing. I have only begun to learn content and peace of mind since I have resolved at all risks to do this.[58]

The characteristic agnostic rejection of all truth claims that lie beyond the reach of fact is plainly in evidence here, but so also are the Protestant sensibilities of the religious culture that Kingsley represented. Had he been explaining this ethic to one of his more like-minded friends, it would have undoubtedly shed these New Testament trappings for the more pantheistic language of Carlyle and Goethe that he had imbibed in his youth.[59] But because he shared the belief of his friend John Morley that the supernaturalism which "stirs men first" would in the "later fulness of years and wider experience of life draw them to a wise and not inglorious acquiescence in Naturalism," he could continue to use the language of orthodoxy in good conscience.[60] And so the hermeneutical ethic of Protestantism remained even as he frankly shifted its basis into nature.

With Huxley's emergence in the late 1860s, the need to link scientific mores with traditional Protestant ones became more pressing. His election at age forty-three as president of the British Association for the Advancement of Science (BAAS) in 1869 signaled the fact that Tory control was giving way to a more autonomous scientific order, much as the positivists had envisioned. But Huxley was too shrewd a political thinker to allow this to be seen as a victory for the Comtians, who were certain to demand a share of this new power, or as a rebuff to the traditional interests that were nervously letting go of control.[61] Science still depended upon the goodwill of the old order, and the Protestant nuances of the agnostic label he had now adopted reflected this balancing act. It was a term that enabled him to express the epistemological exclusivism of positivism upon which this newfound autonomy depended, yet without calling himself a "positivist." It was also a term suggesting an intellectual neutrality that resonated with the Baconian sensibilities that still infused the consciousness of science's traditional patrons. To call the true followers of science agnostics was to say that they abjured those idols of the mind that had formerly established science's moral kinship with the Christian faith.

In this regard it should not surprise us to find that it was before several of England's leading churchmen that the new BAAS president first used this term in 1869. Its invention was occasioned by his participation in the Metaphysical Society, a symposium of English intellectuals organized by James Knowles, the editor of the *Contemporary Review*, which later became *Nineteenth Century*. Knowles' ambition was to bring together men of diverse opinion in the hope that some rapprochement might be achieved between traditional viewpoints and the various new "-isms" that were radicalizing London society. Huxley, along with John Tyndall and Leslie Stephen, had been invited to represent the perspective of the new science in these meetings, and this brought him into polite dialogue with religious conservatives such as Cardinal Manning, the Duke of Argyll, William Gladstone, and, perhaps most notably, William Thomson, the Anglican bishop whose lecture had roused Huxley's anti-Comtian outburst just a few months before.[62] From 1869 until 1880, the "Metaphysicals" met nine times a year to present and discuss papers on all the leading philosophical and religious issues of the day. "Every variety of philosophical and theological opinion was represented," Huxley would later recall, and initially this had caused him some "uneasy feelings." All of his "colleagues were -ists of one sort or another" and he was "without a rag of a label to cover himself with." If natural philosophers were to stand among these others, they would need their own identity, and it was this inventive pressure that inspired his selection of "the appropriate title of 'agnostic.' "[63]

If Huxley did not take a label of his own, he could not forever fend off the attempts of others to do this for him—the very danger he had faced the previous fall in Edinburgh. In his first essay-length attack on positivism that same year, he complained of his constant "irritation" in finding "M. Comte put forward as a representative of scientific thought; and to observe that writers whose philosophy had its legitimate parent in Hume, or in themselves, were labeled 'Comtists' or 'Positivists' by public writers, even in spite of vehement protests to the contrary." Huxley observed that it had already cost John Stuart Mill "hard rubbings to get that label off," though he neglected to mention that Mill had once openly identified his philosophy of science with Comte's, and Herbert Spencer was "ready to tear away skin and all, rather than let it stick." Worst of all, alluding now to the Edinburgh incident, his "own turn might come next; and therefore, when an eminent prelate the other day gave currency and authority to the popular confusion," Huxley made sure to show that Hume had been the true author of this "New Philosophy."[64]

By asserting that the new scientific philosophy predated Comte's and had risen up in fact from British soil, Huxley could weaken the prophetic authority of positivism and distract attention from the similarity that his own notion of scientific agnosticism shared with this movement. English observers were unlikely to notice that the idea of agnosticism was, *via negativa*, the very idea expressed by the term positivism. What made positivism "positive" was its devotion to an ideal of high empiricism that tolerated only the entry of such claims into the realm of genuine knowledge as could show a solid factual basis. But the term agnostic was merely a negative expression of the same limits. The positivists claimed to work on the inside of a circle that delimited certain knowledge from all else, but so did the agnostics. If "positive" facts filled a glass half full of knowledge, the label agnostic merely referenced its empty half. In this regard, Huxley might have just as easily called his position "negativism," but this even more obvious inversion would have drawn unwanted attention to the fundamental similarity of these two positions. The limits of knowledge that positivism imposed and which Huxley had no desire of abandoning were still in effect, but by expressing the same notion under this alternative heading, he gained a sense of neutrality that enabled him to pursue world-building aspirations like those of the positivists even as he appealed to an abiding Baconian sense of science's epistemic modesty.

The enduring and now more familiar association between agnosticism and religious skepticism was undoubtedly part of Huxley's plan for the term. But in its more immediate historical context, it makes just as much sense to interpret this neologism, as both Adrian Desmond and Bernard Lightman have done, as a symbolic act designed to rescue necessary alliances with the Anglican hierarchy that Huxley could ill afford to abandon.[65] If "agnosticism has no creed—in the sense of a statement or conclusions either positive or negative, which the agnostic must hold," as Huxley would write toward the end of his life, then science could remain, as he had privately asserted it ought to, in league with the "radicals," even while it seemed to be the ally of more traditional interests.[66] Huxley was clearly striving to maintain this dual significance even in his first volley against positivism. In "The Physical Basis of Life," his Edinburgh lecture, he had seemed to take hold of materialism with one hand while pushing it back with the other.

> Past experience leads me to be tolerably certain that, when the propositions I have just placed before you are accessible to public comment and criticism, they will be condemned by many zealous persons, and perhaps by some few of the wise and thoughtful. I should not wonder if "gross and brutal materialism" were the mildest phrase applied to them in certain quarters. And, most undoubtedly, the terms of the propositions are distinctly materialistic. Nevertheless two things are certain; the one, that I hold the statements to be substantially true: the other, that I, individually, am no materialist, but, on the contrary, believe materialism to involve grave philosophical error.[67]

What Huxley was pronouncing here was the familiar positivist rejection of all metaphysical claims, but it was the favor of science's more traditional constituents that he sought by making this point. It was the apparent neutrality that was won by claiming to have joined a "materialistic terminology with the repudiation of materialistic philosophy" that enabled him to join with Archbishop Thomson in the next passage in hewing "M. Comte in pieces, as a modern Agag." By portraying himself as a scientific Samuel and Comte as the Amalekite king he would slay in the name of the Lord, Huxley invoked a traditional Baconian vision. Science remained the sword of Christendom wielded against the idols of philosophy. No one listening would have mistaken Huxley for an orthodox Anglican, but this did not really matter. In the Baconian mind-set that he appealed to, science was already metaphysically neutral. So long as it read the book of nature exactly as God had written it, it could not help but be the ally of religion. The personal beliefs even of an infidel like Huxley did not matter.

EVOLUTION PLUS CHRISTIANITY

If English society was in danger of being infected with Comtian positivism, Huxley's cure was to inoculate it with the germ of an indigenous strain of the same thing. Positivism's reincarnation as agnosticism enabled him to work two audiences of prospective constituents simultaneously, the same radical elements that were drawn to positivist scientism and a larger, more moderate representation of the old Protestant order that still resonated to Baconian conceptions of science. To use an adage that Huxley himself sometimes employed, we find him "holding with the hare and hunting with the hounds."

But how do these enduring Protestant themes in Huxley's rhetoric anticipate evolutionism? How do they enable us to understand why evolutionary science was destined to become tied up with the scientific ethos? Part of the answer comes from thinking through the symbolic potential that biological evolution held for a culture already accustomed to regarding nature as a theological text. To the extent that Protestants already regarded empirical science as revelation, historical meaning was likewise a logical complement of scientific knowledge. If special revelation was destined to culminate in the purification of Christ's bride, natural revelation was destined to culminate in the restoration of the creation. This was what had made the millenarian features of Bacon's *New Atlantis* the logical complement to his efforts to link science with the Protestant reform movement. A corresponding historical endpoint for natural revelation was needed to go with the millenarian one that Protestants envisioned in eschatology. Just as the restoration of the Bible was destined to purify the church, science's restoration of natural revelation was destined, via technical application, to

restore humanity to its proper place in the creation. The positivist counterpart to this was the sociocratic millennium that would be realized once
human relationships were ordered by social science. The positivists' greater
optimism regarding social science's ability to order human subjectivity
reflected the Catholic tradition of centering authority within institutions,
and Huxley understood that he could counter positivism's persuasive appeal
by constructing an alternative vision that resonated with indigenous Protestant sensibilities. Evolutionism achieved this by seeming to take its narrative
of history directly from nature, from the substance of biological science.
In this regard it represented a scientific notion of history that carried on a
Baconian cultural tradition rooted in the doctrine of *sola natura*.

What made positivists and agnostics different from their Baconian antecedents was their insistence that history itself had now fallen under science's
command, and this takes us back to my earlier tweaking of Lenzer's claim
that positivism tends to degrade historical consciousness. My own interpretation is that the positivists and their agnostic cousins did not so much
abandon as naturalize preexisting historical conceptions—that they tended
to sublimate history *into* science. Once we suppose that history is capable of
being transposed into theoretical rather than narrative terms, the theory of
history becomes a substitute for the evidences of history. This is something
that has trickled down even into elementary education, where (in the case
of the schools my children attended) "social studies" now seems to be taught
in lieu of history. Since theories explain historical development in terms of
principles or laws rather than in terms of characters and actions, many of
the details of history do not survive such transpositions. This explains why,
as Lenzer points out, contemporary positivists are unlikely to even know
who Auguste Comte was, despite his having founded their worldview.[68] The
aspiration to turn history into a science pushes in the direction of abstraction, leaving us with evolutionary conceptions of intellectual development
like the one that Comte articulated in his law of the three stages. Since it
was now natural law that explained history, there was little reason to understand its particular actors. In the end, we might say that Comte orchestrated
his own disappearance from historical memory.

But my own interpretation of this pattern would predict that this tendency toward abstraction would expunge only some details. Others need to
endure because they play a rhetorical role in drawing attention away from
the mimetic features of agnosticism and positivism. Huxley's place in public
memory is a case in point. He has not been forgotten so much as altered in
historical recollection in order to fit the parameters of the scientized history

he himself worked to create. The lukewarm attitude toward Darwin's theory that we find in the Huxley of history bears little resemblance to the attitude attributed to the Huxley of legend, Darwin's fervent bulldog. Similarly, his agnosticism, though in reality as much an answer to positivism as to religious orthodoxy, has become only the latter. Both of these characteristic distortions (the first of which I will treat more fully in the next chapter) are consistent with what evolutionism requires as an effort to theorize history: the more closely evolutionism is identified with evolutionary science, the more effectively its derivation from religious notions of history must be occulted. Were we to become too cognizant of the fact that Huxley was adapting evolutionary notions to a traditional notion of providence, evolutionism would lose its ability to sustain that identity with nature that upholds science's priestly standing.

Before examining this conflation of history and evolutionary science more closely, I would like to close by looking at the Protestant sensibilities that endured not only in Huxley's own psyche but also in his public polemics. This will set the stage for the next chapter by accounting for why the historical themes that coincide with the Protestant point of view would tend to become so pronounced as evolutionism was being blended into his public treatments of evolutionary science.

Huxley's overt appeals to tradition may have been instrumental in his vigorous campaign to fix the value of science in the English consciousness, but this does not mean that they were therefore merely cynical attempts to make scientism seem compatible with orthodoxy. This attraction was personal, at least in part. Like other positivistic thinkers, Huxley also happened to be a member of the society he was trying to win over to his scientistic way of thinking, and this made it equally difficult for him to transcend that society's habits of thought. If anything, his own personality contributed to this tendency. In a brief autobiographical essay, he conceded the truth of Herbert Spencer's charge that he was possessed of "strong clerical affinities," and even as he maintained that these had "for the most part remained in a latent state," there is ample reason to believe that they fueled his rhetorical aspirations. The small boy who once emulated a favorite local parson by turning his "pinafore wrong side forwards in order to represent a surplice" as he preached to his mother's maids in the kitchen, grew into an adult who genuinely thought to make science the stuff of prophecy.[69] While Huxley was certainly being whimsical when he called himself a "bishop" and in all things a "good Protestant" in his personal correspondence, in public he was inclined to act out these roles in earnest.[70]

Many English Protestants were attracted to this. When R. H. Hutton dubbed him "Pope Huxley" in a *Spectator* editorial, he was not objecting to Huxley's religious posturing. Rather, he was objecting to Huxley's violation of his own Protestant ethos in a heavy-handed response to an anonymous letter writer who had attempted to correct a small point made in his 1870 lecture on the ethnology of Basques, Celts, and Saxons. A fellow "Metaphysical," Hutton had been present at the society's meeting the year before when Huxley first employed the word "agnostic," and the liberal theologian now demonstrated his sympathy for this concept by becoming the first person to use it in print.[71] Hutton expressed admiration for Huxley's determination "to preach to us all the gospel of suspense of judgment on all questions, intellectual and moral," but he thought that Huxley's dogmatic dismissal of the letter writer's point had belied this Protestant ideal. He wondered aloud whether this "tone of bitterness and even virulence is worthy of the very strongest man amongst us" and whether Huxley did not "seem to presume the infallibility of which he is the honest and frank assailant?"[72]

What Hutton had observed in 1870 was merely a momentary lapse. More typically we find Huxley facing down opponents by drawing upon symbolic resources more consistent with his Calvinist upbringing. In 1888, after being attacked by the Reverend Henry Wace as an "infidel" and "unbeliever" for his modernist views of the Bible, he did not hesitate to put on his clerical surplice. Huxley had undoubtedly undertaken these popular expositions of German higher criticism as part of his campaign to undermine the Protestant orthodoxy that Wace represented, but this did not stop him from invoking some of its principles. Never to be outdone in the making of biblical allusions, Huxley turned the tables on Wace by presenting himself as a faithful young David besieged by Anglican Philistines. He protested that he "had the 'Lion and the Bear' to deal with, and it is long since I got quite used to the threatenings of episcopal Goliaths, whose croziers were like unto a weaver's beam." It was he who acted as a true Protestant and his critics were the Sauls who had abandoned God's truth in their lust for earthly power.

> But, nevertheless, my position is really no more than that of an expositor; and my justification for undertaking it is simply that conviction of the supremacy of private judgment (indeed, of the impossibility of escaping it) which is the foundation of the Protestant Reformation, and which was the doctrine accepted by the vast majority of the Anglicans of my youth, before that backsliding towards the "beggarly rudiments" of an effete and

idolatrous sacerdotalism which has, even now, provided us with the sad-
dest spectacle which has been offered to the eyes of Englishmen in this
generation.[73]

Huxley gained additional emotional leverage by parading before his readers'
Protestant eyes the hair-raising specter of the Oxford movement, which was
threatening established interests from another side, but his primary aim
was to maintain the preexistent alignment which had placed science within
this familiar picture of historical destiny. He was arguing that the agnostic
spirit that guided his own inquiries represented the same principle which
had enabled the Reformation to advance beyond such corruptions. It was
the orthodox that were "backsliding," while scientific naturalists remained
at the forefront of progress. To challenge Huxley's right to read the Bible as
he saw fit was not just hypocritical; it was a sin against history.

There is no mistaking the fact that such claims reflected a framework
of historical premises similar to the ones that also sustained the positivists'
faith in progress. Since he shared their belief that all paths of inquiry were
destined to culminate in positive science, he likewise shared their belief that
this was religion's destiny as well. What made Huxley's position different
from Comte's, aside from his Protestant angle, was that he was typically
more circumspect about openly declaring the arrival of a positivist Christendom. But with audiences likely to be more sympathetic to such views,
he spoke more openly. In a letter penned to Kingsley in 1869 as he was
preparing his response to the objections that Congreve had raised after his
Edinburgh speech, Huxley affirmed his agreement with Comte's supposition that the progress of science leads inevitably in this direction—to the
very religious ends he had seemed to ridicule the previous winter.

> I shall endeavour to be just to what there is (as I hold), really great and
> good in his clear conception of the necessity of reconstructing society
> from the bottom to the top "sans dieu ni roi," if I may interpret that
> somewhat tall phrase as meaning "with our conceptions of religion and
> politics on a scientific basis."[74]

In the Fortnightly essay that soon followed, Huxley did not indict Comte's
general religious aspirations at all. He carefully bracketed off from criticism
the general premise that he shared with the Frenchman, their mutual anticipation of a scientific religion to come, before launching a frontal assault
upon the real object of his contempt, the Catholic features of Comte's
vision. In Comte's chapters on "speculative and practical sociology," Huxley

confessed to find "much to arouse the liveliest interest" in one like himself who awaited the arrival of a new faith. As "one whose boat had broken away from the old moorings," he was now "content 'to lay out an anchor by the stern' until daylight should break and the fog clear."

> Nothing could be more interesting to a student of biology than to see the study of the biological sciences laid down as an essential part of the prolegomena of a new view of social phænomena. Nothing could be more satisfactory to a worshipper of the severe truthfulness of science than the attempt to dispense with all beliefs, save such as could brave the light, and seek, rather than fear, criticism; while to a lover of courage and outspo-kenness, nothing could be more touching than the placid announcement on the title-page of the "Discours sur l'Ensemble du Positivisme," that its author proposed
>   "Réorganiser, sans Dieu ni roi,
>   Par le culte systématique de l'Humanité."[75]

Huxley's objection was not to a positivist religion per se. What had disap-pointed him was that the new God, the "Nouveau Grand-Être Suprême" proposed by the French philosopher, was only "a gigantic fetish, turned out brand-new by M. Comte's own hands," in the image of the church of Rome.

> "Roi" also was not heard of; but, in his place, I found a minutely-defined social organization, which, if it ever came into practice, would exert a des-potic authority such as no sultan has rivalled, and no Puritan presbytery, in its palmiest days, could hope to excel. While as for the "culte systéma-tique de l'Humanité," I, in my blindness, could not distinguish it from sheer Popery, with M. Comte in the chair of St. Peter, and the names of most of the saints changed.[76]

The Protestant character of his agnostic answer to Comte would become explicit in later messages. The revolutionary movement of science into the center of higher education that he celebrated in the 1874 address that inaugurated his term as rector at the University of Aberdeen presents an exact parallel to Comte's interpretation of cultural evolution, but now with the Protestant Reformation playing the role that Comte had assigned to the Catholic Church in this process. The scientific revolution in edu-cation was an "act which commenced with the Protestant Reformation," which was now merely giving way through science to "a wider and deeper change than that effected three centuries ago."[77] Just as the Protestant movement was launched when religious reformers began "to awake to the fact that matters of belief and of speculation are of absolutely infinite practical importance," so now the same spirit continued its work in a new "reformation," the scientific revolution:

> It insists on reopening all questions and asking all institutions, however venerable, by what right they exist, and whether they are, or are not, in harmony with the real or supposed wants of mankind. And it is remarkable that these searching inquiries are not so much forced on institutions from without, as developed from within. Consummate scholars question the value of learning; priests contemn dogma; and women turn their backs upon man's ideal of perfect womanhood, and seek satisfaction in apocalyptic visions of some, as yet, unrealised epicene reality.[78]

Comte had made the spiritual authority of the Catholic Church the evolutionary precursor to his emerging priesthood of science. Huxley was now merely substituting the Protestant habit of scrutinizing tradition and dogma as the evolutionary forerunner to scientific method. No less than his French counterpart, he was projecting the ways of science back into a preexisting narrative and, as a consequence of this, advancing the notion that the scientific ways of the present were merely the natural consequence of some process embedded within history's fabric.

The spontaneous fashion in which this emancipation had "developed from within" institutions undoubtedly signaled the natural forces that Huxley regarded as the genuine cause of such changes, but by leaving the philosophical bases of his argument to the imagination, his Scotch Presbyterian audience was free to interpret his message in a traditional Baconian vein. Huxley's claim that science had its moral and historical roots in the Reformation might still signal its ties to providence as the fruition of these reforms within the broader arena of secular learning, but it could also sustain an evolutionary view of history analogous to Comte's, in which science represented the true spirit of the Reformation.

Huxley's commitment to the second of these readings is certainly more apparent in his personal correspondence, where the pressures of rhetorical accommodation were lessened, but even here he did not always abandon Protestant themes. In an 1873 letter sent to his wife, Henrietta, from the Continent as he recuperated from the first of a series of breakdowns brought on by overwork, Huxley declared that the same evolutionary mechanism that had brought about the rebirth of the Christian church was now again giving birth to the age of science.

We are in the midst of a gigantic movement greater than that which pro-
ceeded and produced the Reformation, and really only the continuation
of that movement. But there is nothing new in the ideas which lie at the
bottom of the movement, nor is any reconcilement possible between free
thought and traditional authority. One or other will have to succumb
after a struggle of unknown duration, which will have as side issues vast
political and social troubles. I have no more doubt that free thought will
win in the long run than I have that I sit here writing to you, or that
this free thought will organize itself into a coherent system, embracing
human life and the world as one harmonious whole. But this organisation will be the work of generations of men, and those who further it
most will be those who teach men to rest in no lie, and to rest in no
verbal delusions. I may be able to help a little in this direction—perhaps
I may have helped already.[79]

Here, notably, are all the hallmarks of positivism: (1) a progressive view
of history in which science emerges from but also succeeds religion; (2) the
abandonment of traditional authority for rational authority; (3) the inevitability (naturalness) of this evolutionary process; (4) the destiny of this movement to encompass all arenas of human life—including governance—in one
vast system; and finally (5) the hallmark notion from which positivism takes
its name, that language should only reference empirical data.

In the end, Huxley's polarization of positivism and agnosticism was
really just an inversion of figure and ground. Huxley was not abandoning
positivism any more than Protestant Reformers had abandoned Christianity in ceasing to call it Catholic. The positivists were not infidels for Huxley
but rather papistical idolaters, holders of the received tradition but having
only the form of religion without its substance. His world-building project,
at least as he saw it, was merely a more faithful version of what his French
counterparts had aspired to do. Like them, Huxley merged religious history into scientific history because he looked at the past through similar
developmental glasses. The evolution and ultimate triumph of science, like
everything else, would necessarily have a natural basis of some sort. If history were evolutionary and governed by a scientific *telos*, then some scientific
ingredient would have to be discernable in its record, even if its fabric had
been deeply dyed with the colorings of religion.

7

SCIENTISM SCIENTIZED

Every human society . . . has some form of verbal culture, in which fictions, or
stories, have a prominent place. Some of these stories may seem more important than
others: they illustrate what primarily concerns their society. They help to explain
certain features in that society's religion, laws, social structure, environment, history,
or cosmology. Other stories seem to be less important, and of some at least of these
stories we say that they are told to entertain or amuse.

—Northrop Frye

In the previous chapter I looked at Huxley's ongoing chess match with positivism in an effort to illustrate the features that distinguish it from the alternative ideology of evolutionism. This contrast also illuminates the political
circumstances of the emerging professional culture that made Continental
positivism untenable for natural scientists. The positivists were all about
science, but Huxley clearly recognized that this was a love more likely to
smother than to nurture the object of his affections. The professional culture of science needed something *like* positivism, a scientistic ideology that
could align the ideals of science with the ideals of an emerging secular society, but this needed to be an ideology created by scientists for scientists, not
by outsiders who would use it to rule over them.

As evolutionism emerged in concert with this battle, we are witness to
a revolutionary change in how science related to the larger social world in
which it sought patronage. By seeming to situate within natural history a
version of the Baconian narrative that had traditionally justified science's
place in the world, Huxley was working to collapse scientism into science
itself. This was revolutionary as an effort to resolve a fundamental problem

that had plagued science since the seventeenth century: scientific patronage had always depended upon the public appeal of scientistic movements, and because the motives of such movements were never fully consistent with the interests of scientific inquiry, the need to tap this rhetorical resource had always risked compromise and co-optation. Baconianism was thoroughly scientistic, but as an ideology closely identified with clerical interests, it was also responsible for setting up the social barriers that had frustrated Huxley's early aspirations. The older ideology had made the fate of the scientific laborer dependent upon an Anglican worldview not subject to scientific interpretation and therefore not subject to scientific control. Huxley had come into a scientific world that relied on the goodwill of powers that were blindly disposed to bar its gates against him.

In proposing to substitute a sociological hierarchy for an Anglican one, English positivism threatened to institutionalize a new set of compromises, and it was under the competitive pressure of its rising influence that Huxley began to articulate a more fine-tuned rendition of the old Baconian faith. Agnosticism retained the basic features of Comte's ideology, its radical empiricism, a philosophy of history purporting to have scientific credentials, and even a proposed scientific religion, but it redefined the positivist creed so as to entrust authority only to the natural sciences. The scientific laboratory, Huxley now declared, was "the fore-court of the temple of philosophy," and "whoso has not offered sacrifices and undergone purification there has little chance of admission into the sanctuary." David Hume was the high priest who had represented the faithful in this holy of holies, while Comte illustrated only "the connection of scientific incapacity with philosophical incompetence."[1] Scientific capacity, in fact, now meant the same thing as philosophical competence—science was philosophy.

The emerging evolutionary paradigm symbolized science's absolute supremacy, and thus it invited appropriation by Huxley. The positivists had already proposed a social evolutionary model as the basis for their claim that all the roads of history lead to science, and if Huxley hoped to outdo them in scientizing scientism, the most logical move was to ground history in biological evolution. But this is only one side of his alternative scientism. His constant criticism of the positivist view of history was that its scientific pretensions were undermined by its obvious mimetic basis, but he was unable to resist the allure of an analogous construction. Thus, just as Comte and Saint-Simon had made sociology the evolutionary descendent of Catholicism, Huxley presented his own universalized natural science as the heir of the Reformation. This version of the positivist narrative appealed to his

English constituents because, by imitating the older Baconian one, it spoke to an indigenous cultural tradition that had long regarded science's devotion to empirical fact as an expression of the same hermeneutical ethic that had made Protestant piety distinctive. But because this Baconian model also represented the unfolding of empirical knowledge as the natural counterpart to the unfolding of providence, Huxley's naturalized impersonation of this had similar implications. This is where Darwinism came in. If providence was going to endure as evolutionary progress, Huxley would need to establish a scientific basis for historical meaning, and it was by mythologizing the emerging evolutionary paradigm that he achieved this.

This chapter will explore this symbolic pattern in Huxley's public discourses. But before turning to those, it will be worthwhile to consider how evolutionism's symbolic dependency upon Darwin's science helps to explain the odd anomaly I touched on in the previous chapter, namely Huxley's continued association with a Darwinian thesis that he never fully accepted. While the Huxley of popular legend is everywhere known as "Darwin's bulldog," in reality the Victorian scientist supposed to have taken up the defense of *Origin of Species* on behalf of its reticent author was *not* a Darwinist. As Michael Bartholomew first showed, there was nothing particularly compelling about Huxley's advocacy of the case for natural selection, and his own post-*Origin* science was little different from the science he was doing before 1859.[2] Huxley embraced evolution on other grounds and was never able to accept the mechanism proffered by Darwin. There were scientific reasons for Huxley's lukewarm reception, and these misgivings were admitted whenever he addressed Darwin's thesis. So why does the Huxley of cultural memory endure as Darwinism's great champion? My answer is that his role in forging evolutionism accounts for this anomaly. The truth value of evolutionism is only as good as the truth value of evolutionary science, and so a powerful symbolic association needed to be forged between the foremost author of the first and the foremost pioneer of the second.

In general outline, this thesis has already been suggested by Frank Turner, who surmised that the "immediate social implications of the acceptance of evolution were more important to Huxley than agreement about the mechanism." Huxley had rhetorical as well as scientific reasons for wanting to promote evolution since it had "something to do with the place of science and scientists in Victorian society and intellectual life."[3] That something, in my view, was its power to sustain a historical narrative capable of authorizing science's unbounded patronage. This outcome made it attractive to advance an evolutionary stance that, in his own view at least, still lacked an adequate theoretical basis, and it has ever since made it attractive for the scientific culture to remember Huxley as "Darwin's bulldog."

EVOLUTIONISM'S BULLDOG

In the 1892 "Prologue to Controverted Questions," Huxley denied that he had embraced any "philosophy of evolution," or, for that matter, "any theory of the 'Origin of Species,' much as I value that which is known as the Darwinian theory." He goes on to caution that while it is quite true that "the doctrine of natural selection presupposes evolution," it is "not true that evolution necessarily implies natural selection."[4] With Darwin now entombed beneath the floor of Westminster Abbey, just a stone's throw from Newton's great monument, Huxley could profess what Peter Bowler has called his "pseudo-Darwinian" stance without having to follow up with an apologetic missive to the elder scientist.[5] This cautious refrain still echoed in the 1893 preface to his *Darwiniana*, the volume of his collected works devoted to the Darwinian hypothesis. Here Huxley requests that readers "do me the justice to admit that my zeal to secure fair play for Mr. Darwin, did not drive me into the position of a mere advocate; and that while doing justice to the greatness of the argument I did not fail to indicate its weak points."[6]

Huxley in fact had never minced words on this subject. He had always acknowledged his skepticism regarding natural selection as a viable mechanism of evolution. The scientific bases of these doubts, now thoroughly chronicled in a volume by Sherrie Lyons, were rooted in his commitment to pre-Darwinian notions of type and to his belief that the phenomenon of saltation, or the sudden transformation of species, had to be presumed in order to reconcile an evolutionary model to a very spotty fossil record.[7] Both of these reservations can be detected even in the congratulatory letter that Huxley sent to Darwin in 1859 after reading *Origin of Species*. This letter is frequently cited by popularizers because it contains Huxley's oath that he was "prepared to go to the stake" for Darwin's thesis, but it is only by being taken out of context that this phrase could suggest wholesale approval. A closer examination will show that Huxley's oath was a gesture designed to offset his criticisms. The unswerving loyalty expressed in this sentence applies only to the contents of "chapter IX and most parts of Chapters X, XI, XII"—the sections of *Origin of Species* addressing the geological record and the variation of living species. The chapters on natural selection, Huxley then goes on to declare, represent the "one or two points" upon which "I enter a *caveat* until I can see further into all sides of the question." This was because Darwin had "loaded" himself "with an unnecessary difficulty in adopting *Natura non facit saltum* [nature makes no leaps] so unreservedly," and Huxley expresses the concern that "continual physical conditions"— types, in other words—"are of so little moment" in the book as to make it seem impossible that "variation should occur at all."[8] Without some stability of form, this was to say, the mechanism of natural selection would have nothing upon which to operate.

Huxley's commitment to saltation was rooted both in his extensive knowledge of paleontology, which could not be easily reconciled to the kind of uniformitarianism presupposed by Darwin's theory, and in the morphological doctrines just mentioned. His typological interests reflect the intellectual debt he owed to the developmental morphology of Karl Ernst Von Baer and, to a lesser extent, George Cuvier. He had first brought Von Baer's work to the attention of English scientists with his translation of a key portion of the Estonian embryologist's work. Von Baer's science was attractive for a variety of reasons, but more generally because his work represented science on a purely naturalistic basis. This had been one of the attractions of Darwin's thesis as well, but because he believed that Von Baer's work had a stronger empirical basis, it had the same enduring presence in Huxley's thinking as it did in the anti-Darwinian science of Louis Agassiz.[9] In practical terms, this preference drew Huxley into an area of scientific thought more similar to the science of the old guard, that of Owen and Agassiz, who were favorite objects of his attacks.[10] Although he formally rejected the idealized concepts of type and the implicit sense of design that were associated with the Platonized *Naturphilosophen* of the older generation and of the hated Richard Owen in particular, he was never fully able to escape its spell. The literary romanticism he had imbibed in his youth continued to color those notions of biological order he would advance in adult life.[11]

These reservations are also reflected in how Huxley's understanding of the nature of scientific verification differed from that of Darwin. As a scientist who regarded himself as a descendent of the British empiricists, he was more strongly predisposed than was Darwin, whose philosophy of science is regarded by Mario di Gregorio as a forerunner to that of the pragmatists, to demand more exacting verification for scientific claims.[12] This is not to say that Darwin's own criteria for evaluating scientific hypotheses were all that different from Huxley's, but there seems to have been some important disagreement about the extent to which exact experimental proofs were required before one could assent to natural selection as the *vera causa* of species differentiation. This no doubt was accentuated, especially after 1869, by the fact that Huxley was now invoking this high evidentiary standard to accentuate the boundary he was drawing between his own agnostic stance and the speculative features of positivism. But this ethic of high empiricism is evident even in his first reviews of Darwin's book for the *Times* and for *Macmillan's* late in 1859, where he urged his audience to approach every scientific hypothesis in the spirit of Goethe's *"Thätige skepsis,"* that ethic of "active doubt" that "so loves truth that it neither dares rest in doubting, nor extinguish itself by unjustified belief."[13]

Even though Huxley would always question the efficacy of natural selection, it is not hard to understand why he also cultivated a public association with Darwin's theory. Embryonic theories and comparative anatomy may have offered stronger empirical support for evolution, but an explanatory mechanism like Darwin's could do so much more to symbolize the power of scientific naturalism. His *Origin of Species* created a rhetorical opportunity that Huxley simply could not pass over. It signaled the inevitable triumph of inquiry limited by epistemological agnosticism in unlocking even the deepest mystery of nature, and this made Darwin the poster child for the new professionalized science he was championing. He did not much care, he wrote to Joseph Hooker regarding the anonymous *Times* article he was preparing on Darwin's book, that "as a scientific review the thing is worth nothing" (indeed there is precious little about Darwin's theory in it), "but I earnestly hope it may have made some of the educated mob, who derive their ideas from the *Times*, reflect. And whatever they do, they *shall* respect Darwin."[14] Respecting Darwin meant respecting what he was attempting to do by bringing the question of origins within a naturalistic framework. Writing to Charles Lyell in 1862, Huxley again declared that Darwin was worthy of being supported irrespective of the final verdict on natural selection; "even if he is wrong," Huxley averred, "his sobriety and accuracy of thought will put him on a far different level from Lamarck. I want to make this clear to people."[15] Fervent loyalty to Darwin is clearly manifest in these statements, and what Darwin the person had done exemplified the vision of science's unlimited capacity that Huxley was determined to fix in the public mind.

It may be fair in the end to regard Huxley as *Darwin's* bulldog, if we take this phrase (which itself has ambiguous origins) strictly at face value as expressing his unbounded personal loyalty to the author of *Origin of Species*.[16] The warlike frame of mind that Huxley was working up in 1859 as he was "sharpening his claws and beak in readiness," was being prepared for Darwin's defense, not for the defense of the theory that now bears his name.[17]

However, the defense of Darwin also meant the defense of the naturalistic program that was unfolding south of London at the elder scientist's Down estate, and this was emblematic of Huxley's broader campaign for science.

Darwin's work also symbolized historical progress. This is manifest in the broader context that Huxley gave to his defensive actions when he repeated this phrase to Charles Lyell the following spring in a letter on the question of women's emancipation. "If my claws and beak are good for anything," he told the elder geologist, those who bar the way to women's advancement "shall be kept from hindering the progress of any science I have to do with." Read out of context, as such statements frequently are, we might easily imagine that he meant only "progress" of science in a merely academic sense. In fact Huxley was also speaking of something much broader—the universal "progress" of modernism, the advancement of civilization that would be achieved once the advancing empire of naturalism broke down the gender divide through universal science education. "I don't see how we are to make any permanent advancement while one-half of the race is sunk, as nine-tenths of women are, in mere ignorant parsonese superstitions." By combating feminine superstition, science education would change the world in which "five-sixths of women stop in the doll stage of evolution to be the stronghold of parsondom," and become a "drag on civilisation, the degradation of every important pursuit with which they mix themselves—'intrigues' in politics, and 'friponnes' in science."[18]

If Huxley's sharpened beak and claws were meant to ensure a fair hearing for Darwin's work but also to advance the "evolution" of women, this cause exceeded the scope of biology. We can also see this pattern in his 1860 lecture on Darwin's theory at the Royal Institution. While biological evolution was its topic, what had begun as a public lecture on Darwin's work ended as a sermon, a hortatory discourse urging the public not so much to accept Darwin's theory as to trust in the evolutionary growth of civilization that it signified once naturalism was mapped onto human history. Speaking from this higher summit, Darwin's discovery was just one additional detail within an ever-widening evolutionary panorama, merely a "new link" in the "mighty chain which indissolubly binds us to the rest of the universe."[19] The story Huxley was most interested in at the climax of his presentation was not biological development at all but the unfolding drama of human progress, the success of which would henceforth depend upon the inevitable consolidation of scientific authority.

In saying this, Huxley was once again displacing an indigenous Baconian narrative of history into the naturalistic story that had been presented in Darwin's *Origin of Species*. The older narrative, in which science's obedient hearing of revelation also advanced the course of providence, had become a story about how science's obedience to natural fact partook of an analogous evolutionary process. Thus, to reject the universal scope of naturalism that evolution suggested was to turn away from history. Those so "ashamed" of being connected to the natural world that they would not open themselves to Darwin's great idea were also rejecting "the very noblest use of science as a discipline" that forces human beings to confront difficult truths.

> Laden with our idols, we follow her blithely till a parting in the roads appears, and she turns, and with a stern face asks us whether we are men enough to cast them aside, and follow her up the steep? Men of science are such by virtue of having answered her with a hearty and unreserved, Yea; by virtue of having made their election to follow science whithersoever she leads, and whatsoever lions be in the path.[20]

Even as he seems to set science against the faith of the dominant religious order, Huxley adopts the language of one of faith's great figures. Science has become the "narrow way" of John Bunyan's allegory, the Christian's solitary journey up the steep of "Difficulty" toward natural truth. All those who do not choose this solitary path follow to their doom the broad avenues of "Danger" and "Destruction."[21] Couched in such language, the merely reactionary dismissal of evolution that Huxley was warning against took on new meaning as an act putting religionists (traditional ones at least) on the wrong side of a decisive apocalyptic divide. Anti-evolutionary scoffing was more than just scientific error. Evolutionary biology was history's decisive naturalistic revelation, and this had put England at a millenarian crossroad. It was now revealed that naturalism was life's narrow way and supernaturalism the broad avenue to destruction—and yet the old clerical aristocracy refused to follow science. If the "man of science is the sworn interpreter of nature in the high court of reason," then the opinions handed down from this bench ought to govern public as well as scientific choices. "But of what avail is his honest speech if ignorance is the assessor of the judge, and prejudice foreman of the jury?"[22]

This last rhetorical question reflects the fact that Huxley's broader campaign to restructure the mechanisms of patronage was already working to associate evolutionary science with a positivist conception of history. If the naturalism implied by Darwin's thesis was history's apocalypse, then science was its prophet and those who barred its advancement were the enemies of history. To challenge evolution was to challenge the premise of naturalism, and to challenge naturalism was to reject history's destined course. Thus when Huxley alluded to ecclesiastical resistance to evolution, he was not just reprimanding religionists for opposing scientific truth; he was also making the broader claim that the English oligarchy that still exercised regulatory control over higher education stood against progress itself.

The supposition that the continued regulatory control of science by the Anglican hierarchy was fundamentally at odds with the upward movement of progress required as one of its correlate assumptions the belief that religion and science had always been natural enemies. It was to bolster this premise that Huxley went on to invoke that favorite device of Victorian science, the legend (to which he was no minor contributor) which holds that the science of yesterday had been besieged at every turn by a militant fideism.

> I hardly know of a great physical truth, whose universal reception has not been preceded by an epoch in which most estimable persons have maintained that the phenomena investigated were directly dependent on the Divine Will, and that the attempt to investigate them was not only futile, but blasphemous. And there is a wonderful tenacity of life about this sort of opposition to physical science. Crushed and maimed in every battle, it yet seems never to be slain; and after a hundred defeats it is at this day as rampant, though happily not so mischievous, as in the time of Galileo.[23]

Questionable as this claim might seem given that his country's scientific revolution had unfolded rather successfully in a milieu dominated by faith in "Divine Will," the premise that science and religion are innately polarized is an essential part of Huxley's budding evolutionism. If the unlimited scope of naturalism that Darwin's work symbolized revealed a historical path that could only be followed if science led the way, the past would have to bear witness to this as well. If the science of the past had faced only limited or occasional opposition from religion, one might suppose that the status quo merely needed to be reformed. On the other hand, a foe that was as "rampant" as it was unyielding in its immoral "tenacity" would need to be utterly deposed.

In spite of Huxley's determination to end the regulatory influence that religious institutions exercised over science, the historical meaning of the symbolic polarity he appealed to in doing so was derived from the very theological worldview he was attacking. The theological identity that Bacon had forged between science and religion had disappeared, but the historical narrative that formerly sustained this identity had not. Bacon had presented the conflict between the new science and the older scholasticism as a manifestation of the central theological polarity that was more broadly at issue in the Reformation. True science bore witness to natural revelation, and thus it stood with the Protestants against all those idols of human subjectivity that had corrupted Catholicism. Empirical science had expressed the same ethic of faithful reading that was advancing the Reformation. Huxley was now merely mapping the same narrative onto scientific history, enlarging the older polarity between faithful and idolatrous Christianity, through which Bacon had made sense of the struggle between scholasticism and the new science, into a more general polarity between faith and reason. But because this new representation still engaged the narrative form in which Bacon had embedded it, which Huxley was calling a "new reformation" in this 1860 lecture, it likewise retained the thematic aura of historical providence.[24]

So what had Darwin's theory to do with this new reformation? Framed now within this larger narrative, its scientific truth was no longer the issue. Its value was derived from the fact that it symbolized, as no other scientific idea could, the naturalistic apocalypse that Huxley was proclaiming. Conversely, resistance to Darwin's claims symbolized the tragic lot of those who dared resist the march of history—which now had become the march of nature.

> But to those whose life is spent, to use Newton's noble words, in picking up here a pebble and there a pebble on the shores of the great ocean of truth—who watch, day by day, the slow but sure advance of that mighty tide, bearing on its bosom the thousand treasures wherewith man ennobles and beautifies his life, it would be laughable, if it were not so sad, to see the little Canutes of the hour enthroned in solemn state, bidding that great wave to stay, and threatening to check its beneficent progress. The wave rises and they fly but unlike the brave old Dane, they learn no lesson of humility—the throne is pitched at what seems a safe distance, and the folly is repeated.[25]

The King Canute of legend symbolized the philosophical humility that England's clerical administrators now lacked. To confute the flattering assertion of his courtiers that he could still the ocean's waves by royal command, this Christian monarch had made a public demonstration of his incapacity to rule over nature, thereby affirming the separation of temporal and spiritual powers. Inverting this somewhat, Huxley's "little Canutes" are the ecclesiastics who continue to suppose that their spiritual authority extends into nature. Lacking that humility of place that this ancestral king had shown, they were doomed by the rising tide of naturalistic science that was now sweeping across Britain's intellectual landscape. Darwin's achievement in this regard was the first great sign of the historical swell that was soon to wash aristocratic and clerical privilege into the sea.

> The Origin of Species is not the first, and it will not be the [last] of the great questions born of science, which will demand settlement from this generation. The general mind is seething strangely, and to those who watch the signs of the times, it seems plain that this nineteenth century will see revolutions of thought and practice as great as those which the sixteenth witnessed. Through what trials and sore contests the civilized world will have to pass in the course of this new reformation, who can tell? But I verily believe that come what will, the part which England may play in the battle is a grand and a noble one. She may prove to the world that for one people, at any rate, despotism and demagoguy [sic] are not the necessary alternatives of government; that freedom and order are not incompatible; that reverence is the handmaid of knowledge; that free discussion is the life of truth, and of true unity in a nation.[26]

Given that the "battle" Huxley describes here was overtly one raging between science and religion, it would be easy to overlook the extent to which this passage carries on a narrative rooted in England's Reformation tradition. But to entirely abandon the Christian view of history was not an option. Huxley's determination to make the scientific revolution a "new reformation" enabled him to tap into historical meanings that genuine naturalism could never provide. To let go of the significance that made science a sign of history's preordained plan would be to let go of its role as the instrument of progress.

Sitting in the audience, Darwin was understandably perplexed to see the scientific defense of natural selection that he had expected to hear evaporate into this ideological vapor. He had set great hope on Huxley's lecture and had even paid a fancier to supply him with a variety of bred pigeons, pouters, tumblers, and fantails, as a living illustration of the analogous power of artificial selection.[27] But, as his subsequent correspondence indicates, the talk was a disappointment.

> I succeeded in persuading myself for 24 hours that Huxley's lecture was a success. Parts were eloquent & good & all *very* bold, & I heard strangers say "what a good lecture." I told Huxley so . . . [But] after conversation with others & more reflection I must confess that as an Exposition of the doctrine the Lecture seems to me an entire failure . . . He gave no just idea of *natural* selection.[28]

What Huxley had said on this subject was indeed quite lukewarm, that it is "impossible to admit that the doctrine of the origin of species by Natural Selection stands upon a totally safe & sound physical basis."[29] This was to become a thematic refrain in all his major treatments of the subject. In 1880, when the twentieth anniversary of *Origin of Species* was celebrated, Huxley was again called upon to deliver the doxology, but again his praises were muted by personal ambivalence. Huxley's "The Coming of Age of 'The Origin of Species'" celebrates the general influence of Darwin's theory but says not a word about the theory's central doctrine.[30] The best-remembered passage from this demonstrative oration is Huxley's quip "that it is the customary fate of new truths to begin as heresies and to end as superstitions," but in context the "new truth" that he was warning against *was* Darwin's theory.[31] Darwin could hardly have failed to recognize how wavering was his friend's commitment, and so Huxley wrote him to patch things up, even as he forthrightly acknowledged his reservations.

> I hope you do not imagine because I had nothing to say about "Natural Selection," that I am at all weak of faith on that article. On the contrary, I live in hope that as palæontologists work more and more . . . we shall arrive at a crushing accumulation of evidence in that direction also. But the first thing seems to me to be to drive the fact of evolution home into people's heads; when that is once safe, the rest will come easy.[32]

Huxley's belief in evolution continued to stand on the same basis as it had before 1859, "a generalization of certain facts," which had been accumulated "under the heads of Embryology and Palæontology." Natural selection could not be accepted as the mechanism of evolution, Huxley would again repeat in 1893, "until selective breeding is definitely proved to give rise to varieties infertile with one another."[33]

It seems odd that Huxley should have been determined "to drive the fact of evolution home into people's heads" even while remaining agnostic concerning its mechanism. But this mystery deepens more once we realize the even greater reserve that apparently manifested in his classroom lectures. Father Hahn, a Jesuit priest who studied under him in 1876, noticed that he never discussed evolution in his teaching lectures, even when topics were being treated, such as comparative anatomy, that seemed to lend themselves to this subject.

> But Huxley was so reserved on this subject in his lectures that, speaking one day of a species forming a transition between two others, he

immediately added:—"when I speak of transition I do not in the least mean to say that one species turned into a second to develop thereafter into a third. What I mean is, that the characters of the second are intermediate between those of the others. It is as if I were to say that such and such a cathedral, Canterbury, for example, is a transition between York Minster and Westminster Abbey. No one would imagine, on hearing the word transition, that a transmutation of these buildings actually took place from one into another."[34]

When asked by Hahn why he so frequently addressed evolution in his public lectures but never as an instructor, Huxley explained that, "Here in my teaching lectures . . . I have time to put the facts before a trained audience. In my public lectures I am obliged to pass rapidly over the facts, and I put forward my personal convictions. And it is for this that people come to hear me."[35]

Biological evolution undoubtedly was one of these personal convictions, but since he did not accept the mechanism that Darwin had proposed, why would a self-professed scientific Puritan like Huxley so forcefully push evolution in public? Its relationship to the *other* evolution of evolutionism explains this. Biological evolution had begun to lead a double life. Because the biological doctrine of evolution provided the scientific authority upon which his vision of social evolution stood, it was necessary to promulgate both evolutions for the rising middle class, upon which he was staking the future of science. These consumers needed a worldview in which to frame science as much as they needed to understand its substance. Their curiosity about evolution created an opportunity for Huxley's exposition of an analogous ideology.

Were we to sift out the essence of this social evolutionary tale, it would be fair to say that it is a version of the positivist story, a narrative about the unyielding expansion of scientific naturalism in history. But in Huxley's hands this story had become evolutionism—a Darwinian narrative tied up with the story of science itself. Within this narrative, the absolute rule of naturalism, certified now by the apparent triumph of evolutionary biology, also signaled a similar naturalistic hegemony that was overtaking historical understanding more generally.

This is the decisive symbolic move that sets evolutionism off from its Enlightenment and positivist antecedents. Formerly, the unbounded authority that was claimed for science in the governance of human affairs stood upon assertions about the universal applicability of its methods and its metaphysical reserve. This was mere philosophical scientism, a powerful discourse to be sure, and one frequently enlisted by Huxley himself. But with evolutionism, scientism was now tied up with evolutionary fact, and this meant that biological science itself had become the ground of a scientistic myth.

EVOLUTIONARY METAPHOR AND EVOLUTIONARY MYTH

We will return to Huxley's rhetorical career in a moment, but in preparing to look more closely at how evolutionism retains traditional religious meanings while seeming to advance scientific ones, we may first wish to consider the theory of metaphor which I believe best accounts for such mythical transformations. In rhetorical Darwinism, as I pointed out in chapter 1, evolutionary science becomes a "living" narrative, as Mircea Eliade describes myth, that "supplies models for human behavior and, by that very fact, gives meaning and value to life."[36] In emphasizing the rhetorical side of this narrative, our concern is to understand how these mythical meanings and values help to create the kind of public or social knowledge that sustains the professional interests of scientists.

Evolutionism achieves such potency by conflating the cultural being of science (*nomos*) with that of nature (*cosmos*), and the language mechanism that sustains this is metaphor, or more specifically metaphor's potential for *transparency*, its ability to render invisible the verbal mediation (the metaphorical "vehicle," to use I. A. Richards' terminology) through which the "tenor" of culture is conceptualized in natural terms. This is to say that evolution becomes myth when various terms representing biological evolution are also applied to the realm of culture. Such ties become transparent (and thus fully mythical) when users become unable to recognize that what the language evolutionary biology has abandoned is its scientific meaning. When evolutionary terms express social knowledge, they take on more traditional historical meanings that could have no scientific grounding, yet because the language expressing these meanings seems to have a natural basis in biology, it serves to conflate evolutionism with evolution.

To say that Huxley mythologized evolutionary concepts is not to say that these ideas were not also scientific. In fact, it was precisely because evolutionary constructs had gained scientific standing that he could transform them into mythical symbols. Living myths must reference a viable understanding of nature, and for this reason the one Huxley was fashioning was dependent upon the truth value of evolutionary science. The flip side of this, which will undoubtedly trouble some readers, is the inherent ambiguity of motivation that necessarily arises from this consideration. If

evolutionism can only live as myth, within the confines of which the sound-
ness of its scientific counterpart is presumed, how do we know that we are
not only embracing evolution in order to make evolutionism more compelling? Since I mean to stick to the premise that the merits of evolutionary
science must be weighed independently, this is not a question I would dare
to answer. While the prevalence of evolutionism and the obvious validation
it gains from its associations with science must draw attention to this problem, my only purpose here is to draw attention to how evolutionism exceeds
evolution—not to claim that it diminishes it.

The reality of this problem becomes especially apparent once we take
into account John Greene's finding that the nineteenth century's great
champions of evolution all subscribed to social evolutionary doctrines
even before they came to accept biological evolution. No less than Darwin,
Spencer, and other prominent naturalists of the Victorian era, Huxley had
been a social evolutionist even before he embraced evolution as a scientific
hypothesis.[37] The arrival of a plausible mechanism for evolution in Darwin's
Origin of Species did not convert him to evolutionism; it only enabled science
to more fully animate this preexisting worldview. Darwin brought science
into harmony with an incipient myth of origins that at first lacked a compelling scientific correlate. His theory provided a symbolic catalyst capable
of more powerfully fusing the *nomos* of a preexisting positivist evolutionism
with the scientific *cosmos*.

This was nothing new. Throughout Western history, if not in all times
and cultures, myth has sought to relate itself to science, simply because
mythologies that are shown to comport with technical conceptualizations
of nature will always carry greater force than those that do not. In principle
this should be all the more true for philosophical positivists, who contend
that knowledge of the universe attained through scientific means is the only
knowledge. Taken at face value, positivism professes to abolish mythological modes of thought as speculative and unscientific, but if myth is not a
mere philosophical idol that can be voluntarily cast off, but is, in fact, as
native to human consciousness as reason, imagination, or libido, it will not
disappear merely because it contradicts the professed scientific ideals of its
adherents. If the mythic impulse endures even for the metaphysical skeptic,
this could mean that the very principle of epistemic skepticism that would
seem to cast doubt upon myth may instead be the authority structure that
masks its presence.

The fact that positivists and naturalists disparage myth cannot change
the fact that their language patterns affirm it. When they employ terms

from evolutionary biology to produce metaphors that are no longer consistent with a merely scientific description of the world, they enter into the
basic linguistic modality of myth. Evolutionism professes to speak in a scientific idiom but in fact speaks in a mythological one. This shift, as explained
through Max Black's and Paul Ricoeur's expansions of I. A. Richards'
well-known interactionist theory of metaphor, may be regarded as a cross-
categorizing event by which the transference of meaning that occurs when
one thing is called by the name of another creates some mutual signification, a new "combining" of meanings.[38] This means that when one subject
of concern (some "tenor," in Richards' vocabulary) figuratively appropriates
a name (or "vehicle") usually assigned to something else, that subject or
tenor achieves a new meaning that is the result of its interaction with the
preexisting meanings of this vehicle. Thus when economists say that "confidence in the dollar is eroding," they bring together whatever meaning we
have already assigned to the tenor of "confidence" with meanings already
assigned to "erosion." Our preexisting notions of gradual geological change
become part of our thinking about those mental states tied up with the idea
of declining confidence. Two typically unrelated concepts are taken together
interactively in what Ricoeur calls a "planned category mistake" in which
"'the similar' is perceived *despite* difference, *in spite of* contradiction."[39]

Such devices of metaphor are so ubiquitous, in fact, that we scarcely
notice them until they are forced upon our attention. At some *level* of consciousness, we recognize that tenor and vehicle are distinct categories of
thought artificially brought into interaction, but we do not have to be mindful of these interactions in order for metaphors to work. This is shown by
my use of the word "level" in the previous sentence to represent a category
of thought. As a metaphorical vehicle, "level" imagines thought as something stratified, like the floors of a building or like layers of sediment laid
down on some extinct ocean bed. But such further explanation is unlikely
to be needed. Such comparisons work spontaneously. Consequently, I was
not at first aware of the fact that I was using metaphor when I composed
that sentence, nor was the reader likely to notice that "level" was metaphorical before I drew attention to this fact.

It is the payoff of meaning that results from thinking across categories
in this way that makes such technical contradictions pervasive. But their
spontaneity also causes us to lose sight of the essentially fictitious bases of
metaphors. In an influential treatment of this problem, the philosopher Earl
MacCormac has argued that it is the greater difficulty of recognizing this
pattern of identification in certain metaphors that turns them into myths.

Myth for MacCormac is "the mistaken attribution of reality to a diaphoric metaphor," in other words, to those sorts of metaphors, even scientific ones, that are incapable of reduction to any merely nonmetaphorical form.[40] It is when cognition is most dependent upon seeing one thing through another that we lose sight of the fact that we are looking "through" anything at all. The transparency that sustains myths, in other words, is of a different order from that which is at work in many everyday metaphors. While the identification of dissimilar things may be recognized by conscious reflection, as in the "level" example above, we are more resistant to such awareness when more vital meanings are at stake. Diaphoric metaphors, whether mythic or not, cannot be cast off without eradicating the meanings they sustain, and in consequence those who most depend upon them will be less likely to recognize their figurative character. The "universe as machine" metaphor in science, I would surmise, is an example. While contemporary physicists often say that this metaphor was made obsolete by relativity and quantum theory, in reality it seems as pervasive as ever. The term "mechanics" (as in "quantum mechanics," for instance) still governs physical thought simply because it is impossible (or at least nearly so, since an "organism" metaphor might accomplish much the same meaning) for modern science to think of nature other than as a kind of vast mechanism. To abandon it altogether would be to make it difficult to think of nature as having an intelligible order, and this is a vital presupposition of science.

MacCormac's understanding of myth enables us to appreciate what is symbolically necessary when evolution becomes evolutionism. However, I wish to suppose that myth is more than a particular operation of metaphor. Traditionally myths are also regarded as having sacred significance, and some metaphors that invite the collapse of tenor and vehicle do not achieve this. For example, Aristotle's use of "air" or *aether* as a metaphor for space seems to fit MacCormac's definition of myth, but I am not aware that this idea ever had any significance reaching beyond science. A better example from classical science might be Aristotle's notion that the earth was the "center" of the natural universe. If those interpreters are right who believe that Galileo was persecuted because his unseating of this physical truth was taken as an affront to Catholic notions of human dignity, then we might say that geocentrism truly was a myth. It involved a collapse of vehicle and tenor (physical "centrality" and the "centrality" of humanity's place in the created order), and the resultant meaning had to do with the usual substance of myth, the "sacred, exemplary, [and] significant," as Eliade describes it. Eliade's more conventional view takes into account the important recognition that a myth is only "living" when it "supplies models for human behavior and, by that very fact, gives meaning and value to life."[41] Another way to put this would be to say that myth is always a symbolic ordering of reality that elevates and secures those supreme human values which anchor a particular culture's existence. It provides a basic "meaning and orientation," to borrow a phrase from Jacques Ellul, that creates a "topography of the world," an "organization of action in a space, and at the same time . . . the establishment of a geography of that space in which the action can be undertaken," and, more importantly, in which the human experience of good and evil can be meaningfully interpreted.[42]

Whether this sacred reality is otherworldly, as it is in traditional religious thought, or immanent, as it has tended to be in modernist redactions, its conceptualization will always depend upon a metaphorical mode of imagining to the extent that it posits an essential reality beyond the reach of any simpler cognition—a *noumenal* that is not equal to any of its *phenomenal* referents. Mythic consciousness always entails thought stretching beyond itself, from the realm of ordinary being into the realm of the "other." Looked at this way, the loss of tension between tenor and vehicle that Mac-Cormac identifies as myth's defining feature makes sense, not because it is definitive but because it describes a linguistic pattern that is necessary for communicating higher meanings.

Metaphor is always a way of "seeing through." When we look out upon the earth though an airplane window, we are in some sense looking at two things, a windowpane and the visage of the terrestrial landscape that it mediates. The passenger has the power to choose which of these objects will have presence. One can alternate between looking *at* the windowpane and *through* it, but most of the time one simply forgets the window. In such instances it becomes "empty" of meaning, as Roland Barthes has said of mythic symbolism, so that one loses sight of its role in mediating what is seen through it.[43] It is likewise this transparency in metaphorical vehicles that naturalizes their signification. In this, Barthes writes, we reach "the very principle of myth: it transforms history into nature." The reader of myth experiences it as "innocent speech: not because its intentions are hidden . . . but because they are naturalized."[44] The playful intentionality of the metaphorical imagination disappears when metaphor becomes myth. Rather than treating B "as if" it were A, the mythic thinker will have collapsed A and B. The linguistic tension that preserves this "as if" sense will have ceased to operate.

What authorizes such transformations will differ from one culture to the next. The special role played by the dominant windows of metaphor through which Western religion has looked upon supernatural reality—God as "Father" and "Lord," nature as "creation," human beings as "fallen," and the like—are validated by the premise of revelation, the supposition of the faithful that the canonical texts which ratify these metaphors represent the divine breaking in upon profane experience. Being habituated to the notion of revelation as the dynamic principle of Western mythologizing, we are less likely to recognize the same sort of symbolism emanating from a scientific culture that professes metaphysical neutrality. However, it is not a particular kind of authority structure that turns metaphor into myth; any kind of authority may work. Scientific cultures merely rely upon the truth value of scientific discovery to justify suspending the "as if" tension that otherwise enables us to recognize metaphor as such.

SCIENCE'S PLACE IN NATURE

To illustrate how evolutionism achieves this transparency, I would like to examine the metaphors of "place" that appear in key sections of Huxley's influential 1863 book, *Man's Place in Nature*. This volume is significant in the history of evolutionary thought because, in tandem with Lyell's *Geological Evidences of the Antiquity of Man*, which was published the same year, it was an important first effort to explore the human implications of Darwin's thesis—even though, in typical form for its author, it gives natural selection only the slightest attention. Although intended for general audiences, it is unmistakably also a scientific treatment, a fairly technical one, in fact, that compiles detailed evidences for human evolution from zoology, ethnology, paleontology, and embryology. Customarily we would not go looking for mythical symbolism in a book that details how the close-fitting polygonal bones in the human *carpus* compare with measurements of Neanderthal frontal sinuses and the thickness of the bone at its parietal protuberance. But it is precisely the authoritative cover provided by the volume's scientific purposes that gives its author the freedom to step out of science into a mythical modality. No one comes to such messages expecting to find myth, and so the reader is unlikely to notice that its scientific content sometimes serves as a symbolic window inviting them to look out upon a scientistic landscape.

This mythical aspect coincides with another extra-scientific goal. *Man's Place in Nature* also played a part in Huxley's ongoing chess match with the scientific old guard. In the opinion of James Paradis, it was the endpoint of Huxley's campaign to "transform the theoretical basis of British biology from the speculative tradition of the nature-philosophers and from the traditionalism of men like Lyell, to a new empirical, naturalistic basis."[45] As a powerful demonstration of the viability of a strictly naturalistic science of life, one that now encompassed even human nature, the book was his checkmate against the hated Richard Owen's transcendentalist anatomy that had dominated natural history. But Paradis also shows Huxley's broader ambitions.

> Like Matthew Arnold, Huxley dreamed of the "harmonious whole," doubting, however, the powers of Victorians or their immediate twentieth-century descendants to achieve it. Nevertheless, he invested considerable energy in an attempt to discover the outline of a "coherent system" which would unify "human life and the world," and set out to enlist the scientist as an ally of intellectual freedom in the archetypal struggle between free thought and traditional or ideological authority. Such a unity, he had hoped early in his career, might take the form of a naturalistic system in which ethical order was established as the premise of social order, historical processes of nature and human society were shown to be uniform, and the universal order of nature was accepted by all as the great absolute of existence. Extensive notes Huxley left behind in his manuscripts reveal that his system would have borrowed from Greek Stoical thought and from the philosophy of Spinoza, incorporating the principle of evolutionary progression as the driving force of the whole.[46]

This is the broader ideological backdrop against which *Man's Place in Nature* was written. To regard it as a mere scientific treatise or even as part of Huxley's internal struggle against Owen's blending of Continental *Naturphilosophen* with an indigenous Platonism would be to overlook an important feature of the book.[47] This is likely to happen simply because scientistic arguments always pull their ideological claims back within the compass of science. In Huxley's case, this occurs largely through the devices of metaphor just outlined, when historical notions are couched in the same scientific language that the author employs to discuss biological evolution. Seen through the window of biological evolution, the evolutionism that Huxley is also promulgating becomes invisible.

One of the terms that sustains this mythical transparency is the notion of "place" that is featured in the book's title. As a spatial metaphor, "place" supports Huxley's scientific purposes by signifying the relative position that organisms occupy within the continuum of development that Darwin had imposed upon the animal world. But "place" does not easily shake off its culturally laden meaning as a hierarchical metaphor, and Huxley exploits this by simultaneously advancing a parallel narrative in which this term denotes a historical order. This hierarchical "place," since it is built upon the term's more primary signification in evolutionary theory, has a share in the scientific authority of the first. The two meanings run together metaphorically to found a myth.

Although the interaction of these two narratives becomes most visible in the second of the book's three chapters, it is prefigured in Huxley's opening essay, "The Natural History of the Man-like Apes." The scientific purpose of this chapter is to summarize the current state of knowledge about the great apes as a prelude to exploring evidence of their common ancestry with human beings. However, a striking oddity in its content and narrative form belies this merely technical purpose. Laid over the chapter's lessons on primate biology is a second message about science's own evolution. Rather than merely recounting what anatomists and field biologists then knew about chimpanzees, gorillas, and orangutans, Huxley opens with a narrative on the emergence of primate science itself, one that seems to parallel the biological history which is his professed subject. Just as human beings have descended from primate ancestors, we discover that primate science has *evolved* from certain prescientific antecedents—those mixtures of truth and legend that were part of the cargo unloaded in European ports as sailors returned from early excursions into the African continent in the sixteenth and seventeenth centuries. His story about how we came to our current reliable knowledge of the great apes, in other words, has a developmental theme all its own that runs in metaphorical parallel with the narrative of biological evolution.

By his own admission, these accounts have little scientific relevance. Early explorers were so inclined to exaggerate the human attributes of apes as to create the impression of organisms like the centaurs and satyrs of antiquity, a kind of "mythical compound" of human and animal traits. But Huxley mentions this scientific prehistory, as he explains in his prefatory comments, to make a historical point. "Ancient traditions, when tested by the severe processes of modern investigation, commonly enough fade away into mere dreams: but it is singular how often the dream turns out to have been a half-waking one, presaging a reality."[48] In the end there is some continuity between the prescientific past and the scientific present that Huxley wishes to have his readers recognize.

But why? The answer to this question goes back to the historical suppositions that Huxley shared with the positivists. He was as anxious as they were to show that science was the end of a natural evolutionary process, and he was equally impatient to show that modern humans had a primate ancestry. By placing the flawed inquiries of past travelers within a developmental progression leading up to the certainties of contemporary science, he could show that modern science was itself the product of a natural development—and thus the heir to all former enterprises of discovery. Implicitly, then, Huxley constructs an evolutionary analogy or metaphor that mythologizes the unfolding world of human knowledge by identifying it with the model of biological evolution. Biological evolution has become the window through which the reader sees the history of learning. The fact that the untrained and misguided observors of past generations got something right when they recognized human-like features in the great apes signals their social evolutionary connection to the positive science of the present day. All paths of inquiry lead to modern science, and through it back to nature.

Much as with the cycles of myth or literary fiction, the book's central drama of biological evolution is recapitulated in the gradual evolution of primate biology out of crude travelers' tales. To use an analogy offered by Claude Lévi-Strauss, each such evolutionary iteration, much like the variations on a single theme that unify a musical composition, finds some connection with every other similar statement.[49] For Huxley this means that just as these ancestral "dreams" presaged the primate science that Darwin had awakened, they also reflected the evolutionary rhythms of the natural world itself. Intellectual evolution recapitulated biological evolution and thus resonated with its natural overtones.

An example of one such recapitulation in the Bible and its derivative literature will give us a better idea of what Huxley is doing. Each of the six days that are recounted in the Genesis narrative of creation (1:1-31) also coincides with an act of separation. On the first day, God created light and also "separated the light from the darkness": and on the second day he made the firmament, which "separated the waters which were under the firmament from the waters which were above the firmament." This pattern reaches its climax on the sixth day when Adam and Eve are made in God's own image and then *separated* from all other living things by being given dominion over the creation. To the extent that each primordial act of creation gives way to an ordering act of separation, it makes sense that this pattern would also manifest in the Bible's subsequent narratives of redemption, since these are themselves secondary acts of divine creativity, albeit creative acts now performed to repair a fallen order. These echoes of the primordial creation, we might suppose, serve to remind the reader that the work performed by biblical heroes is still God's work more primarily. The symbolism of creation and separation, once brought into the flood or exodus narratives, reiterates the more basic theological point that salvation comes from above and that Noah, Moses, and all others who work the restoration of the fallen creation are only God's human instruments. Thus we see that the primordial separation of "the waters from the waters" (Genesis 1:6) is also the context in which a small remnant of living things is saved from the great flood. Even though it is through Noah's heroics that these survivors float between the "fountains of the great deep" and the rains falling from the "windows of the heavens" (Genesis 7:11), it is not Noah but rather God who saves. Similar imagery appears when the infant Moses is cast upon the Nile in a boat of reeds, and even more vividly when Israel departs from Egypt through the parted waters of the Red Sea. This association of rebirth or salvation with the separation of waters plays out once again in the Christian rite of baptism, which finds the initiate buried in water and then drawn out from it as a new creature. Outside the Bible, we see this primordial symbolism in the boat journey that precedes Dante's ascent up the mount of purgatory and in the river that separates heaven from earth in Bunyan's allegory. Not every biblical event does this; it is only when human deeds are particularly exalted that an event's superseding divine origins need to be reiterated, lest there should be theological confusion.

The counterparts to this in Huxley's book are those echoes of the evolutionary story that resound whenever he takes up the subject of human and scientific history. He recapitulates the root act of creation—nature's evolutionary work of bringing the new from the old—in certain human acts, scientific ones specifically, by bringing them into symbolic coincidence with this primordial model. The evolving world of science is symbolically harmonized with the biological world. Thus regarded, the various moments in which Huxley seems to turn aside from his overt scientific subject matter are not deviations from his subject so much as variations upon the book's evolutionary theme.

One might think that these symbolic associations were merely accidental, but the pattern of analogy is too persistent and too obvious to tolerate such an explanation. To wave this off would be like supposing that Emily Brontë's descriptions of the English moors in *Wuthering Heights* are mere side notes on ecological land classification and that the verbal association between the barrenness of the story's rocky and heath-covered setting and the name "Heathcliff" was merely coincidental. We expect such associations in fiction and may even look for them, but the fact that Huxley's book presents itself as a work of science will make us much less likely to notice such symbolic coincidences. Nevertheless, since we can detect their presence, we should suppose similar effects. If the heroism of biblical and romantic protagonists is elevated and the hubris of tragic ones deepened by such associations with nature, Huxley's use of a similar literary technique may also transform scientists into actors belonging to a superintendent order of being. In fact, the serious scientific work that Huxley also appears to perform in doing so would only magnify this mythical effect. We know that the romantic hero's identification with spring is an effect of imagination, but the linkages between science and nature in *Man's Place in Nature* purport to have their basis in evolutionary science. Readers introduced to the heading of its second chapter, "On the Relations of Man to the Lower Animals," will expect to find in what follows a summary of evidence supporting the evolutionary kinship of human beings and primates—and of course they do. But the genuine science that is reviewed as it unfolds also occults its mythical treatment of this same material. Having been asked to suppose that they are approaching a scientific discourse, those who read the chapter's first paragraph will hardly notice that they have been transported into a different sphere of meaning. Having entered through the merely zoological door signaled by Huxley's title, they are less likely to notice the mythical terrain they are stepping onto.

> The question of questions for mankind—the problem which underlies all others, and is more deeply interesting than any other—is the ascertainment of the place which Man occupies in nature and of his relations to the universe of things. Whence our race has come; what are the limits of our power over nature, and of nature's power over us; to what goal are we tending; are the problems which present themselves anew and with undiminished interest to every man born into the world.[50]

Nothing in this statement refers to any of the technical details of the new evolutionary theory. Thus if we were to read this out of context, we would be apt to regard it as the beginning of a religious or philosophical discourse. Huxley's supposition that he is opening up a discussion of ultimate concern having to do with our "place" in the universe and the "goal" of history would in such circumstances call to mind the traditional speculations of theology and philosophy rather than science. This is because terms like "place" and "goal" belong to the traditional metaphorical vocabulary of metaphysics. But what makes our reading of this statement different is precisely the fact that the reader is left to presume that this *is a* science book. Because Huxley has set these lines within a book devoted to biological science, their mythical dimension of meaning will seem to stand upon a scientific authority. Except for its teleologically pregnant phrase concerning the "goal" of human history, this paragraph's other claims might seem to outline merely scientific objectives. And perhaps even here we might allow the author some poetic license in assuming that by "goals" he does not refer to a purpose embedded in natural history but merely to what can be predicted once certain mechanisms of biological evolution are understood. But the solemnity of the utterance and the grandeur of its framing as the "question of questions" should tip us off to an equivocation, that what Huxley gives with one hand as science he takes back with the other as myth. He seems to want the ambiguities of the term "place" to have free play, so as to suggest that natural evolution is capable of giving human life some of the meaning traditionally assigned to it by this metaphor. This interpretation gains further support as he goes on to intimate that his own questions about "place" are those same perennial ones that "present themselves anew and with undiminished interest to every man born into the world."[51] If the new evolutionary science covers the same ground that was formerly trod by religious and philosophical thinkers, then implicitly, at least, it is their natural successor.

Once "place" takes on this dual significance, the title phrase "man's place in nature" no longer denotes just a zoological category. The evolutionary meaning of "place" has become a metaphor of hierarchy, a version of what Arthur Lovejoy dubbed the "Great Chain of Being."[52] But unlike more traditional versions of the *scala naturae* that explicitly integrated scientific understanding with theology, the value hierarchy that Huxley proposes presents itself as something entirely of science's making. Scientific authority seems to be self-affirming: science illuminates a natural hierarchy, and in doing so also finds itself perched atop it.

This is reinforced by the placement of this famous icon of evolution (reproduced in figure 6 below) which appears on the page just opposite his paragraph on the "question of questions."

Rather than being situated amidst the anatomical discussion it references, which does not appear for another twenty pages, this image by Waterhouse Hawkins, the celebrated Victorian illustrator of dinosaurs, is adjacent to Huxley's remarks about the "goal" of human history.[53] Consequently, the reader who first turns the page to contemplate this parade of primate skeletons and is next ushered into Huxley's discourse on our "place" in the universe, is likely to give this image a similar metaphorical significance. Contextualized in this fashion, the Hawkins lithograph invites reading

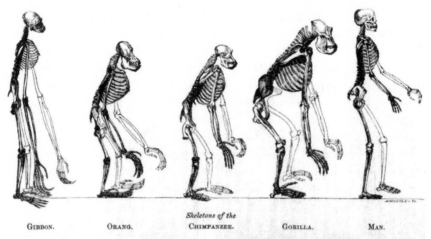

Skeletons of the

GIBBON.   ORANG.   CHIMPANZEE.   GORILLA.   MAN.

Photographically reduced from Diagrams of the natural size (except that of the Gibbon, which was twice as large as nature), drawn by Mr. Waterhouse Hawkins from specimens in the Museum of the Royal College of Surgeons.

Figure 6

both as an iconographic representation of human evolution (in the biological sense) and as a mythical representation of the social evolutionary vision that Huxley has verbalized.

Each step of the traditional chain of being, ranging from nonliving things at the bottom to humans and sometimes angels at its highest point, symbolized the relative value accorded to creatures by virtue of their ordained proximity to the uncreated author of all things. The analogous value that arises from Huxley's image is found in the metaphorical significance of each creature's position relative to some imagined end of evolution. But what is this end? As would seem fitting for an agnostic chain of being, these skeletal figures advance toward that unseen future into which the human figure at the forefront of this parade seems to step, perhaps toward the "Unknowable" spiritual *telos* of Spencer's philosophy. But while this ordering principle remains unseen, the greater proximity that evolution has created between the human figure and this presupposed end signals the higher value that Huxley accords to the scientific worldview on the opposite page.

In this modernist chain of being, science has become the measure of all things. As the discoverer of evolution, it has command of the principle of hierarchy. The ascending movement that we find in the traditional image is now represented as an evolutionary march of knowledge toward an answer to Huxley's "question of questions." The steps of this *scala naturae* no longer climb steeply toward the heavens. Having been turned on its side to better accord with the evolutionary doctrine, these steps have become historical moments rising toward the human form that leads this procession, the evolutionary engine of scientific humanity that has put the rest of the biological world in its train. As both evolution's discoverer and its ultimate product, only science is fully erect and fully capable of peering down the track of natural history into the future.

Of course I am not asserting that the Hawkins lithograph manifests such ideas by itself. Rather, it is because it has been placed alongside the vision of intellectual development that Huxley proffers on the next page that it invites such a metaphoric reading. Huxley in fact gives further encouragement to this interpretation of Hawkins' marching skeletons as he goes on to describe a progression of antecedent types that has led up to the modern "natural philosopher." The mass of humanity trapped in "respectable tradition" has been succeeded in history by a small minority of "restless spirits," the "genius" and the "skeptic" who broke away from tradition but failed to find any satisfactory alternative. From their ranks those seekers after "true knowledge" have emerged who are Huxley's natural philosophers. We might think of Huxley's traditionalists as the social-evolutionary counterparts to the gibbon in the Hawkins lithograph. In this evolutionary scheme, they are the furthest removed from true science, inclined to flee from fact whenever faced by those "difficulties and dangers which beset the seeker after original answers to these riddles." These less evolved thinkers are content to ignore "original answers" or to "smother the investigating spirit under the featherbed of respected and respectable tradition." The various "restless spirits" who are their heirs are closer in this evolutionary hierarchy to the true natural philosopher, much as the gorilla and chimpanzee are to the human form in Hawkins' drawing. But these are failed scientists marked by an obvious inferiority. In anticipation of the modern scientific spirit, these hulking and beetle-browed ancestors, the theologians, philosophers, and poets of the past and present, dared to "strike out into paths of their own." But while they were "blessed with that constructive genius, which can only build on a secure foundation, or cursed with the spirit of mere scepticism" that refused to follow in the "comfortable track" of tradition, they were also "unmindful of thorns and stumbling-blocks." Their destiny was not scientific truth.

> The sceptics end in the infidelity which asserts the problem to be insoluble, or in the atheism which denies the existence of any orderly progress and governance of things: the men of genius propound solutions which

grow into systems of Theology or of Philosophy, or veiled in musical language which suggests more than it asserts, take the shape of the Poetry of an epoch.[54]

These persons are not scientists but only their kin, ancestral forms or perhaps evolutionary dead ends. Their ways of seeking are failed efforts doomed to die out by and by, but as links in an evolutionary progression they have passed along traits that endure in the scientific temperament.

Here again we see how closely Huxley emulates the historical thinking of the positivists. The more primitive religious stage in Comte's tripartite narrative of history finds its counterpart in what Huxley now calls "tradition," and the transitional metaphysical stage of Comte's history has become one dominated by philosophers, theologians, and poets whose brilliance anticipates science but is held back by its intermingling with mere skepticism and non-naturalistic thought. And just as Comte admired the contributions to social knowledge wrought by the Catholic Church, Huxley likewise gives the theological geniuses of old their due by naming them among the natural ancestors of modern science.

No less than Comte, Huxley purports to naturalize history, but it was not in his interest to do so fully. Were naturalism to be purchased at the cost of abandoning all notions of historical purpose, scientism would be unable to attain the kind of cultural authority that could sustain scientific patronage. This trapped Huxley in a version of Durkheim's paradox. He wished to appeal to evolution so as to naturalize other domains of inquiry as lesser precursors to science, but the whole point of doing this was to enable science to take possession of a historical authority like that claimed by these ancestral forms. Huxley found his solution in the metaphorical potential of evolution. Although evolution implied a naturalism that could depose religion, it also implied an ordered process of development that enabled Huxley to depict science as an undertaking capable of understanding the "goals" of history. Even as his efforts to situate religion and philosophy within a naturalized chain of being subordinated them to the social authority of science, the fact that this hierarchy had an evolutionary basis kept alive some of the validity of these ancestral epistemologies. Once made into stages within a unified evolutionary ladder, these older modes of inquiry would seem to pass down their mantle of authority to the natural sciences.

Superficially, this evolutionary perspective did not abolish so much as rework the traditional *providential, apocalyptic, universal,* and *periodized* meanings that Christianity had formerly breathed into history. What Huxley had in fact done was to continue to invoke these categories of historical ideation while keeping the biological world of science within sight so as to maintain the appearance that these concepts referenced natural truths. He naturalizes the notion of *providence*, for instance, by aligning the patient and reserved gradualism that enables scientific inquiry to advance with the gradualism of evolutionary development. He does this by employing the term "Time" as a metaphor (or more properly, as a metonym) to stand in simultaneously for both the unfolding of events in natural history and the gradual enlargement of scientific knowledge. While each "answer to the great question" promulgated by lower forms of inquiry may purport "to be complete and final," and may remain for many centuries "in high authority and esteem,"

> Time proves each reply to have been a mere approximation to the truth— tolerable chiefly on account of the ignorance of those by whom it was accepted, and wholly intolerable when tested by the larger knowledge of their successors.[55]

To say that it is "Time" that corrects the answers proffered in the past is to push human agency out of this historical picture. The progress of science in this regard appears to follow a preordained course and to keep pace, so to speak, with biological evolution. Unlike the ossified knowledge that manifested in the ancestral inquiries of tradition and genius, science alone moves in harmony with the natural rhythms of evolutionary growth.

By implying that science was the incarnation of natural time, that the ways of evolution had now entered into human self-consciousness, Huxley was asserting that science was the *apocalypse* of history, the vital intersection of *nomos* and *cosmos* from which all of history could now be understood. Because such inquiry self-consciously stood with "Time" by virtue of its singular devotion to those methods that forever hold inquiry open to correction, it now stood in the gap between nature and culture and was prepared to guide history into the future. Being of one mind with the universe, science was the only enterprise of learning that was always in step with natural history. Like evolution itself, it never presumed to hold "complete and final" truth but was always kept in motion by being "tested."

Once regarded as playing this prophetic role, the scientific perspective on history likewise achieved a *universal* scope. In the Christian worldview, all merely human understandings of history needed to be rejected, as Collingwood explains this, because they were governed by a "particularistic centre of gravity."[56] Those without revelation could only understand the passage of

time as they experienced it, but prophecy enabled the Christian to understand, if only through a glass darkly, the universal plan of creation. If Christians understood something of the whole plan of history, it was because
they looked down upon it from above, from a divinely ordered perspective
capable of situating each of history's passing moments within an unfolding
plan. The vantage point of evolutionary knowledge, now enlarged by Huxley to account for intellectual as well as biological development, provided
the naturalized counterpart to this divine point of view. Since the Darwinian revolution had put science in possession of the very principle of history,
science was uniquely able to appreciate its whole and thus to overturn those
more particularistic understandings promulgated by others.

Universalism implies a historical continuity that the facts of history
will always seem to belie, and it is for this reason that Huxley also needed
to *periodize* the past. By interpreting these various periods of knowledge as
stages within a developmental process leading up to science, he could create
unity within disunity. We might say that his construction of these various
epochs functions as a kind of theodicy of history. They account for the
unscientific character of the past while affirming the scientific end toward
which history is leading.

The need to maintain these traditional elements of historical understanding stood at odds with the scientific purposes of Huxley's book, and
his negotiation of this tension required some carefully selected symbols. His
solution was to mask these historical ideas in biological metaphors. Thus
he opens the section of his book entitled "The Mental Ecdyses of Man"
by proclaiming a "parallel" between the past stages of religious speculation
that gave way to philosophy, theology, and art in "the mental progress of the
race," and those stages comprising "the metamorphosis of the caterpillar
into the butterfly."

> History shows that the human mind, fed by constant accessions of knowl-
> edge, periodically grows too large for its theoretical coverings, and bursts
> them asunder to appear in new habiliments, as the feeding and growing
> grub, at intervals, casts its too narrow skin and assumes another, itself but
> temporary. Truly the imago state of Man seems to be terribly distant, but
> every moult is a step gained, and of such there have been many.[57]

As a biological comparison, the butterfly device effectively keeps the
premise of evolutionary naturalism before Huxley's readers even as it sustains religious associations as a metaphor. Without this alternative meaning,
Huxley's world picture would be in danger of evaporating back into mere

deterministic causality. It would be a hollow victory to declare science's rule over a world despoiled by reductionism. The interactive attributes of metaphor ensure that this does not happen by taking advantage of what Kenneth Burke once described as its ability simultaneously to bring out the "thisness of a that" but also the "thatness of a this."[58] At one level, Huxley's caterpillar metaphor, by seeming to say that "history is biology," reduces history to nature, thus maintaining science's absolute authority in the human realm. But because metaphors cut both ways, Huxley's image also projects a more traditional notion of historical purpose upon the biological world. The tacit notion that "biology is history," in other words, keeps the traditional religious meaning of Huxley's "well-worn metaphor" alive: since history is contained within biology, it retains its traditional sense of purpose.

One subtlety of Huxley's metaphor that sustains the latter impression is the fact that it is an image of *ontogeny* rather than of *phylogeny*. Despite the blind determinism that biological evolution presupposes, the preprogrammed character of the individual organism's development conveys an abiding sense of "design." In this regard, while Huxley's image is consistent with naturalism, it also tends to overreach it. Once ontogeny becomes a metaphor for phylogeny, the provisional teleology that is recognizable in the unfolding of the individual organism is projected upon all of biological history—and by Huxley's butterfly allegory, upon all of intellectual history as well. So long as the periodic infusions of life that have forced a slumbering humanity to shed outworn layers of knowledge were events bringing it ever closer to some "imago" state, the ontogenetic end conveyed by this metaphor could draw back into a seemingly naturalistic view some of the teleological meaning already present within the reader's historical consciousness.

The progression of historical stages envisioned by Huxley bears an obvious similarity, as Ruth Barton has pointed out, to the scheme popularized by Condorcet. But the biological metaphors that Huxley has laid over this eighteenth-century vision of progress reinforce his more specific claim that the social authority that had been emerging in these stages was destined to culminate in the rule of the natural sciences.[59] After the discovery of science in antiquity, "whereby the Western races of Europe were enabled to enter upon that progress towards true knowledge, which was commenced by the philosophers of Greece," learning was "arrested" as humanity fell into "subsequent long ages of intellectual stagnation, or, at most gyration." All through time, and now especially with the "revival of learning . . . the human larva has been feeding vigorously, and moulting in proportion," but as its "imago" state draws nearer in modernity, it has become evident that these transformations are being brought about by a succession of revolutions in physical science.

> A skin of some dimension was cast in the 16th century, and another towards the end of the 18th, while, within the last fifty years, the extraordinary growth of every department of physical science has spread among us mental food of so nutritious and stimulating a character that a new ecdysis seems imminent. But this is a process not unusually accompanied by many throes and some sickness and debility, or, it may be, by graver disturbances; so that every good citizen must feel bound to facilitate the process, and even if he have nothing but a scalpel to work withal, to ease the cracking integument to the best of his ability.[60]

Condorcet's narrative had certainly been open to such an interpretation, but Huxley's is carefully designed to ensure that the future rule of the natural sciences is its *only* interpretation. Rather than stating this openly, Huxley allows the reader to infer this stance from the heroic posture he now attributes to science. He closes this introductory section on humanity's mental ecdyses, in fact, by writing himself into this biological narrative, declaring that "duty" is his "excuse for the publication of these essays." Every scientist was called upon to wield the scalpel of evolutionary knowledge so as to release humanity from its prescientific bondage. Knowledge of humanity's "position in the animate world," he declares, is an "indispensable preliminary to the proper understanding of his relations to the universe," an understanding that ultimately "resolves itself" into an "inquiry into the nature and the closeness of the ties which connect him with those singular creatures whose history has been sketched in the preceding pages."[61] Evolutionary biology is no mere technical subject. Because it is also the apocalypse which reveals history's universal pattern, scientists have a special responsibility to make it known.

In this curious mystical conflation, the end of the evolution of science is the discovery of biological evolution, and the end of biological evolution is the discovery of science. The succession of "moults" through which science has developed culminates in the discovery of biological evolution, and in this revelation the natural evolutionary basis of science is likewise made known. Each hill mounted by past learning has been leading upward toward evolutionary knowledge, and as science has approached this final summit, it has come face to face with itself. History's final apocalypse is the discovery that science was created in the image of nature—because it was nature.

Having now realized this historical destiny, science bears responsibility for guiding evolution's future course.

It is only after Huxley has forged this identification that he finally turns to the scientific exposition which makes up the body of his essay. Thus, even before his readers learn anything about the evidences for human evolution, this scientific subject matter has already been framed within a larger social-evolutionary narrative. Huxley's scientific message flows out of myth, and in its peroration flows back into it as well. His announced purpose in the chapter's conclusion is to address the popular "repugnance" that many express when faced with their animal ancestry, and so we might superficially suppose that he is merely acknowledging his duty to comment on this salient clash of religious and scientific views. But upon closer inspection, we see that this topic merely provides an occasion for picking up where he had left off at the beginning. Huxley does not merely reject the charge of traditional religionists that an animal ancestry deprives humans of spiritual dignity; his closing in fact turns the tables by insisting that it is in the evolutionary viewpoint that such dignity is found.

A key signpost indicating that evolution is about to be transfigured again into evolutionism can be found in the sudden shift into argument from analogy that occurs just as Huxley is about to transition into the chapter's conclusion. Having spent seventy pages summarizing the evolutionary implications of comparative anatomy, paleontology, and the geographical distribution of primates, the author concludes, again adopting the cautious posture he always took on this subject, with four additional pages on "Darwin's hypothesis." Natural selection cannot yet be accepted, Huxley explains, because a "true physical cause" can be admitted only "on one condition—that it shall account for all the phenomena which come within the range of its operations," and Darwin's mechanism had not lived up to this standard. These reservations are put "as strongly as possible before the reader" lest the author should seem to "smooth over real difficulties, and to persuade where he cannot convince."[62] But he then goes on to compensate for this tepid assessment in closing by outlining a surer basis for accepting evolution.

> But even leaving Mr. Darwin's views aside, the whole analogy of natural operations furnishes so complete and crushing an argument against the intervention of any but what are termed secondary causes, in the production of all the phenomena of the universe; that, in view of the intimate relations between Man and the rest of the living world, and between the

forces exerted by the latter and all other forces, I can see no excuse for
doubting that all are co-ordinated terms of Nature's great progression,
from the formless to the formed—from the inorganic to the organic—from
blind force to conscious intellect and will.[63]

Having just cautioned that Darwin's theory should not gain full acceptance
until it could stand up to the highest evidentiary standards, it seems odd
that Huxley would then go on to assert that a "complete and crushing"
proof for evolution is found in a much less rigorous argument, the basis of
which was founded on analogy. But this move makes rhetorical sense once
we recognize that Huxley is now transitioning back into the same mythic
mode with which he had begun the chapter.

The mythical potential of this argument may be detected in the similarity that Huxley's phrase "whole analogy of natural operations" bears to the
"whole analogy of nature" that had been the basis for Joseph Butler's (1692–
1752) influential defense of Christianity.[64] Against the popular deism of the
eighteenth century, which had rejected the revelations of the Bible, Bishop
Butler had advanced the supposition that one could argue by analogy "from
that part of the Divine government over intelligent creatures which comes
under our view" to the sacred revelation which discloses "that larger and
more general government over them which is beyond it."[65] Butler's *Analogy
of Religion* (1736) still weighed heavily upon English thought well into the
middle of the nineteenth century, and like other theological arguments that
Huxley admired, it invited emulation.

No similar meaning might at first seem to be afoot in the above paragraph since Huxley is employing analogy to argue for an all-encompassing
naturalism. He seems only to argue that the universality of evolution followed inductively from the ever-growing number of natural explanations
that science had already amassed. What the reader may not notice, however,
is that the innate ambiguity of analogy as an argumentative form has also
enabled Huxley to entertain a notion of evolution that goes far beyond anything that could be reasoned out from Darwin's mechanism. While Huxley's analogy brings "conscious intellect and will" within the compass of
secondary causation, he does not address what this seems to imply, namely
that the transcendent freedom that notions of will and consciousness typically denote have evaporated into a deterministic mist. This leaves open
two alternative meanings, one materialistic and one pantheistic: either the
universal compass of evolution has abolished those qualitative features that
traditionally set consciousness and will apart, or consciousness and will are

being incorporated into nature as innate features. Since Huxley is speaking as a scientist, we might suppose that he means to advance materialism, but the traditional theistic language that is also present when he speaks of "Nature's great progression" points in the direction of pantheism.

Huxley hinted at his willingness to entertain such a deified universe in his private correspondence with Charles Kingsley later that same year. He conceded that he was "too much a believer in Butler and in the great principle of the 'Analogy' . . . to have any difficulty about miracles," and he therefore had not "the least sympathy with the *a priori* reasons against orthodoxy."[66] Of course, in tossing this bone to religious tradition, Huxley was only appeasing his theologian friend, and he goes on to clarify that he was not about to consider a supernatural worldview. But his rejection of Kingsley's views did not stand on anything like an agnostic refusal to suppose that religious knowledge is possible; rather, it stood upon his preference for a different analogical reading of nature.

> I cannot see one shadow or tittle of evidence that the great unknown underlying the phenomena of the universe stands to us in the relation of a Father—loves us and cares for us as Christianity asserts. On the contrary, the whole teaching of experience seems to me to show that while the governance (if I may use the term) of the universe is rigorously just and substantially kind and beneficent, there is no more relation of affection between governor and governed than between me and the twelve judges. I know the administrators of the law desire to do their best for everybody, and that they would rather not hurt me than otherwise, but I also know that under certain circumstances they will most assuredly hang me; and that in any case it would be absurd to suppose them guided by any particular affection for me.[67]

Huxley did not reject Butler's natural theology because he rejected the analogical reasoning that sustained it; rather, it was because analogical reasoning was pushing him in another direction. Huxley only questioned whether the ruler of the universe was so completely benevolent as to be comparable to a "Father," and, as he would clarify in his next missive to Kingsley, whether this deity was transcendent rather than immanent. Materialism and pantheism were equivalent readings of nature, "according as you turn it heads or tails," and pantheism "chimes in better with the rules of the game of nature" than any other cosmology.[68]

The outcomes of meaning that Huxley achieved by shifting into this analogical mode of argument are by no means distinctive to *Man's Place in Nature.* Lightman has shown that similar religious themes were commonly taken up within the broader agnostic movement, by such members of Huxley's inner circle as Leslie Stephen, William Clifford, and John Tyndall.[69] A chief source of this religious inspiration came not so much from Huxley as from the "natural supernaturalism" that he and other agnostics had imbibed from Thomas Carlyle.[70] But the manner in which this pattern arises in *Man's Place in Nature* stands apart in one critical way. Unlike Carlyle and other romantic thinkers such as Goethe, Schiller, and Fichte, who had also influenced the similarly pantheistic *Naturphilosophie* movement, Huxley was weaving these themes into a scientific treatment of human evolution, and this is what makes evolutionism distinctive. It is by virtue of its entry into a scientific genre that this metaphorical impersonation of evolutionary history gains its greater mythical and rhetorical force. The technical authenticity of evolutionary science enabled such pantheistic meanings to maintain a scientific transparency. Those reading Goethe or Carlyle would easily recognize that the religious ideas encountered there arose out of literary imagination, but those reading *Man's Place in Nature* would not.

The attentive reader might notice the relaxation of scientific rigor that occurs as Huxley turns from those concrete evidences for evolution elaborated in the chapter's middle section to the "analogy of natural operations" that frames its closing. But the presumption of an overarching scientific standard overshadows this shift. Even as Huxley begins to move back once again into the realm of evolutionary myth, he works to keep scientific standards in sight by reminding his readers of the empirical discipline that reigns over science.

> Science has fulfilled her function when she has ascertained and enunciated truth; and were these pages addressed to men of science only, I should now close this Essay, knowing that my colleagues have learned to respect nothing but evidence, and to believe that their highest duty lies in submitting to it, however it may jar against their inclinations.
>
> But, desiring as I do, to reach the wider circle of the intelligent public, it would be unworthy cowardice were I to ignore the repugnance with which a majority of my readers are likely to meet the conclusions to which the most careful and conscientious study I have been able to give the matter, has led me.[71]

If we pay close attention, we will notice that Huxley is performing a sleight of hand as he transitions into his peroration. He gestures with one hand toward the "careful and conscientious study" that has formed the foundation of his previous evolutionary arguments, and by doing so he draws the reader's attention away from the fact that the claims about human "dignity" that he holds out with the other hand could not fall within the compass of such scientific knowledge. Logically speaking, we might say that his argument (albeit tacit) goes like this: since scientists "respect nothing but evidence," and since the arguer is a scientist, his conclusions about the dignity of the human person must also fall within science's scope. Thus a vital ambiguity of meaning persists as he goes on to say that it would be folly to base "Man's dignity upon his great toe, or to insinuate that we are lost if an Ape has a hippocampus minor." Could not a "sensible child confute by obvious arguments" the supposition that the poet or the philosopher is,

> degraded from his high estate by the historical probability, not to say certainty, that he is the direct descendent of some naked and bestial savage, whose intelligence was just sufficient to make him a little more cunning than the Fox, and by so much more dangerous than the Tiger? Or is he bound to howl and grovel on all fours because of the wholly unquestionable fact, that he was once an egg, which no ordinary power of discrimination could distinguish from that of a Dog? Or is the philanthropist, or the saint, to give up his endeavours to lead a noble life, because the simplest study of man's nature reveals, at its foundations, all the selfish passions, and fierce appetites of the merest quadruped? Is mother-love vile because a hen shows it, or fidelity base because dogs possess it?[72]

This series of rhetorical questions would seem to say that science is fundamentally limited, that the implications of evolution that many people find offensive cannot be deduced from its teachings. But Huxley only *seems* to say this; he never states in any overt way that these human qualities lie beyond the scope of scientific explanation. His claims about the limits of science are really only the diversion that enables this rhetorical magician to pull meanings about love, creativity, and humanity's sense of its higher place in nature from a scientistic hat. With their gaze firmly fixed upon the idea that biological explanations have nothing to do with questions of value or ultimate meaning, Huxley's nodding readers are unlikely to notice that the opposite assumption appears to govern what comes next.

> Healthy humanity, finding itself hard pressed to escape from real sin and degradation, will leave the brooding over speculative pollution to the cynics and the "righteous overmuch," who, disagreeing in everything else, unite in blind insensibility to the nobleness of the visible world, and in inability to appreciate the grandeur of the place Man occupies therein.[73]

Huxley has turned the tables. It is science that truly appreciates the "noble-ness of the visible world" and the grandeur of humanity's "place" within it, and it is the foes of evolution who "unite in blind insensibility" against virtue. More "thoughtful men, once escaped from the blinding influences of traditional prejudice," will discover in the "lowly stock whence Man has sprung, the best evidence of the splendour of his capacities; and will discern in his long progress through the Past, a reasonable ground of faith in his attainment of a nobler Future."[74]

The analogy of nature, we might say, has occasioned a kind of equivo-cation. Evolution means the merely observable development of life when Huxley wishes to remind his readers of the special scientific rigors that sus-tain the more general case laid out in his book, but at other moments the concept of evolution is imbued with qualities of "splendour," "nobleness," and "grandeur of place" that a science so conceived could never detect.

Since materialism and pantheism were, to Huxley's mind, not distin-guishable categories, this dual use of the evolutionary concept reflected no personal dishonesty. This pattern misleads only in its tendency to cloak what it is doing behind a professional scientific cover. Having prefaced these metaphysical speculations by insisting that scientists "respect nothing but evidence," he invites his readers to suppose that these claims arise somehow from evidence.

The same pattern of adding allegorical interpretation to straightforward scientific claims continues as Huxley closes. Still working to confute the "passion and prejudice" that resisted the new evolutionary perspective, he ends by representing humanity's elevated state as "that great Alps and Andes of the living world." The opponent of human evolution is likened to the Alpine traveler who cannot fathom the geologist's assertion that something so grand could have arisen by evolutionary gradualism, that "the mountains soaring into the sky" are but the "hardened mud of primeval seas or the cooled slag of subterranean furnaces. . . but raised by inward forces to that place of proud and seemingly inaccessible glory." Superficially, the point of this analogy is to show that just as the beauty and grandeur of the mountains is not lessened once we discover their gradual formation, neither should our appreciation of human nature be diminished once its animal origins are recognized. The fact that a mountain range evolved across eons cannot erase the features that now make it so striking. In fact, the evolutionary perspec-tive complements rather than diminishes "our reverence and our wonder" by adding "all the force of intellectual sublimity to the mere æsthetic intuition of the uninstructed beholder."[75]

Huxley's argument that science adds a dimension of intellectual sublimity to the uninstructed observer's intuitions of beauty is also a transition from analogy into myth. The ground of his analogy now shifts from biological evolution to the evolution of science itself, and the evolutionary mountain that grew up to become humanity now transforms into something even higher, the scientific enterprise that stands atop this summit.

> Our reverence for the nobility of manhood will not be lessened by the knowledge that Man is, in substance and in structure, one with the brutes; for, he alone possesses the marvellous endowment of intelligible and rational speech, whereby, in the secular period of his existence, he has slowly accumulated and organised the experience which is almost wholly lost with the cessation of every individual life in other animals; so that, now, he stands raised upon it as on a mountain top, far above the level of his humble fellows, and transfigured from his grosser nature by reflecting, here and there, a ray from the infinite source of truth.[76]

The scientific lesson of Huxley's book, that even human beings are products of natural evolution, has given way as he closes this chapter to the notion that science is in fact the end of this evolutionary epic. Science is both the prophet of evolution and its chosen one; it has discovered an answer to the mystery of mysteries, and a key part of this answer is that science itself is the protagonist of evolutionary history.

8

THE CONTINUING EVOLUTION OF EVOLUTIONISM AND SCIENCE'S BATTLE FOR THE PUBLIC MIND

From Thomas Henry Huxley and Herbert Spencer down to William Hamilton and Edward O. Wilson, evolution took on the trappings of a religious faith. It offered a story of the origins of life and a meaning to existence. The Alpha and Omega. A religion of evolutionary naturalism that was thoroughly postmillennialist, in the sense that it pointed to a brighter tomorrow if only we would do what is demanded of us.

—Michael Ruse

Symbolism, then, is not just a nuisance to be got rid of. It is essential. Facts will never appear to us as brute and meaningless; they will always organize themselves into some sort of story, some drama. These dramas can indeed be dangerous. They can distort our theories, and they have distorted the theory of evolution perhaps more than any other. The only way in which we can control this kind of distortion is, I believe, to bring the dramas themselves out into the open, to give them our full attention, understand them better and see what part, if any, each of them ought to play both in theory and in life. It is no use merely to swipe at them from time to time like troublesome insects, while officially attending only to the theoretical questions. This will not make them go away, because they are a serious feature of life.

—Mary Midgley

Perhaps we should not begrudge Mr. Huxley the expression of such hopes—his vision of science rising to approach the "infinite source of truth." In arguing that his religiosity functioned to sustain the campaign to overhaul English science, I am certainly not saying that it was insincerely professed. The threads of religious meaning that I have detected in *Man's Place in Nature* were clearly and openly expressed in his private correspondence. Readers only exposed to the folklore that has typically shaped public memory of this great man might think otherwise, but clearly Huxley was as fully

239

preoccupied with spiritual matters as any of the religious leaders he so vigorously opposed. This has been known by Huxley scholars for some time, and it was something he himself plainly acknowledged. Late in life, he would profess to Wilfrid Philip Ward, the son of one of the "metaphysicals" who had become his neighbor and intimate during his seacoast retirement to Eastbourne, that his opposition had only been against theology, not religion. Huxley denied that he had ever, except by force of appearances, been a mere scoffer; he had in fact always been a firm believer in Spinoza's God.[1] In the early decades of his public life, it had been necessary to carry forward a "literary militancy" against the religious establishment that controlled the purse strings of scientific patronage.[2] Now, with these forces neutralized, science's elder statesman was free to openly affirm the alternative religiosity that he had more surreptitiously advanced in *Man's Place in Nature*.

Those somewhat acquainted with the best-known work of Huxley's later years, the Romanes lecture given just two years before his passing, might suppose that it offers evidence against the religious themes that I have detected in this earlier treatment—or perhaps, at minimum, that it contains something like a death-bed conversion to a more genuine materialism. Indeed, many contemporaries who heard or read "Evolution and Ethics" thought that it marked the scientist's rejection of evolutionary progress. It upset some of the agnostic faithful, and it comforted opponents like St. George Mivart, a former pupil (now turned Darwinian apostate) who saw Huxley's apparent separation of natural evolution from ethics as a concession to supernaturalism.[3] But what Mivart saw was really only a refinement of his teacher's earlier evolutionism. The mistake here is the supposition that terms like "nature" and "evolution" had ever merely denoted a mundane physical realm for Huxley. He had declared in his 1869 lecture, "The Physical Basis of Life," that while his terms were "distinctly materialistic," he himself was "no materialist" and believed "materialism to involve grave philosophical error."[4] In reality, Huxley was a Spinozean pantheist; he just happened to be in the habit of using scientific language to represent his faith in this immanent deity. His materialistic language did reference the *phenomena* of natural evolution, but it also referenced, as *noumena*, the personified Cosmos of Goethe that Huxley put on display that same year when he quoted the German poet to open the first issue of *Nature*. She was a goddess who "without asking, or warning . . . snatches us up into her circling dance, and whirls us on until we are tired and drop from her arms."[5] When Huxley later seemed to set Darwinian natural evolution and ethical progress at odds in his Romanes lecture, he was not genuinely retreating from this earlier mythical conflation. In 1893, he was simply clarifying that not every aspect of evolution manifested progress. Darwinian natural selection, in particular, did not account for ethical advancement. But so far as Huxley was personally concerned, this did not mean that he had let up on the supposition that progress is grounded in nature—only that Darwin's theory did not account for the whole of evolution.

In his earlier days, he had seemed to suggest otherwise, most famously in the Darwinian-sounding "chess-board" metaphor he plied in his 1868 working man's lecture on "Liberal Education." For the younger Huxley, the biological world was an opponent but one that was "always fair, just and patient," a "calm strong angel" who repays the one who obeys its laws with that "overflowing generosity with which the strong shows delight in strength" and who checkmates the "one who plays ill . . . without haste but without remorse."[6] But this earlier "analogical naturalism," as Paradis has called it, had only given way to a different kind of evolutionary ethics three decades later.[7] In his Romanes lecture, Huxley may have exerted more caution than Spencer and Stephen had about supposing that the material forces described by biologists could always be applied in the human arena, but this never amounted to denying that morality and civilization were the ends of natural evolution. If "Evolution and Ethics" was "the missing chapter of *Man's Place in Nature*, filled in after 30 years," as Adrian Desmond has suggested, this was not because the author had abandoned evolutionary naturalism.[8] He still believed that evolution accounted for moral progress; he was only insisting that this was not the same evolutionary mechanism that had been responsible for biological life.

Huxley was more willing to make this distinction in 1893 because science's different rhetorical context now made it less risky to do so. As Ruth Barton admonishes us, any examination of Huxley's messages "must take account of their polemical context," and must not assume that they represent "judicially-balanced analyses of philosophical and theological problems."[9] New circumstances had inspired him to present a more nuanced version of the earlier evolutionism. In the 1860s, as the battle for science was reaching its peak, Huxley was more willing to draw evolutionary science wholesale into a moral vision of history.

His predominant concern in the peak years of his public career with reinventing the scientific ethos makes *Man's Place in Nature* more representative of his abiding rhetorical aims than the Romanes lecture. More importantly, this book also represents the creation of a new genre of scientific communication. For the first time, the work of scientific exposition and the constitution of the scientific identity were conjoined in one message. *Man's Place in Nature* was at once both a science book and a scientism book— science in the service of the mythopoeic, a literary form designed to put the serious and academic purposes of communicating evolutionary science to work in order to underwrite the ideological purposes of evolutionism. As such, the book mirrors the labors of institutional revitalization that were making Huxley the face of Victorian science.

Man's Place in Nature certainly taught many scientific lessons, but set within the larger pattern of Huxley's public life, it takes on a different significance. The ship of science that was steaming out of the nineteenth century had Huxley at its tiller, and in this regard it would be more accurate to sum up his career by calling him "science's bulldog." It was in order to advance the place of science, not evolution, that he gave thirty-six lectures to schoolmasters in just June and July of 1871, as his son Leonard described it, so "that they might set about scientific instruction in the right way," and this was only a fraction of the workload that would soon lead to a series of breakdowns.[10] Huxley's devotion to the scientific cause found him accepting an endless succession of society presidencies, advisory board positions, school board posts, and royal commissions, and forever moving behind the scenes to influence the administrations of even the most remote municipalities of English science.[11] This was also the impetus for his many battles with politicians and churchmen who envisioned a lesser role for science in the new industrial empire that was expanding in step with England's territorial imperialism.

Since Huxley's death, the same ideological needs that kept him him so busy have worked to create him in the image of the evolutionism he helped to create. We remember him as "Darwin's bulldog" in large part because the internal symbolic mechanisms that continue to sustain evolutionism demand that he should be seen simply as an advocate of science rather than of a scientific worldview. The scientific ethos that Huxley was fashioning invited mythogenesis, the wholesale identification of science with progress and of progress with nature. But like other symbolic creations of this kind, it needed to maintain the belief that this was a work of *cosmos* building rather than of *nomos* building—a work of scientific discovery rather than mere human invention. Were historical memory to attend too closely to Huxley's extensive political efforts to promote science's place in the world, the bonds that hold culture and nature together would be more likely to come undone. Evolutionism sustains the idea that the scientific identity springs spontaneously from the natural world, and this belief is more consistent with what is supposed about the Huxley of legend than about the Huxley of fact.

RULES TO LIVE BY

Michael Ruse's monumental effort to chronicle evolutionism's ubiquitous growth since the nineteenth century bears witness to the rhetorical vitality of what Huxley set in motion a century and a half ago. For Huxley evolutionism was the symbolic correlative of his efforts to build a scientific empire, and it has continued to expand and diversify as science has continued to grow. It has done so because institutional cultures, no less than other human inventions, are maintained by replicating the symbol systems that first built them.

As I bring this book to a close, I wish to consider some of the important implications of evolutionism both for the present world of science and for the nonscientific world that now relies so significantly upon scientific understanding. To do this, of course, requires some consideration of a vast store of scientific rhetoric that has arisen since the nineteenth century, and a fair treatment of this subject would require several more volumes of this length. Having space for only a few examples, I mean to highlight three of evolutionism's symbolic patterns that I believe to be especially pervasive and meaningful:

1. The allure of evolutionism tempts scientists to exaggerate the scope and meaning of evolutionary science, especially when concerns of scientific identity are at stake.
2. Evolutionism and creationism are mutually reinforcing. The existence of each fosters the existence of the other.
3. As a kind of meta-paradigm for science, evolutionism closes itself off from criticism by identifying itself with evolutionary science.

Let me begin with the first proposition. Evolutionary science in the service of the scientific identity will have difficulty remaining faithful to the normative standards that science otherwise avows. This is because more than the truth value of evolutionary science is at stake. Because evolutionism derives its mythical potency from evolutionary science, its vitality depends upon that science. I do not presume that the messages of evolutionary science are directly influenced by these identity concerns when they appear in the professional contexts of scientific communication, and so this proposition only pertains to the public communication of evolutionary ideas. In other words, I am not alleging that evolutionism is a fatal problem for evolutionary science. Although I am by no means qualified to judge its scientific merits fully, I take its integrity on faith because I think it is reasonable (if not prudent and honorable) to give presumption, at least provisionally, to the consensus of professional practitioners. It is only when evolutionary science goes public that its scientistic potency is likely to become manifest.

I suspect that the allure of scientism has distorted one particular treatment of evolutionary science in Chicago's Field Museum. In addition to covering the basic principles of Darwinian selection, the museum's evolution exhibit also summarizes the well-known experimental program launched by Stanley Miller and Harold Urey in 1953 in an effort to determine whether the basic amino acids making up RNA and DNA could have formed spontaneously in the earth's early atmosphere. The conclusions that the exhibitors draw from this famous research project seem to reach well beyond its scientific scope. While it would seem reasonable to say that the Miller-Urey experiment demonstrated that one vital condition necessary for the origin of life, the natural generation of amino acids, had been shown to exist, one does not need to be a scientific expert to recognize that this study did not *demonstrate* that life can or did evolve from nonlife. But this is precisely where the Field Museum's language seems to take us.

How Could Life Begin?

A breakthrough in 1953 let us imagine life beginning as a natural event. Stanley Miller built this terrarium of ancient lifeless Earth. Simulated lightning striking its atmosphere of water, ammonia, methane and hydrogen left a sum of amino acids. A simple thunderstorm had produced the building blocks of life.

A chemical reaction started everything. Miller's experiment broke our imagination barrier. Its message? Life could begin from chemical reactions between common materials found anywhere on earth. In fact the building blocks of life are even found in outer space! When this meteorite crashed to earth in 1969, it was carrying amino acids as passengers.[12]

Did these experiments really show that "a chemical reaction started everything," or that "life *could* begin from chemical reactions"? We might plausibly believe, independent of any definitive information about the earth's primitive atmosphere, that a "simple thunderstorm had produced the building blocks of life," but Miller's synthesis of amino acids certainly did not tell us anything about "how life could begin." To insist that it did would be a bit like saying that knowledge of the physical origins of silicon tells us something meaningful about how the microcomputer *could* begin. A necessary but remote cause has been put forth in place of more sufficient and immediate ones that still remain unknown.

I am not faulting the Field Museum's curators for the simplicity of this summation. The plain significance of the Miller-Urey experiment could have easily been adapted to the understanding of the average fifth grader without any meaningful distortion of its explanatory scope. But in this instance, simplicity has been achieved at the expense of basic logicality. Upon close inspection, it is apparent that the fallacy on display at the Field Museum is the naturalistic counterpart to the God-in-the-gaps reasoning sometimes invoked by biblical creationists. Scientists will say that creationists argue from irrelevant grounds when they suppose that supernatural intervention can be inferred from various lacunae in the fossil record. In doing so, they are attempting to deduce a positive from a negative: "We do not know what bridged these gaps, so let us suppose that it was God." But the Field Museum has responded in kind—with a Nature-in-the-gaps argument. In the absence of any concrete explanatory basis for the origin of life, the reader is asked to suppose that prebiotic molecules could spontaneously assemble themselves into living organisms. To declare that "Nature did it" without any information about how is hardly any more rigorous than to assert that "God did it" absent any scientific means for testing supernatural causation.

Some will say that the Field Museum's language is merely reactionary, that it may be faulted only for being overzealous in its efforts to combat the doubts that many Americans harbor about evolution. But it seems unlikely that scientists could hope to combat those who reject evolutionary science by flying from science themselves. A more plausible explanation is that the generative force responsible for this language lies beyond reason, in a mythogenic impulse that wishes to envision infinite horizons for science. Some hint of this can be detected in this adjacent bullet-point summary.

Rules to Live By

- Living things are controlled by the same physical and chemical laws as nonliving things.
- Experiments show that life could have begun as a chemical reaction.
- Exactly how or where that reaction took place still is a mystery.[13]

The final of these three statements might at first seem to back away from the notion that the Miller-Urey experiment demonstrated the certainty of abiogenesis, but the first two propositions show that this is at most a slight modification of that claim. If all living things are governed by natural laws and if experiments have shown that "life could have begun as a chemical reaction," then any remaining puzzles about "how or where" will seem fairly insignificant. Rather than introducing caution, the curators in fact push out the boundaries of science even further. So definitive is the scope of the naturalism established by this famous experiment that it now even encompasses "rules to live by." Scientific naturalism is made to seem a normative premise. Since "physical and chemical laws" govern all living things, they govern every human judgment, the realm of "ought" just as much as the realm of "is."

Rather than clarifying where science leaves off and broader speculations begin, the museum seems intent on sustaining just enough ambiguity and misdirection to maintain the appearance of professional reserve even as it invites visitors into the realm of evolutionism. Its scientific pretensions provide a cover for its scientism. Much as Huxley had done in *Man's Place in Nature*, the curators of the Field Museum have created a message that has scientific markings, but this is precisely what enables it to pursue such mythopoeic themes.

A different language surrounds public discussions of evolutionary science, a language disposed to pass outside the bounds of material causality that are usually regarded as the defining limits of scientific explanation. The scientific credibility of evolutionary ideas may be jeopardized when they pass into this outer frontier, but the identity needs of scientists tempt them to lose sight of this fact. A strictly mechanical conception of evolution would make the scientists who teach it mere technicians of nature, whereas evolutionary ideas about "place," "order," and "rules to live by" make scientists into authorities capable of pointing the way to historical progress. Only a science that dealt with the subject of natural history could so easily transition into the language of history as it is more traditionally rendered.

I do not have space here to examine a representative body of such public treatments, but I would like to discuss one more that seems to fairly represent this pattern of narration: Joseph Levine and Kenneth Miller's textbook, *Biology: Discovering Life*. Their chapter introducing evolutionary science, entitled "Darwin's Dilemma: The Birth of Evolutionary Theory," actually contains two birth narratives. It chronicles the process of discovery that culminated in the publication of Darwin's *Origin of Species*, but it is also about the birth of a new epoch. In fact, Levine and Miller open with this second claim when they declare that Darwin's book "shook the world" because of

its "profound practical and philosophical implications for humanity." Quoting the philosopher J. Collins, the authors explain that "there are no living
sciences, human attitudes or institutional powers that remain unaffected by
the ideas . . . catalytically released by Darwin's book."[14]

For this reason, the authors add that to "understand why Darwin's
work was so important, we must first place his theory within the context
of eighteenth- and nineteenth-century Western philosophy." But the reader
will soon discover that the authors' reason for setting Darwin's work in
history is to sustain the notion that it launched a new epoch that would
forever divide us from the past. Darwin's work did not just upset the biological preconceptions of the Victorian world; it overturned a view of the
"material world as rigid, static and innately flawed" that stretched back
into classical antiquity. One legitimate reason for delving into this deep
past is the need to explain the philosophical and theological ideas that
shaped biological thinking before Darwin. The reader learns, accordingly,
how the classical notion of "ideal types" and the Christian doctrine of
creation "*necessarily* implied stability; things that were divine and perfect
should not change."[15] But Levine and Miller's exposition clearly exceeds
this instructional purpose. They are not content merely to show why biological thinking had previously given presumption to the notion of fixed
species. They go out of their way, as they close their opening section, to
remind us that these preconceptions were also responsible for some of the
notorious evils of the premodern world.

> This view of a divinely ordered and stable world governed not only the
> natural world but social systems as well. Just as the human race had domin-
> ion over creation, kings ruled over humanity by "divine right." The rigid
> system of upper and lower social classes was thus seen as an extension of
> the immutable world order represented by the Great Chain of Being. Talk
> of change was immoral; such change was unthinkable, whether in the
> human social order or the natural world.[16]

As this paragraph transitions into the authors' discussion of Darwin's
career, we notice that the term "change" has shifted its meaning. What had
a plain scientific sense in the chapter's first sentence, where the authors
explain that a "theory of evolution is nothing more (or less) than a theory of
biological change," has taken flight as metaphor. In strict scientific terms,
the "change" mediated by natural selection could never denote (except as an
article of faith) what we mean to say when we demand that people "change"
their ways. The theory of evolution accounts for what must happen once the

patterns of natural causation are recognized; it does not account for what we think *ought* to happen in human choice-making.

Levine and Miller seem to have slipped into verbal equivocation. They have done so, I would surmise, because the creative impulse that has taken over their exposition is a mythical one. If the same entrenched ideas about stability that were responsible for science's failure to address the question of origins also accounted for the rigidity and injustice of the social world, then the story of evolution *is* the story of progress, and Darwin is history's savior. They have suggested to their readers that the dynamics of change that science has demonstrated in the biological world are vitally the same as those accounting for the rise of democracy.

When Levine and Miller turn next to their narrative on the life and discoveries of Charles Darwin, they adopt the device, quite familiar in romantic fiction, of setting their hero within but also in opposition to a fallen world. They begin by reminding us that Darwin "was born and raised in a privileged family within a society growing uncomfortable with the rigid status quo." The world was struggling to set itself free from the oppression of "stability," and this made Darwin, as one more thoroughly trapped in it than others, the most unlikely of heroes. All the world was struggling against this Goliath, but there was no one who could slay it. By the time he was born, "the merchant class created by the Industrial Revolution was not satisfied with the hereditary social structure and struggled to change it, while philosophers searched for a new world view that could accommodate the emerging competitive social order." Science was likewise busily attacking the old "static, divinely ordered world" on every front "except biology."[17]

With the stage thus set, the reader knows where this story is headed, but a vital tension in its dramatic form holds our attention. The world awaited the decisive blow that would bring down the dragon of stability, and Darwin, the candidate tapped for this role, seemed to have no promise of success. But this only magnifies the grandeur of the triumph to come. It has already been determined that the scientific adventure that is about to unfold in the next ten pages will be about something bigger than biology. This is because Levine and Miller have ordered these historical elements into a literary form that invites their interpretation as metaphors of progress. The assortment of signs from geology and natural history that were beginning to point toward evolution, Darwin's gradual conversion to transmutation during his journey aboard the HMS *Beagle*, and his eventual piecing together of the theory of natural selection, may still do much to explain how the idea of evolution took hold, but the social drama in which they have been set gives them mythical significance. They now symbolize the essential supposition of evolutionism that science is what drives progress. Darwin's courage in overcoming the "dilemma" of the chapter's title by following a path of evidence that was certain to lead this "pious man" away "from the commonly accepted religious views," and just as certain to undermine the privileged standing of his own class, occurs within a story that has already conflated the natural "change" discovered by science with the "change" of progress.[18]

In the end, this narrative advances a very clear lesson: not only are natural evolution and social progress the same thing, the second also depends upon the first. It was not until Darwin established the fact of evolution in the biological realm that the world was set free from the oppressive ideological forces that hindered the advance of civilization. Darwin discovered the principle of progress. In suggesting this, Levine and Miller are not therefore denying that evolution does not equal naturalism. "Darwin knew that accepting his theory required believing in *philosophical materialism*, the conviction that all mental and spiritual phenomena are its by-products. Darwinian evolution was not only purposeless but also heartless—a process in which the rigors of nature ruthlessly eliminate the unfit." To deny this would undermine the whole point of evolutionism. If knowledge is not bounded by naturalism, scientism cannot hold. But Levine and Miller also understand, at some level at least, that determinism also undermines the rhetorical payoff they seek, and so they round things off with this statement.

> Yet as pointed out by evolutionary scholar Douglas Futuyma, seldom do the detractors of the Darwinian world view take note of its positive implications. In Darwin's world we are not helpless prisoners of a static world order, but rather masters of our own fate in a universe where human action can change the future. And from a strictly scientific point of view, rejecting evolution is no different from rejecting other phenomena such as electricity and gravity.[19]

Ordinary reasoning would see an obvious contradiction here. How can evolution hold that thoughts are mere "by-products" of material determinants and yet show us that we are "masters of our own fate"? How could free will exist in a world bounded by philosophical materialism? But ordinary reasoning has been trumped by premises that come prepackaged within the larger narrative form they have appropriated; the romantic story form that Levine and Miller have introduced to make these points derives from a mythical tradition that belies such limits. Thus, while I claimed in chapter 1 (and still hold) that evolutionism entails both scientism and naturalism, the fact that it is enfolded within a narrative form that presumes neither of these positions always enables it to defy its own logic.

EVOLUTIONISM AND CREATIONISM

My second proposition suggests a more complicated understanding of the relationship between evolutionary science and creationism. Since religionists are more attuned than others to the language patterns of religion, they are also more likely to sense the shroud of evolutionism that hovers around public treatments of evolutionary science. If we add to this the fact that scientific actors are not particularly vigilant in distinguishing evolutionary science from evolutionism, we should not be surprised to find that religionists will endeavor to throw out the science with the scientism. . In consequence, public efforts to promote evolutionary science tend to have the opposite of their intended effect: rather than assuaging the suspicions of religionists, they tend to encourage them.

Anyone who has listened to the messages of biblical creationists will have also heard the charge that "evolution is a religion too." I disagree with this claim simply because I wish to take scientists at their word when they insist that evolutionary claims are subject to the rigors of scientific scrutiny. But principle and practice are different things. The halo of religiosity (evolution reaching toward evolutionism) that creationists detect in evolutionary discourses is certainly there, and so long as scientists persist in sustaining its presence, the general public will never come around to what evolutionary biology teaches. I realize that there are other factors, hermeneutical ones primarily, that give rise to such skepticism. So long as a significant percentage of American religionists believe that the inspiration or inerrancy of Scripture depends on it being both scientifically and theologically precise, evolution will remain untenable. But this lies outside the control of scientists. What they can control is how evolutionary science is presented, but they seem to make only half-hearted and sometimes insincere efforts to respect their own professional limits.

This is certainly bad for scientists, but it is also bad for the rest of us when confusion about the nature of science results in ill-considered public policies. This was apparent in the most famous anti-evolutionary backlash in American history, the popular movement to banish evolution from public education that culminated in the Scopes trial of 1925. The principle architect of this movement and the anti-evolution laws it inspired, the three-time Democratic nominee for president, William Jennings Bryan (1860-1925), also played an important role in the judicial pageant that played out in Dayton, Tennessee. But prior to the early 1920s, Bryan had been at most a passive opponent of Darwinism and had not taken a rigidly fundamentalist position in understanding science's relationship to the Bible. In his 1913 "Prince of Peace" lecture, he had stated, "While I do not accept the Darwinian theory, I shall not quarrel with you about it."[20] He only became an anti-evolution crusader after learning about the role played by evolutionary ideas in sustaining the Prussian militarism that had fueled the Great War.[21] Social applications of Darwin's theory had not only undermined German belief in free will but also the sanctity of the human person and the dignity and transcendence of moral consciousness; Bryan thought that it had also sustained the historical myth that evolution, as one popular social Darwinist put it, would soon "oust the unfit from this planet" so that German "high culture" could progress globally.[22] It was in this way, Bryan had declared in his best selling book, *In His Image* (1922), that Darwinism had helped to "destroy the faith of Christians and lay the foundation for the bloodiest war in history."[23]

We are no longer likely to mistake the German social Darwinism of this period for science, but this is only because the evolutionism of every historical period is adapted to reflect the cultural tolerances (or intolerances) of its own day. The evolutionism of the 1920s is not our evolutionism. It has always been variable, but it is constant in its determination to link some sort of evolutionary ideology with evolutionary science. As with his descendants, Bryan was given little meaningful encouragement by the scientists of his day to distinguish one from the other. Had he done so, he might have responded by supporting education policies designed to ensure greater adherence to the normative standards that scientists everywhere profess to honor. Instead, he chose the imprudent course of challenging Darwinism's scientific footings. The fact that the author of *In His Image* had precious little background in science did not stop him from closing his book with an extended attack on Darwinism's scientific credentials. Bryan's followers followed suit, and the anti-evolution laws that were soon adopted in Tennessee and other states executed in policy what such arguments had presupposed: since these malodorous philosophies of social evolution were a direct outgrowth of the evolutionary doctrine, evolutionary science had to be reined in.

This has been a familiar pattern ever since, and in thousands of books and articles scientists have responded by blaming such popular antipathy on religious fundamentalism. Certainly that is an important part of the problem. A substantial number of evangelical Christians operate upon a concept of inerrancy that assumes that the language of science can be true to God only if it is also true to the Bible. The very name of one popular creationist website, "Answers in Genesis," reflects this assumption: no scientific account of origins will be vouchsafed which does not reflect the Bible's language of creation. However, the historical record shows that even quite conservative approaches to the Bible have not always ruled out evolution. Important contributors to *The Fundamentals*, the volumes from which this movement took its name, did not reject it. The fundamentalist theologians Augustus Hopkins Strong (1836-1921), Benjamin B. Warfield (1851-1921), James Orr (1844-1913), and George Frederick Wright (1838-1921) may have promoted biblical inerrancy, but they did not suppose that it precluded evolution.[24] Even Bryan's views were not as extreme as those of his fictional counterpart in *Inherit the Wind*, the demagogic Matthew Harrison Brady. One of the embarrassments that the Great Commoner faced when called as Clarence Darrow's surprise witness on the last day of the Scopes trial was the public exposure of a cosmology not quite in keeping with the young-earth creationism of his followers.[25] It had been Darrow's intention merely to expose Bryan's scientific ignorance, but he also managed to expose some remnants of the Nebraska politician's earlier openness to the evolutionary perspective.

Fundamentalist notions of the Bible have done much to prejudice Americans against evolutionary science, but evolutionism contributes as well. An evolutionary outlook that proposes to encompass religious or philosophical questions of meaning automatically falsifies every alternative viewpoint. Scientism in this way mirrors the bibliolatry it so likes to attack. A pattern analogous to the hermeneutical positivism that causes many religionists to suppose that scientific answers are found in Genesis invites scientists to suppose that religious ones are found in science. Bryan certainly detected this, and he could quote from Huxley's *Man's Place in Nature* to back himself up.

> The materialist has always rejected the Bible account of Creation and, during the last half century, the Darwinian doctrine has been the means of shaking the faith of millions. It is important that man should have a correct understanding of his line of descent. Huxley calls it the "question of questions" for mankind. He says: "The problem which underlies all others, and is more interesting than any other—is the ascertainment of the place which man occupies in nature and of his relation to the universe of things. Whence our race has come, what are the limits of our power over nature, and of nature's power over us, to what goal are we tending,

are the problems which present themselves anew with undiminished interest to every man born in the world."[26]

While Bryan's assertion that the integrity of the Bible depended upon a "correct understanding" of the human "line of descent" certainly reflects his fundamentalism, Huxley's evolutionism reinforced this idea. If a scientific figure of Huxley's stature would freely assert that patterns of evolutionary descent provided clues about the "goal" of human history, how could we expect Bryan to suppose any less?

Closer to home, this supposition was being affirmed by one of Huxley's former students, the eminent paleontologist Henry Fairfield Osborn (1857-1935), who challenged Bryan's anti-evolution crusade in numerous lectures and newspaper columns. Judging by the book title under which several of these messages were collected in 1925, *The Earth Speaks to Bryan*, one might expect to find an amassment of fossil evidence sufficient to crush Bryan's quixotic attacks, but the Columbia University scientist and president of the American Museum of Natural History offered nothing of the kind. Osborn's answer to fundamentalism is evolutionism, not evolutionary science. The title, which paraphrases Job's "speak to the earth and it shall teach thee" (12:18), reaffirms science's traditional role as a resource for natural theology.[27] Osborn's goal is not to refute the scientific pretensions of fundamentalism but rather to reassert the religious role of evolutionary science. "Nature's firm foundations for religion and morals" are found in evolutionary science, and he identifies this claim with the same Baconian tradition that had made Bishop Paley's *Evidences* standard reading in his own student days—a book that even Huxley had "always kept . . . at his bedside for last reading at night."[28]

It is an evolutionism substantially like Huxley's that we find in Osborn's books. Although he affiliates himself with Christianity more directly than Huxley ever did, his natural theology is just as unorthodox as that of his British mentor. When he invokes St. Augustine to denounce Bryan's conflations of science and revelation, he sounds the voice of a respected Christian tradition, but such appeals to mainstream theology are only subordinate elements within what is, hermeneutically speaking, only a reverse fundamentalism.[29] In arguing that the Bible is only "an infallible source of spiritual and moral knowledge," he takes a position that many respected theologians of that time would have invoked against Bryan. What makes Osborn's position different is the fact that he does not honor the scientific correlative of this precept. He asks the reader to reject the notion that scientific truth is found in the Bible, while at the same time acting out the idea that sacred truth *is* found in science—that science is ultimately infallible and comprehensive.

What the earth says to Bryan in Osborn's book is prophecy, not science. Osborn answers Bryan's religious objections by saying that science is the truer source of spiritual truth. The "simple, direct teaching of Nature is full of moral and spiritual force, if we keep the element of human opinion out of it," but what this amounts to when Osborn spells it out is the moral elevation of survival of the fittest.

> The moral principle inherent in evolution is that nothing can be gained in this world without an effort; the ethical principle inherent in evolution is that only the best has the right to survive; the spiritual principle in evolution is the evidence of beauty, of order, and of design in the daily myriad of miracles to which we owe our existence.[30]

This was meant to refute fundamentalism, but by insisting that evolutionary science is an alternative source of ethical meaning, Osborn was affirming the very premise that had inspired Bryan's attacks. The author goes out of his way to argue that his own position should not be confused with the merely speculative vitalism of Henri Bergson because it had a scientific foundation. Osborn's own doctrine of "creative evolution" was, in fact, "the outstanding result of forty years" of his "own observation."[31] He believed that his own research had repaired the rift that Huxley seemed to open up in his Romanes lecture between "moral and spiritual evolution" and Darwin's "struggle for existence."[32] This meant that those who did not accept evolution were not merely against science; they were also incapable of finding their way upon the moral and spiritual course it mapped. This was why "in the Tennessee case, the governor, the legislators, the courts, and the majority of the people, including certain of the teaching class, were pursuing a course quite fatal both to religion and morals. No code of morals, however Draconian, can stand up against the laws of Nature."[33]

The tragedy of Osborn's scientistic fundamentalism may be found in the equally Draconian morality that these "laws of Nature" were already inspiring in the United States. His belief that science had found moral truth in biology sustained his lifelong support for the eugenics movement and, in his final years, his sympathy for Hitler and Mussolini.[34] But this was also a tragedy for the American religionists he opposed. Both the predominant scientism and the predominant fundamentalism of 1925 partook of a common premise, and in consequence of a common blindness. Because religionists like Bryan also believed that scientific truth was religious truth and religious truth scientific truth, they expended great energy attacking evolutionary science that might have been more productively marshaled against its scientistic misapplications. Had Bryan been more discerning, he might have recognized that it was careless political aspirations that had caused evolutionary ideas to slip from the grasp of scientific discipline. The poison of Prussian imperialism came not from science but from a perverse alchemy experiment. Had he recognized that it was only a mythologized doppelgänger of evolutionary science that was inspiring the downward spiral of civilized mores in Europe and the United States, he might have staged a more meaningful spiritual and political campaign.

Second guessing history is a dicey business. But let us imagine what might have happened in 1925 had Bryan been capable of distinguishing evolutionary science from evolutionism. It turns out that a contemporary example of this convergence of science and ideology was right under his nose in the very textbook that the prosecution introduced as evidence against John Scopes, George W. Hunter's *Civic Biology*. There is in fact surprisingly little information about evolution in Hunter's book. Its entire treatment of the subject accounts for only three pages, and when evolution does come into view, evolutionism is always in tow. This becomes evident in the book's opening section entitled "Biology in its Relation to Society," where the author asserts that "society itself is founded upon the principles which biology teaches."

> Plants and animals are living things, taking what they can from their surroundings; they enter into competition with one another, and those which are best fitted for life outstrip the others. Animals and plants tend to vary each from its nearest relative in all details of structure. The strong may thus hand down to their offspring the characteristics which make them winners. Health and strength of body and mind are factors which tell in winning.[35]

We soon learn that this biological fitness is the basis of social success as well, that because "unselfishness exists in the natural world as well as among the highest members of society" we will be made "better men and women" through the study of biology.

> Animals, lowly and complex, sacrifice their comfort and their very lives for their young. In the insect communities the welfare of the individual

is given up for the best interests of the community. The law of mutual give and take, of sacrifice for the common good, is seen everywhere. This should teach us, as we come to take our places in society, to be willing to give up our individual pleasure or selfish gain for the good of the community in which we live. Thus the application of biological principles will benefit society.[36]

This might sound well intentioned, even noble, were we not so familiar with the odious social policies that these idealistic-sounding ideas supported in the 1920s. The two chief lessons that biology teaches, we soon learn, are that regnant notions of fitness have an evolutionary basis and that state-sponsored oversight of human reproduction is therefore an exercise of public goodwill. Evolutionary science reveals a biological *scala naturae* in which "animal forms may be arranged so as to begin with very simple one-celled forms and culminate with a group which contains man himself. " In the human part of this spectrum, "Causasians, represented by the civilized white inhabitants of Europe and America," are the "highest type of all."[37] The social policy demanded now that science has uncovered the biological bases of these hierarchical structures was eugenic selection, which proposed to make the practices of animal breeding already familiar to Hunter's rural readers a model for the "improvement of the future race." To demonstrate the urgency of such programs, Hunter summarizes two genealogical case studies of his day that show the widespread "mental and moral defects" that have followed from the unregulated breeding of the Jukes and Kallikaks. "Margaret, the mother of criminals," began a Jukes family that in seventy-five years "has cost the state of New York over a million and a quarter of dollars" besides "giving over to the care of prisons and asylums considerably over a hundred feeble-minded, alcoholic, immoral, or criminal persons." The descendants of Kallikaks include "33 . . . sexually immoral, 24 confirmed drunkards, 3 epileptics, and 143 *feeble-minded*," who, like the defective progeny of hundreds of other families, "have become parasitic on society." They not only "do harm to others by corrupting, stealing, or spreading disease, but they are actually protected and cared for by the state out of public money." Were such people "lower animals, we would probably kill them off to prevent them from spreading." But since "humanity will not allow this," policies must be put in place that will "have the remedy of separating the sexes in asylums or other places and in various ways preventing intermarriage and the possibilities of perpetuating such a low and degenerate race." Hope for the adoption of such policies was growing. Hunter notes that "remedies of this sort have been tried successfully in Europe and are now meeting with success in this country."[38]

Had Bryan merely protested such social applications of evolutionary science, he might have a more favorable place in historical memory since we now recognize that the scientific authority that the eugenics movement took from evolution was unwarranted. But Bryan chose to go after evolutionary science instead. Bryan agreed with Hunter, Osborn, and the vast majority of their scientific contemporaries that evolution had moral implications of this kind, but for him this was only one additional sign of its falsehood. It seems not to have occurred to him that perhaps much that was claimed for evolution came from cultural sources far removed from the scientific enterprise. The temptation to locate the root of such evils in evolutionary science itself was simply irresistible. We are likely to blame this on his religious fundamentalism, but his convictions were just as strongly reinforced by the evolutionism of his day. The alternative notion that evolution is one thing and evolutionism another was closed off to actors on both sides of this controversy. Once this had occurred, there was no point in challenging the justice of eugenics policies, racism, or any other might-makes-right social philosophy on merely moral grounds; such abuses could only be remedied by toppling evolutionary science itself.

THE SCIENTIFIC META-PARADIGM

From a historical standpoint, we might explain conflicts between science and religion such as occurred in 1925 by saying that creationism and evolutionism descend from a common tradition of natural theology. The fact that this tradition once provided a vital basis for scientific patronage is key to understanding its durability. This also means that evolutionism is not entirely expendable. It is a constitutive ideology; to discard it would be to abandon a set of ideas that has become a crucial part of the scientific identity.

This brings me to my third proposition, that evolutionism functions as a kind of *meta-paradigm* for science and is therefore especially likely to infiltrate science education. Evolutionism is *not* a paradigm in the exact sense that Thomas Kuhn meant that term. It is something larger, the ideological center of an analogous and superordinate system of meanings that is indirectly crucial to the advancement of science because it sustains its professional ethos. As systems, Kuhnian paradigms are not just particular bodies of theory; more precisely, they consist of the various intellectual, methodological, and institutional apparatuses that emerge to sustain the "normal science" undertaken to investigate established theoretical models. Because these symbolic infrastructures of science need to be reworked whenever an established theory is supplanted, scientific revolutions can never succeed at a merely intellectual level. Every scientific theory advances within its own entourage of methodologies, grants, journals, departments, social networks, and philosophical premises, and so all of these may be at stake whenever an established theory is called into question.[39] The researcher confronted by a new theory is not just being asked to amend or abandon some outdated set of concepts but also to abandon the whole framework of an older paradigm.

What I am calling a meta-paradigm consists of those constituent elements that sustain the scientific enterprise more broadly. To identify evolutionism as the central feature of this meta-paradigm is not to say that a mythologized evolutionary science by itself defines the contemporary scientific identity and its place in the world. Like paradigms, meta-paradigms are comprised by more than just the theories they sustain. Evolutionary science, as the body of theory that has been symbolically enlarged to sustain crucial beliefs about the scientific ethos, is evolutionism's central element, but science's place in the world also depends upon many other things, such as its established place in university curricula, formal lines of public and private patronage, its prestige as a professional vocation, and the general attitude of hopeful expectation that sustains its public support. In identifying this meta-paradigm with evolutionism, I am only saying that mythical representations of evolutionary science hold all of this together. Once evolution becomes evolutionism, it sustains scientism, naturalism, and, most importantly of all, the notion that science is the animating soul of natural history. Evolutionism situates science within a closed system of ideas that ensures science's worldly supremacy.

Those familiar with Kuhn's thesis will remember that established scientific paradigms are a kind of mixed blessing, vitally needed for the continued work of "normal science" but just as vitally obstructive to "revolutionary science," to the emergence of new theories and the paradigm shifts that sustain them. The same can be said of ideological meta-paradigm shifts. The first scientific meta-paradigm, the one based in the Baconian natural theology that I outlined in chapters 2 and 3, played a significant role in making England safe for science, but it was also destined to become a crucial obstacle that stood in Huxley's way two centuries later as he worked to transform science into the institutional giant that it is today. The chief rhetorical problem with Baconianism rested in the fact that it placed the center of scientific authority outside of science by continuing to identify its work with theology. This older meta-paradigm gave science tremendous prestige but little autonomy. To overcome this limitation, the new meta-paradigm has retained those spiritual resources that made science a transcendent authority but also transformed them to give it greater autonomy. Instead of abandoning natural theology, evolutionism has scientized it by perpetuating the notion that evolutionary science and evolutionism are one and the same. Huxley did not want to abandon the great idea that Bacon had brought to science, the belief that it advanced God's work. Why would any scientist want to give up the already widely held belief that science had prophetic significance? What he needed to do was to reinvent this idea. The logical solution was to naturalize natural theology, and the emerging field of evolutionary science provided an ideal material that he could manipulate to accomplish this goal.

If evolutionism lies at the center of this contemporary meta-paradigm, then it will be important to consider the means by which this core is protected. The fact that evolutionism can exist only so long as it is thought to be identical with evolutionary science means that the teaching of evolutionary science is vital to its survival. If nothing in *biology* makes sense except in the light of evolution, as Theodosius Dobzhansky (1900–1975) proclaimed in the title of his famous essay, we might also add that *science's place in the world* only makes sense in the light of evolutionism. Dobzhansky's influential article, in fact, conjoins both ideas.[40] The body of the essay defends evolutionary science by showing, as the PBS "Evolution Library" summarizes it, that "evolution is the cornerstone which supports and unifies the many fields within biology."[41] But evolution gives way to evolutionism in its concluding paragraph.

> One of the great thinkers of our age, Pierre Teilhard de Chardin, wrote the following: "Is evolution a theory, a system, or a hypothesis? It is much more—it is a general postulate to which all theories, all hypotheses, all systems must henceforward bow and which they must satisfy in order to be thinkable and true. Evolution is a light which illuminates all facts, a trajectory which all lines of thought must follow—this is what evolution is." Of course, some scientists, as well as some philosophers and theologians, disagree with some parts of Teilhard's teachings; the acceptance of his worldview falls short of universal. But there is no doubt at all that

Teilhard was a truly and deeply religious man and that Christianity was the cornerstone of his worldview. Moreover, in his worldview science and faith were not segregated in watertight compartments, as they are with so many people. They were harmoniously fitting parts of his worldview. Teilhard was a creationists [sic], but one who understood that the Creation is realized in this world by means of evolution.[42]

By providing the example of this Jesuit paleontologist as evidence of the compatibility of evolution and faith, Dobzhansky gives voice to a familiar pattern in scientific efforts to combat creationism. But he does more than just claim that one can be "truly and deeply religious" and accept evolution—he also makes evolution identical with Teilhard's faith. It is not just "a theory, a system or a hypothesis" but also a "worldview," "a general postulate" to which mere science must bow.

Written by one of the giants of the modern evolutionary synthesis and published in *American Biology Teacher*, a journal devoted to science pedagogy, Dobzhansky's article is undoubtedly invoked more frequently than any other message in public campaigns to promote the teaching of evolution. Should we therefore be surprised to find it endorsing Teilhard's speculative mysticism? Not at all. I do not doubt that the scientists who create such messages wish to promote evolutionary science, but its capacity for mythical enlargement does much more than this.

The temptation to use science education as an occasion for promoting evolutionism is also witnessed by two other features of these campaigns: 1) the fact that they tend to make the case for evolution mean the same thing as the case for science more broadly, and 2) the fact that they seem to be more concerned with refuting creationism than with teaching about evolutionary biology. We would certainly expect an organization called the National Center for Science Education (NCSE) to address creationism, since it is certainly an obstacle to science education, but the fact that fighting creationism is *all* the NCSE does seems a little odd. Its website provides information about the dangers of doubting evolution and much guidance about how to answer those who do, but (excepting the various suggested library sources that it urges visitors to seek out) the NCSE offers almost no scientific information. The little scientific education that the website does include in its many editorial messages pertains *only* to evolutionary science—never to physics, chemistry, geology, astronomy, or any other field. But it makes sense to reduce the cause of science education to the defense of evolution against creationism if "evolutionary science" symbolizes a broader scientistic worldview. For the proponent of scientism, creationism represents more than just public skepticism about evolutionary science; it also represents the rejection of the sort of absolute public authority that evolutionism sustains.

Outwardly, the messages displayed on the NCSE website profess to seek a kind of diplomacy with religionists. They present themselves as religion-friendly and intending only to demarcate science from theology. The site boasts of the 12,690 Christian clergy and 473 rabbis who have signed a petition supporting evolution under the auspices of the "Clergy Letter Project," and this certainly would seem to affirm that, for these religionists at least, the doctrinal traditions of theism are capable of being reconciled with evolutionary science.[43] But if we look more closely at how such religious accommodations are interpreted by the NCSE, we get a different meaning; what it seems to say, in fact, is that the beaches of traditional religious belief are fast receding before a rising tide of scientific understanding. This appears to be the direction the NCSE is taking when it enlists the help of its "faith project director," the theologian Peter Hess, to explain the bases of a supposed ecclesiastical truce.

> Theologians from many traditions hold that science and religion occupy different spheres of knowledge. Science asks questions such as "What is it?" "How does it happen?" "By what processes?" In contrast, religion asks questions such as "What is life's meaning?" "What is my purpose?" "Is the world of value?" These are complementary rather than conflicting perspectives.[44]

What Hess may have meant to describe here is the traditional distinction between secondary and primary knowledge that has been used, more or less since the time of Galileo, to set science off from philosophy and theology. Another way to express this idea would be to say that science deals with questions of material causality but not with metaphysical questions of being, or, using Kant's language, with *phenomena* but not *noumena*. Superficially, Hess' questions might seem to honor this mode of demarcation, but this is only because he has presented them as abstract categories. Once we put more flesh on the kinds of questions he assigns to science, we will discover that he is actually ceding areas of inquiry to science that are traditionally of religious concern. The question "What is it?" might find a zoological answer (human beings are primates), but it could just as easily find a metaphysical or theological one (human beings are children of God). The questions "How does it happen?" and "By what processes?" may be answered by saying that humans evolved from apes through natural selection, but to wholly give these categories of inquiry over to science is also to deny, tacitly at least, theology's fundamental premise of supernatural causation.

Perhaps it was not Hess' intention to cede this ground to science; perhaps this ambiguity arises only because he has tried to communicate a difficult philosophical distinction in the everyday language of the typical web user. But our concern is with effects, not motives. By asserting that all questions of being and process belong to science, Hess has done more to open the door to evolutionism than to open the religious reader's mind to evolutionary science. Those who buy into the supposition that religion only asks questions about purpose, meaning, and value, but never about being, means, and process, will have also surrendered to science much of what theologians have traditionally held. If questions about what "is" can only have scientific answers, then not only creationism will have to be thrown out; the doctrine of creation (the most central theological answer to the "What is it?" question) will have to go as well.

The informal positivism that this message passes along may be rendered invisible by the fact that it comes from a theologian. General readers recognizing a religion-friendly voice in Hess will not be on the lookout for such encroachments. It is only when we step outside the confines of the NCSE's public relations efforts that we are likely to realize that this attendant philosophical baggage does not appear by accident. The professional decorum of the NCSE website's messages and its science education orientation draw attention away from these implications, but this guard comes down in different contexts of communication. When not speaking directly to the broader public that the NCSE seeks to reach, even its executive director, Eugenie Scott, does not shy away from the symbols of evolutionism. A decade ago, her letter asking supporters to renew their NCSE memberships offered a "Darwin fish" refrigerator magnet as a bonus for those contributing fifty dollars or more (figure 7).

Scott later defended this in a *Firing Line* debate with Phillip Johnson by calling it an "ecumenical" symbol that signals the organization's official profession of making peace between science and religion. However, it seems odd to say that an object that so clearly parodies a traditional religious symbol should be thought to signal rapprochement.[45] Symbols can be made to mean different things, of course, but my own survey research on the meanings intended by those who display the Darwin fish emblem belies Scott's claim. Users typically explained it as a symbol displayed (playfully for some, more aggressively for others) to mock religious people—a Darwinian version

Figure 7

of Tina Fey doing Sarah Palin.[46] This does not necessarily mean that it was employed as an antireligious symbol, but when these respondents explained what they thought it meant, the contours of evolutionism instantly became visible. In addition to representing support for evolutionary science, it is also likely to stand for a set of moral and spiritual principles that could have no basis in biology: a "progress" involving the "integration and connection of all life on earth," an "irreverence for organized religion," the "oneness of everything in the universe," or a Dawkinsesque solidarity of human beings with even "bacteria" and "moss and mollusks." Some professed that it stood for an alternative set of "religious beliefs," or a "philosophy and goal of trying to evolve as a human being." These respondents frequently repudiated the historical pretensions of religionists who presumed that they "should have dominion over other living things," but they also seemed to think that evolutionary knowledge equipped them for a similar role. One respondent said that evolution inspires us to "take care of the earth, our home." If those who question evolution cannot "be expected to make wise decisions in the 21st century," certainly those who understand this scientific theory will. To display this symbol is therefore to "take a stand, as small as it is, for science and rationalism," and to recognize that "while science will not solve all our problems," it is "the best tool for the job."

Nothing that sounds quite like this will be found on the NCSE's website. But why should it? If it is already commonly believed that the truth of evolutionary biology simply entails the truth of evolutionism, any campaign for the first will entail public acceptance of the second. Some slight fear of professional embarrassment perhaps explains why Scott has circulated this symbol of evolutionism among friends and refrained from doing so on the NCSE website. But Scott's personal evolutionism is no secret. She has been recognized as one of the "notable signers" of "Humanism and its Aspirations," a revised version of the American Humanist Association's (AHA) "Humanist Manifesto" of 1933 that is not at all reticent about expressing this creed.[47]

So far as the AHA is concerned, scientism is the vital key to human prosperity. Humanism is a "progressive philosophy of life that, without supernaturalism, affirms our ability and responsibility to lead ethical lives of personal fulfillment that aspire to the greater good of humanity," and the knowledge needed to sustain such progress "is derived by observation, experimentation, and rational analysis." Since "science is the best method for determining this knowledge as well as for solving problems and developing beneficial technologies," it stands to reason that the evolutionary science that accounts for human origins would be the keystone in humanism's arch.

> Humans are an integral part of nature, the result of unguided evolutionary change. Humanists recognize nature as self-existing. We accept our life as all and enough, distinguishing things as they are from things as we might wish or imagine them to be. We welcome the challenges of the future, and are drawn to and undaunted by the yet to be known.[48]

In spite of the evolutionary determinism and the positivist view of knowledge avowed by the manifesto's signatories (twenty-two of whom are Nobel laureates), the group does not hesitate to proclaim the following moral ideals.

> Ethical values are derived from human need and interest as tested by experience. Humanists ground values in human welfare shaped by human circumstances, interests, and concerns and extended to the global ecosystem and beyond. We are committed to treating each person as having inherent worth and dignity, and to making informed choices in a context of freedom consonant with responsibility.[49]

There is nothing particularly novel about what is expressed here. What makes this utterance different is the fact that the moral ideas it expresses are being made to stand upon the scientific truth of evolution. Thus by signing this statement, the foremost leader of the NCSE seems therefore to openly acknowledge that her commitment to evolutionary science entails a similar commitment to evolutionism.

Were we to ask Eugenie Scott about this, I suspect that she would answer by appealing to some notion of a public/private split. She would insist that she speaks for evolutionary science in her public capacity as executive director of the NCSE and endorses the evolutionism of the Humanist Manifesto as a private citizen. It certainly may be honorable to make such distinctions when one's professional responsibilities to an institution conflict with one's personal convictions. We expect judges who privately disagree with the laws they apply in the courtroom to refrain from any expression of dissent lest they prejudice their juries. But it would hardly be honorable for a judge who held her peace in the courtroom to take out a newspaper advertisement to publicize her objections, and this is what Scott has done. In her capacity as the leading voice of the NCSE, she publicly presents evolution merely as a scientific theory, but by signing the Humanist Manifesto she has just as publicly acknowledged that she has no intention of abiding by this claim.

We can be sure that the scientific community in the United States will be unlikely to gain much ground with an already skeptical public so long as evolutionism is voiced alongside the case for evolutionary science. Scientists would be more likely to gain such support by rising up with one voice to repudiate the notion that evolutionary science supports evolutionism, but, if the thesis of this book has any merit, it would be just as naive to suppose that this is likely to happen soon. The evolution-evolutionism identity is simply too alluring. The idea that science can derive a meta-paradigm from its own researches promises to give the scientific community absolute control over the public imagination. So long as scientific patronage figures to benefit when citizens are willing to make this leap from the "is" of evolution to the "ought" of rhetorical Darwinism, then both things are likely to retain equal importance for the scientific community.

Those already inclined to share the AHA's distrust of traditional religious views are unlikely to see evolutionism as a problem. Those weary of seeing secular political ideologies sanctioned by theological ones are unlikely to recognize that they have themselves retreated into something similar. The perennial attraction of evolutionary worldviews comes from their apparent grounding in a scientific perspective that, while nearly as hallowed as religion, also seems to be independent of individual prejudice or ideology. For this reason, contemporary believers in evolutionism are not likely to suppose that they are in any danger of being seduced by the category mistakes that enabled their grandparents to embrace the politics of eugenics as a mere application of scientific truth. But this is because category mistakes are impossible where scientism holds. Once people believe that their decisions follow from evolutionary principles that are presumed to be universal, it becomes impossible to recognize their unscientific aspects. A century ago people commonly mistook hierarchical notions of race for scientific truths. Seized by enthusiasm for the scientistic implications of evolutionary biology, they failed to recognize that they had appropriated an idea that imposed a metaphysical *scala naturae* upon this Darwinian picture.

That specific danger has now passed out of the mainstream, but similar evils are likely to arise so long as this more rudimentary error persists. These threats are easy enough to spot in the messages of the most extreme Darwinists. Daniel Dennett, for instance, has proposed under the heading of "universal Darwinism" a framework of evolutionary causality that takes no metaphysical prisoners. Since Darwinism is that "universal acid" of legend that eats through everything it touches, even the sorts of questions that more moderate proponents of evolution might leave to others are taken away. In principle, this might seem to mean that questions about purpose, meaning, and value would simply no longer be raised; if Darwinism explains all things, all things must be reduced to their mechanistic properties. But what Dennett clearly rejects in principle, he does not refrain from doing in practice. One still finds him making proposals that appear to the ordinary reader's sensibilities as teleological and ethical. Dennett's vision of the future, for instance, is typical of evolutionism. Like Condorcet, Saint-Simon, and Comte before him, he presumes that the pattern of history is the pattern of scientific growth, and this means that Darwinism is destined to realize a universal scope of command—or at least nearly so. There are bound to be a few religious holdouts, and so we face a moral dilemma. As the full force of evolutionary truth takes hold, we will be "faced with a difficult choice" about what to do with the few dissenters who remain. While the scientific rulers of the future will certainly be "eager to preserve" religion in some appropriate "'denatured' state—in churches and cathedrals and synagogues, built to house huge congregations of the devout, and now on the way to being cultural museums"—they will also need to protect society from those who refuse to accept its peaceful retirement. These holdouts may need to be set apart in "zoos" where they will be less likely to harm themselves and others.[50]

I am not particularly worried lest Dennett's vision should soon come to pass. Although we should not be tempted to forget past instances in which scientifically authorized social engineering of this kind became public policy, there seems to be little danger that the Supreme Court will soon be accepting briefs from the likes of Steven Pinker, E. O. Wilson, and Daniel Dennett when it interprets the Bill of Rights. Oliver Wendell Holmes Jr. may have let down his guard a century ago when he upheld the state of

Virginia's right to sterilize Carrie Buck, but memory of the disasters wrought by that era's unrestrained scientism (one would hope) will continue to sustain greater public caution. However, if European and American consumers of science are now repulsed by the prospects of scientific social engineering, this has been due to external factors—to the shocking marriage of eugenics with National Socialism and a civil rights movement that awakened our better angels. The scientific culture itself has never entirely backed away from the underlying framework of ideas that rationalized such initiatives. It has only become more reluctant to advance, except under the cover of abstract academic tomes on sociobiology, the moral and political authority that evolutionism always claims for itself.

Evolutionism does not persist because those who subscribe to it are bad people—or at least not intrinsically any worse than the rest of us—but because it is a mainstay of the contemporary scientific identity. For this reason, it is hard to envision a time when scientists will be willing to abandon it. Without evolutionism, science would be without its institutional self, and while another similar grand narrative might be found, it is hard to imagine one as potent as this. Any alternative construction of the scientific identity, much like the Baconian one that came before it, would require that scientists surrender to outside symbolic resources of public authority that currently seem to arise from within.

My argument will sound to some like a conspiracy theory, but it is not. The conspiracy theorist typically accuses an institution, say an office of the federal government, of hatching a plot that others do not perceive and that authorities formally disavow—a systematic effort to blackball opponents, to cover up some crime, or to obscure the fact that its policies are genuinely grounded in Marxist ideology or in secret alliances with a Masonic cult. In order for a conspiracy theory to be plausible, one must also believe that the accused institution has constructed, more or less in secret but also by design, a vast infrastructure of relationships, plans, and materials capable of perfectly executing its misdeeds. The outsider must also believe that the institution has simultaneously managed to cover all this up—which explains why conspiracy theorists never feel obliged to produce concrete evidence for such plots.

Were I proposing evolutionism as a kind of scientific conspiracy, I would have to suppose that scientists intentionally promulgate lies when they claim that evolutionary science reveals the progressive order of history and promises to deliver a new blueprint for social existence and moral values. I would also have to suppose that they are just as intentionally covering up when they claim that all these proposals rest on a scientific ground. What *will* sound conspiracy-like is my supposition that scientists are almost certain to deny that they are rhetorical Darwinists—and of course many are not. But while I am fairly certain that they do actively promulgate evolutionism, I doubt whether they are truly aware of the pseudoscientific character of these efforts. Rhetorical Darwinists, rather, are true believers. They belong to an academic culture that socializes its members to be insensible to the difference between evolutionary science and evolutionism. As products of a scientistic movement that was beginning to break off from the rest of intellectual culture a century and a half ago, they have lost the capacity to look critically at the positivist underpinnings that sustain their faith. When C. P. Snow decried this split fifty years ago, it was largely because he was concerned about the intellectual deprivations suffered by humanists once they had lost touch with science.[51] In evolutionism we see the flip side of this, a scientific culture tempted by the interests of self-preservation to resist any meaningful conversation with the broader world of thought.

NOTES

Preface

1   See "Understanding Evolution for Teachers," University of California, Berkeley, http://evolution.erkeley.edu/evosite/misconceps/IIIBmight.shtml. Accessed December 15, 2008. Image used with permission of the UC Museum of Paleontology's Understanding Evolution.

2   "Understanding Evolution for Teachers," http://evolution.berkeley.edu/evosite/nature/I3basicquestions.shtml. Accessed December 15, 2008.

3   This definition of culture draws upon the work of Peter Berger, *The Sacred Canopy: Elements of a Sociological Theory of Religion* (Garden City, N.Y.: Doubleday, 1967), 6.

4   Michael Ruse, *Monad to Man: The Concept of Progress in Evolutionary Biology* (Cambridge, Mass.: Harvard University Press, 1996).

5   John Angus Campbell, "Scientific Revolution and the Grammar of Culture: The Case of Darwin's *Origin*," *Quarterly Journal of Speech* 72 (1986): 351-76.

Chapter 1

Epigraph: Mary Midgley, *Evolution as a Religion: Strange Hopes and Stranger Fears* (London: Methuen, 1985), 3-4.

1   Stephen Jay Gould, *Wonderful Life: The Burgess Shale and the Nature of History* (New York: Norton, 1989), 28-34.

2   Jeanne Fahnestock, *Rhetorical Figures in Science* (New York: Oxford University Press, 1999), 95-98.

3   Jeffrey Walker, "Dionysio de Halicarnaso y la Idea de Crítica de la Retórica," *Anuario Filosófico* 31, no. 2 (1998): 581-601; the original English version of

269

Walker's essay is posted on his website: https://webspace.utexas.edu/jw2893/www/index.htm. See also Dilip Gaonkar, "The Idea of Rhetoric in the Rhetoric of Science," *Southern Communication Journal* 58 (1993): 258–95.

4   Aristotle, *On Rhetoric*, trans. George A. Kennedy (New York: Oxford University Press, 1991), 39 [1356a]. The nonrational aspect of this authority suggests some coincidence between Aristotle's notion of ethos and what Max Weber has called "charismatic authority" in *The Theory of Social and Economic Organization*, trans. A. M. Henderson and Talcott Parsons (New York: Free Press, 1947), 106, 358–73.

5   Berger, *Sacred Canopy*, 24–25.

6   *The Outer Limits*, season 1, episode 5, "The Sixth Finger."

7   Arthur C. Clarke, *2001: A Space Odyssey* (New York: New American Library, 1968), 168–69. In Clarke's sequel, *2010*, a different explanation is introduced, a schizophrenia resulting from mixed messages in HAL's programming.

8   Jacob Bronowski, *The Ascent of Man* (Boston: Little, Brown, 1973); Carl Sagan, *Cosmos* (New York: Random House, 1980). Both programs closely follow the accompanying books.

9   Bronowski, *Ascent*, 374.

10   Jacob Bronowski, *Magic, Science, and Civilization* (New York: Columbia University Press, 1978), 1–2.

11   William Poundstone, *Carl Sagan: A Life in the Cosmos* (New York: Henry Holt, 1999), 256–61; John Marsh, "The Universe and Dr. Sagan," *Commentary* 71 (1981): 64.

12   Sagan, *Cosmos*, xii.

13   Martin Buber, *I and Thou*, trans. Ronald Gregor Smith (Edinburgh, U.K.: T&T Clark, 1947).

14   Stephen Toulmin, *The Return to Cosmology: Postmodern Science and the Theology of Nature* (Berkeley: University of California Press, 1982), 21–85, 165–75, 211.

15   Sagan, *Cosmos*, 338.

16   Sagan, *Cosmos*, 3.

17   Sagan, Cosmos, 12

18   Sagan, *Cosmos*, 12.

19   Ruse, *Monad to Man*, 1–83.

20   Michael Ruse, *The Evolution-Creation Struggle* (Cambridge, Mass.: Harvard University Press, 2005), 265.

21   Ruse, *Monad to Man*, 526–39.

22   Ruse, *Monad to Man*, 427–28, 467–70, 511–14.

23   Karl Giberson and Mariano Artigas, *Oracles of Science: Celebrity Scientists versus God and Religion* (Oxford: Oxford University Press, 2007), 19.

24 Davi Johnson, "Dawkins' Myth: The Religious Dimensions of Evolutionary Discourse," *Journal of Communication and Religion* 29 (2006): 285-314.

25 Richard Dawkins, *The Ancestor's Tale: A Pilgrimage to the Dawn of Evolution* (Boston: Houghton Mifflin, 2004), 4-6.

26 Johnson, "Dawkins' Myth," 293-96.

27 Dawkins, *Ancestor's Tale*, 8.

28 Dawkins, *Ancestor's Tale*, 111.

29 F. Newport, "Half of Americans Believe in Creationist Origins of Man," *Gallup Poll Monthly* 336 (1993): 24-28. The scientific account of human evolution is rejected by 47% of Americans and 53% of Canadians in favor of the biblical story of creation. In the United States, a quarter of all college graduates believe that "God created man pretty much in his present form at one time within the last 10,000 years." A more recent poll by *Newsweek*, December 4, 2004, shows a similar percentage of doubters, 45% in total.

30 Thomas M. Lessl, "The Priestly Voice," *Quarterly Journal of Speech* 75 (1989): 183-97.

31 Ronald C. Tobey, *The American Ideology of National Science, 1919-1930* (Pittsburgh: University of Pittsburgh Press, 1971).

32 Alexis de Tocqueville, *Democracy in America*, trans. Richard Heffner (New York: Penguin, 1984), 164-65.

33 Émile Durkheim, *Rules of Sociological Method*, trans. Sarah A. Solovay and John H. Mueller, ed. George E. G. Catlin (Glencoe, Ill.: Free Press, 1964); Émile Durkheim, *The Elementary Forms of the Religious Life*, trans. Joseph Ward Swain (London: Allen & Unwin, 1915).

34 Durkheim, *Elementary Forms*, 419.

35 Émile Durkheim, *Suicide: A Study in Sociology*, trans. J. A. Spaulding and G. Simpson (London: Routledge & Kegan Paul, 1951), 312.

36 Clifford Geertz, *The Interpretation of Cultures* (New York: Basic Books, 1973), 131.

37 Geertz, *Interpretation*, 127.

38 Berger, *Sacred Canopy*, 11.

39 Durkheim, *Elementary Forms*, 422.

40 Geertz, *Interpretation*, 126.

41 Geertz, *Interpretation*, 126.

42 Mary Douglas, *Implicit Meanings: Essays in Anthropology* (London: Routledge & Kegan Paul, 1975), xvi. Durkheim does appear to acknowledge this himself when he states that "the fundamental categories of thought, and consequently of science, are of religious origin." *Elementary Forms*, 466.

43 Émile Durkheim, *Pragmatism and Sociology*, trans. J. C. Whitehouse, ed. John B. Allcock (Cambridge: Cambridge University Press, 1983), 91.

44 René Girard, *Things Hidden since the Foundation of the World*, trans. Stephen Bann and Michael Metteer (Stanford, Calif.: Stanford University Press, 1987), 32.

45 G. Thomas Goodnight, "The Personal, Technical, and Public Spheres of Argument: A Speculative Inquiry into the Art of Public Deliberation," *Journal of the American Forensic Association* 18 (1982): 214-27.

46 Karl Mannheim, *Ideology and Utopia: An Introduction to the Sociology of Knowledge*, trans. Louis Wirth and Edward Shils (New York: Harcourt, Brace & World, 1936), 125.

47 Thomas M. Lessl, "Incommensurate Boundaries: The Rhetorical Positivism of Thomas Huxley," in *Rhetoric and Incommensurability*, ed. Randy Allen Harris (West Lafayette, Ind.: Parlor, 2005), 198-237.

48 Hayden White, *Tropics of Discourse: Essays in Cultural Criticism* (Baltimore, Md.: Johns Hopkins University Press, 1978), 88.

49 Dawkins, *Ancestor's Tale*, 8.

50 White, *Tropics of Discourse*, 88.

51 Northrop Frye, *Anatomy of Criticism: Four Essays* (Princeton, N.J.: Princeton University Press, 1957), 187.

52 Frye, *Anatomy of Criticism*, 187.

53 Bronowski, *Ascent*, 24.

54 Bronowski, *Ascent*, 56.

55 For a summary of these patterns of historical misrepresentation, see Thomas M. Lessl, "The Galileo Legend as Scientific Folklore," *Quarterly Journal of Speech* 85 (Spring 1999): 146-68.

56 Hayden White, *The Content of the Form : Narrative Discourse and Historical Representation* (Baltimore, Md.: Johns Hopkins University Press, 1987).

57 Bronowski, *Ascent*, 202, 205.

58 Giorgio de Santillana, *The Crime of Galileo* (Chicago: University of Chicago Press, 1955).

59 Bronowski, *Ascent*, 218.

60 Bronowski, *Ascent*, 437.

61 The following represent just a small sample of the historical studies that have explored this relationship: John Hedley Brooke, *Science and Religion: Some Historical Perspectives* (Cambridge: University of Cambridge Press, 1991); John Hedley Brooke, *Reconstructing Nature: The Engagement of Science and Religion* (Oxford: Oxford University Press, 2000); Reijer Hooykaas, *Religion and the Rise of Modern Science* (Edinburgh, U.K.: Scottish Academic, 1972); Reijer

Hooykaas, *Robert Boyle: A Study in Science and Christian Belief* (Lanham, Md.: Academic Press of America, 1997); Reijer Hooykaas, *Faith, Fact and Fiction in the Development of Science: The Gifford Lectures Given in the University of St. Andrews* (Boston: Kluwer Academic, 1999); David Lindberg and Ronald Numbers, eds., *God and Nature: Historical Essays on the Encounter Between Christianity and Science* (Berkeley: University of California Press, 1986); Thomas M. Lessl, "Francis Bacon and the Biblical Origins of the Scientific Ethos," *Journal of Communication and Religion* 15 (1992): 87–98. This historical connection has been shown to reflect the scientific culture's need of certain metaphysical ideas that underpin its epistemology, as well as its need to maintain alliances with various social values of its patrons. See, for instance, Edwin Burtt, *The Metaphysical Foundations of Modern Physical Science: A Historical and Critical Essay* (London: Routledge & Kegan Paul, 1924); Friedrich Wilhelm Nietzsche, *The Gay Science: With a Prelude in Rhymes and an Appendix of Songs*, trans. with commentary by Walter Kaufmann (New York: Random House, 1974), 344; Toulmin, *Return to Cosmology*, 191–92; Robert K. Merton, *Science, Technology and Society in Seventeenth-Century England* (Bruges, Belgium: Saint Catherine, 1938); Margaret Jacob, *The Cultural Meaning of the Scientific Revolution* (Philadelphia: Temple University Press, 1987); Joseph Ben-David, *The Scientist's Role in Society: A Comparative Study*, rev. ed. (Chicago: University of Chicago Press, 1984).

62   Geertz, *Interpretation* 351.

63   Sagan, *Cosmos*, 27.

64   R. G. Collingwood, *The Idea of History* (Oxford: Oxford University Press, 1946), 50.

65   Bronowski, *Ascent*, 437.

66   Sagan, *Cosmos*, 339, 345.

67   Richard Weaver, *The Ethics of Rhetoric* (South Bend, Ind.: Regnery/Gateway, 1953), 212–15.

68   Weaver, *Ethics of Rhetoric*, 212–15.

69   Northrop Frye, "Myth, Fiction, and Displacement," in *Theories of Myth*, vol. 4 of *Literary Criticism and Myth*, ed. Robert A. Segal (New York: Garland, 1996), 119–37; Frye, *Anatomy of Criticism*, 77–78.

70   Frye, *Anatomy of Criticism*, 186.

71   Janice Hocker Rushing, "The Rhetoric of the American Western Myth," *Communication Monographs* 50 (1983): 14–32.

72   White, *Content of the Form*, 11.

73   Campbell, "Scientific Revolution," 351–76; John Angus Campbell, "Of Orchids, Insects, and Natural Theology: Timing, Tactics and Cultural Critique in Darwin's Post-'Origin' Strategy," *Argumentation* 8 (1994): 63–80.

Chapter 2

Epigraph: W. A. Sessions, *Francis Bacon Revisited* (New York: Twayne, 1996), 26.

1   Benjamin Nelson, "Discussion: Philosophical and Theological Backgrounds," in *The Nature of Scientific Discovery: A Symposium Commemorating the 500th Anniversary of the Birth of Nicolas Copernicus*, ed. Owen Gingerich (Washington, D.C.: Smithsonian Institution, 1975), 377.

2   René Descartes, *Discourse on the Method of Conducting One's Reason Well and Seeking the Truth in the Sciences*, ed. and trans. George Heffernan (Notre Dame, Ind.: University of Notre Dame Press, 1994), 53-61.

3   William T. Lynch, "A Society of Baconians?: The Collective Development of Bacon's Method in the Royal Society of London," in *Francis Bacon and the Refiguring of Early Modern Thought*, eds. Julie Robin Solomon and Catherine Gimelli Martin (Aldershot, U.K.: Ashgate, 2005), 173-202; Antoinette Mann Paterson, *Francis Bacon and Socialized Science* (Springfield, Ill.: Charles C. Thomas, 1973); Lisa Jardine, *Francis Bacon: Discovery and the Art of Discourse* (Cambridge: Cambridge University Press, 1974); Mary Hesse, "Francis Bacon's Philosophy of Science," in *A Critical History of Western Philosophy*, ed. D. J. O'Connor (New York: Macmillan, 1964), 141-52.

4   See Karl R. Wallace, *Francis Bacon on Communication and Rhetoric* (Chapel Hill: University of North Carolina Press, 1943); Brian Vickers, "Bacon and Rhetoric," in *The Cambridge Companion to Bacon*, ed. Marakku Peltonen (Cambridge: Cambridge University Press, 1996), 200-231.

5   C. S. Lewis, *English Literature in the Sixteenth Century Excluding Drama* (Oxford: Clarendon, 1954), 307.

6   Quoted in Vickers, "Bacon and Rhetoric," 205.

7   Thomas Sprat, *The History of the Royal-Society of London for the Improving of Natural Knowledge* (London: 1667).

8   Michel Malherbe, "Bacon's Method of Science," in *The Cambridge Companion to Bacon*, ed. Marakku Peltonen (Cambridge: Cambridge University Press, 1996), 75-98; William T. Lynch, "A Society of Baconians?: The Collective Development of Bacon's Methods in the Royal Society of London," in *Francis Bacon and the Refiguring of Early Modern Thought: Essays to Commemorate the Advancement of Learning (1605-2005)*, eds. Julie Robin Solomon and Catherine Gimelli Martin (Burlington, Vt.: Ashgate Publishing, 2006), 173-202.

9   Sprat, *History of the Royal Society*, 35-36.

10   Sprat, *History of the Royal Society*, 35.

11   Francis Bacon, *The Works of Francis Bacon*, eds. James Spedding, Robert Leslie

Ellis, and Douglas Denon Heath (1870; reprint, New York: Garrett, 1968), 3:264.

12   Bacon, *Works*, 3:264.

13   Bacon, *Works*, 3:264-65.

14   Bacon, *Works*, 3:265. Eccl 3:11 (emphasis in original).

15   Bacon, *Works*, 3:265. Eccl 3:11; Prov 20:27 (emphasis in original).l

16   The popularity of this trope among Renaissance scientists is explored by Benjamin Nelson, "The Quest for Certitude and the Books of Scripture, Nature, and Conscience," in *The Nature of Scientific Discovery: A Symposium Commemorating the 500th Anniversary of the Birth of Nicolas Copernicus*, ed. Owen Gingerich (Washington, D.C.: Smithsonian Institution, 1975), 355-72. It was first used to justify the separation of science from theology in the twelfth century by Adelard of Bath. See A. C. Crombie, *Robert Grosseteste and the Origins of Experimental Science: 1100-1700* (Oxford: Clarendon, 1961), 11-12.

17   This is a commonplace probably going back to Tertullian. "We postulate that God ought first to be known by nature, and afterward further known by doctrine—by nature through His works, by doctrine through official teaching." Quintus Tertullian, *Against Macion*, trans. and ed. Ernest Evans (Oxford: Clarendon, 1972), 1:18. The metaphor also harkens back to St. Paul's well-known declaration in the Letter to the Romans (1:20) that "Ever since the creation of the world [God's] invisible nature, namely his eternal power and deity, has been clearly perceived in the things that have been made."

18   Bacon, *Works*, 3:221 (emphasis in original).

19   Bacon, *Works*, 3:266.

20   Bacon, *Works*, 3:268.

21   Bacon, *Works*, 3:267-68.

22   When Bacon does use the "handmaid" image in his *Novum Organum* (4:89), he also mixes this metaphor with language that is more suggestive of partnership than clear-cut subordination. Bacon asserts that when Jesus reprimands the Sadducees as men who "know not the Scriptures and the power of God," he was "thus coupling and blending in an indissoluble bond information concerning his will and meditation concerning his power."

23   Maurice A. Finocchiaro, ed. and trans., *The Galileo Affair: A Documentary History* (Berkeley: University of California Press, 1989).

24   William E. Carroll, "Galileo and the Interpretation of the Bible," *Science and Education* 8 (1999): 151-87.

25   Richard J. Blackwell, *Galileo, Bellarmine, and the Bible* (Notre Dame, Ind.: University of Notre Dame Press, 1991), 67-68.

26   Bacon, *Works*, 3:287.

27   Stephen Toulmin, "Introduction: The End of the Copernican era?" in *The Nature of Scientific Discovery: A Symposium Commemorating the 500th Anniversary of the Birth of Nicolaus Copernicus*, ed. Owen Gingerich (Washington, D.C.: Smithsonian Institution, 1975), 189–98.

28   Ben-David, *Scientist's Role*, 75–87.

29   On Bacon as the mediator of the Puritan perspective, see especially John Channing Briggs, "Bacon's Science and Religion," in *The Cambridge Companion to Bacon*, ed. Marakku Peltonen (Cambridge: Cambridge University Press, 1996), 172–99; Jacob, *Cultural Meaning*, 76–84; see also Richard Westfall, *Science and Religion in Seventeenth-Century England* (New Haven, Conn.: Yale University Press, 1958), 106–45; Charles Webster, *The Great Instauration: Science, Medicine and Reform 1626–1660* (New York: Holmes & Meier, 1976), 12–25; Antonio Pérez-Ramos, *Francis Bacon's Science and the Maker's Knowledge Tradition* (Oxford: Clarendon, 1988), 12–16.

30   Harold Fisch, *Jerusalem and Albion: The Hebraic Factor in Seventeenth-Century Literature* (New York: Schocken, 1964), 86.

31   Jacob, *Cultural Meaning*, 78.

32   Bacon, *Works*, 4:372.

33   Bacon, *Works*, 4:104, 11.

34   Webster, *Great Instauration*, 508.

35   Daniel Murphy, *Comenius: A Critical Assessment of His Life and Work* (Dublin: Irish Academic, 1995), 70–78.

36   Robert Fitzgibbon Young, *Comenius in England* (1932; reprint, New York: Arno, 1971), 25–48; Dorothy Stimson, *Scientists and Amateurs: A History of the Royal Society* (New York: Henry Schuman, 1948), 8; G. H. Turnbull, *Hartlib, Dury and Comenius: Gleanings from Hartlib's Papers* (London: University Press of Liverpool, 1947), 1–88.

37   The term appears in the correspondence of Robert Boyle on three different occasions between 1646 and 1647. Harold Hartley, ed., *The Royal Society: Its Origins and Founders* (London: Royal Society, 1960), 21–23.

38   Young, *Comenius in England*, 64; Stephen Clucas, "In Search of 'The True Logick': Methodological Eclecticism Among the 'Baconian Reformers,'" in *Samuel Hartlib and Universal Reformation: Studies in Intellectual Communication*, ed. Mark Greengrass, Michael Leslie, and Timothy Raylor (Cambridge: Cambridge University Press, 1994), 53; Malcolm Oster, "Millenarianism and the New Science: The Case of Robert Boyle," in Greengrass, Leslie, and Raylor, *Samuel Hartlib*, 137–48.

39   John Amos Comenius, *Via Lucis*, trans. E. T. Compagnac (London: Hodder & Stoughton, 1938), 173.

40 John Amos Comenius, *Panorthosia or Universal Reform: Chapter 1-18 and 27*, trans. A. M. O. Dobbie (Sheffield, U.K.: Sheffield Academic, 1995), 47.

41 Robert K. Merton, *The Sociology of Science: Theoretical and Empirical Investigations*, ed. Norman Storer (Chicago: University of Chicago Press, 1973), 228-53. Originally published as "Motive Forces of the New Science," chap. 5 in *Science, Technology and Society in Seventeenth-Century England* (Bruges, Belgium: Saint Catherine, 1938).

42 Merton, *Sociology of Science*, 233.

43 Two prominent historians of seventeenth-century science have come to the support of Merton's thesis. See Webster, *Great Instauration*; and Christopher Hill, *The Century of Revolution: 1603-1714* (Edinburgh, U.K.: T. Nelson, 1961).

44 Chaim Perelman, *The Realm of Rhetoric*, trans. W. Kluback (Notre Dame, Ind.: University of Notre Dame Press, 1982), 36.

45 S. F. Mason, "The Scientific Revolution and the Protestant Reformation," in *Puritanism and the Rise of Modern Science: The Merton Thesis*, ed. I. Bernard Cohen (New Brunswick, N.J.: Rutgers University Press, 1990), 184-88.

46 Kenneth Burke, *Language as Symbolic Action: Essays on Life, Literature and Method* (Berkeley: University of California Press, 1966), 45.

47 Hugh F. Kearney, "Puritanism, Capitalism and the Scientific Revolution," *Past and Present* 28 (1964): 81-101. In this particular essay, Kearney is largely responding to the work of Hill, *Century of Revolution*.

48 James W. Carroll, "Merton's Thesis on English Science," *American Journal of Economics and Sociology* 13 (1954): 427-32; T. K. Rabb, "Puritanism and the Rise of Experimental Science in England," *Journal of World History* 7 (1962): 46-66; A. Rupert Hall, "Merton Revisited, or Science and Society in the Seventeenth Century," *History of Science* 2 (1963): 1-16; Westfall, *Science and Religion*, 7.

49 John Henry, "The Scientific Revolution in England," in *The Scientific Revolution in National Context*, ed. Roy Porter and Mikuláš Teich (Cambridge: Cambridge University Press, 1992), 181-82.

50 Yakov Rabkin, "The Interaction of Scientific and Jewish Cultures: An Historical Overview," in *The Interaction of Scientific and Jewish Cultures in Modern Times*, ed. Yakov Rabkin and Ira Robinson (Lewiston, N.Y.: Edwin Mellen, 1995), 3-30.

51 Ben-David, *Scientist's Role*, 16-17.

52 Gary A. Abraham, "Misunderstanding the Merton Thesis: A Boundary Dispute between History and Sociology," *Isis* 74 (1983): 368-87; Joseph Ben-David, "Puritanism and Modern Science: A Study in the Continuity and Coherence of Sociological Research," in *Comparative Social Dynamics*, ed. Eric

Cohn, Moshe Lissak, and Uri Almagor (Boulder, Colo.: Westview, 1985), 207–23.

53 Henry, "Scientific Revolution," 179.

54 Merton, *Sociology of Science*, 250–53; Max Weber, *The Protestant Ethic and the Spirit of Capitalism*, trans. Talcott Parsons (New York: Charles Scribner's Sons, 1958), 95–154.

55 Sessions, *Bacon Revisited*, 5.

56 *Aubrey's Brief Lives*, ed. Oliver Lawson Dick (Ann Arbor: University of Michigan Press, 1962), 130.

57 Donald C. Bryant, "Rhetoric: Its Functions and Its Scope," *Quarterly Journal of Speech* 39 (1953): 413.

Chapter 3

Epigraphs: Charles Whitney, *Francis Bacon and Modernity* (New Haven, Conn.: Yale University Press, 1986), 5; Bacon, *Works*, 3:136.

1 G. R. Elton, *Reformation Europe 1517–1559* (New York: Harper Torchbooks, 1966), 15–22.

2 Whitney, *Francis Bacon*, 23.

3 Whitney, *Francis Bacon*, 23–54.

4 Bacon, *Works*, 4:261.

5 Webster, *Great Instauration*, 6–8. On the role of millenarian prophecy in the English Civil War, see J. F. McGregor and B. Reays, eds. *Radical Religion in the English Revolution* (Oxford: Oxford University Press, 1988); Bernard S. Capp, *The Fifth Monarchy Men: A Study of Seventeenth-Century Millenarianism* (London: Faber and Faber, 1972); Paul Christianson, *Reformers and Babylon: Apocalyptic Visions from the Reformation to the Eve of the Civil War* (Toronto: University of Toronto Press, 1978); and Christopher Hill, *The World Turned Upside Down: Radical Ideas During the English Revolution* (New York: Vintage, 1972).

6 Joseph Glanvill, *Scepsis Scientifica* (London, 1665), 22.

7 Samuel Hartlib to Robert Boyle, May 8, 1556, in *The Works of the Honourable Robert Boyle*, ed. Thomas Birch (London, 1772), 6:88.

8 R. W. Gibson, *Francis Bacon: A Bibliography of His Works and of Baconiana to the Year 1750* (Oxford: Scrivener, 1950), xv, 147–58, 184–87.

9 Webster, *Great Instauration*, 45.

10 Bacon, *Works*, 3:129.

11 Bacon, *Works*, 3:156–64.

12 Bacon, *Works*, 3:165–66.

13 Whitney, *Francis Bacon*, 30–32.

14   Bacon, *Works*, 3:409–10.

15   Bacon, *Works*, 3:411.

16   Bacon, *Works*, 3:343.

17   Bacon, *Works*, 3:343–44.

18   Robert Faulkner, *Francis Bacon and the Project of Progress* (Boston: Rowman & Littlefield, 1993), 236–39.

19   Bacon, *Works*, 3:129 (emphasis in original).

20   Bacon, *Works*, 4:7.

21   Bacon, *Works*, 4:247–48.

22   Sagan, *Cosmos*, 345.

23   E. O. Wilson, *Consilience: The Unity of Knowledge* (New York: Knopf, 1998), 262.

24   Bacon, *Works*, 3:141–43.

25   Bacon, *Works*, 3:146.

26   Mircea Eliade, *The Myth of the Eternal Return*, trans. W. R. Trask (New York: Pantheon, 1954), 7, 17.

27   Bacon, *Works*, 3:144.

28   Bacon, *Works*, 3:151–54.

29   Merton, *Sociology of Science,"* 273–75. Jerry Weinberger has interpreted this negatively as an indication of the moral and spiritual dangers coinciding with scientific development. Weinberger, Introduction to *New Atlantis and the Great Instauration*, by Francis Bacon, ed. Jerry Weinberger, rev. ed. (Wheeling, Ill.: Harlan Davidson, 1989), xxxii. Faulkner (*Project of Progress*, 235) interprets Bensalemite secrecy as serving the "rhetorical function" of sustaining its visionary aspirations by masking those operations about which it does not wish to speculate. Whitney (*Francis Bacon*, 198) regards this as an anticipation of modernism with its "one-way flow of profit and sovereignty of transnational capital over nations."

30   Bacon, *Works*, 3:285–87. Robert Ellis, in this edition (287n), derives this interpretation of Bacon's "fierce with dark keeping" from the supposition that it alludes to a corresponding Latin fragment that is also quoted in this paragraph.

31   *Teaching about Evolution and the Nature of Science* (Washington, D.C.: National Academies, 1998), 29. Quotation courtesy of the National Academies Press.

32   Collingwood, *Idea of History*, 49–50.

33   Bacon, *Works*, 3:221.

34   Bacon, *Works*, 4:91–92. Bacon quotes Luke 17:20.

35   Bacon, *Works*, 4:91.

36   Bacon, *Works*, 4:92.

37   Bacon, *Works*, 3:220-1, 340.
38   Sessions, *Bacon Revisited*, 153.
39   Bacon, *Works*, 3:343.
40   Bacon, *Works*, 3:137-38.
41   Bacon, *Works*, 3:137-38.
42   Bacon, *Works*, 3:137.
43   Scholars who focus on the modernist features of Bacon's rhetoric certainly do recognize its millenarian features, but they discount their relevance. Hans Blumenberg achieves this by treating this aspect of Bacon's writing as a mere indulgence of his audience, and Robert Faulkner does so by attributing the religious elements to a Machiavellian motive. Hans Blumenberg, *The Legitimacy of the Modern Age*, trans. Robert Wallace (Cambridge, Mass.: MIT Press, 1983); see also Faulkner, *Project of Progress*, 15. Whitney's understanding of the modern aspects of Bacon's thought (*Francis Bacon*, 9–15) is more consistent with my own reading.
44   Margarita Mathiopoulos, *History and Progress: In Search of the European and American Mind* (New York: Praeger, 1989), 13.

Chapter 4

Epigraph: Reinhold Niebuhr, *Human Nature*, vol. 1 of *The Nature and Destiny of Man* (1941; reprint, New York: Charles Scribner's Sons, 1964), 95.
1   Quoted in Richard H. Popkin, "Condorcet and Hume and Turgot," in *Condorcet Studies II*, ed. David Williams (New York: Peter Lang, 1984), 61; Louis de Bonald, *Observations sur un ouvrage posthume de Condorcet, intitulé Esquisse d'un Tableau historique des progrès humain*, in *Œuvres complète de M. de Bonald*, (Petit Montrouge: Migne, 1859), 1:721-22.
2   Carl Becker, *The Heavenly City of the Eighteenth-Century Philosophers* (New Haven, Conn.: Yale University Press, 1932), 102. This theme comprises much of Eric Voegelin's *From Enlightenment to Revolution*, ed. John H. Hallowell (Durham, N.C.: Duke University Press, 1975), 3–194.
3   Jacob Salwyn Schapiro, *Condorcet and the Rise of Liberalism* (New York: Octagon, 1963), 105.
4   Steve Fuller, *Concepts in the Social Sciences: Science* (Buckingham, U.K.: Open University Press, 1998), 4–6.
5   Roger Hahn, *The Anatomy of a Scientific Institution: The Paris Academy of Sciences, 1666–1803* (Berkeley: University of California Press, 1971), 162–68, 193, 205–22.
6   This has been noted by two historians of the French Enlightenment, Peter

Gay, in passing, and Henry Vyverberg, as the thesis of a book-length mono-graph; both reason from the vantage point of a fairly comprehensive view of this period. Peter Gay, *The Party of Humanity: Essays in the French Enlightenment* (New York: Knopf, 1964); Henry Vyverberg, *Historical Pessimism in the French Enlightenment* (Cambridge, Mass.: Harvard University Press, 1958).

7   Jean-Jacques Rousseau, *Discourse on Political Economy and the Social Contract*, trans. Christopher Betts (Oxford: Oxford University Press, 1994), 1.

8   Vyverberg, *Pessimism*, 69.

9   Renée Waldinger, "Condorcet: The Problematic Nature of Progress," *Condorcet Studies I*, ed. Leonora Cohen Rosenfield (Atlantic Heights, N.J.: Humanities Press, 1984), 121-23.

10   Quoted in Becker, *Heavenly City*, 101; Marquis de Condorcet, *Œuvres* (Stutt-gart-bad Cannstatt: Friedrich Frommann Verlag, 1968), 8:188-89.

11   Theodore Olson, *Millenialism, Utopianism and Progress* (Toronto: University of Toronto Press, 1982), 219-20.

12   Charles Frankel, *Faith of Reason: The Idea of Progress in the French Enlightenment* (New York: King's Crown, 1948), 126.

13   Frank Manuel, *The Prophets of Paris* (Cambridge, Mass.: Harvard University Press, 1962), 13, 16.

14   Popkin, "Condorcet and Hume and Turgot," 54.

15   Ann Robert Jacques Turgot, *Turgot on Progress, Sociology, and Economics*, ed. Ronald Meek (Cambridge: Cambridge University Press, 1973), 58.

16   Quoted in Frankel, *Faith of Reason*, 122; Anne Robert Jacques Turgot, *Œuvres de Turgot* (Paris: Librairie Félix Alcan, 1913), 1:194-214.

17   Quoted in Frankel, *Faith of Reason*, 122.

18   Frye, "Myth," 132.

19   Frye, "Myth," 123.

20   Frye, "Myth," 121 (emphasis in original).

21   Frye, *Anatomy of Criticism*, 77-78 (emphasis in original).

22   Frye, *Anatomy of Criticism*, 137.

23   Isak Dinesen, *Anecdotes of Destiny* (New York: Random House, 1958), 23-68.

24   Dinesen, *Anecdotes of Destiny*, 61.

25   Mircea Eliade, *Myths, Dreams, and Mysteries: The Encounter Between Contemporary Faiths and Archaic Realities*, trans. Philip Mairet (New York: Harper & Row, 1960), 27.

26   Frye, "Myth," 135.

27   White, *Tropics of Discourse*, 61-62, 88.

28   White, *Content of the Form*, 2.

29   White, *Tropics of Discourse*, 88 (emphasis in original).

30   White, *Content of the Form*, 21; Kenneth Burke, *A Grammar of Motives* (Berkeley: University of California Press, 1945).

31   Collingwood, *Idea of History*, 49–50.

32   Antoine-Nicolas de Condorcet, *Sketch for a Historical Picture of the Progress of the Human Mind*, trans. June Barraclough (London: Weidenfeld and Nicolson, 1955), 3.

33   Condorcet, *Sketch*, 3 (emphasis added).

34   Condorcet, *Sketch*, 4.

35   Condorcet, *Sketch*, 49.

36   Antoine-Nicolas de Condorcet, "The Nature and Purpose of Public Instruction," in *Condorcet: Selected Writings*, ed. Keith Michael Baker (Indianapolis, Ind.: Bobbs-Merrill, 1976), 114.

37   Condorcet, *Sketch*, 3–4.

38   Collingwood, *Idea of History*, 51.

39   Condorcet, *Sketch*, 45.

40   Condorcet, *Sketch*, 63.

41   Niebuhr, *Human Nature*, 9.

42   Condorcet, *Sketch*, 63–64.

43   Frye, *Anatomy of Criticism*, 195.

44   Condorcet, *Sketch*, 104–5.

45   Condorcet, *Sketch*, 104–5.

46   Condorcet, *Sketch*, 121–22.

47   Condorcet, *Sketch*, 122.

48   Condorcet, *Sketch*, 9.

49   Condorcet, *Sketch*, 121–23.

50   Condorcet, *Sketch*, 175.

51   Condorcet, *Sketch*, 4.

52   Karl R. Popper, *The Poverty of Historicism* (Boston: Beacon, 1957).

53   Condorcet, *Sketch*, 4.

54   Condorcet, *Sketch*, 45.

55   William Keith Chambers Guthrie, *The Fifth-Century Enlightenment*, vol. 3 of *A History of Greek Philosophy* (Cambridge: Cambridge University Press, 1969), 407.

56   Condorcet, *Sketch*, 45–46. For a discussion of the various sources from which historical information concerning Socrates is drawn, see Guthrie, *Enlightenment*, 323–77; on the use of characterization in Greek comedy, see Francis Macdonald Cornford, *The Origin of Attic Comedy* (Cambridge: Cambridge University Press, 1934).

57   Condorcet, *Sketch*, 45.

58   Condorcet, *Sketch*, 17–18.

59   Condorcet, *Sketch*, 17–18.

60   Karl Marx, *Early Writings*, trans. T. B. Bottomore (London: Watts, 1963), 43.

61   Condorcet, *Sketch*, 22.

62   Condorcet, *Sketch*, 44–45.

63   The classicist Louis Dyer tells us that the relation of politics to religion in Athens was "ritualistic rather than ethical" and that Anytus and Meletus, Socrates' accusers, were motivated by personal grudges. Louis Dyer, introduction to *Apology of Socrates and Crito, with Extracts from the Phaedo and Symposium and from Xenophon's Memorabilia*, ed. Louis Dyer (Boston: Ginn, 1908), 15, 23–24. Dyer also notes that Greek religion had no "dogmatic theology" and raised no questions of "orthodoxy or heterodoxy," such as Condorcet here alleges. Dyer, *Apology*, 15. See also Jan N. Bremmer, *Greek Religion* (Oxford: Oxford University Press, 1994), 1–10; and John M. Wickersham and Dora C. Pozzi, introduction to *The Myth and the Polis*, ed. Dora Pozzi and John M. Wickersham (Ithaca, N.Y.: Cornell University Press, 1991), 1–15.

64   Condorcet, *Sketch*, 179.

65   Condorcet, *Sketch*, 147.

66   Ben-David, *Scientist's Role*, 89–94, 102, 126–29.

67   Ben-David, *Scientist's Role*, 100–102.

Chapter 5

Epigraph: Marie-Joseph Chénier, quoted in Becker, *Heavenly City*, 156–57; *Œuvre de M. J. Chénier* (Paris: Guillaume, 1824) 3:377.

1   Iain McLean and Fiona Hewitt, trans. and eds., *Condorcet: Foundations of Social Choice and Political Theory* (Brookfield, Vt.: Edward Elgar, 1994), 17–31.

2   Eric Voegelin, *From Enlightenment to Revolution*, ed. John H. Hallowell (Durham, N.C.: Duke University Press, 1975), 10.

3   Reinhold Niebuhr, *Faith and History: A Comparison of Christian and Modern Views of History* (New York: Charles Scribner's Sons, 1949), 6.

4   Collingwood, *Idea of History*, 129.

5   Collingwood, *Idea of History*, 129.

6   Frank E. Manuel, *The New World of Henri Saint-Simon* (Cambridge, Mass.: Harvard University Press, 1956), 117.

7   Émile Durkheim, *Socialism and Saint-Simon*, ed. Alvin Gouldner, trans. Charlotte Sattler (Yellow Springs, Ohio: Antioch, 1958).

8   Claude Henri de Saint-Simon, *Introduction aux travaux scientifiques*, in *Œuvres Choisies* (Hildesheim: Georg Olms Verlag, 1973), 1:109.

9   Saint-Simon, *Mémoire sur la science de l'homme*, in *Œuvres Choisies*, 2:111–12; Manuel, *Saint-Simon*, 139–47.

10 Claude Henri de Saint-Simon, *Esquisse d'une nouvelle encyclopédie, ou Introduction à la philosophie du XIXe siècle*, quoted in Mary Pickering, *Auguste Comte: An Intellectual Biography* (Cambridge: Cambridge University Press, 1993), 1:72.

11 This was announced in one of Saint-Simon's earliest pamphlets, his *Extrait d'un ouvrage sur l'organization social* of 1804. It is translated as "Extract on Social Organization," in *Henri Saint-Simon (1760–1825): Selected Writings on Science, Industry and Social Organization*, ed. and trans. Keith Taylor (New York: Holmes & Meier, 1975), 83–85.

12 Claude Henri de Saint-Simon and Augustin Thierry, *De la réorganisation de la société Européenne*, in *Œuvres Choisies*, 2:253–328. Portions of this tract are translated as "The Reorganization of the European Community," in *Henri Comte de Saint-Simon (1760–1825): Selected Writings*, trans. F. M. H. Markham (New York: Macmillan, 1952), 28–68.

13 Saint-Simon, "Reorganization," in Markham, *Selected Writings*, 29. The scientific principle in this case is what Manuel interprets this law of 'alternativity' as a notion similar to the historical dialectic of Hegel—though invented independently. See Manuel, *Saint-Simon*, 139–47.

14 Keith Taylor, introduction to Taylor, *Saint-Simon*, 30.

15 We see in Saint-Simon the beginnings of the positivist reduction of the notion of "universalism" to its methodological component. This is the sense of the term as it has been appropriated by sociologists of science to describe the methodological norm which supposes that a common standard applies to scientific claims in all times and cultures. See Robert K. Merton, "The Normative Structure of Science," in *Sociology of Science*, 270.

16 The general character of Saint-Simon's appeals to these various audiences is discussed in Manuel, *Saint-Simon*, 189–98, 283–84. On his efforts to influence Napoleon and his campaign to influence the French *industriels*, see also Mathurin Dondo, *The French Faust Henri de Saint-Simon* (New York: Philosophical Library, 1955), 104, 131–48.

17 Georg G. Iggers, introduction to *The Doctrine of Saint-Simon: An Exposition First Year, 1828–1829*, trans. Georg G. Iggers (Boston: Beacon, 1958), ix–xii. Two years before, Saint-Simon had dedicated his *Travail sur la gravitation universelle* to "his Majesty the Emperor." In likening Napoleon to Charlemagne, Saint-Simon enjoins him to extend the reign of his own new Christianity over all of Europe. Translated as "Study in Universal Gravitation," in Taylor, *Saint-Simon*, 124–27. See also Manuel, *Saint-Simon*, 120.

18 Claude Henri de Saint-Simon and Augustin Thierry, "The Reorganization of

European Society," in Taylor, *Saint-Simon*, 130–36; Saint-Simon, "Letter to the Minister of the Interior," in Taylor, *Saint-Simon*, 141–44.

19   Saint-Simon and Thierry, "Reorganization," in Taylor, *Saint-Simon*, 132.

20   The inversion of this meaning of *idéology* that would eventually become the false consciousness of Marxist social theory first arose from Napoleon's reaction against this movement.

21   The presumption that there was direct contact between de Staël and Saint-Simon is based upon the testimony of his disciples, but is not corroborated in any of the surviving writings or correspondence of either party. However, it is known that Saint-Simon spent time in Geneva, where Madame de Staël had relocated her Parisian salon after falling out with Bonaparte. See Dondo, *French Faust*, 99–102.

22   Madame de Staël's speculations on such a positivist system are in her *De la littérature considérée dans ses rapports avec les institutions sociales, suivi de L'Influence des passions sur le bonheur, des individus et des nations* (Paris: InfoMédia Communication, 1998). See Pickering, *Auguste Comte*, 1:65–66; Manuel, *Saint-Simon*, 59–61.

23   Pickering, *Auguste Comte*, 1:88–89; Manuel, *Saint-Simon*, 67–69.

24   The earliest presentation of this scheme is found in Saint-Simon's *Lettres d'un habitant de Genève à ses contemporains*, published in 1802–1803. It is translated as "Letters from an Inhabitant of Geneva to his Contemporaries," in Taylor, *Saint-Simon*, 66–82; Manuel, *Saint-Simon*, 73–75, 124, 164.

25   Saint-Simon and Thierry, "Reorganization," in Markham, *Selected Writings*, 28–68. This was first published as *De la réorganisation de la société Européenne* in 1814.

26   Charles François Dupuis, *The Origin of All Religious Worship*, ed. and trans. Robert Richardson (1872; facsimile, New York: Garland, 1984).

27   Manuel, *Saint-Simon*, 124–25.

28   Voegelin, *Enlightenment to Revolution*, 174, 186–94.

29   Pickering, *Auguste Comte*, 1:73.

30   Becker, *Heavenly City*, 82.

31   Saint-Simon, "Memoir," in Taylor, *Saint-Simon*, 113.

32   Saint-Simon, *De la réorganisation de la société Européenne*, in *Œuvres Choisies*, 1:198.

33   Saint-Simon, "Memoir," in Markham, *Selected Writings*, 21.

34   Saint-Simon, *Travaux Scientifiques*, in *Œuvres Choisies*, 1:199.

35   Saint-Simon, "Scientific Studies," in Taylor, *Saint-Simon*, 95 (emphasis in original).

36   Saint-Simon, "Scientific Studies," in Taylor, *Saint-Simon*, 95.

37 Saint-Simon, *Travaux Scientifiques*, 1:206.
38 Saint-Simon, *Travaux Scientifiques*, 1:206.
39 Auguste Comte, *The Positive Philosophy*, trans. Harriet Martineau, 3rd ed. (London: Kegan Paul, 1893), 1:1-2.
40 Comte, *Positive Philosophy*, 1:2.
41 Comte, *Positive Philosophy*, 1:1-2, 2:142-43.
42 Saint-Simon, "New Christianity," in Markham, *Selected Writings*, 102.
43 Saint-Simon, "New Christianity," 116.
44 Recorded, according to Markham, by Saint-Simon's disciples. *Selected Writings*, xvii.
45 Voegelin, *Enlightenment to Revolution*, 136-42.
46 Pickering, *Auguste Comte*, 1:415.
47 Leah Ceccarelli, "Polysemy: Multiple Meanings in Rhetorical Criticism," *Quarterly Journal of Speech* 84 (1998): 407-9.
48 Burke, *Grammar of Motives*, 507.
49 Saint-Simon, *Lettres d'un habitant de Genève à ses contemporains*, in *Œuvres Choisies*, 1:40.
50 Burke, *Grammar of Motives*, 509.
51 Manuel, *Saint-Simon*, 349.
52 Émile Durkheim, *Socialism and Saint-Simon*, 193-94. See also Durkheim, *Elementary Forms*, 466.
53 Voegelin, *Enlightenment to Revolution*, 22.
54 Voegelin, *Enlightenment to Revolution*, 90.
55 Auguste Comte, *System of Positive Polity*, trans. Frederic Harrison (New York: Burt Franklin, 1875), 1:309-10, 322, 329-30, 332, 334-36.
56 Comte, *System of Positive Polity*, 1:325-26 (emphasis added).
57 Comte, *System of Positive Polity*, 1:310.
58 Comte, *System of Positive Polity*, 1:309.
59 Comte, *System of Positive Polity*, 1:309-12.
60 Comte, *System of Positive Polity*, 1:309-10.
61 Auguste Comte, *Œuvres d'Auguste Comte* (Paris: Éditions Anthropos, 1968), 7:iv.

Chapter 6

Epigraph: Gertrud Lenzer, ed., *Auguste Comte and Positivism: The Essential Writings* (Chicago: University of Chicago Press, 1975), xvii.
1 Thomas H. Huxley, "The Physical Basis of Life," in *Methods and Results*, vol. 1 of *Selected Works of Thomas H. Huxley* (New York: Appleton, 1893), 156. For a

brief summary of Huxley's ongoing feud with positivism, see James G. Paradis, *T. H. Huxley: Man's Place in Nature* (Lincoln: University of Nebraska Press, 1978), 80–86; and Sydney Eisen, "Huxley and the Positivists," *Victorian Studies* 7 (1964): 337–58.

2   Thomas H. Huxley, "Agnosticism: A Symposium," *Agnostic Annual*, 1884.

3   Michael Bartholomew, "Huxley's Defence of Darwin," *Annals of Science* 32 (1975): 425–35; Sherrie L. Lyons, *Thomas Henry Huxley: The Evolution of a Scientist* (Amherst, N.Y.: Prometheus, 1999), 13–24; Adrian Desmond, *Huxley: From Devil's Disciple to Evolution's High Priest* (Reading, Mass.: Addison-Wesley, 1997), 627.

4   See especially J. Vernon Jensen, *Thomas Henry Huxley: Communicating for Science* (Newark: University of Delaware Press, 1991), 166–85; Leonard Huxley, *Thomas Henry Huxley: A Character Sketch* (1920; reprint, Freeport, N.Y.: Books for Libraries, 1969), 43–50; Ed Block Jr., "T. H. Huxley's Rhetoric and the Popularization of Victorian Scientific Ideas: 1854–1874," *Victorian Studies* 29 (1986): 363–86; and Walter Houghton, "The Rhetoric of T. H. Huxley," *University of Toronto Quarterly* 18 (1949): 159–75.

5   Adrian Desmond, introduction to *Scientific Papers and Correspondence of Thomas Henry Huxley, c. 1843–1895, from the Imperial College of Science, Technology, and Medicine, London*, units 1 and 2 of *Darwin, Huxley and the Natural Sciences* (London: Research Publications, 1990), 5 (emphasis in original).

6   Paul White, *Thomas Huxley: Making the "Man of Science"* (Cambridge: Cambridge University Press, 2003), 69–75; Desmond, *Huxley*, 190, 192–93, 195–97, 204–5, 219–20, 224–25, 261–62.

7   These are published as Thomas H. Huxley, "The Darwinian Hypothesis," *Selected Works*, 2:1–21; and Thomas H. Huxley, "The Origin of Species," *Selected Works*, 22–79.

8   Thomas H. Huxley to John Morley, February 7, 1878, in *Life and Letters of Thomas Huxley*, ed. Leonard Huxley (New York: Appleton, 1901), 1:523.

9   Huxley to Herbert Spencer, November 7, 1886, in *Life and Letters*, 2:154.

10   Huxley to Ray Lankester, December 6, 1888, in *Life and Letters*, 2:227.

11   Huxley to Charles Darwin, November 14, 1880, in *Life and Letters*, 2:15.

12   Huxley to Ernst Haeckel, May 20, 1867, in *Life and Letters*, 1:309–10 (emphasis is in original).

13   Adrian Desmond, introduction to *Scientific Papers and Correspondence*, 5.

14   John Fiske to Abby Fiske, December 31, 1873, in *The Letters of John Fiske*, Ethel F. Fiske, ed. (New York: Macmillan, 1940), 296; John Fiske to Abby Fiske, November 12, 1873, in *Letters of John Fiske*, 270–71.

15   Cyril Bibby, "Thomas Henry Huxley and University Development," *Victorian Studies* 2 (1958): 107.

16   Bibby, "University Development," 98.

17   Huxley to Henrietta Heathhorn, March 1851, in *Life and Letters*, 1:72.

18   Ben-David, *Scientist's Role*, 89–94, 102–3, 126–29.

19   Desmond, *Huxley*, 185–87; White, *Man of Science*, 72–73; Thomas H. Huxley, "Science," *Westminster Review* 5 (1854): 254–57.

20   White, *Man of Science*, 69–75.

21   George Eliot to George Combe, November 28, 1853, in *The George Eliot Letters*, ed. Gordon Haight (New Haven, Conn.: Yale University Press, 1954), 8:89–90 (emphasis in original).

22   Huxley, "Darwinian Hypothesis," 20.

23   Lester Kurtz, *The Politics of Heresy: The Modernist Crisis in Roman Catholicism* (Berkeley: University of California Press, 1986); Kai Erikson, *Wayward Puritans: A Study in the Sociology of Deviance* (New York: John Wiley, 1966).

24   T. R. Wright, *The Religion of Humanity: The Impact of Comtean Positivism on Victorian Britain* (Cambridge: Cambridge University Press, 1986), 1, 273.

25   Thomas H. Huxley, "The Scientific Aspects of Positivism," in *Lay Sermons, Addresses, and Reviews* (New York: Appleton, 1871), 147.

26   Desmond, *Huxley*, 193; Eliot to John Chapman, December 17, 1853, in *Eliot Letters*, 2:132–33. Lewes' response was published in *Leader*, January 14, 1854, 40.

27   Huxley to Charles Kingsley, April 12, 1869, in *Life and Letters*, 1:323.

28   Desmond, *Huxley*, 487–88, 625–28.

29   Charles Kingsley to F. D. Maurice, October 23, 1868, in *Charles Kingsley: His Letters and Memories of His Life*, ed. Frances E. Kingsley (London: Henry King, 1877), 2:214.

30   Kingsley to Dr. Rigg, May 16, 1871, in *Letters and Memories*, 2:367.

31   See Desmond, *Huxley*, 373; and George Eliot to Frederic Harrison, January 5, 1866, in *Eliot Letters*, 4:214–15. Huxley, of course, was not always adverse to such arguments himself. See, for instance, his "On the Advisableness of Improving Natural Knowledge," in *Methods and Results*, 18–41.

32   Eisen, "Huxley and the Positivists," 343.

33   Thomas H. Huxley, "Science and Culture," in *Science and Education: Essays*, vol. 3 of *Selected Works of Thomas H. Huxley* (New York: Appleton, 1893), 155.

34   Robert Gilpin, "The Atlantic Imbalance in Science and Technology," in *Comparative Studies in Science and Society*, ed. Sal Restivo and Christopher Vanderpool (Columbus, Ohio: Merill, 1974), 289–305.

35   Thomas Gieryn's case study, in fact, revolves around the similar messages of

Huxley's close friend, the Irish physicist John Tyndall. Gieryn, "Boundary-Work and the Demarcation of Science from Non-Science: Strains and Interests in Professional Ideologies of Scientists," *American Sociological Review* 48 (1983): 781-95.

36   Ruth Barton, "'An Influential Set of Chaps': The X-Club and Royal Society Politics 1864-85," *British Journal of the History of Science* 23 (1990): 72.

37   Barton, "X-Club," 58; Huxley to W. H. Flower, July 7, 1883, in *Life and Letters,* 2:57.

38   Paul White, "Ministers of Culture: Arnold, Huxley and Liberal Anglican Reform of Learning," *History of Science* 43 (2005): 115-38.

39   Huxley, "Physical Basis of Life," 156 (emphasis in original).

40   Eisen, "Huxley and the Positivists," 341 (emphasis in original).

41   William Irvine, *Apes, Angels, and Victorians: The Story of Darwin, Huxley, and Evolution* (New York: McGraw-Hill, 1972), 250.

42   Edward Beesly to Huxley, February 8, 1869, in *Huxley Papers*, College Archives, Imperial College London, 10:270-71.

43   Richard Congreve, "Mr. Huxley on M. Comte," *Fortnightly Review* 5 (1869): 407.

44   Huxley, "Scientific Aspects of Positivism," 123-72.

45   Congreve, "Mr. Huxley," 415.

46   Huxley to Henrietta Huxley, August 8, 1873, in *Life and Letters,* 1:428.

47   Thomas H. Huxley, "On the Study of Biology," in *Science and Education,* 270-71.

48   Ernst Cassirer, *The Problem of Knowledge: Philosophy, Science, and History since Hegel*, trans. William H. Woglom and Charles W. Hendel (New Haven, Conn.: Yale University Press, 1950), 245-46.

49   Thomas H. Huxley, "An Apologetic Irenicon," *Fortnightly Review* 52 (November 1892): 557.

50   Huxley, "Apologetic Irenicon," 557.

51   Huxley, "Apologetic Irenicon," 559.

52   Bryant, "Rhetoric," 413.

53   Campbell, "Scientific Revolution"; Campbell, "Orchids, Insects, and Natural Theology."

54   Campbell, "Orchids, Insects, and Natural Theology," 66.

55   Henry Longueville Mansel, *The Limits of Religious Thought Examined in Eight Lectures* (London: John Murray, 1858); Bernard Lightman, *The Origins of Agnosticism: Victorian Unbelief and the Limits of Knowledge* (Baltimore, Md.: Johns Hopkins University Press, 1987), 7-9, 32-67.

56   Charles Lyell to George Ticknor, March 11, 1859, in *Life, Letters and Journals*

of Sir Charles Lyell, ed. K. M. Lyell (London: John Murray, 1881), 2:321–22. See also Huxley to Charles Kingsley, September 23, 1860, *Life and Letters*, 1:234–35.

57 Lightman, *Origins of Agnosticism*, 181.

58 Huxley to Charles Kingsley, September 23, 1860, in *Life and Letters*, 1:235.

59 James G. Paradis writes that the extensive notes left behind in Huxley's manuscripts reveal his aspiration to construct a "system" that "would have borrowed from Greek Stoical thought and from the philosophy of Spinoza, incorporating the principle of evolutionary progression as the driving force of the whole." Paradis, *Man's Place*, 4, 185. Paradis also discusses Carlyle's influence on Huxley as a spiritual mentor (48–49).

60 John Morley, *Critical Miscellanies* (London: Macmillan, 1886), 1:179.

61 Desmond, *Huxley*, 375–76.

62 Leonard Huxley, *Life and Letters*, 1:336–45; Lightman, *Origins of Agnosticism*, 10–16; Desmond, *Huxley*, 374.

63 Thomas H. Huxley, "Agnosticism," in *Science and Christian Tradition*, vol. 5 of *Selected Works of Thomas H. Huxley* (New York: Appleton, 1893), 239.

64 Huxley, "Scientific Aspect of Positivism," 130–31.

65 Desmond, *Huxley*, 372–74; Lightman, *Origins of Agnosticism*, 120, 158, 181.

66 *Huxley Papers*, College Archives, Imperial College London, 47:148; Huxley to Michael Foster, November 10, 1883, in *Life and Letters*, 2:65.

67 Huxley, "Physical Basis of Life," 154–55.

68 Lenzer, *Auguste Comte*, xiii.

69 Thomas H. Huxley, "Autobiography," in *Methods and Results*, 5.

70 See, for instance, his correspondence with two of his children while he was touring the Vatican in Rome. Huxley to his daughter Mrs. Roller, January 11, 1885, in *Life and Letters*, 2:95; and Huxley to his son Leonard, January 20, 1885, in *Life and Letters*, 2:98.

71 Tener and Woodfield, *A Victorian Spectator*, 280– 81n1, 281n2.

72 R. H. Hutton, "Pope Huxley," *Spectator*, January 29, 1870, 135–36. Reprinted in Tener and Woodfield, *Victorian Spectator*, 180–84.

73 Thomas H. Huxley, "Agnosticism: A Rejoinder," in *Science and the Christian Tradition*, 267; Desmond, *Huxley*, 567.

74 Huxley to Charles Kingsley, April 12, 1869, in *Life and Letters*, 1:323.

75 Huxley, "Scientific Aspect of Positivism," 128–29.

76 Huxley, "Scientific Aspect of Positivism," 129–30.

77 Thomas H. Huxley, "Universities: Actual and Ideal," in *Science and Education*, 191–92.

78   Huxley, "Universities," 192.
79   Huxley to Henrietta Huxley, August 8, 1873, in *Life and Letters*, 1:427–28.

Chapter 7

Epigraph: Northrop Frye, *The Secular Scripture: The Study of the Structure of Romance* (Cambridge, Mass.: Harvard University Press, 1976), 6.

1   Thomas H. Huxley, *Hume: With Helps to the Study of Berkeley*, vol. 6 of *Selected Works of Thomas H. Huxley* (New York: Appleton, 1893), 61.
2   Bartholomew, "Huxley's Defence of Darwin," 525–35.
3   Frank Turner has touched on the same idea in his "Public Science in Britain: 1880–1919," in *Contesting Cultural Authority: Essays in Victorian Intellectual Life* (Cambridge: Cambridge University Press, 1993), 20.
4   Thomas H. Huxley, "Prologue to Controverted Questions," in *Science and the Christian Tradition*, 41.
5   Peter Bowler, *The Non-Darwinian Revolution* (Baltimore, Md.: Johns Hopkins University Press, 1988), 72–77.
6   Thomas H. Huxley, preface to *Darwiniana*, vol. 2 of *Selected Works of Thomas H. Huxley* (New York: Appleton, 1893), v–vi.
7   Lyons, *Huxley*.
8   Huxley to Charles Darwin, November 23, 1859, *Life and Letters*, 1:188–89 (emphasis in original).
9   Lyons, *Huxley*, 49–53, 60–72; Bartholomew, "Huxley's Defence of Darwin," 525–26; Mario A. di Gregorio, *T. H. Huxley's Place in Natural Science* (New Haven, Conn.: Yale University Press, 1984), 26–33, 123–24; Louis Agassiz, "Evolution and Permanence of Type," *Atlantic Monthly*, January 1874, 92–101.
10   Lyons, *Huxley*, 49–90.
11   Ruth Barton, "Evolution: The Whitworth Gun in Huxley's War for the 'Liberation of Science from Theology,'" in *The Wider Domain of Evolutionary Thought*, ed. D. R. Oldroyd and I. Langham (Dordrecht: Reidel, 1983), 268.
12   di Gregorio, *Huxley's Place*, 60–65.
13   Huxley, "Darwinian Hypothesis," 20. This essay first appeared as "Darwin on the Origin of Species," *London Times*, December 26, 1859. Thomas H. Huxley, "Time and Life: Mr. Darwin's 'Origin of Species,'" *Macmillan's Magazine* 1 (1859): 142–48.
14   Huxley to Joseph Dalton Hooker, December 31, 1859, in *Life and Letters*, 1:190 (emphasis is in original).
15   Huxley to Charles Lyell, August 17, 1862, in *Huxley Papers*, College Archives, Imperial College London, 30:41.

16 Leonard Huxley, *Life and Letters*, 1:391. In the passage where Leonard Huxley attributes the phrase "Darwin's bull-dog" to his father, he is discussing an instance in which Huxley was responding to the treatment of Darwin in a *Quarterly Review* article that his father regarded as "unjust and unbecoming."

17 Huxley to Charles Darwin, November 23, 1859, in *Life and Letters*, 1:189.

18 Huxley to Charles Lyell, March 17, 1860, in *Life and Letters*, 1:228.

19 Thomas H. Huxley, "On Species and Races," in *The Scientific Memoirs of Thomas Henry Huxley*, eds. Michael Forster and Ray Lankester (London: Macmillan 1898–1901), 2:392.

20 Huxley, "On Species and Races," 2:392–93.

21 John Bunyan, *The Pilgrim's Progress from This World to That Which Is to Come* (1667; reprint, London, J. M. Dent, 1907), 47–48.

22 Huxley, "On Species and Races," 2:393.

23 Huxley, "On Species and Races," 2:393.

24 Huxley, "On Species and Races," 2:393.

25 Huxley, "On Species and Races," 2:393.

26 Huxley, "On Species and Races," 2:393–94.

27 Desmond, *Huxley*, 268–69.

28 Charles Darwin to J. D. Hooker, February 14, 1860, in *The Correspondence of Charles Darwin*, ed. Frederick Burkhardt and Sydney Smith (Cambridge: Cambridge University Press, 1985–1994), 8:80, 84 (emphasis in original).

29 Thomas H. Huxley, "On Species and Races," in *Huxley Papers*, College Archives, Imperial College London, 41:9–56.

30 Thomas H. Huxley, "The Coming of Age of the 'Origin of Species,'" in *Darwiniana*, 227–43.

31 Huxley, "Coming of Age," 229.

32 Huxley to Charles Darwin, May 10, 1880, in *Life and Letters*, 2:13.

33 Huxley, "Controverted Questions," 42.

34 Quoted in Leonard Huxley, *Life and Letters*, 2:428

35 Quoted in Leonard Huxley, *Life and Letters*, 2:428.

36 Mircea Eliade, *Myths, Dreams, and Mysteries*, 2.

37 John C. Greene, *Science, Ideology, and World View: Essays in the History of Evolutionary Ideas* (Berkeley: University of California Press, 1981), 60–193. This interpretation is also supported by Ruse, *Monad to Man*, 145–50, 187–91.

38 I. A. Richards, *Philosophy of Rhetoric* (Oxford: Oxford University Press, 1965), 89–112; Max Black, *Models and Metaphors* (Ithaca, N.Y.: Cornell University Press, 1962), 25–47. "Combining" is Paul Ricoeur's term; see Ricoeur, *The Rule of Metaphor: Multi-Disciplinary Studies of the Creation of Meaning in Language*,

trans. Robert Czerny, Kathleen McLaughlin, and John Costello (Toronto: University of Toronto Press, 1977), 180.

39 Ricoeur, *Rule of Metaphor*, 196–97 (emphasis in original).

40 Earl R. MacCormac, *Metaphor and Myth in Science and Religion* (Durham, N.C.: Duke University Press, 1976), 102. A diaphor is a "metaphor that *suggests* possible meanings rather than expresses meanings that are confirmed by hearers" (85) (emphasis in original). It is a metaphor that is incapable of becoming "dead." Once the tension is lost between tenor and vehicle, the figure ceases to mean. This distinction comes from Philip Wheelright, *Metaphor and Reality* (Bloomington: University of Indiana Press, 1962), 57.

41 Mircea Eliade, *Myth and Reality*, trans. W. R. Trask (New York: Harper & Row, 1963), 1–2.

42 Jacques Ellul, *The New Demons*, trans. E. Edward Hopkin (New York: Seabury, 1975), 51–52.

43 Roland Barthes, *Mythologies*, trans. Annette Lavers (London: Jonathan Cape, 1972), 109–59. The window analogy is Barthes' as well (124–25).

44 Barthes, *Mythologies*, 129, 131. Barthes does not use the vocabulary of "tenor" and "vehicle" in his discussion of myth. He defines mythic metaphors, in the language of semiotics, as "second order signifiers."

45 Paradis, *Man's Place*, 121.

46 Paradis, *Man's Place*, 4.

47 Michael Ruse, *Darwin and Design: Does Evolution Have a Purpose?* (Cambridge, Mass.: Harvard University Press, 2003), 81–82.

48 Huxley, *Man's Place in Nature*, vol. 7 of *Selected Works of Thomas H. Huxley* (New York: Appleton, 1893), 1.

49 Claude Lévi-Strauss, *Myth and Meaning*, ed. Wendy Doniger (1978; reprint, New York: Schocken, 1995), 44–54.

50 Huxley, *Man's Place in Nature*, 77–78.

51 Huxley, *Man's Place in Nature*, 77–78.

52 Arthur O. Lovejoy, *The Great Chain of Being* (Cambridge, Mass.: Harvard University Press, 1953).

53 The Hawkins illustration appears on p. 76, and Huxley's comparisons of primate and human anatomy begin on p. 97.

54 Huxley, *Man's Place in Nature*, 78.

55 Huxley, *Man's Place in Nature*, 78–79.

56 Collingwood, *Idea of History*, 49.

57 Huxley, *Man's Place in Nature*, 79.

58 Burke, *Grammar of Motives*, 503.

59 Barton, "Whitworth Gun," 275.

60 Huxley, *Man's Place in Nature*, 79–80.
61 Huxley, *Man's Place in Nature*, 80.
62 Huxley, *Man's Place in Nature*, 149.
63 Huxley, *Man's Place in Nature*, 150–51.
64 Joseph Butler, *The Analogy of Religion, Natural and Revealed, to the Constitution and Course of Nature* (Oxford: Clarendon, 1874), 205.
65 Butler, *Analogy of Religion*, 6.
66 Huxley to Kingsley, May 5, 1863, in *Life and Letters*, 1:259.
67 Huxley to Kingsley, May 5, 1863, in *Life and Letters*, 1:260.
68 Huxley to Kingsley, May 22, 1863, in *Life and Letters*, 1:263.
69 Lightman, *Origins of Agnosticism*, 152–60.
70 Lightman, *Origins of Agnosticism*, 147–49.
71 Huxley, *Man's Place in Nature*, 151.
72 Huxley, *Man's Place in Nature*, 152–54.
73 Huxley, *Man's Place in Nature*, 154.
74 Huxley, *Man's Place in Nature*, 154.
75 Huxley, *Man's Place in Nature*, 155.
76 Huxley, *Man's Place in Nature*, 155–56.

Chapter 8

Epigraphs: Ruse, *Evolution-Creation Struggle*, 265; Midgley, *Evolution as a Religion*, 4.
1   Wilfrid Ward, *Problems and Persons* (Freeport, N.Y.: Books for Libraries, 1903), 240–41.
2   Huxley, "Controverted Questions," 2.
3   Desmond, *Huxley*, 598.
4   Huxley, "Physical Basis of Life," 155.
5   Thomas H. Huxley, "Nature: Aphorisms by Goethe," *Nature* 1 (1869): 9.
6   Thomas H. Huxley, "A Liberal Education and Where to Find It," in *Science and Education*, 82.
7   James Paradis, "Evolution and Ethics in Its Victorian Context," in *T. H. Huxley's Evolution and Ethics With New Essays on Its Victorian and Sociobiological Context*, ed. James Paradis and George C. Williams (Princeton, N.J.: Princeton University Press, 1989), 52.
8   Desmond, *Huxley*, 597.
9   Barton, "Whitworth Gun," 261.
10 Leonard Huxley, *Life and Letters*, 1:383–84.
11 Appendix iv to Leonard Huxley, *Life and Letters*, 2:499–503.
12 Chicago: Field Museum of Natural History.

13 Chicago: Field Museum of Natural History.

14 Quoted in Joseph S. Levine and Kenneth R. Miller, *Biology: Discovering Life* (Lexington, Mass.: D. C. Heath, 1991), 140.

15 Levine and Miller, *Biology*, 140 (emphasis in original).

16 Levine and Miller, *Biology*, 140.

17 Levine and Miller, *Biology*, 141.

18 Levine and Miller, *Biology*, 144.

19 Levine and Miller, *Biology*, 152.

20 William Jennings Bryan, "Prince of Peace," *New York Times*, September 7, 1913.

21 Paolo E. Coletta, *William Jennings Bryan* (Lincoln: University of Nebraska Press, 1964), 3:200.

22 Klaus Wagner, *Kried: Eine politish-entwicklungsgeschichtliche Untersuchung* (Jena: Hermann Constenoble, 1906), 53, quoted in Richard Weikart, *From Darwin to Hitler: Evolutionary Ethics, Eugenics and Racism in Germany* (New York: Palgrave Macmillan, 2004), 172.

23 William Jennings Bryan, *In His Image* (Chicago: Fleming H. Revell, 1922), 125.

24 John Moore, *The Post-Darwinian Controversies: A Study of the Protestant Struggle to Come to Terms with Darwin in Great Britain and America, 1870–1900* (New York: Cambridge University Press, 1979), 71–76.

25 Edward Larson, *Summer for the Gods: The Scopes Trial and America's Continuing Debate Over Science and Religion* (New York: Basic Books, 1997), 187–91; see also Ronald Numbers, *The Creationists: From Scientific Creationism to Intelligent Design*, rev. ed. (Cambridge, Mass.: Harvard University Press, 2006), 13.

26 Bryan, *In His Image*, 88–89.

27 Henry Fairfield Osborn, *The Earth Speaks to Bryan* (New York: Charles Scribner's Sons, 1925), 5, 25, 35–37.

28 Osborn, *Earth Speaks*, 64.

29 Osborn, *Earth Speaks*, 24–25.

30 Osborn, *Earth Speaks*, 51–52.

31 Osborn, *Earth Speaks*, 53.

32 Osborn, *Earth Speaks*, 62–63.

33 Henry Fairfield Osborn, *Evolution and Religion in Education: Polemics of the Fundamentalist Controversy of 1922 to 1926* (New York: Charles Scribner's Sons, 1926), 152.

34 Ruse, *Monad to Man*, 272; Stephen Jay Gould, *The Mismeasure of Man*, rev. and exp. ed. (New York: Norton, 1996), 261.

35 George W. Hunter, *A Civic Biology* (New York: American Book, 1914), 18.

36   Hunter, *Civic Biology*, 18.

37   Hunter, *Civic Biology*, 194–96.

38   Hunter, *Civic Biology*, 260–66 (emphasis in original).

39   Thomas S. Kuhn, *The Structure of Scientific Revolutions* (Chicago: University of Chicago Press, 1962).

40   Theodosius Dobzhansky, "Nothing in Biology Makes Sense Except in the Light of Evolution," *American Biology Teacher* 35 (1973): 125–29.

41   "Nothing in Biology Makes Sense Except in the Light of Evolution," Evolution Library, PBS.org, http://www.pbs.org/wgbh/evolution/library/10/2/l_102 _01.html.

42   Dobzhansky, "Light of Evolution," 129.

43   The Clergy Letter Project, http://www.butler.edu/clergyproject/Resources/ sci_expert_data_base.htm, accessed April 21, 2009.

44   Peter M. J. Hess, "Science and Religion," http://ncseweb.org/religion, accessed April 21, 2009.

45   I have the parodic intent of the symbol on the authority of its creator, Chris Gilman, president of Global Effects. E-mail correspondence, June 15, 2000.

46   Thomas M. Lessl, "The Culture of Science and the Rhetoric of Scientism: From Francis Bacon to the Darwin Fish," *Quarterly Journal of Speech* 93 (May 2007): 123–49. A questionnaire was distributed to users of the symbol which asked the following three questions:

      1. Please explain why you chose to put this emblem on your car.

      2. Is there a specific group of persons you wish to say something to by displaying this emblem?

      3. Would you please explain what the Darwin-fish emblem means to you.

47   "Notable Signers," American Humanist Association, http://www .americanhumanist.org/Who_We_Are/About_Humanism/Humanist_ Manifesto_III/Notable_Signers

48   "Humanism and Its Aspirations," American Humanist Association, http:// www.americanhumanist.org/Who_We_Are/About_Humanism/Humanist _Manifesto_III.

49   "Humanism and Its Aspirations," American Humanist Association, http:// www.americanhumanist.org/Who_We_Are/About_Humanism/Humanist _Manifesto_III.

50   Daniel Dennett, *Darwin's Dangerous Idea: Evolution and the Meanings of Life* (New York: Simon and Schuster, 1995), 63, 514–15.

51   C. P. Snow, *The Two Cultures: And a Second Look* (Cambridge: Cambridge University Press, 1964).

BIBLIOGRAPHY

Abraham, Gary A. "Misunderstanding the Merton Thesis: A Boundary Dispute between History and Sociology." *Isis* 74 (1983): 368–87.

Agassiz, Louis. "Evolution and Permanence of Type." *Atlantic Monthly*, January 1874, 92–101.

Aristotle. *On Rhetoric*. Translated by George A. Kennedy. New York: Oxford University Press, 1991.

Bacon, Francis. *The Works of Francis Bacon*. Edited by James Spedding, Robert Leslie Ellis, and Douglas Denon Heath. 14 vols. 1870. Reprint, New York: Garrett, 1968.

Barthes, Roland. *Mythologies*. Translated by Annette Lavers. London: Jonathan Cape, 1972.

Bartholomew, Michael. "Huxley's Defence of Darwin." *Annals of Science* 32 (1975): 425–35.

Barton, Ruth. "Evolution: The Whitworth Gun in Huxley's War for the Liberation of Science from Theology." In *The Wider Domain of Evolutionary Thought*, edited by D. R. Oldroyd and I. Langham, 261–87. Dordrecht: Reidel, 1983.

———. "'An Influential Set of Chaps': The X-Club and Royal Society Politics 1864–85." *British Journal of the History of Science* 23 (1990): 53–81.

Becker, Carl. *The Heavenly City of the Eighteenth-Century Philosophers*. New Haven, Conn.: Yale University Press, 1932.

Ben-David, Joseph. "Puritanism and Modern Science: A Study in the Continuity and Coherence of Sociological Research." In *Comparative Social Dynamics*, edited by Eric Cohn, Moshe Lissak, and Uri Almagor, 207–23. Boulder, Colo.: Westview, 1985.

———. *The Scientist's Role in Society: A Comparative Study.* Rev. ed. Chicago: University of Chicago Press, 1984.

Berger, Peter. *The Sacred Canopy: Elements of a Sociological Theory of Religion.* Garden City, N.Y.: Doubleday, 1969.

Bibby, Cyril. "Thomas Henry Huxley and University Development." *Victorian Studies* 2 (1958): 97–116.

Birch, Thomas, ed. *The Works of the Honourable Robert Boyle.* London, 1772.

Black, Max. *Models and Metaphors.* Ithaca, N.Y.: Cornell University Press, 1962.

Blackwell, Richard J. *Galileo, Bellarmine, and the Bible.* Notre Dame, Ind.: University of Notre Dame Press, 1991.

Block, Ed Jr. "T. H. Huxley's Rhetoric and the Popularization of Victorian Scientific Ideas: 1854–1874." *Victorian Studies* 29 (1986): 363–86.

Blumenberg, Hans. *The Legitimacy of the Modern Age.* Translated by Robert Wallace. Cambridge, Mass.: MIT Press, 1983.

Bonald, Louise de. *Œuvres complète de M. de Bonald.* 9 vols. Petit Montrouge, France: Migne, 1859.

Bowler, Peter. *The Non-Darwinian Revolution.* Baltimore, Md.: Johns Hopkins University Press, 1988.

Bremmer, Jan N. *Greek Religion.* Oxford: Oxford University Press, 1994.

Briggs, John Channing. "Bacon's Science and Religion." In *The Cambridge Companion to Bacon,* edited by Marakku Peltonen, 172–99. Cambridge: Cambridge University Press, 1996.

Bronowski, Jacob. *The Ascent of Man.* Boston: Little, Brown, 1973.

———. *Magic, Science, and Civilization.* New York: Columbia University Press, 1978.

Brooke, John Hedley. *Reconstructing Nature: The Engagement of Science and Religion.* Oxford: Oxford University Press, 2000.

———. *Science and Religion: Some Historical Perspectives.* Cambridge: Cambridge University Press, 1991.

Bryan, William Jennings. *In His Image.* Chicago: Fleming H. Revell, 1922.

Bryant, Donald C. "Rhetoric: Its Functions and Its Scope." *Quarterly Journal of Speech* 39 (1953): 401–24.

Buber, Martin. *I and Thou.* Translated by Ronald Gregor Smith. Edinburgh, U.K.: T&T Clark, 1947.

Bunyan, John. *The Pilgrim's Progress from This World to That Which Is to Come.* 1667. Reprint, London: J. M. Dent and Sons, 1907.

Burke, Kenneth. *A Grammar of Motives.* Berkeley: University of California Press, 1945.

———. *Language as Symbolic Action: Essays on Life, Literature and Method*. Berkeley: University of California Press, 1966.

Burkhardt, Frederick, and Sydney Smith, eds. *The Correspondence of Charles Darwin*. 16 vols. Cambridge: Cambridge University Press, 1985–1994.

Burtt, Edwin. *The Metaphysical Foundations of Modern Physical Science: A Historical and Critical Essay*. London: Routledge & Kegan Paul, 1924.

Butler, Joseph. *The Analogy of Religion, Natural and Revealed, to the Constitution and Course of Nature*. Oxford: Clarendon, 1874.

Campbell, John Angus. "Of Orchids, Insects, and Natural Theology: Timing, Tactics and Cultural Critique in Darwin's Post-'Origin' Strategy." *Argumentation* 8 (1994): 63–80.

———. "Scientific Revolution and the Grammar of Culture: The Case of Darwin's Origin." *Quarterly Journal of Speech* 72 (1986): 351–76.

Capp, Bernard S. *The Fifth Monarchy Men: A Study of Seventeenth-Century Millenarianism*. London: Faber & Faber, 1972.

Carroll, James W. "Merton's Thesis on English Science." *American Journal of Economics and Sociology* 13 (1954): 427–32.

Carroll, William E. "Galileo and the Interpretation of the Bible." *Science and Education* 8 (1999): 151–87.

Cassirer, Ernst. *The Problem of Knowledge: Philosophy, Science, and History since Hegel*. Translated by William H. Woglom and Charles W. Hendel. New Haven, Conn.: Yale University Press, 1950.

Ceccarelli, Leah. "Polysemy: Multiple Meanings in Rhetorical Criticism." *Quarterly Journal of Speech* 84 (1998): 395–415.

Chénier, Marie-Joseph. *Œuvre de M. J. Chénier*. 3 vols. Paris: Guillaume, 1824.

Christianson, Paul. *Reformers and Babylon: Apocalyptic Visions from the Reformation to the Eve of the Civil War*. Toronto: University of Toronto Press, 1978.

Clarke, Arthur C. *2001: A Space Odyssey*. New York: New American Library, 1968.

Clucas, Stephen. "In Search of 'The True Logick': Methodological Eclecticism Among the 'Baconian Reformers.'" In *Samuel Hartlib and Universal Reformation: Studies in Intellectual Communication*, edited by Mark Greengrass, Michael Leslie, and Timothy Raylor. Cambridge: Cambridge University Press, 1994.

Coletta, Paolo E. *William Jennings Bryan*. Lincoln: University of Nebraska Press, 1964.

Collingwood, R. G. *The Idea of History*. Oxford: Oxford University Press, 1946.

Comenius, John Amos. *Panorthosia or Universal Reform: Chapter 1–18 and 27.* Translated by A. M. O. Dobbie. Sheffield, U.K.: Sheffield Academic, 1995.

———. *Via Lucis.* Translated by E. T. Compagnac. London: Hodder & Stoughton, 1938.

Comte, Auguste. *Œuvres d'Auguste Comte.* 12 vols. Paris: Éditions Anthropos, 1968.

———. *The Positive Philosophy.* Translated by Harriet Martineau. 2 vols. 3rd ed. London: Kegan Paul, 1893.

———. *System of Positive Polity.* Translated by Frederic Harrison. 4 vols. New York: Burt Franklin, 1875.

Condorcet, Antoine-Nicolas de. *Condorcet: Selected Writings.* Edited by Keith Michael Baker. Indianapolis, Ind.: Bobbs-Merrill, 1976.

———. *Œuvres.* 12 vols. Stuttgart-bad Cannstatt: Friedrich Frommann Verlag, 1968.

———. *Sketch for a Historical Picture of the Progress of the Human Mind.* Translated by June Barraclough. London: Weidenfeld & Nicolson, 1955.

Congreve, Richard. "Mr. Huxley on M. Comte." *Fortnightly Review* 5 (1869): 407-18.

Cornford, Francis Macdonald. *The Origin of Attic Comedy.* Cambridge: Cambridge University Press, 1934.

Crombie, A. C. *Robert Grosseteste and the Origins of Experimental Science: 1100–1700.* Oxford: Clarendon, 1961.

Dawkins, Richard. *The Ancestor's Tale: A Pilgrimage to the Dawn of Evolution.* Boston: Houghton Mifflin, 2004.

Dennett, Daniel. *Darwin's Dangerous Idea: Evolution and the Meanings of Life.* New York: Simon & Schuster, 1995.

Descartes, René. *Discourse on the Method of Conducting One's Reason Well and Seeking the Truth in the Sciences.* Edited and translated by George Heffernan. Notre Dame, Ind.: University of Notre Dame Press, 1994.

Desmond, Adrian. *Huxley: From Devil's Disciple to Evolution's High Priest.* Reading, Mass.: Addison-Wesley, 1997.

———. Introduction to *Scientific Papers and Correspondence of Thomas Henry Huxley, c. 1843–1895, from the Imperial College of Science, Technology, and Medicine, London.* Units 1 and 2 of *Darwin, Huxley and the Natural Sciences.* London: Research Publications, 1990.

Dick, Oliver Lawson, ed. *Aubrey's Brief Lives.* Ann Arbor: University of Michigan Press, 1962.

di Gregorio, Mario A. *T. H. Huxley's Place in Natural Science*. New Haven, Conn.: Yale University Press, 1984.

Dinesen, Isak. *Anecdotes of Destiny*. New York: Random House, 1958.

Dobzhansky, Theodosius. "Nothing in Biology Makes Sense Except in the Light of Evolution." *American Biology Teacher* 35 (1973): 125–29.

Dondo, Mathurin. *The French Faust Henri de Saint-Simon*. New York: Philosophical Library, 1955.

Douglas, Mary. *Implicit Meanings: Essays in Anthropology*. London: Routledge & Kegan Paul, 1975.

Dupuis, Charles François. *The Origin of All Religious Worship*. Edited and translated by Robert Richardson. 1872. Facsimile, New York: Garland, 1984.

Durkheim, Émile. *The Elementary Forms of the Religious Life*. Translated by Joseph Ward Swain. London: Allen & Unwin, 1915.

———. *Pragmatism and Sociology*. Translated by J. C. Whitehouse. Edited by John B. Allcock. Cambridge: Cambridge University Press, 1983.

———. *Rules of Sociological Method*. Translated by Sarah A. Solovay and John H. Mueller. Edited by George E. G. Catlin. Glencoe, Ill.: Free Press, 1964.

———. *Socialism and Saint-Simon*. Edited by Alvin Gouldner. Translated by Charlotte Sattler. Yellow Springs, Ohio: Antioch, 1958.

———. *Suicide: A Study in Sociology*. Translated by J. A. Spaulding and G. Simpson. London: Routledge & Kegan Paul, 1951.

Dyer, Louis, ed. *Apology of Socrates and Crito, with Extracts from the Phaedo and Symposium and from Xenophon's Memorabilia*. Boston: Ginn, 1908.

Eisen, Sydney. "Huxley and the Positivists." *Victorian Studies* 7 (1964): 337–58.

Eliade, Mircea. *Myth and Reality*. Translated by W. R. Trask. New York: Harper & Row, 1963.

———. *Myths, Dreams, and Mysteries: The Encounter Between Contemporary Faiths and Archaic Realities*. Translated by Philip Mairet. New York: Harper & Row, 1960.

———. *The Myth of the Eternal Return*. Translated by W. R. Trask. New York: Pantheon, 1954.

Eliot, George. *The George Eliot Letters*. Edited by Gordon Haight. 9 vols. New Haven, Conn.: Yale University Press, 1954.

Ellul, Jacques. *The New Demons*. Translated by E. Edward Hopkin. New York: Seabury, 1975.

Elton, G. R. *Reformation Europe 1517–1559*. New York: Harper Torchbooks, 1966.

Erikson, Kai. *Wayward Puritans: A Study in the Sociology of Deviance.* New York: John Wiley, 1966.

Fahnestock, Jeanne. *Rhetorical Figures in Science.* New York: Oxford University Press, 1999.

Faulkner, Robert. *Francis Bacon and the Project of Progress.* Boston: Rowman & Littlefield, 1993.

Finocchiaro, Maurice A., ed. and trans. *The Galileo Affair: A Documentary History.* Berkeley: University of California Press, 1989.

Fisch, Harold. *Jerusalem and Albion: The Hebraic Factor in Seventeenth-Century Literature.* New York: Schocken, 1964.

Fiske, John. *The Letters of John Fiske.* Edited by Ethel F. Fiske. New York: Macmillan, 1940.

Frankel, Charles. *Faith of Reason: The Idea of Progress in the French Enlightenment.* New York: King's Crown, 1948.

Frye, Northrop. *Anatomy of Criticism: Four Essays.* Princeton, N.J.: Princeton University Press, 1957.

———. "Myth, Fiction, and Displacement." In *Theories of Myth*, vol. 4 of *Literary Criticism and Myth*, edited by Robert A. Segal, 119–37. New York: Garland, 1996.

———. *The Secular Scripture: The Study of the Structure of Romance.* Cambridge, Mass.: Harvard University Press, 1976.

Fuller, Steve. *Concepts in the Social Sciences: Science.* Buckingham, U.K.: Open University Press, 1998.

Gaonkar, Dilip. "The Idea of Rhetoric in the Rhetoric of Science." *Southern Communication Journal* 58 (1993): 258–95.

Gay, Peter. *The Party of Humanity: Essays in the French Enlightenment.* New York: Knopf, 1964.

Geertz, Clifford. *The Interpretation of Cultures.* New York: Basic Books, 1973.

Giberson, Karl, and Mariano Artigas. *Oracles of Science: Celebrity Scientists versus God and Religion.* Oxford: Oxford University Press, 2007.

Gibson, R. W. *Francis Bacon: A Bibliography of His Works and of Baconiana to the Year 1750.* Oxford: Scrivener, 1950.

Gieryn, Thomas. "Boundary-Work and the Demarcation of Science from Non-Science: Strains and Interests in Professional Ideologies of Scientists." *American Sociological Review* 48 (1983): 781–95.

Gilpin, Robert. "The Atlantic Imbalance in Science and Technology." In *Comparative Studies in Science and Society.* Edited by Sal Restivo and Christopher Vanderpool, 289–305. Columbus, Ohio: Merill, 1974.

Girard, René. *Things Hidden since the Foundation of the World.* Translated by Stephen Bann and Michael Metteer. Stanford, Calif.: Stanford University Press, 1987.

Glanvill, Joseph. *Skepsis Scientifica.* London, 1665.

Goodnight, G. Thomas. "The Personal, Technical, and Public Spheres of Argument: A Speculative Inquiry into the Art of Public Deliberation." *Journal of the American Forensic Association* 18 (1982): 214-27.

Gould, Stephen Jay. *The Mismeasure of Man.* Rev. and exp. ed. New York: Norton, 1996.

———. *Wonderful Life: The Burgess Shale and the Nature of History.* New York: Norton, 1989.

Greene, John C. *Science, Ideology, and World View: Essays in the History of Evolutionary Ideas.* Berkeley: University of California Press, 1981.

Guthrie, William Keith Chambers. *The Fifth-Century Enlightenment.* Vol. 3 of *A History of Greek Philosophy.* Cambridge: Cambridge University Press, 1969.

Hahn, Roger. *The Anatomy of a Scientific Institution: The Paris Academy of Sciences, 1666–1803.* Berkeley: University of California Press, 1971.

Hall, A. Rupert. "Merton Revisited, or Science and Society in the Seventeenth Century." *History of Science* 2 (1963): 1-16.

Hartley, Harold, ed. *The Royal Society: Its Origins and Founders.* London: Royal Society, 1960.

Henry, John. "The Scientific Revolution in England." In *The Scientific Revolution in National Context,* edited by Roy Porter and Mikuláš Teich, 178-209. Cambridge: Cambridge University Press, 1992.

Hesse, Mary. "Francis Bacon's Philosophy of Science." In *A Critical History of Western Philosophy,* edited by D. J. O'Connor, 141-52. New York: Macmillan, 1964.

Hill, Christopher. *The Century of Revolution: 1603–1714.* Edinburgh, U.K.: T. Nelson, 1961.

———. *The World Turned Upside Down: Radical Ideas During the English Revolution.* New York: Vintage, 1972.

Hooykaas, Reijer. *Faith, Fact and Fiction in the Development of Science: The Gifford Lectures Given in the University of St. Andrews.* Boston: Kluwer Academic, 1999.

———. *Religion and the Rise of Modern Science.* Edinburgh, U.K.: Scottish Academic, 1972.

———. *Robert Boyle: A Study in Science and Christian Belief.* Lanham, Md.: Academic Press of America, 1997.

Houghton, Walter. "The Rhetoric of T. H. Huxley." *University of Toronto Quarterly* 18 (1949): 159–75.

Hunter, George W. *A Civic Biology.* New York: American Book, 1914.

Huxley, Leonard. *Thomas Henry Huxley: A Character Sketch.* 1920. Reprint, Freeport, N.Y.: Books for Libraries, 1969.

Huxley, Thomas H. "Agnosticism: A Symposium." *Agnostic Annual,* 1884.

———. "An Apologetic Irenicon," *Fortnightly Review* 52 (November 1892): 557–71.

———. *Huxley Papers,* College Archives, Imperial College London.

———. *Lay Sermons, Addresses, and Reviews.* New York: Appleton, 1871.

———. *Life and Letters of Thomas Huxley.* Edited by Leonard Huxley. 2 vols. New York: Appleton, 1901.

———. "Nature: Aphorisms by Goethe." *Nature* 1 (1869): 9–11.

———. "Science." *Westminster Review* 5 (1854): 254–57.

———. *Selected Works of Thomas H. Huxley.* 9 vols. New York : Appleton, 1893.

———. "On Species and Races." In *The Scientific Memoirs of Thomas Henry Huxley,* edited by Michael Forster and Ray Lankester. 2:388-94. London: Macmillan, 1898-1901.

———. "Time and Life: Mr. Darwin's 'Origin of Species.'" *Macmillan's Magazine* 1 (1859): 142–48.

Iggers, Georg G. Introduction to *The Doctrine of Saint-Simon: An Exposition First Year; 1828–1829,* translated by Georg G. Iggers. Boston: Beacon, 1958.

Irvine, William. *Apes, Angels, and Victorians: The Story of Darwin, Huxley, and Evolution.* New York: McGraw-Hill, 1972.

Jacob, Margaret. *The Cultural Meaning of the Scientific Revolution.* Philadelphia: Temple University Press, 1987.

Jardine, Lisa. *Francis Bacon: Discovery and the Art of Discourse.* Cambridge: Cambridge University Press, 1974.

Jensen, Vernon J. *Thomas Henry Huxley: Communicating for Science.* Newark: University of Delaware Press, 1991.

Johnson, Davi. "Dawkins' Myth: The Religious Dimensions of Evolutionary Discourse." *Journal of Communication and Religion* 29 (2006): 285–314.

Kearney, Hugh F. "Puritanism, Capitalism and the Scientific Revolution." *Past and Present* 28 (1964): 81–101.

Kingsley, Charles. *Charles Kingsley: His Letters and Memories of His Life.* Edited by Frances E. Kingsley. 2 vols. London: Henry King, 1877.

Kuhn, Thomas. *The Structure of Scientific Revolutions.* Chicago: University of Chicago Press, 1962.

Kurtz, Lester. *The Politics of Heresy: The Modernist Crisis in Roman Catholicism.* Berkeley: University of California Press, 1986.

Larson, Edward. *Summer for the Gods: The Scopes Trial and America's Continuing Debate Over Science and Religion.* New York: Basic Books, 1997.

Lenzer, Gertrud, ed. *Auguste Comte and Positivism: The Essential Writings.* Chicago: University of Chicago Press, 1975.

Lessl, Thomas M. "The Culture of Science and the Rhetoric of Scientism: From Francis Bacon to the Darwin Fish." *Quarterly Journal of Speech* 93 (2007): 123–49.

———. "Francis Bacon and the Biblical Origins of the Scientific Ethos." *Journal of Communication and Religion* 15 (1992): 87–98.

———. "The Galileo Legend as Scientific Folklore." *Quarterly Journal of Speech* 85 (1999): 146–68.

———. "Incommensurate Boundaries: The Rhetorical Positivism of Thomas Huxley." In *Rhetoric and Incommensurability*, edited by Randy Allen Harris, 198–237. West Lafayette: Ind.: Parlor, 2005.

———. "The Priestly Voice." *Quarterly Journal of Speech* 75 (1989): 183–97.

Levine, Joseph S., and Kenneth R. Miller. *Biology: Discovering Life.* Lexington, Mass.: D. C. Heath, 1991.

Lévi-Strauss, Claude. *Myth and Meaning.* Edited by Wendy Doniger. 1978. Reprint, New York: Schocken, 1995.

Lewis, C. S. *English Literature in the Sixteenth Century Excluding Drama.* Oxford: Clarendon, 1954.

Lightman, Bernard. *The Origins of Agnosticism: Victorian Unbelief and the Limits of Knowledge.* Baltimore, Md.: Johns Hopkins University Press, 1987.

Lindberg, David, and Ronald Numbers, ed. *God and Nature: Historical Essays on the Encounter Between Christianity and Science.* Berkeley: University of California Press, 1986.

Lovejoy, Arthur O. *The Great Chain of Being.* Cambridge, Mass.: Harvard University Press, 1953.

Lyell, K. M., ed. *Life, Letters and Journals of Sir Charles Lyell.* London: John Murray, 1881.

Lynch, William T. "A Society of Baconians?: The Collective Development of Bacon's Method in the Royal Society of London." In *Francis Bacon and the Refiguring of Early Modern Thought: Essays to Commemorate the Advancement of Learning (1605–2005)*, edited by Julie Robin Solomon and Catherine Gimelli Martin, 173–202. Aldershot, U.K.: Ashgate, 2005.

Lyons, Sherrie L. *Thomas Henry Huxley: The Evolution of a Scientist.* Amherst, N.Y.: Prometheus, 1999.

MacCormac, Earl R. *Metaphor and Myth in Science and Religion.* Durham, N.C.: Duke University Press, 1976.

Malherbe, Michel. "Bacon's Method of Science." In *The Cambridge Companion to Bacon,* edited by Marakku Peltonen, 75–98. Cambridge: Cambridge University Press, 1996.

Mannheim, Karl. *Ideology and Utopia: An Introduction to the Sociology of Knowledge.* Translated by Louis Wirth and Edward Shils. New York: Harcourt, Brace & World, 1936.

Mansel, Henry Longueville. *The Limits of Religious Thought Examined in Eight Lectures.* London: John Murray, 1858.

Manuel, Frank E. *The New World of Henri Saint-Simon.* Cambridge, Mass.: Harvard University Press, 1956.

———. *The Prophets of Paris.* Cambridge, Mass.: Harvard University Press, 1962.

Marsh, John. "The Universe and Dr. Sagan." *Commentary* 71 (1981): 64–68.

Marx, Karl. *Early Writings.* Translated by T. B. Bottomore. London: Watts, 1963.

Mason, S. F. "The Scientific Revolution and the Protestant Reformation." In *Puritanism and the Rise of Modern Science: The Merton Thesis,* edited by I. Bernard Cohen, 184–88. New Brunswick, N.J.: Rutgers University Press, 1990.

Mathiopoulos, Margarita. *History and Progress: In Search of the European and American Mind.* New York: Praeger, 1989.

McGregor, J. F., and B. Reays, eds. *Radical Religion in the English Revolution.* Oxford: Oxford University Press, 1988.

McLean, Iain, and Fiona Hewitt, trans. and eds. *Condorcet: Foundations of Social Choice and Political Theory.* Brookfield, Vt.: Edward Elgar, 1994.

Merton, Robert K. *Science, Technology and Society in Seventeenth-Century England.* Bruges, Belgium: Saint Catherine, 1938.

———. *The Sociology of Science: Theoretical and Empirical Investigations.* Edited by Norman Storer. Chicago: University of Chicago Press, 1973.

Midgley, Mary. *Evolution as a Religion: Strange Hopes and Stranger Fears.* London: Methuen, 1985.

Moore, John. *The Post-Darwinian Controversies: A Study of the Protestant Struggle to Come to Terms with Darwin in Great Britain and America, 1870–1900.* New York: Cambridge University Press, 1979.

Morely, John. *Critical Miscellanies.* 4 vols. London: Macmillan, 1886.

Murphy, Daniel. *Comenius: A Critical Assessment of His Life and Work.* Dublin: Irish Academic, 1995.

Nelson, Benjamin. "The Quest for Certitude and the Books of Scripture, Nature, and Conscience/Discussion: Philosophical and Theological Backgrounds." In *The Nature of Scientific Discovery: A Symposium Commemorating the 500th Anniversary of the Birth of Nicolas Copernicus*, edited by Owen Gingerich, 355–91. Washington, D.C.: Smithsonian Institution, 1975.

Newport, F. "Half of Americans Believe in Creationist Origins of Man." *Gallup Poll Monthly* 336 (1993): 24–28.

Niebuhr, Reinhold. *Faith and History: A Comparison of Christian and Modern Views of History*. New York: Charles Scribner's Sons, 1949.

———. *Human Nature*. Vol. 1 of *The Nature and Destiny of Man*. 1941. Reprint, New York: Charles Scribner's Sons, 1964.

Nietzsche, Friedrich Wilhelm. *The Gay Science: With a Prelude in Rhymes and an Appendix of Songs*. Translated with commentary by Walter Kaufmann. New York: Random House, 1974.

Numbers, Ronald. *The Creationists: From Scientific Creationism to Intelligent Design*. Rev. ed. Cambridge, Mass.: Harvard University Press, 2006.

Olson, Theodore. *Millenialism, Utopianism and Progress*. Toronto: University of Toronto Press, 1982.

Osborn, Henry Fairfield. *The Earth Speaks to Bryan*. New York: Charles Scribner's Sons, 1925.

———. *Evolution and Religion in Education: Polemics of the Fundamentalist Controversy of 1922 to 1926*. New York: Charles Scribner's Sons, 1926.

Oster, Malcolm. "Millenarianism and the New Science: The Case of Robert Boyle." In *Samuel Hartlib and Universal Reformation: Studies in Intellectual Communication*, edited by Mark Greengrass, Michael Leslie, and Timothy Raylor, 137–49. Cambridge: Cambridge University Press, 1994.

Paradis, James G. "Evolution and Ethics in Its Victorian Context. " In *T. H. Huxley's Evolution and Ethics With New Essays on Its Victorian and Sociobiological Context*, edited by James Paradis and George C. Williams. Princeton, N.J.: Princeton University Press, 1989.

———. *T. H. Huxley: Man's Place in Nature*. Lincoln: University of Nebraska Press, 1978.

Paterson, Antoinette Mann. *Francis Bacon and Socialized Science*. Springfield, Ill.: Charles C. Thomas, 1973.

Perelman, Chaim. *The Realm of Rhetoric*. Translated by W. Kluback. Notre Dame, Ind.: University of Notre Dame Press, 1982.

Pérez-Ramos, Antonio. *Francis Bacon's Science and the Maker's Knowledge Tradition*. Oxford: Clarendon, 1988.

Pickering, Mary. *Auguste Comte: An Intellectual Biography*. Cambridge: Cambridge University Press, 1993.

Popkin, Richard H. "Condorcet and Hume and Turgot." In *Condorcet Studies II*, edited by David Williams, 47–62. New York: Peter Lang, 1984.

Popper, Karl R. *The Poverty of Historicism*. Boston: Beacon, 1957.

Poundstone, William. *Carl Sagan: A Life in the Cosmos*. New York: Henry Holt, 1999.

Pozzi, Dora, and John M. Wickersham, eds. *The Myth and the Polis*. Ithaca, N.Y.: Cornell University Press, 1991.

Rabb, T. K. "Puritanism and the Rise of Experimental Science in England." *Journal of World History* 7 (1962): 46–66.

Rabkin, Yakov. "The Interaction of Scientific and Jewish Cultures: An Historical Overview." In *The Interaction of Scientific and Jewish Cultures in Modern Times*, edited by Yakov Rabkin and Ira Robinson, 3–30. Lewiston, N.Y.: Edwin Mellen, 1995.

Richards, I. A. *Philosophy of Rhetoric*. Oxford: Oxford University Press, 1965.

Ricoeur, Paul. *The Rule of Metaphor: Multi-Disciplinary Studies of the Creation of Meaning in Language*. Translated by Robert Czerny, Kathleen McLaughlin, and John Costello. Toronto: University of Toronto Press, 1977.

Rousseau, Jean-Jacques. *Discourse on Political Economy and the Social Contract*. Translated by Christopher Betts. Oxford: Oxford University Press, 1994.

Ruse, Michael. *Darwin and Design: Does Evolution Have a Purpose?* Cambridge, Mass.: Harvard University Press, 2003.

———. *The Evolution-Creation Struggle*. Cambridge, Mass.: Harvard University Press, 2005.

———. *Monad to Man: The Concept of Progress in Evolutionary Biology*. Cambridge, Mass.: Harvard University Press, 1996.

Rushing, Janice Hocker. "The Rhetoric of the American Western Myth." *Communication Monographs* 50 (1983): 14–32.

Sagan, Carl. *Cosmos*. New York: Random House, 1980.

Saint-Simon, Claude Henri Comte de. *Henri Comte de Saint-Simon (1760–1825): Selected Writings*. Translated by F. M. H. Markham. New York: Macmillan, 1952.

———. *Henri Saint-Simon (1760–1825): Selected Writings on Science, Industry and Social Organization*. Edited and translated by Keith Taylor. New York: Holmes & Meier, 1975.

———. *Œuvres Choisies*. 3 vols. Hildesheim: Georg Olms Verlag, 1973.

Santillana, Giorgio de. *The Crime of Galileo*. Chicago: University of Chicago Press, 1955.

Schapiro, Jacob Salwyn. *Condorcet and the Rise of Liberalism.* New York: Octagon, 1963.

Sessions, W. A. *Francis Bacon Revisited.* New York: Twayne, 1996.

Snow, C. P. *The Two Cultures: And a Second Look.* Cambridge: Cambridge University Press, 1964.

Sprat, Thomas. *The History of the Royal-Society of London for the Improving of Natural Knowledge.* London, 1667.

Staël, Madame de. *Speculations on such a positivist system are in her De la littérature considérée dans ses rapports avec les institutions sociales, suivi de L'Influence des passions sur le bonheur, des individus et des nations.* Paris: InfoMédia Communication, 1998.

Stimson, Dorothy. *Scientists and Amateurs: A History of the Royal Society.* New York: Henry Schuman, 1948.

Teaching about Evolution and the Nature of Science. Washington, D.C.: National Academies, 1998.

Tener, Robert H., and Malcolm Woodfield, eds. *A Victorian Spectator: Uncollected Writings of R. H. Hutton.* Bristol, U.K.: Bristol Press, 1989.

Tertullian, Quintus. *Against Macion.* Translated and edited by Ernest Evans. Oxford: Clarendon, 1972.

Tobey, Ronald C. *The American Ideology of National Science, 1919–1930.* Pittsburgh: University of Pittsburgh Press, 1971.

Tocqueville, Alexis de. *Democracy in America.* Translated by Richard Heffner. New York: Penguin, 1984.

Toulmin, Stephen. "Introduction: The End of the Copernican era?" in *The Nature of Scientific Discovery: A Symposium Commemorating the 500th Anniversary of the Birth of Nicolaus Copernicus,* ed. Owen Gingerich (Washington, D.C.: Smithsonian Institution, 1975), 189–98.

———. *The Return to Cosmology: Postmodern Science and the Theology of Nature.* Berkeley: University of California Press, 1982.

Turgot, Anne Robert Jacques. *Œuvres de Turgot.* 3 vols. Paris: Librairie Félix Alcan, 1913.

———. *Turgot on Progress, Sociology, and Economics.* Edited by Ronald Meek. Cambridge: Cambridge University Press, 1973.

Turnbull, G. H. *Hartlib, Dury and Comenius: Gleanings from Hartlib's Papers.* London: University Press of Liverpool, 1947.

Turner, Frank. *Contesting Cultural Authority: Essays in Victorian Intellectual Life.* Cambridge: Cambridge University Press, 1993.

Vickers, Brian. "Bacon and Rhetoric." In *The Cambridge Companion to*

Bacon, edited by Marakku Peltonen, 200–231. Cambridge: Cambridge University Press, 1996.

Voegelin, Eric. *From Enlightenment to Revolution*. Edited by John H. Hallowell. Durham, N.C.: Duke University Press, 1975.

Vyverberg, Henry. *Historical Pessimism in the French Enlightenment*. Cambridge, Mass.: Harvard University Press, 1958.

Waldinger, Renée. "Condorcet: The Problematic Nature of Progress." In *Condorcet Studies I*, edited by Leonora Cohen Rosenfield, 117–29. Atlantic Heights, N.J.: Humanities Press, 1984.

Walker, Jeffrey. "Dionysio de Halicarnaso y la Idea de Crítica de la Retórica." *Anuario Filosófico* 31, no. 2 (1998): 581–601.

Wallace, Karl R. *Francis Bacon on Communication and Rhetoric*. Chapel Hill: University of North Carolina Press, 1943.

Ward, Wilfrid. *Problems and Persons*. Freeport, N.Y.: Books for Libraries, 1903.

Weaver, Richard. *The Ethics of Rhetoric*. South Bend, Ind.: Regnery/Gateway, 1953.

Weber, Max. *The Protestant Ethic and the Spirit of Capitalism*. Translated by Talcott Parsons. New York: Charles Scribner's Sons, 1958.

———. *The Theory of Social and Economic Organization*. Translated by A. M. Henderson and Talcott Parsons. New York: Free Press, 1947.

Webster, Charles. *The Great Instauration: Science Medicine, and Reform 1626–1660*. New York: Holmes & Meier, 1976.

Weikart, Richard. *From Darwin to Hitler: Evolutionary Ethics, Eugenics and Racism in Germany*. New York: Palgrave Macmillan, 2004.

Weinberger, Jerry. Introduction to *New Atlantis and the Great Instauration*, by Francis Bacon. Edited by Jerry Weinberger, xiii–xxxiii. Rev. ed. Wheeling, Ill.: Harlan Davidson, 1989.

Westfall, Richard. *Science and Religion in Seventeenth-Century England*. New Haven, Conn.: Yale University Press, 1958.

Wheelright, Philip. *Metaphor and Reality*. Bloomington: University of Indiana Press, 1962.

White, Hayden. *The Content of the Form: Narrative Discourse and Historical Representation*. Baltimore, Md.: Johns Hopkins University Press, 1987.

———. *Tropics of Discourse: Essays in Cultural Criticism*. Baltimore, Md.: Johns Hopkins University Press, 1978.

White, Paul. "Ministers of Culture: Arnold, Huxley and Liberal Anglican Reform of Learning." *History of Science* 43 (2005): 115–38.

———. *Thomas Huxley: Making the "Man of Science."* Cambridge: Cambridge University Press, 2003.

Whitney, Charles. *Francis Bacon and Modernity.* New Haven, Conn.: Yale University Press, 1986.

Wilson, E. O. *Consilience: The Unity of Knowledge.* New York: Knopf, 1998.

Wright, T. R. *The Religion of Humanity: The Impact of Comtean Positivism on Victorian Britain.* Cambridge: Cambridge University Press, 1986.

Young, Robert Fitzgibbon. *Comenius in England.* 1932. Reprint, New York: Arno, 1971.

INDEX